ECO-GLOBAL CRIMES

To Tinga and Singa
In memory of Ronja

Eco-global Crimes

Contemporary Problems and Future Challenges

Edited by

RUNE ELLEFSEN
University of Oslo, Norway

RAGNHILD SOLLUND
University of Oslo, Norway

GURI LARSEN
University of Oslo, Norway

Routledge
Taylor & Francis Group
LONDON AND NEW YORK

First published 2012 by Ashgate Publishing

Published 2016 by Routledge
2 Park Square, Milton Park, Abingdon, Oxfordshire OX14 4RN
711 Third Avenue, New York, NY 10017, USA

First issued in paperback 2016

Routledge is an imprint of the Taylor & Francis Group, an informa business

British Library Cataloguing in Publication Data
Eco-global crimes : contemporary problems and future
challenges. -- (Green criminology)
1. Offenses against the environment. 2. Environmental law--
Criminal provisions. 3. Animal welfare.
I. Series II. Ellefsen, Rune. III. Sollund, Ragnhild
Aslaug, 1959- IV. Larsen, Guri.
364.1'45-dc23

Library of Congress Cataloging-in-Publication Data
Eco-global crimes : contemporary problems and future challenges / [edited] by Rune Ellefsen, Ragnhild Sollund and Guri Larsen.
p. cm.
Includes bibliographical references and index.
ISBN 978-1-4094-3492-4 (hbk) 1. Offenses against the environment. 2. Animal welfare.
3. Criminology--Environmental aspects. I. Ellefsen, Rune. II. Sollund, Ragnhild Aslaug, 1959- III. Larsen, Guri.
HV6401.E26 2012
364.1'45--dc23

2012014724

ISBN 13: 978-1-138-27154-8 (pbk)
ISBN 13: 978-1-4094-3492-4 (hbk)

Contents

List of Figures and Tables

Figures

Tables

List of Contributors

Elisa Aaltola, PhD, has concentrated on animal philosophy in her research, and in particular animal ethics. She is currently interested in the problems related to the representation and mediation of, and the normative persuasion concerning both human and non-human suffering. Aaltola works as a Senior Lecturer in Philosophy in the University of Eastern Finland. She is also a Fellow at the Oxford Centre for Animal Ethics.

Kristian Bjørkdahl is a PhD Fellow at the University of Oslo, where he is completing a dissertation on neopragmatism and human–animal relations. He is a researcher at the Centre for Development and the Environment (SUM) at the same institution. His background is in interdisciplinary cultural studies, and his main research interest is Richard Rorty's pragmatism, pragmatic sociology and the rhetoric of the animal and environmental movements.

Sigurd S. Dybing holds a Master's Degree in Criminology from Oslo University. His research interests within the field of green criminology are the development of environmental laws and knowledge, how environmental impacts from business activities will affect society and strategies for corporate environmental regulation.

Rune Ellefsen is employed as a researcher at the Department of Criminology and Sociology of Law, University of Oslo. His research interests, besides eco-global criminology in general, are focused on criminalisation and repression developing as a result of new conflicts between social movements, state control and various industries. Ellefsen is currently writing a book about Norwegian animal welfare legislation, animal rights theory and the various strategies of the Norwegian animal protection movement.

Researcher **Johanna Hagstedt** and **Lars Korsell** both work at the Swedish National Council for Crime Prevention in Stockholm. The Council works to reduce crime and improve levels of safety by producing data on and disseminating knowledge about crime and crime prevention work and the justice system's response to crime. Johanna Hagstedt is a researcher at the Department for Research and Development and Dr Lars Korsell is head of the Department for Economic and Organized Crime as well as of the judicial section. Both authors have previous research experience within the field of green and eco-global criminology, including the illegal hunting of large carnivores and the trade in endangered species.

Guri Larsen is a professor in Criminology at the University of Oslo. Larsen's main focus has been on social defence and the marginalisation of different social groups. She has addressed topics such as immigration policies, violence among young immigrants, the school systems and minority families and the history and development of the Norwegian Child Care Legislation. In her current research she is studying the abuse of animals, both in the forms of criminal offences and legal action. Furthermore, she seeks to develop a theoretical perspective in order to understand how it is possible to inflict pain on living creatures as a legal and – in general – approved praxis.

Marte Qvenild works as a researcher at the Norwegian Institute for Nature Research and is a PhD Fellow in the Department of Geography at the Norwegian University of Science and Technology (NTNU). She is a human geographer with special interests in political and social aspects of biodiversity management and nature-society relations.

Ingvill H. Riise has an MA in cultural studies, and her Master's thesis focuses on how the exploitation of animals is made to seem natural through the use of conceptual power. She is currently working on a book on the same topic and living in Sweden.

Ragnhild Aslaug Sollund is a professor in Criminology at the University of Oslo. She has also worked at the Institute for Social Research (ISF) and the Norwegian Social Research Institute (NOVA). Her doctoral thesis was about the occupational mobility of immigrant women and she has also researched the relationship between the police and ethnic minorities. She has published books and articles on migration, violence, police racism and, lately, green criminology, including *Global Harms. Ecological Crime and Speciesism* (ed.). (Nova Science Publishers) and 'Expressions of speciesism: the effects of keeping companion animals on animal abuse, animal trafficking and species decline', in *Crime, Law and Social Change*, 55(5), 437–51.

Per-Anders Svärd is a PhD Fellow in political science at Stockholm University, Sweden. His work focuses on the reproduction of speciesist ideology in national politics.

Gro Birgit Ween is employed as a Postdoctoral Fellow on the project 'Newcomers to the Farm: Atlantic salmon between the wild and the industrial', headed by Prof. Marianne Lien, in the Department of Social Anthropology at the University of Oslo. Her previous work involves issues of natural resource management conflicts, legal anthropology and identity politics.

Rob White is a professor of Criminology in the School of Sociology and Social Work at the University of Tasmania, Australia. He is also the editor of *Controversies in Environmental Sociology* (Cambridge University Press), as well as author of *Transnational Environmental Crime: Towards an Eco-global Criminology* and *Crimes Against Nature: Environmental Criminology and Environmental Justice*.

Per Jørgen Ystehede is employed in the Department of Criminology and Sociology of Law, University of Oslo. Ystehede has an MPhil degree in criminological research from Cambridge University and a research degree (Candidatus philologiae) in History of Ideas, from the University of Oslo. He has published a monograph on Cesare Lombroso in English: 'In The Twilight of Good and Evil: Cesare Lombroso and the Criminological Imagination' (VGM 2008) and articles on Lombroso in English, Italian and Norwegian. Together with Dr. Paul Knepper, University of Sheffield, he is currently co-editing an anthology entitled *The Cesare Lombroso Handbook* to be published in 2012.

Preface and Acknowledgements

The purpose of this book is to contribute to the development of the growing field of eco-global criminology, also known as green criminology. This anthology expands the discussions, research and core issues of the field with original contributions from scholars and academics from various countries, backgrounds and disciplines. This is the first book being published in Ashgates' new Green Criminology book series, edited by Michael J. Lynch and Paul B. Stretesky.

As editors, we wish to acknowledge the crucial support of the Scandinavian Research Council for Criminology (SRCC). We owe special thanks to SRCC for their grants, making the realisation of this book possible. Their commitment has been invaluable and even made it possible to gather most of the book's contributors for a workshop where draft versions of the book's chapters were discussed and further elaborated.

Rune Ellefsen, Ragnhild Aslaug Sollund and Guri Larsen
October, 2012

Part I
Introduction to Eco-global Criminology

Chapter 1

Introduction

Ragnhild Aslaug Sollund[1]

Over the past three decades there has been a growing body of literature within what is known as *green criminology* (Lynch 1990, South and Beirne 2006, Beirne and South 2009) and *eco-global criminology* (White 2008, 2009, 2011). The present book seeks to build knowledge within this field, by both empirical examples and theoretical discussions. The goal of this book is to illustrate the scope of environmental crime, and how local environmental problems are also transnational in their effects.

This is a reason for the title: *Eco-global Crimes: Contemporary Problems and Future Challenges*. In Chapter 2 of this book, Rob White defines eco-global criminology as the following: 'Eco-global criminology refers to a framework of analysis where the emphasis is on the ecological, the transnational and questions of justice. The substantive focus of eco-global criminology is transgressions against ecosystems, humans and animals'. Eco-global crimes are often transnationally organized, with damage being caused by legal transnational corporations, such as British Petroleum in the Gulf of Mexico, and the destruction of the soil and forest in the Ecuadorian Amazon caused by Chevron and Texaco.

The topics addressed by eco-global criminologists are many and various; relating to air, water and space-pollution (Walters 2007), toxic waste (White 2011), legal and illegal deforestation (Boekhout van Solinge 2008 a, b) and legal and illegal animal abuse (Beirne 1995, 1995, 1999, 2009; see also White this volume). Because of the multivariate character of problems relating to eco-global crimes, it is necessary to expand the boundaries of criminology as a discipline, and thus also the perspective of what crime is and what should be perceived as a crime, as well as the notions of harm and justice. For example, moral and utilitarian philosophy (Regan 1988, Singer 1977) have been important points of departure for non-speciesist criminologists (Beirne 1999, Cazaux 1999 and Sollund 2008), and observations and fieldwork done by biologists and ornithologists have been important in providing an empirical basis for discussions of crime prevention regarding the illegal parrot trade (Pires and Clark 2010).

The concept of crime relates to that which is a breach of law, yet eco-global harms, such as those committed by states and corporations, often eclipse the scope and reach of criminal law (South 2008, O'Brien 2008, Sollund 2008, White

1 I owe thanks to my co editors, Rune Ellefsen and Guri Larsen, as well as the series editors Michael Lynch and Paul Stretesky for comments to this chapter.

2011). This book seeks to broaden the perspectives of the research topics falling within the fields of eco-global criminology and assumes that these issues must be addressed with the same theoretical weight found in, for example, the study of deviance and other more traditional criminological topics. One example is an examination of how laws and regulations which actually uphold and legitimize intolerable exploitation of non-human animals and of nature are passed by means of the legislation processes supported by capitalist and consumerist interests, despite the increasing importance of environmental issues in modern contexts.

To do so, interdisciplinary approaches are required, as different disciplines have different epistemologies which all have something to offer. Empirical knowledge from, for example, biologists, botanists and oceanographers can provide a basis for 'building a case' relevant to an eco-global criminological analysis, while a theoretical contribution may come from humanistic sciences such as ethics and philosophy. Interdisciplinary thought may help create a firm theoretical and empirical ground from which to develop convincing arguments and effective strategies for altering the present course of exploitation which endangers so many people, plants and animals, both now and in the future.

Building on and including interdisciplinary contributions, however, does not mean that critical criminology should be ignored, since its tradition of speaking for the weak and pointing to structural injustice is a central issue addressed in eco-global criminology. Critically speaking, perspectives relating to the prevention of crime/harm and victimology may be useful, while the principle of precaution directs attention to what lies beyond the horizon (White 2011).

In addition, related criminology concepts such as those related to globalization and migration (crimmigration, Aas 2011), a phenomenon closely related to structural differences between the north and the south, may prove useful. For instance, partly as a consequence of the effects of climate change, migration will increase in the decades to come, unless we manage to remedy the situation. These migration patterns have important criminological implications such as exclusion and criminalization of the 'deviant other – the asylum seeker'– whereby refugees are put in detention centers, or are forced to live 'undocumented' and deprived of basic human rights (Engbersen et al. 1999).

The establishment of green/eco-global criminology followed broader the green and animal liberation movements four decades ago, and owes much to those traditions. Prior to this, criminologists showed little interested in studying for example the pollution caused by the coal industry during the industrial revolution, though the damage caused by pollution then became evident. While the early animal welfare movements that were connected to feminist movement in the UK emerged (Donovan 1993), criminologists studied human deviance. Environmental problems and animal abuse thus existed long before green/eco-global criminology emerged. Nevertheless, these environmental problems, though studied across various disciplines, have criminological implications.

The effects of the exploitation of nature – the senseless polluting of the seas, of fresh water and of the earth, and the pollution of the air which has led to global warming, have become common knowledge – they are not, strictly speaking, the results of criminological research. In addition, we are constantly made aware of the rapid decline of other species because they are regarded as legitimate objects for human consumption of some kind – as trophies, food, medicine, or clothing. These harms are now obviously caused by the expansion of the human species, which is in turn bound up with the globalization of the economy and the capitalist system. The present-day actions of humans against nature and other species may not be fundamentally different from the way humans have always taken advantage of their superior position *vis-à-vis* nature and other species in an historical sense. However, new historical conditions such as advanced technologies produced an imaginative capacity to develop innumerable new ways of exploiting natural resources and other species, multiplying the effects of humans on the environment so that now these effects appear catastrophic.

Many human cultures have been anthropocentric (Sollund 2008), though native Americans, for example, appeared to regard all creatures as sacred and entitled to fundamental respect (Donovan 1993: 181–192). In the present day we are seeing the large-scale consequences of the anthropocentric world view. This goes parallel to an increased knowledge of, and conscience about, non-human species which seriously questions the 'right' humans have previously accorded themselves to use other species as they please. So far, however, this knowledge has not had any general impact on people's daily practices, which to a large extent are colored by denial, whether with regard to the relationship between global warming and human carbon emissions, or the systemic and widespread physical and psychological abuse of non-human animals. A driving force behind the abuse of the world around us is the belief that human welfare can only be achieved by increased consumption, which has been increasingly fueled by global capitalism and neo-liberalism. According to this logic, the only way to bring about 'justice' between the peoples of the south and north is to increase consumption for those living in underdeveloped regions. This view, however, overlooks the volume of waste and pollution this form of 'justice' creates. This logic may in a sense seem fair to the extent that the countries of the south are those which suffer most from the consumption of the western world with respect to, for example, climate change and electronic waste, but the consequences of consumptive justice are fatal. Humans, it seems, generally behave like the three wise monkeys;[2] *Mizaru*, *Mikazaru*, and *Mazaru*, refusing to see, hear or speak evil, but forgetting the fourth, the monkey who by crossing his/her arms, *does* no evil. Indeed, we refuse to see, refuse to listen, remain silent, and therefore see no reason why we should not proceed with our actions. The rejection of facts is caused by denial Cohen (2000). Consumption has been encouraged by political leaders,

2 There are different interpretations of the monkeys' actions, either as above, as refusing to see/acknowledge facts, or as pointing towards agency; morally encouraging one to speak no evil, hear no evil, and do no evil. See Wikipedia: http://en.wikipedia.org/wiki/Three_wise_monkeys.

who, typically, saw no other answer to the global financial crisis than to increase consumption, to 'make the wheels run faster'.

As a counterblast to this view we seek with this book to direct attention towards eco-global crimes and the abuse of non-human species, and to look at the causes of these behaviors and the challenges they present now and in the future. The fact that the book is being published may point to a more positive trend, exemplified also by the afore-mentioned growing body of literature in the field. By expanding the agenda for criminology in this way, and by not leaving eco-global problems to environmental and animal rights movements alone, we also seek to give these issues further academic weight, and consequently to increase the impact of this kind of research and these ideas.

As the topics which need to be addressed in order to secure the health of Tellus and its inhabitants are challenging, we can in this book only point to some crucial immediate issues. In this we share in building knowledge, stone by stone, which hopefully will inspire other social scientists, and also influence social movements, politicians and decision-makers.

Outline of the Book

The book is divided into three parts. This said, it is important to add that themes may overlap, and be treated from different perspectives in the different sections. The first part of the book – Introduction to Eco-global Criminology – is theoretical, starting with Rob White's chapter, *The Foundations of Eco-global Criminology,* in which he provides an overview of the different kinds of crimes/harms which can be encompassed within the field of eco-global criminology. In this he shows precisely the transnational, global character of eco-global crimes/harms, and how an action in one local context may impact other places and people far from where the harm was initiated. In demonstrating the multiversity of eco-global crimes, White also emphasizes the urgency with which these problems must be met. He provides us with the theoretical tools to discuss eco-global crimes through a justice perspective by using the terms ecological justice, environmental justice and species justice. These are important concepts which need to be further developed by means of empirical examples, and to be absorbed deeper into the theoretical basis of eco-global criminology through discussion and amplification.

The latter is illustrated by Guri Larsen in Chapter 3, *The Most Serious Crime: Eco-genocide*, in which she critically scrutinizes the inherent meaning of the different concepts used in the field, such as the concepts of *harm*, *green criminology,* and *eco-global criminology*, and provides arguments for why the concept eco-global criminology is better equipped to address eco-crimes than the previously more established concept *green criminology.* In her discussion Larsen also makes the point that ecological justice includes an emphasis on environmental and species justice. Ecological justice reflects the interdependence between all kinds of life on the planet, whether life is part of nature or culture. She distinguishes between *ecocrime* as a legal category, and *ecocide* as a moral category. However, as legal acts may be even more destructive, she introduces a new concept: *eco-genocide*, which she sees as a unifying category for both illegal and legal damage that cause harm to nature-culture unit, that is, to the environment, animals, the climate and to humans and human societies.

In Chapter 4, *Constructing a Meta-history of Eco-global Criminology – On Brute Criminologists, Mortified Bunnies, Nature and its Discontent*, Per Jørgen Ystehede traces the historical and theoretical roots of eco-global criminology, by creating a genealogy of eco-global criminological research spanning 150 years. He suggests that the history of eco-global criminology, especially the part encompassing the human–animal–nature relationship, may be divided into three main intellectual historical developments, or stages, which can be seen as partly shadowing the history of the science of criminology in general. In the first stages animals, as being nature, were regarded as criminal agents. This view was heavily influenced by the tendency of 18th century men of letters value comparisons between moral temperament, and the physical appearance of humans and animals. In this stage, though recognizing humans' relatedness to nature, humans still distinguished themselves from animals and nature by regarding them as criminal. Thus man when criminal was closer to nature – nature being criminal. In the second stage, attention focused on sexual crimes: bestiality or zoophilia, as it was called by Richard von Krafft-Ebing, with animals being of interest as objects acted upon by men's sexually deviant desires, and regarded as symptoms of deviance rather than victims. We are now in the third stage, in which non-human animals and nature are gradually acquiring victim status. These three stages represent shifts in thinking about eco-global crime.

In the second part of the book, *Speciesism, Animal Abuse and Social Movements*, the human–animal relationship's theoretical roots are further examined, starting with Chapter 5 *The Rhetorical Making of a Crime Called Speciesism* by Kristian Bjørkdahl. Bjørkdahl examines letters sent to animal activist and academic Peter Singer to gain an understanding of his role in pioneering the modern animal rights movement by publishing *Animal Liberation* in 1975. In presenting his reading of these letters, Bjørkdahl analyses how the book came to have so great an impact by providing/spreading a new concept – speciesism – which also gave new meaning to the human–animal relationship. Through the publication of this book, the systematic discrimination against animals on the basis of species differences was publicly acknowledged and given academic weight. However, despite the attention and recognition the book received, and its success in putting animal rights on the agenda, it has, as Bjørkdahl observes, nonetheless had little practical influence on the lives of billions of animals worldwide. Animals are used in agribusiness and as research tools on a larger scale than ever before.

The reasons why animal abuse and speciesism persist on such a large scale are discussed by Ragnhild Aslaug Sollund in Chapter 6 of the book: *Speciesism as Doxic Practice Versus Valuing Difference and Plurality*. In it she discusses how techniques of neutralization and denial serve to preserve doxic practices of animal abuse and exploitation, thus being precisely the reasons why Singer's book has not had greater practical impact. Critical of the logic of Peter Singers' and Tom Regan's argument that animals should be accorded similar rights to humans because they are anthropocentrically similar and that this view presupposes that similarity to humans is required if rights are to be accorded, Sollund instead claims that animals should have equal rights because of their different species' *genuine* individuality and specific features and capacities. Consequently, one should argue for equal rights not only because other animals have the same capacities as humans to experience pain, suffering and joy, but also because of *different* interests and different capacities worthy of equal, or even greater respect – precisely because of this difference. By arguing for the valuing of difference, she also argues for the appreciation of plurality and heterogeneity.

In Chapter 7 of the book, *The Ideological Fantasy of Animal Welfare, a Lacanian Perspective on the Reproduction of Speciesism*, Per-Anders Svärd examines animal welfare ideology and asks, if everyone publicly disavows animal abuse, how can we explain persistent abusive practices directed at animals? Counter to what one would intuitively believe, one reason may be the animal welfare ideologies which, by giving people a fantasy image of how animals are treated, serve to reinforce and uphold speciesist ideology and practice. Another reason is that by regarding animal abusers as 'The Other', those who commit these acts of cruelty are in fundamental ways regarded as different from 'us', the animal welfarists. Thus 'we' can continue our practices because the guilt is placed on the 'Other'. The animal welfare ideology is hegemonic – it is one the majority of people can espouse. But at the same time, Svärd says, it is equally taken for granted that we are free to use animals for food and other purposes, as long as we treat them 'humanely'. The stability of this particular articulation of appropriate human–animal relations is remarkable.

In Chapter 8, *Natural Exploitation: the Shaping of the Human-animal Relationship through Concepts and Statements*, Ingvill H. Riise discusses discourse as a shaping element in thehuman–animal relationship, with its inherent domination and exploitation. She applies discourse analysis to a central political document *Report to the Storting nr. 12 (2002–03): On animal husbandry and animal welfare.* Riise discusses how speciesist practices are being upheld through the use of conceptual power, while also noting the role of some ethically significant concepts and terms in the process of legitimization of animal exploitation. At the same time she also shows how debate about fundamental ethical questions is being avoided. For example, statements such as: 'Humans have always used animals' stress the 'correctness' and 'unavoidability' of exploiting non-humans and stigmatize opponents, thus facilitating the avoidance of ethical debate. However, the fact that animal exploitation seeks legitimization in this way can also indicate a positive trend, because the exploitation of animals, previously taken for granted, now apparently needs justification.

Strong interests are involved in these matters, both those of states and those of capitalist industry, which is often supported by state law enforcement agencies, and states and capitalists work hard and deliberately to counteract those who protest against animal abuse and exploitation. This is documented in Chapter 9 by Elisa Aaltola: *Differing Philosophies: Criminalization and the Stop Huntingdon Animal Cruelty Debate.* The conflict between those who profit from animal abuse and those who oppose it increases because, on the one hand activists argue that certain forms of animal use are, or should be, illegal, while corporations, states and many within the news media suggest that activists should be criminalized for their animal activism, as indeed they are. The case studied by Aaltola involves the effective protest campaign by Stop Huntingdon Animal Cruelty (SHAC) against the company Huntingdon Life Sciences (HLS), a big laboratory that tests the toxicity of various chemicals on animals. Particular attention is given to how and with what means the activists were criminalized in the attempt to silence their disclosure of HLS' practices, which led to sentences of up to 11 years in prison for some involved in this activist process.

The criminalization of animal rights activists and the political repression of green social movements more generally is also a focus in Rune Ellefsen in Chapter 10, *Green Movements as Threats to Order and Economy? Animal Activists Repressed in Austria and Beyond.* This chapter builds on a case study of political repression against Austrian animal advocates, when activists were charged under anti-mafia law (§ 278a). At least 40 people were singled out for surveillance before police raids and arrests. The case received massive media attention, seven of those arrested began hunger strikes, solidarity groups were established and in numerous countries across the world there was action in support of the detainees. The arrested activists were held in custody for more than one hundred days of pre-trial detention, and not until a year after their release were the charges made official. After years of intense police investigations and a trial lasting for over hundreds of days, the verdict was finally announced by the judge on 2 May 2011: it acquitted the 13 accused of all charges, both that of membership of a criminal organization, and those relating to other individual offences. Ellefsen explores how repression was brought to bear, and examines some of its possible aims and motives. In his description of the Austrian events he points to the international trend for increased surveillance and criminalization of animal rights and ecological resistance movements across Europe and the USA, something also documented by Aaltola in the previous chapter.

Ellefsen argues that the repression and persecution of the activists became so intense because of economic costs for individual animal industries that resulted from the achievements of animal advocates. Thus the industries see activists as threats. By pushing for stricter legislation, animal advocates also indirectly threaten the financial interests of animal-based industries, such as those based on animal testing and fur production. They damage the public image of animal agribusinesses by revealing the suffering of the animals which are used, thus adversely affecting sales and reducing trust in such companies.

Following this focus on the repression of opinions and viewpoints which create opposition to widespread animal abuse, the third part of the book, *Biodiversity,*

Environmental and Species Justice, considers policy processes which aim to control nature and the creatures living in it through regulations, while at the same time producing regulations which preserve and maintain the use of 'natural resources', mostly from an anthropocentric viewpoint.

This section begins with Chapter 11, entitled *Unlawful Hunting of Large Carnivores in Sweden* by Lars Korsell and Johanna Hagstedt. The chapter is based upon empirical data provided by a large number of interviews with people in Sweden who illegally kill predators – wolves, lynx, wolverines and golden eagles. It also includes analysis of verdicts given at trials of these crimes. The existence and protection of large predators is a source of conflict and debate, both in Sweden and Norway. Much is at stake, historically and culturally, in the case of the wolf because it is an animal to which a lot of superstition and fear is attached. There is also a tension between farmers, who want to keep their sheep outside without supervision, and environmentalists, who want to ensure that Sweden (and Norway) act according to the Berne convention. The predator issue has also become a symbol for the conflict between urban and rural areas, between the governed and the governors and between local governance and globalization in the form of EU directives and legislation.

Both the direct threats mentioned above, as well as the larger contextual conflicts are factors that affect the incidence of unlawful hunting. The study reveals that there are many motivations for people to kill the predators illegally: hatred of the predators, the taste for trophy hunting and the status it brings in the social context, the interests of 'life-stylers' and animal owners who see predators as a threat to their lifestyle and of 'businessmen', who organize hunts for their business partners. Life-stylers are perhaps the most serious threat to predators, since they have both the will and the means to engage in illegal hunting, as hunting is part of their lifestyle. They are also able to hide the crime. An important finding is that law enforcement of these crimes is weak.

In Chapter 12, *Native Nature and Alien Invasions: Battling with Concepts and Plants at Fornebu* by Marte Qvenild, we leave animals in favour of plant species and see how the question of preserving biodiversity and native species was approached and debated in the aftermath of the construction of the new airport in Oslo. When the old airport, *Fornebu*, was left empty, this opened discussion about how the land should be used. Following the closing of the airport, 'alien' plant species were used by the Norwegian Directorate of Public Construction and Property (Statsbygg) to refurbish the former landing strip. During the reconstruction process the environmental NGO, SABIMA, reported Statsbygg to the police for an environmental crime. Globally, the spread of invasive alien species is currently viewed in the light of scientific biological knowledge as a collective threat to national biodiversity. This has resulted in eco-nationalistic approaches to biodiversity protection which creates new legal and moral borders for the exclusion, inclusion and spread of species. The Fornebu case raises questions as to what type of environmental crime the introduction of invasive alien plant species is, and how such introductions are categorized, and this illuminates how conflicts over environmental harm in Norway are morally and socially charged.

In Chapter 13, *Industrializing Greenland: Government and Transnational Corporations vs Civil Society*, Mikkel Myrup discusses another topic of great current interest, which has relevance in places other than Greenland, the geographical context of this particular case. The question posed is whether, and to what extent, natural resources such as minerals should be extracted for human benefit, when this exploitation is at the same time highly polluting and damaging to human and animal life, as well as to the environment. In May 2009 there was a referendum on whether Greenland should obtain the status of a self-governing body within the Danish Commonwealth. This status is considered to be the final step before full independence. Two thirds of the votes were in favour of self-government. Mikkel Myrup shows how great tension has arisen in Greenland society because of conflicting interests: the desire on the one hand to be economically independent from Denmark, through the exploitation of natural minerals and hydro power, and on the other, the wish to preserve the environment. This is not much different from the situation in other parts of the world when mining in territories of indigenous peoples are involved. Depletion of shrimp and halibut stocks and plummeting prices on the world market have led to an increased interest in attracting transnational corporation (TNC) investments, mainly in the mineral and hydrocarbon extraction sector. Hydropower potential is also attractive to heavy industry requiring vast amounts of cheap energy, such as primary aluminum-producing TNCs (for example, Alcoa Inc). The situation in Greenland is thus a fresh example of how a 'goldrush', facilitated by liberalism and deregulation, is benefiting capitalist interests as such as those of Alcoa, and harming the environment and living beings.

In Chapter 14, *Environmental Harm: Social Causes and Shifting Legislative Dynamics*, Sigurd Dybing discusses pollution produced by large corporations. He presents three cases: the polluting of Norwegian fiords with PCB and mercury, the catastrophic oil spill in the Gulf of Mexico in 2010 caused by the explosion of the oil rig *Deepwater Horizon*, owned by British Petroleum and the explosion of a tank of Cocker Gasoline owned by the company Vest Tank in Gulen, Norway, in May 2007. The contents of the tank that exploded in Gulen are alleged to have been the same material that was dumped in 2006 in the Ivory Coast, causing the deaths of 14 people, and injuring several hundred more. The Netherland-based company Trafigura, which was responsible for the toxic waste dumping in the Ivory Coast, entered into an agreement with Vest Tank after the dumping, because no other company in the world wanted the toxic waste. This is a very good example of the transnational character of ecological crimes, and of the fact that, while the trade in electronic waste is *per se* not illegal, it will often have illegal consequences, as when Vest Tank was trading in toxic waste without permission. Though the two last examples happened suddenly, and thus aroused a great deal of attention, pollution more often has long-term effects, which take time to be recognized, as is often the case with PCB pollution, and consequent poisoning. The aim of sustainable development is to ensure that environmental regulation meets social needs both economically and existentially. The absence of a balanced focus on the core issues of environmental protection may have real social consequences for humans and other beings, in the present, and most certainly in the future. Actions that for decades were viewed as normal business practice are now forbidden, but this does not mean that law enforcement is not often complicated.

In Chapter 15, *Enacting Human and Non-Human Indigenous: Salmon, Sami and Norwegian Natural Resource Management*, Gro Birgit Ween describes a particular bureaucratic incident from 2010 in Norway, which juxtaposes environmental justice in terms of the rights of indigenous people to survive in the same way they have always done, in this case by catching wild salmon, and species justice in terms of the rights of a specific stock of wild salmon to survive. This conflict arose when the Directorate of Nature Management, in an effort to establish a new wild salmon management regime, was forced to consider Coastal Sami fishermen's cultural rights in relation to the economic potential of salmon as a resource. Here, the survival of the indigenous fish intersects with the rights of the human indigenes. Ween's research into this bureaucratic problem shows that the environmental institutions involved approached the two indigenous categories in much the same way. Although the indigenous humans and salmon were poised as co-constituted, the emphasis on economic benefits served increasingly to foreground the salmon indigenes, thus affecting bureaucratic perceptions of the nature of human indigeneity. The nature of indigeneity was made dependent on context, on questions asked, legal documents referred to, statistics recited, academic writings adduced and definitions invoked. As the economic argument gained significance, when the value of the salmon in economic terms became evident, the Directorate attempted to devalue human indigeneity by ranking human and non-human indigeneity according to the same criteria. They felt that the purity of both kinds of indigeneity was that which legitimized species survival: when wild salmon became hybrids and when the human indigenes used the same fishing gear as non-indigenous people, the ordered purity that legitimized existing categories dissolved.

The chapters of this book provide an interesting collection which add to the literature, and answer some questions, but raise new ones which need further study. For example, what are the rights *to* nature and the rights *of* nature, and how should these relate to the individual rights of humans and animals? These may produce the same dilemmas as the rights of the individual – whether human or non-human – versus the rights of ethnic groups and species, but on an even wider scale. How can justice *between* people in different parts of the world be achieved while at the same time ecological, environmental and species justice is ensured? And how can justice be achieved for and between non-human species, as habitats are restricted? How can ecological, environmental and species justice be secured under the prevailing liberal capitalist system? The ways in which nature and other species are currently exploited conflict with new (in reality old) ways of perceiving nature which respect a more holistic world view, such as that represented by recent Ecuadorian and Bolivian legislation granting eco-systems and mother nature – *Pachamama* – rights.[3] How may such a view be extended globally? How can the securing of individual rights on the global level – whether those of animals or humans – become a reality, rather than a vision, without further harming the ecological balance? While contemplating these questions, we believe that this book will provide new ideas and new insight.

References

Aas, K.F. 2011. 'Crimmigrant' Bodies and Bona fide Travelers: Surveillance, Citizenship and Global Governance, in *Theoretical Criminology*, 15(3), 331–46.

Beirne, P. 1995. The Use and Abuse of Animals in Criminology, in *Social Justice*, 22(1), 5–31.

Beirne, P. 1999. For a Non-speciesist Criminology: Animal Abuse as an Object of Study, in *Criminology: An Interdisciplinary Journal.* The official publication of the American Society of Criminology, 37(1), 117–48.

Beirne, P. 2009. *Confronting Animal Abuse.* Lanham: Rowman & Littlefield.

Boekhout van Solinge, T. 2008a. Crime, Conflicts and Ecology in Africa, in *Global Harms: Ecological Crime and Speciesism*, edited by R. Sollund. New York: Nova Science Publishers, 13–35.

Boekhout van Solinge, T. 2008b. The Land of the Orangutan and the Bird of Paradise Under Threat, in *Global Harms: Ecological Crime and Speciesism*, edited by R. Sollund. New York: Nova Science Publishers, 51–71.

Cazaux, G. 1999. Beauty and the Beast: Animal abuse from a non-speciesist criminological perspective, in *Crime, Law and Social Change*, 31(2), 105–26.

Cohen, S. 2000. *States of Denial.* London: Cambridge Polity Press.

Donovan, J. 1993. Animal Rights and Feminist Theory, in *Ecofeminism: Women, Animals, Nature*, edited by G.C. Gaard. Philadelphia: Temple University press, 167–94.

Engbersen, G., van San. M. and Leerkes, A. 1999. A Room with a View: Irregular Immigrants in the Legal Capital of the World, in *Ethnography*, 7(2), 209–42.

Lynch, M. 1990. 'The Greening of Criminology': A Perspective for the 1990s, in *Critical Criminologist*, 3(2), 1–5.

O'Brien, M. 2008. Criminal Degradations and Consumer Culture, in *Global Harms: Ecological Crime and Speciesism*, edited by R. Sollund. New York: Nova Science Publishers, 35–50.

Pires, S. and Clark, R. 2010. Are Parrots Craved? An Analysis of Parrot Poaching in Mexico, in *Journal of Research in Crime and Delinquency*, 48(4).

Regan, T. 1988. *The Case for Animal Rights:* London: Routledge.

3 See http://www.foxnews.com/world/2011/04/18/prepares-debate-rights-mother-earth/, and http://www.rightsofmotherearth.com/rights-nature/ecuador-rights/ [Accessed 10 September 2011].

Singer, P. 1977. *Animal Liberation*. New York: Avon.

Sollund, R. 2008. Causes for Speciesism: Difference, Distance and Denial, in *Global Harms: Ecological Crime and Speciesism*, edited by R. Sollund. New York: Nova Science Publishers, 109–30.

South, N. 2008. Nature, Difference and the Rejection of Harm: Expanding the Agenda for Green Criminology, in *Global Harms: Ecological Crime and Speciesism*, edited by R. Sollund. New York: Nova Science Publishers, 187–200.

Walters, R. 2007. Politics, Economy and Environmental Crime, *Criminal Justice Matters*, 70(1), 27–8.

White, R. 2008. *Crimes Against Nature: Environmental Criminology and Ecological Justice*. Devon: Willan Publishing.

White, R. 2010. Globalisation and Environmental Harm, in *Global Environmental Harm: Criminological Perspectives*. Devon: Willan.

White, R. 2011. *Transnational Environmental Crime. Toward an Eco-global Criminology*. London: Routledge.

Chapter 2
The Foundations of Eco-global Criminology

Rob White

Introduction

A concern with environmental crime inevitably leads the analytical gaze to acknowledge the fusion of the local and the global, and to ponder the ways in which such harms transcend the normal boundaries of jurisdiction, geography and social divide. This observation is important because so much environmental harm is intrinsically transnational. Contemporary discussions of environmental crime, for example, deal with issues such as the illegal transport and dumping of toxic waste, the illegal traffic in radioactive or nuclear substances, the proliferation of 'e'-waste generated by the disposal of tens-of-thousands of computers and other electronic equipment, trans-border pollution that is systematic (via location of factories) or accidental (for example, chemical plant spills), the illegal trade in plants and non-human animals, and illegal fishing, hunting and logging. This list goes on, but the point is that environmental harm, whether conceptualised in conventional legal terms or based upon more encompassing ecologically-based conceptions of harm, is by nature mobile and easily subject to transference.

The systemic causal chains that underpin much environmental harm are located at the level of the global political economy – within which the transnational corporation stands as the central social force – and this, too, is reflected in the pressing together of the local-global at a practical level. For example, the agribusiness company Monsanto has come under scrutiny by those who are concerned about genetically modified organisms (GMOs). Not only has study revealed the huge extent of Monsanto's reach and power in the GMO area in many different countries around the world, but also specific breaches of the law, including major acts of environmental harm (Engdahl 2007, Robin 2010, Smith 2003). International systems of production, distribution and consumption generate, reinforce and reward diverse environmental harms and those who perpetrate them (White 2002, 2008). These production-distribution systems include the distribution of unsafe toys, the increasing reliance on genetically modified grains, the destruction of out-of-date ships and planes and the transportation and dumping of hazardous chemicals that were central to production. A basic premise of green or environmental criminology is that we need to take environmental harm seriously, and that in order to do this we need conceptualisations of harm that go beyond conventional understandings of crime (Beirne and South 2007). Green criminology emphasises 'environmental justice, with a special focus on human rights and social equity; and ecological justice, with a special focus on the biosphere generally and the rights of non-human as well as human' (White 2007: 50). However, the doing of green criminology also requires a sense of scale, and of the essential interconnectedness of issues, events, people and places.

The intention of this chapter is to provide an introduction and outline of the key concepts and broad methodological approach of eco-global criminology. The chapter is based upon and draws from a recent book, *Transnational Environmental Crime: Toward an Eco-global Criminology* (White 2011). Eco-global criminology is a framework of analysis that emphasizes the ecological, the transnational and questions of justice. The substantive focus of eco-global criminology is transgressions against ecosystems, humans and non-human animals. The chapter explicates the core concerns of the paradigm as these relate to the concepts of harm, crime and justice from legal, ecological and green criminological perspectives.

The chapter then explores the methodological implications of a framework that purports to be global in scope. For example, issues of space and time are discussed in the context of the transference of harm across borders and over time. The question of scale is associated with particular types of crime and harm, ranging from the global (for example, climate change) to the local (for example, specific events and incidents such as oil spills). Cross-national and cross-cultural research and networks are crucial in the light of common experiences and shared interests around ecological issues.

The chapter concludes by discussing the importance of horizon scanning to the doing of eco-global criminology. This refers to a process of looking over the horizon at those issues and trends that are likely to involve environmental crime and harm now and in the future. For example, global warming may impact the extent and intensity of 'natural' disasters such as floods, tsunami, earthquakes, heat-waves, landslides and cyclones. Accompanying such disasters are a broad range of criminal activities, including rape, mob violence, company fraud, misappropriation of crisis aid and the formation of armed gangs. Many such crimes happened in the aftermath of Hurricane Katrina in New Orleans and the earthquake in Haiti, and in both cases the safety and wellbeing of non-human animals (especially animal companions such as dogs and cats) were largely ignored. Futures analyses are essential to strategic planning and early intervention if we are to adequately deal with such risks and harms.

A word about language is warranted before proceeding. Any survey of green criminology literature must recognise that language is socially constructed and describes the world in a particular way. This is perhaps most evident in regards to how criminologists and others speak about 'animals'. From a conventional 'natural resource' perspective (see for example, Gibbs et al. 2010, Herbig and Joubert 2006) the language used to speak about animals tends to be anthropocentric and instrumental. Thus, animals are categorised in terms of 'wildlife' and 'fisheries'. Environmental laws and laws specifically about animals likewise tend to define animals in ways that determine their 'value' through reference to human conceptions and human uses (Sankoff and White 2009). By contrast, green criminologists who write primarily about animal rights and animal welfare issues describe such anthropocentric descriptions as a form of 'specieism' (see Beirne 2007, Sollund 2008). From this perspective, it is the suffering of non-human animals – whether construed as wild, domestic or commercial – that is of central concern, not whether the suffering stems from illegal criminal acts or not (since much animal suffering is linked to legal activities such as abattoirs and factory farms that rely upon animals as food sources).

The moral standing of non-human animals thus varies, not only within criminology generally, but within green criminology specifically. So, too, the presence of animals in green criminology analyses will vary greatly depending upon the specific writer and the specific topic being discussed. The differences in conceptual and practical emphasis on animals within green criminology are reflected to some degree in the discussions that follow and in the variability of language used to discuss different topics.

Ecology

Eco-global criminology provides a 'framework of analysis' that directs our attention to particular problems and ways of seeing and analysing the world around us. It is based upon three intertwined conceptual categories: the ecological, the transnational and the criminal/harmful. Eco-global criminology is not a 'theory' as such, since it does not purport to offer an overarching causal explanation for transnational environmental crime (for example, to blame it on 'capitalism' or 'overpopulation' or 'specieism'). It does not seek to answer the question of why things happen or occur in this more general sense; rather, it is concerned with matters of how things are as they are. Answers to the 'why' question are instead devolved to lower levels of abstraction (that is, concrete cases relating to prosecution of offenders) and are specific to the topic at hand (for example, explanations for the low penalties assigned to environmental offenders). Eco-global criminologists want to get to the bottom of environmental harm by identifying what happened, how it happened, why it happened and who knew it and when.

What makes eco-global criminology distinctive is the attention given to specifically ecological considerations of harm, as well as its concern with a global perspective on issues and events. Accordingly, this section briefly elaborates on some key ecological harms in order to illustrate the major threats to planetary wellbeing posed by climate change, diminished biodiversity and pollution.

Climate Change

A key problem identified by the United Nations Environment Programme (2007) is that of climate change. According to UNEP there are several interrelated dimensions to the problem. These include ozone depletion, climate change linked to various kinds of emissions and the impact of air pollution on global warming.

In large measure, the problem of climate change is directly related to how humans across the globe produce and consume, distribute and exchange the fruits of their labour. While, to date, the impact of climate change on humans has been felt disproportionately in the developing countries, recent estimates indicate that the more affluent countries of the West are now beginning to experience climate-related disasters (see UNEP 2007). Plants and animals are affected not only by global warming (for example, through threats to habitat and weather changes), but by human efforts to mitigate and adapt to climate change (for example, deforestation linked to planting of GMO crops). Coping with climate change means dealing with the unexpected. This poses a major challenge for planners, policymakers, regulators and others tasked with the job of minimising the potential threats, while considering possible solutions. Criminologists, likewise, have a role in these processes.

The Problem of Biodiversity

Commodification is taking place in regards to all aspects of human life, and in all parts of the globe. The global political economy of genetically modified organisms (GMOs) provides a case in point, insofar as the promotion of GMOs by large transnational corporations has continued apace, regardless of serious reservations being raised about significant potential risks to human health and safety, antibiotic immunity and contamination of the environment (Walters 2011). These kinds of developments ultimately lead to reliance upon fewer species (of plant and of animal) in regards to food production for humans. That is, the transformation of genetic material via science and biotechnology also tends toward homogenisation of species composition – it is more profitable to reduce variety at the same time as increase quantitative productivity with the 'winners'. The overall result is an attitude of 'fewer species is better' (and more profitable), especially if control over these is vested in private hands. In more conventional environmental and criminal law terms, the illegal trade in plants and animals represent their own kind of threat, as well. The threat here is both to biodiversity in relation to endangered species, and to the economic viability of industries such as agriculture, forestry and fisheries. In this scenario, both individual members of, and species as a whole, are potentially harmed. Humans are destroying what is anthropocentrically viewed as their 'natural resources'. Whether contaminants enter into the food production system through illegal importation of banned organic substances or the legal use of patented materials, the result will be the same – devastation to the basic requirements of life.

The Problem of Waste

A third major area of environmental concern has to do with the problems associated with waste and pollution (White 2008, 2009a). Some of the more pressing issues include the proliferation of 'e-waste' generated by the disposal of tens-of-thousands of computers and other equipment, and more generally widespread pollution of air, land and water. Much of the transfer of waste has been from advanced industrialised countries to developing countries (Clapp 2001). So, too, the most polluted places on earth tend to likewise be developing countries. Meanwhile, hazardous residues and contaminated sludge are most likely to find a foreign home in a Third World country. We can add to the list of trans-border problems the threats to health posed by smog, and more generally indoor and outdoor pollutants. These have been shown to have a major impact on human and animal health and wellbeing, and the negative health consequences are apparent in both developing and the more developed countries (UNEP 2007: 55). Air pollution also adversely affects agriculture, among other things, which impacts food quality and quantity. Thus, trends in hazardous waste releases have major implications for the nature of crime, the dynamics of criminality and the operations of criminal justice systems (in terms of prosecutions as well as dealing with transnational organised crime).

Geography

To appreciate fully the nature of global environmental crime it is essential to consider the physical location of harm within particular geographical contexts. On a world map, it is possible to plot out a myriad of different types of harms, some of which are common across the surface, others of which, however, are specific to particular locales, regions and countries. This is illustrated in Table 2.1. Layers of harm, present and potential, can be determined by, on the one hand, investigating ecological trends that involve degradation and destruction of environments (such as clear-felling of forests), and on the other, by considering existing documentation of specific types of environmental crime (such as illegal international trade in plants and animals).

Table 2.1 Geographical scale and environmental harm

Scale	Example
The Local	Lobster poaching in Nova Scotia, Canada. Abalone theft in Tasmania, Australia.
The National	Pollution related to pastoral industry in New Zealand. Issues of drinking water in Palestine, Israel and Jordan.
The Regional	Logging in the forests of the Amazon. Killing of elephants for their tusks in Africa.
The Global	Global warming and natural disasters. Formation of huge plastic dumps in oceans.
The Transnational	Global trade in toxic waste. Shifting of dirty industries to developing countries.

The harms described in Table 2.1 are interconnected and intertwined in various ways: the 'butterfly effect' is real in more ways than one. What happens at the local level has consequences for those on the other side of the planet. What happens in any one place is thus intrinsically important to what happens worldwide.

Locality is important and refers to those places where we live, work and play. Around the world, different countries tend to have different types of environmental problems and issues. In New Zealand, for example, important concerns have arisen over the use of pesticides and overuse of land for agriculture and pastoral purposes. Land and water is being contaminated through existing systems of production. By contrast, pressing issues of concern in Canada relate to the ecological impact of the huge oil tar sands projects in Alberta, and to the impact of insect blights on the pine trees of British Columbia. National context is important in both the objective nature of the problems at hand (for example, pollution, deforestation, lack of adequate water), and in regards to subjective processes relating to the politicisation of issues (for example, the role of social movements in shaping public consciousness and state action on specific issues).

Most countries of the world share at least one border with another country. Rivers flow, mountains soar, air currents weave their way through the atmosphere and animals move across artificial boundaries that do not exist in an ecological sense. There are issues that are specific to particular regions of the world. Huge tropical forests are found in the Amazon, an area that encompasses several different countries such as Brazil and Columbia. Such forests also cover parts of South-East Asia, spanning Indonesia, Malaysia, Thailand and Burma, amongst other countries. Africa is home to elephants, reptiles, giraffe and other creatures that are unique to particular parts of that continent, and not the preserve of any one country. Desertification and drought are phenomena associated with the dry lands of Northern Africa and the island continent of Australia. Meanwhile, cross-border pollution in Europe, and between China and Russia, are matters that demand a regional rather than simply national response. Acid rain traverses provincial and state demarcations and can affect environments, animals and humans many kilometres away. A nuclear accident in the Ukraine makes its presence felt in Britain, as well as the immediate vicinity of Chernobyl. Radioactivity stemming from nuclear meltdown in Japan moves around the globe via waterways and air currents.

The opportunities for certain types of crime are influenced by very specific local and regional factors. For example, the penetration and dominance of the Mafia in the waste disposal industry in Italy provides a unique but devastating illustration of national difference (compared to countries where organised crime is not involved in this industry) that has an international impact (through dumping of toxic waste in international waters). In Central and Western Africa, the global bush meat trade is driven by several different factors and has dire consequences for apes, chimpanzees, gorillas and other primates especially, which are threatened with extinction. Local habitats for these non-human animals are being lost through logging and commercial developments. Not only are the adult primates being killed for food and body parts, but orphaned primates are being sold on the exotic pet market, further contributing to the degradation of these species.

The production of global environmental harm is partly determined through complex processes of transference (Heckenberg 2010). Harm can move from one place to another. The recent toxic incident in Hungary provides a tragic illustration of this, when a thick red torrent of sludge burst from a reservoir at a metals plant 100 kilometres south of Budapest in early October 2010. At least nine people died as a result of the sludge surge, some went missing and over one hundred persons were physically injured as the toxic substance flowed into nearby villages and towns. The toxic sludge reached the Danube River several days later, from where it could flow into six other European countries before reaching the Black Sea: Croatia, Serbia, Romania, Bulgaria, Ukraine and Moldova. Meanwhile, a recent report by the Norwegian Radiation Protection Authority has concluded that if only 1 per cent of the liquid radioactive waste stored at the Sellafield nuclear power plant in Britain was released to air, the radioactive fallout in Western Norway could be five times higher than in the areas of Norway that were worst affected by the Chernobyl accident (Norway Ministry of the Environment 2011).

Harm can also be externalised from producers and consumers in ways that make it disappear from their sight and oversight. The global trade in toxic waste (often under the cover of recycling), the illegal dumping of radioactive waste, carbon emission trading and the shifting of dirty industries to developing countries constitute some of the worst aspects of the 'not in my backyard' syndrome. The result is a massive movement of environmentally harmful products, processes and wastes to the most vulnerable places and most exploited peoples of the world. The transnational also provides the context for the emergence of specific types of criminal activity. For instance, the decline in the number of fish off the coast of Somalia, due to over-fishing by many different nations and groups of fishers, has robbed the local people of their main traditional livelihood. One consequence of this has been the move into another line of work – the most notorious being piracy on the high seas. Environmental harm, whether legal or not, can generate its own spin-off crimes.

Specific places demand specific analysis, yet these are intrinsically linked into considerations that are universal in their relevance and application. For instance, transnational environmental harm is always located somewhere. That is, while risk and harm can be analysed in terms of movements and transference from one place to another, it is nonetheless imperative that threats to the environment be put into specific regional and national contexts. This is important for several reasons. First, environmental threats originate in particular factories, farms, firms, industries and localities. Second, the political and policy context within which threats to the environment emerge is shaped by the nature of and interplay between local, national, regional and international laws and conventions. What happens at the local and regional level counts – whether we are referring to the Nordic countries, those of South Eastern Europe, Australasia or Latin America.

What happens at the local level is likewise implicated in decisions and processes that transcend the merely local, given the complex international ties and connections between businesses, governments, workers and activists. For example, Australian conservationists have linked with their activist counterparts in Japan to influence the relationship between Japanese paper companies and a Tasmanian forestry company engaged in the clear-felling of old growth forest. Protests have effectively been internationalised, although the destruction occurs in a specific place (White 2005). Business associations and cross-national environmental campaigns are illustrative of how closely connected we all are in an increasingly globalised world.

Examination of transnational environmental harm also needs to take into account geographical locations of varying environmentally harmful practices. This might include analysis of origins (of toxic materials, of the location of particular unique species of plant), transit points (illegal trade – at sea, on land, in particular regions) and end points (for waste dumping, for exotic plant collectors). A global mapping of harmful practices can serve to provide useful insights into how harm is transferred around the planet, and ultimately who or what is responsible for which kinds of harm. Simultaneously, the combined effects of human transformations of nature are having repercussions well beyond the local and regional.

Crime and Justice

To speak of environmental crime or eco-crime is to acknowledge some kind of specificity in the act or omission that makes it distinctly relevant to environmental considerations. Yet, as with crime generally, there is much dispute over what gets defined as environmentally harmful and what ends up with the legal status as 'crime' *per se*. The definition of transnational environmental crime is contentious and ambiguous. Much depends upon who is defining the harm, and what criteria are used in assessing the nature of the activities so described (for example, legal versus ecological, criminal justice versus environmental justice) (see Situ and Emmons 2000, Beirne and South 2007, White 2008). As mentioned earlier, the language used also shapes how 'harm' and 'value' are socially constructed in regards to (specific groups of) humans, specific biospheres and non-human animals.

From the point of view of eco-global criminology, analysis of transnational environmental crime needs to incorporate different, albeit interrelated notions of harm. This is shown in Table 2.2. These include *legal conceptions* of harm informed by laws, rules and international conventions, and that pertain to things such illegal fishing and the transportation of banned substances (this is the substance of conventional criminology). They include consideration of *ecological wellbeing* and holistic understandings of harm that are informed by the interrelationship between species and environments, and that see the key issue of ecological sustainability in the light of global warming and species extinction (this the main focus for ecology and environmental studies). They include *justice conceptions* of harm that are informed by notions of human, ecological and animal rights, and egalitarian concerns, and that are concerned with preserving complex ecosystems for their own sake and preventing animal abuse (the main concerns of green criminology). These three approaches incorporate at times competing yet overlapping notions of harm (both within and between each approach) that one way or another have to be acknowledged in eco-global criminological research.

Table 2.2 Three approaches to conceptualising environmental harm

Conventional Criminology

- Illegal taking of flora and fauna – which includes activities such as illegal, unregulated and unreported fishing, illegal logging and trade in timber and illegal trade in wild plants and animals.
- Pollution offences – which relates to issues such as fly-tipping (illegal dumping) through to air, water and land pollution associated with industry.
- Transportation of banned substances – which refers to illegal transport of radioactive materials and the illegal transfer of hazardous waste.

Ecological Conceptions

- Problem of Climate Change – in which the concern is to investigate those activities that contribute to global warming, such as the replacement of forests with cropland.
- Problem of Waste and Pollution – in which the concern is with those activities that defile the environment, leading to things such as the diminishment of clean water.
- Problem of Biodiversity – in which the concern is to stem the tide of species extinction and the overall reduction in species through application of certain forms of human production, including use of genetically modified organisms.

Green Criminology

- Environment rights and environmental justice – in which environmental rights are seen as an extension of human or social rights so as to enhance the quality of human life, now and into the future.
- Ecological citizenship and ecological justice – in which ecological citizenship acknowledges that human beings are merely one component of complex ecosystems that should be preserved for their own sake via the notion of the rights of the environment.
- Animal rights and species justice – in which environmental harm is constructed in relation to the place of non-human animals within environments and their intrinsic right to not suffer abuse, whether this be one-on-one harm, institutionalised harm or harm arising from human actions that affect climates and environments on a global scale.

The argument underpinning Table 2.2 is that if ecological (and social and economic, and human and non-human) welfare is to be maximised, then we need to expand our notions of what actually constitutes an environmental crime. Harm, as conceived by critical green criminologists for example, demands more encompassing definitions than that offered by conventional law and mainstream criminology. This is because some of the most ecologically destructive activities, such as clear-felling of old growth forests, are quite legal; while more benign practices, such as growing of hemp (an extremely strong fibre), are criminalised. When criminalisation does occur, it often reflects very limited anthropocentric (human-centred) notions of what is best (for example, protection of legal fisheries and legal timber coups) that treat 'nature' and 'wildlife' simply and mainly as resources for human exploitation. It is about private property and business interests and monopolies and sustainable development. The intrinsic value of specific ecological areas and non-human species tends to be downplayed or ignored. Furthermore, exploitation of environments, plants and animals are treated as if they were equivalent – based upon their use-value to humans – rather than in the light of individual suffering and the lived experiences of harm.

Nevertheless, recent years have seen greater legislative and judicial attention being given to the rights of the environment *per se*, and to the rights of certain species of non-human animal to live free from human abuse, torture and degradation. This reflects both the efforts of eco-rights activists (for example, conservationists) and animal rights activists (for example, animal liberation movements) in changing perceptions, and laws, in regards to the natural environment and non-human species. It also reflects the growing recognition that centuries of industrialisation and global exploitation of resources are transforming the very basis of world ecology – global warming threatens us all, regardless of where we live or our specific socio-economic situation. The transnational nature and consequences of pollution, resource depletion and threats to biodiversity have likewise over the past few decades called forth a variety of international legal responses.

For eco-global criminology, the biggest threat to environmental rights, ecological justice and non-human animal wellbeing are system-level structures and pressures that commodify all aspects of social existence, that are based upon the exploitation of humans, non-human animals and natural resources and that privilege the powerful minority over the interests of the vast majority – in a word, the global capitalist political economy. Those who determine and shape the law are very often those whose activities need to be criminalised for the sake of planetary wellbeing. Environmental harm is thus intrinsically contestable, both at the level of definition, and in terms of visions of what is required for desired social and ecological change.

Doing Eco-global Criminology

What recent global study has demonstrated is that methodologically it is essential to have both a sense of history and a sense of place in the study of the phenomenon at hand. Specific historical and material conditions shape how particular activities come to predominate in particular places around the world. It is through global, comparative and historical analyses that not only differences in environmental crime, but also differences in the study of, and state and civil society responses to environmental harm, are best understood.

There are at least three different ways in which transnational research can be approached (White 2009b).

- *Global research* – examines transnational harms such as climate change and radioactive fall-out, and includes transference of harms worldwide into the open seas of our oceans as well as to nation-states everywhere.
- *Comparative research* – examines particular differences and commonalities between nation-states and specific regions of the world, identifying where the more worrisome environmental harms reside, whether related to pollution, wildlife or other issues.
- *Historical research* – examines fundamental changes in the global systems of production and consumption over time such as the shift from feudalism to mercantile capitalism to industrial capitalism, and the different environmental harms associated with these such as the proliferation of genetically modified organisms.

The first 'global' approach focuses on globalisation as a far-reaching process in which crime can be traced in its movements across the world and its presence documented in many different locales (Larsen and Smandych 2008). For example, the idea of globalisation incorporates consideration of transnational harms, processes and agencies that span the globe. It implies that there are universal effects (such as climate change) that require collaborative responses worldwide.

The second 'comparative' approach has a comparative focus, with a concern to study particular countries and regions, including failed states, in relation to each other (Gros 2008). The nature of similarities and differences is fundamental to this kind of study. Thus, the differences between nation-states and regions must be acknowledged and explained in their own right. For example, some countries and regions are more liable to be polluted than others; in others, the key issue might be the killing of elephants as part of the ivory trade.

The third 'historical' approach is based upon historical appreciation of social change and social differences (Wright Mills 1959, Cornforth 1976). It views trends and issues in terms of major epochs, such as the transitions from feudalism to capitalism, or the shift from competitive capitalism to global monopoly capitalism. There are differences in modes of production and global trends (for example, peasant-based feudal agriculture versus capitalist agribusiness), and it is important to track systemic changes over time, within and between different types of social formation.

The researching of transnational environmental crime involves a combination of these approaches. After all, environmental harm crosses borders to incorporate all nation-states on Planet Earth (as evident in ozone depletion and global warming, and the illegal trade in animals). Comparative analysis shows us where some of the 'weak links' are (especially failed states, states at war, civil unrest) and thus hot spots for particularly worrisome environmental problems (such as dumping of toxic waste). Historical studies can alert us to the ways in which 'growth states' churn up natural resources, but also how ecological consciousness can grow out of affluence and a growing middle class. And a global awareness of environmental harm may direct our concern to not only particular nation-states and regional issues, but to non-state environments, such as the open seas, that require our attention as well.

The study of transnational environmental crime has to incorporate investigation of the different types of crime that occur under this umbrella label and the different scales or levels at which crimes may occur. With respect to the latter, it is important not to focus solely on one level. Problems such as climate change, for example, are not just a global problem but a multilevel problem that has harmful (and criminal) impacts across the local, regional, national, international and transnational spheres (Bulkeley and Newell 2010).

Engaging in research into transnational environmental harm involves a number of practical, scientific, empirical and political challenges (see for examples, White 2011). So, too, does another useful methodological approach to the study of transnational environmental crime – namely, horizon scanning (White 2011, see also White and Heckenberg 2011). The use and need for horizon scanning as an intellectual exercise and planning tool is related to the idea that many threats and opportunities are presently poorly recognised and are addressed in an *ad hoc* and reactive fashion. A more systematic approach is required (see Sutherland et al. 2009). Horizon scanning can provide insight into risks (potential problems) and harms (actual problems). It provides a mechanism to discern where emerging threats (and positive opportunities) may arise and potential ways to mitigate or adapt to these.

Collectively there are nine analytical signposts that provide a useful conceptual framework for assessing and analysing risks and harms as part of the exercise of looking over the horizon (see White and Heckenberg 2011). The framework simultaneously incorporates the key values of eco-global criminology. Table 2.3 provides a summary of these key ideas.

Table 2.3 The conceptual framework for environmental horizon scanning

Substantive Orientation

Risk – a prediction or expectation that includes the perspectives of those affected about what is important to them, concerning a potential hazard or danger in which there is uncertainty over occurrence but which may involve adverse consequences as the possible outcome within a certain time period.
Harm – an actual danger or adverse effect, stemming from direct and indirect social processes, that negatively impinges upon the health and wellbeing and ecological integrity of humans, specific biospheres and non-human animals.
Cause – analysis of causal chains that may involve many interrelated variables, but which ultimately are linked to specific practices and human responsibility for environmental harm.

Justice Orientation

Environment justice – in which environmental rights are seen as an extension of human or social rights so as to enhance the quality of human life, now and into the future.
Ecological justice – in which it is acknowledged that human beings are merely one component of complex ecosystems that should be preserved for their own sake via the notion of the rights of the environment.
Species justice – in which harm is constructed in relation to the place of non-human animals within environments and their intrinsic right to not suffer abuse, whether this be one-on-one harm, institutionalised harm or harm arising from human actions that affect climates and environments on a global scale.

Futures Orientation

Intergenerational equity – refers to the principle of ensuring that the generations to follow have at least the same or preferably better environments in which to live than those of the present generation.
Precautionary principle – when an activity raises threats of harm to human health, non-human animals or the environment, precautionary measures should be taken even if some cause and effect relationships are not fully established scientifically.
Transference over time – in this context refers to the transfer of harm involving both cumulative impacts and compounding effects.

Source: White 2011

This analytical approach provides a broad methodological framework that can inform the study of specific environmental issues. The various orientations in the model – substantive, justice, futures – are intended to provide direction and the conceptual building blocks for more detailed analysis of specific issues and trends. As a whole, they constitute the basis for the particular questions that are relevant to an environmental horizon scanning exercise.

In terms of practical research considerations, for example, the conceptual framework for environmental horizon scanning (see White 2011) translates into a stepped approach as illustrated in Table 2.1.

Table 2.4 describes a research process that is more or less generic to any social research process. That is, the study of environmental harm – whether retrospective or prospective – demands a systematic approach to data collection and analysis. The challenge for eco-global criminology is to marshal ideas and evidence from many different sources and disciplines in order to identify where harms and risks are emerging as matters of possible social and political importance, and to develop pre-emptive strategies to begin to address potential problems before they create further harms and risks pertaining to humans, environments and animals.

Table 2.4 Steps to doing environmental horizon scanning

Process		Example 1	Example 2
Step 1	Identify broad ecological issue.	Land use.	Climate change.
Step 2	Ask what harm is related to this now and in the future?	Types of land use that threaten ecological wellbeing and social justice.	Differential effects of climate change on specific population groups, particular ecosytems and particular species.
Step 3	Draw upon a wide variety of sources (for example, cross-disciplinary, multi-jurisdictional, cross-cultural), to investigate a broad ecological issue.	Different types of land use, including for example, replacement of forests by biofuel crops, use of subterranean spaces for radioactive waste.	Conflict over resources, climate-induced migration, radical shifts in weather patterns.
Step 4	Refine analysis by drilling down to a specific topic.	Analysis of specific forms of land use, such as those that diminish biodiversity.	Analysis of natural disasters associated with changing weather patterns.
Step 5	Read widely on specific topic.	Literature on genetically modified organisms and the role of transnational corporations, including for example United Nations reports on global biodiversity and literature on deforestation.	Disaster studies literature that links climate change to specific types of disaster (for example, floods, cyclones) and that expounds issues surrounding cause and effect.
Step 6	Collect information and data relevant to specific topic.	Information about GMO crop substitution in countries such as Brazil, Argentina and Indonesia.	Information about specific natural disasters such as floods in Pakistan, or hurricane Katrina and associated storms in the United States.

Step 7	Systematically investigate the phenomenon in question using the conceptual framework of environmental horizon scanning (for example, substantive, justice and futures orientations).	Identify which species are threatened, the reasons why this is so and the key variables that together have generated the harm in question (for example, global agriculture markets).	Identify which places and populations are most at risk, the reasons why this is the case, the key variables that together have generated the harm in question (for example, lack of infrastructure).
Step 8	Analyse and interpret the information and data in the light of eco-global criminological considerations (for example, transgressions against humans, ecosystems and animals).	Displacement of endemic species from habitat (including humans), and replacement of multiple species (plant and animal) with monoculture.	Analysis of environmental victimisation involving particularly vulnerable groups (for example, women, children, poor, ethnic minorities), and effects of disasters on local ecosystems and species wellbeing.
Step 9	Extrapolate the key emerging patterns associated with the information and data on the particular topic.	Forced removal of people from traditional lands, substitution of existing species with single species and further diminishment of biodiversity.	Breakdown in law and order, prevalence of chaotic living conditions and massive changes to local ecosystems and species composition.
Step 10	Analyse the information in the light of the varied discourses surrounding cause, harm and victimisation from the point of view of relationships of power.	Examine statements by governments, corporations, communities, experts and others about land use issues .	Examine statements by media outlets, governments, non-government organizations and global agencies about a particular disaster.
Step 11	Theorise the findings in relation to anthropogenic causes (for example, human responsibility for harm, specific perpetrators and degrees of culpability).	Transnational corporations and governments that privilege sectional interests over those of local communities and particular species.	Government officials and local building contractors who have a duty of care *vis-à-vis* requisite construction standards and provision of adequate preventive measures.
Step 12	Reflect on possible avenues for action or strategic intervention that will best forestall or mitigate the impact and consequences of the future trend (for example, application of the precautionary principle).	Community engagement in local and regional planning processes, including environmental impact assessments, United Nations involvement in protecting traditional ownership and land uses.	Regulation of building codes and instigation of community policing models based around local participation and neighbourhood security.
Step 13	Communicate the findings, bearing in mind the varied audiences for the particular research topic.	Local communities, local councils, regional governments.	Planning and municipal decision-makers, construction companies, law enforcement officials, non-government aid organisations.

Source: White and Heckenberg (2011: 98–9)

Conclusion

Eco-global criminology provides a distinctive type of analytical lens for the study of transnational environmental crime. As a perspective, it requires one to be highly conscious of the specifically ecological basis of environmental crime or harm, and to incorporate this into the core concerns of its criminological analysis. As an approach, it demands that one be highly sensitive to the intricacies of doing research on a global scale (even if localised to specific regions), and to develop methodologies that are socially and culturally inclusive while maintaining a strong critical edge. New concepts of harm, as informed by ecological sciences and environmental values, will inevitably be developed as part of this process.

References

Beirne, P. and South, N. (eds) 2007. *Issues in Green Criminology: Confronting Harms Against Environments, Humanity and other Animals*. Devon: Willan Publishing.

Bulkeley, H. and Peter, N. 2010. *Governing Climate Change*. London: Routledge.

Clapp, J. 2001. *Toxic Exports: The Transfer of Hazardous Wastes from Rich to Poor Countries*. Ithaca and London: Cornell University Press.

Cornforth, M. 1976. *Dialectical Materialism: An Introduction – Volume 2: Historical Materialism*. London: Lawrence and Wishart.

Engdahl, F.W. 2007. *Seeds of Destruction: the Hidden Agenda of Genetic Manipulation*. Montreal: Global Research.

Gibbs, C., Gore, M., McGarrell, E. and Rivers III, L. 2010. Introducing Conservation Criminology: Towards Interdisciplinary Scholarship on Environmental Crimes and Risks, in *British Journal of Criminology*, 50(1), 124–44.

Gros, J. 2008. Trouble in Paradise: Crime and Collapsed States in the Age of Globalization, in *Global Criminology and Criminal Justice: Current Issues and Perspectives*, edited by N. Larsen and R. Smandych. Peterborough, Ontario: Broadview Press, 43(1), 63–80.

Heckenberg, D. 2010. The Global Transference of Toxic Harms, in *Global Environmental Harm: Criminological Perspectives*, edited by R. White. Devon: Willan Publishing, 37–61.

Herbig, F. and Joubert, S. 2006. Criminological Semantics: Conservation Criminology – Vision or Vagary?, in *Acta Criminologica*, 19(3), 88–103.

Larsen, N. and Smandych, R. (eds) 2007. *Global Criminology and Criminal Justice: Current Issues and Perspectives*. Peterborough, Ontario: Broadview Press.

Norway Ministry of the Environment 2011. New Report on Hypothetical Sellafield Accident. [online] Available at: http://www.norway.org.uk/News_and_events/Current-Affairs/sellafield/ [accessed 15 March 2011].

Robin, M. 2010. *The World According to Monsanto: Pollution, Corruption and the Control of Our Food Supply*. New York: The New Press.
Sankoff, P. and White, S. (eds) 2009. *Animal Law in Australasia: A New Dialogue*. Sydney: The Federation Press.
Situ, Y. and Emmons, D. 2000. *Environmental Crime: The Criminal Justice System's Role in Protecting the Environment*. Thousand Oaks: Sage.
Smith, J. 2003. *Seeds of Deception: Exposing Industry and Government Lies about the Safety of the Genetically Engineered Foods You're Eating*. Fairfield, Iowa: Yes! Books.
Sollund, R. 2008. Causes for Speciesism: Difference, Distance and Denial, in *Global Harms: Ecological Crime and Speciesism*, edited by R. Sollund. New York: Nova Science Publishers, 109–30.
Sutherland, W.J. et al. 2009. A Horizon Scan of Global Conservation Issues for 2010, in *Trends in Ecology and Evolution*, 25(1), 1–7.
United Nations Environment Programme (UNEP) 2007. *Global Environment Outlook*. New York: UNEP.
Walters, R. 2011. *Eco Crime and Genetically Modified Food*. New York: Routledge.
White, R. 2002. Environmental Harm and the Political Economy of Consumption, in *Social Justice*, 29(1 and 2), 82–102.
White, R. 2005. Stifling Environmental Dissent: On SLAPPS and Gunns, in *Alternative Law Journal*, 30(6), 268–73.
White, R. 2007. Green Criminology and the Pursuit of Social and Ecological Justice, in *Issues in Green Criminology*, edited by P. Beirne and N. South (eds). Devon: Willan Publishing.
White, R. 2008. *Crimes against Nature: Environmental Criminology and Ecological Justice*. Devon: Willan Publishing.
White, R. 2009a. Toxic Cities: Globalising the Problem of Waste, in *Social Justice*, 35(3), 107–19.
White, R. 2009b. Researching Transnational Environmental Harm: Toward an Eco-Global Criminology, in *International Journal of Comparative and Applied Criminal Justice*, 33(2), 229–48.
White, R. 2011. *Transnational Environmental Crime: Toward an Eco-global Criminology*. London: Routledge.
White, R. and Heckenberg, D. 2011. Environmental Horizon Scanning and Criminological Research and Practice, in *European Journal of Criminal Policy and Research*, 17(2), 87–100.
Wright Mills, C. 1959. *The Sociological Imagination*. New York: Oxford University Press.

Chapter 3
The Most Serious Crime: Eco-genocide Concepts and Perspectives in Eco-global Criminology

Guri Larsen[1]

Introduction

'A beloved child has many names' is a Norwegian saying describing the way we give pet names to living beings that are dear to us. I have a lot of names for my dog Singa, a big brown curly-coated retriever: 'little sparrow', 'little cinnamon', 'little lunatic', 'little storm' and so forth. The names are my expressions of love for her and I do not use the word 'little' because of her small brain, but because of her vulnerability as an animal: particularly as an animal forced to live in captivity according to my daily regime and not in the way she would probably prefer to live. I use this story about Singa's many names to introduce my discussion of eco-genocide. In some ways, the terms that criminologists use to define the study of environmental harm and damage are similar and convey the importance of the subject, just as all my names for Singa convey my love for her. However, unlike the interchangeable nature of my names for Singa, I argue that the different terms that criminologists use to define the study of environmental harm within the field of criminology have consequences for the development of the field. The terms that criminologists use which shape the study of environmenal harm are examined in this chapter. First, I review commonly used terms, including green criminology and eco-global criminology. I suggest that the term eco-global criminology, as developed by Rob White (2007, 2008, 2009, 2010, 2011), is the best choice to describe the criminological area of study that examines environmental harm. The concept eco-global criminology is most appropriate because it best conveys the interplay between nature and human society/the societal or culture (from now on, I use the term *culture* as a term for nature which humans have turned into cultivated landscape and human societies/the societal, that is, the part of nature that humans have cultivated and domesticated either to urbanization, industrialization, food production or other ways humans have exploited nature). However, eco-global

1 I would like to thank Sigri Lund, Unni Rustad, Arni Hole, Rune Ellefsen, Ragnhild Aslaug Sollund, Charles Husband and Paul Stretesky for constructive comments and help in the process of writing this chapter.

criminology does not yet have a term that adequately addresses the problem of environmental damage and harm in the context of the interconnectedness of nature and culture. I therefore examine the weaknesses of eco-global criminology by examining the problem of harm and the anthropocentric concept of crime in penal law, as well as the historical significance of critical global studies that discuss the definition of crime in the context of power relations. Thus the core of this analysis pivots around the centrality of law and its role in the definition and ranking of crimes in framing the interface of violations of the integrity of life: ecological, animal and human. Through this progressive interrogation of emerging concepts a critical sense of the limitations of specific formulations will lead to an understanding of the range of issues at play in the search to understand this inherently contentious area of political analysis which, amongst other things, fundamentally challenges the socially constructed dualism of nature and culture. The capacity of the conceptual development traced below to transcend this historically hegemonic and damaging dichotomy is one of its merits. I conclude my chapter by examining the strengths of the term *eco-genocide*, a term that describes the destruction of the nature-culture unit. The crucial point of this work, then, is to show how the term eco-genocide advances the field of criminology within the worldwide interdisciplinary research of the interplay between damage to the environment, animals, climate, and to societies and humans.

Green Criminology: Problems with the Term 'Green'

The term *green criminology* was initially coined by Michael J. Lynch in 1990. The term green in criminology was originally a way to link this field of research to what in some countries are defined as green political movements (Lynch 1990; in Norway we do not use the term green to identify such movements, we call them environmental protection movements). In 1999 Piers Beirne contributed to green criminology by expanding the concept to include the study of animal abuse. Initially Beirne described his research as *non-speciesist criminology* but in a subsequent publication (Beirne 2007) he used the term green criminology and described the emerging area of study as *a green field of criminology*. The green designation has been gradually adopted by most researchers concerned with environmental harm. However, as noted below, Rob White broke with this tradition by using the term *environmental criminology* in 2008. In 2009 White began to use the term *eco-global criminology* (or eco-global criminology in 2010). Others have refered to the study of environmental harm as *conservation criminology* (Herbig and Joubert 2006, Gibbs, Gore, Mcgarrell and Rivers 2009).

I see the creation of the different terms used to describe the study of environmental harm within the field of criminology as a result of the way the field has developed. The diversity of terms is interesting, but it is time to examine the discourse and politics that go along with these terms, as well as the role of power in supporting the use of certain concepts rather than others. Green criminology, for instance, is a unique and separate area of criminological research, but not one that is as yet coherently defined as such through the development of new theories and concepts designed to analyze the interaction between humans and nature (Lynch 1990). The pioneers of the field, Lynch (1990), Beirne (1999) and South (2004), have been followed by many others from different disciplines who use theories and concepts derived from those disciplines (among other authors in this book). When different terms and concepts are currently used to describe identical or similar phenomena, I think this may be a consequence of how this field of research is known: through *the topics* of the research. The shared critical eco-global perspective of the analysis of global harms is the core characteristic. This perspective is also shared with other scientific disciplines, both in the social and natural sciences. As noted, the use of different concepts and perspectives reflects the diversity of this research. It is highly interdisciplinary and has different theoretical perspectives and approaches. As White (2008) points out, there are several different approaches and research designs, empirical as well as theoretical.

This study of environmental harm within the context of criminology has become established and recognized both internationally and in the Nordic countries as green criminology. In recent decades, the 'green' designation has been adopted by various commercial sectors: we have, for example, green technology, green chemistry, green economy, green energy, green lifestyles and so on (see Lynch and Stretesky 2003). Thus the use of the term green may be seen as a way to make people believe that commercial products and processes really mean that the environment is being protected or improved. Over time, then, the term green has become increasingly ideological and is mainly used to legitimate industrial products in order to increase profit rather than to convey the importance of environmental protection. As a result, terms like *greenwashing* have emerged, to highlight harmful practices that are described as green. The term was originally coined by New York environmentalist Jay Westervelt in 1986. According to Ecolife dictionary, 'Greenwashing is the process by which organizations spread misleading perception about their products or services that suggests they are more environmentally responsible than is the reality. The practice of greenwashing is used regularly by corporations, governments, and other entities to deceive the public into believing that they are doing more for the environment than they truly are in order to gain better public perception.' Jed Greer and Kenny Bruno (1996) provide in their book *Greenwash: The reality Behind Corporate Environmentalism* an overview of how international corporations in the global economy have been greenwashing their dismal environmental performance by posing as friends of the environment.

The notion of greenwashing has, for example, been used to describe the so-called 'green' technology of the oil industry that is supposed to mean that there is little need to reduce oil production. Another example of greenwashing is the Monsanto description of their genetically modified plants that withstand climate change as 'green"although these plants require significant use of chemical fertilizers and pesticides produced by the same company (Naerstad 2011). I see the 'green' industry as a pretext or a lightning rod for not addressing what is really necessary to prevent environmental degradation and climate change. Thus criminological research documenting damage to nature should not be associated with this industry by the use of a similar term. In short, I argue that Lynch and Stretesky's (2003) observations concerning the definition of green have come true: the term green has been captured and reflects corporate interests as opposed to environmental justice interests.

Unfortunately, the term green criminology has a long history and is hard to get rid of, despite the fact that the name tends to conceal issues of power rather than clarify those issues. Moreover, the term is misleading and does not indicate the content of the research.

Eco-Global Criminology: Perception of the Interaction between Nature and Culture

Problems with the term green have led me to favour the use of White's term eco-global criminology. The term implies a global perspective that sees ecology and criminology combined, that is, nature is linked more directly to society by examination of how humans interact and govern the nature. Thus eco-global criminology contributes an important alternative perspective that helps criminologists interested in the study of environmental harm to understand the interconnectedness of nature and culture, and how economic globalization, which is fostered by systems of international governance, may pose a threat to both humans and nature. In order to understand the importance of eco-global criminology, the dialectical relationship between nature and culture must be explored in more detail.

The Interconnectedness of Nature and Culture

In order to understand environmental harm in the context of the interconnectedness of nature and culture, my starting point is the damage inflicted by perceptions arising from the socially constructed dualism of nature and culture: I indicate why it is necessary to trandscend this dualism. As mentioned above, from the perspective of eco-global criminology, I see culture as being all that part of nature that humans have cultivated or domesticated, whether this is the development of cities and infrastructure, the extraction of natural resources, industrial development or other ways humans use nature and animals, for example, for food production, or in the management of 'wild' animals.

The term dualism, 'in general, is the idea that, for some particular domain, there are two fundamental kinds or categories of things or principles' (Stanford Encyclopedia of Philosophy). Constructions of dualism have a long history: the dualism of Good and Evil in theology, the mind-body dualism in philosophy where René Descarte's (1596–1650) description of all organisms as automata or machines is central. The exception is humans who have consciousness, and this gives humans unlimited authority over the whole of nature. Francis Bacon (1561–1626), in his *Essays* of 1597, claimed that humanity has to regain the right over nature which belongs to humanity by divine decree. The Christian doctrine, well supported by philosophical interpretations, helped in a fundamental way to put humans not only outside nature but also above nature. Darwin's *The Origin of Species* of 1859 revolutionized this view of humans as outside and above nature: humans are part of nature (Hessen 2008, 2000).

Nevertheless, unfortunately the dualistic way of understanding the relationship between nature and culture still underlies humans thinking about and use of nature. The dualism of nature-culture separates humans – and all that humanity has created and cultured – from nature. According to this understanding, humans are perceived as part of culture – alienated from nature – and as representing the highest level of evolution and as qualitatively different from all parts of nature, including other animals. In this view, humans have dominion over all of nature and this legitimates humans' right to control nature. This instrumental and anthropocentric view of nature allows humans to exploit nature for our own interests and for economic interests.

The value of nature is a central question. How can biodiversity and ecosystems be valued? Are they to be valued on the basis of nature's use to humans – that is, from an anthropocentric view? Or valued on the basis of nature's intrinsic value – that is, from an ecocentric view? Should moral status only be given to humans, or can all living creatures and organisms be recognized as moral entities?[2] Answers to these questions among others can be found in the field of *deep ecology* or *ecosophy* that was originally coined by the Norwegian philosopher Arne Naess (1974, 1989). Ecosophy ties together all life and nature, Naess says that what is needed is *ecological wisdom*. By ecological wisdom he means the right of all forms of life to live being held as a universal right that cannot be quantified. No single species has more right to live and unfold than any other. Another philosopher, J. Baird Callicott (1989, 1994), espouses a holistic, non-anthropocentric environmental ethic. Callicot offers a subjectivist theory of nature's intrinsic value that focuses on transorganismic entities (endangered species, threatened biotic communities and ecosystems, rivers and lakes, oceans and atmosphere), and not on individual organisms. He claims that an adequate environmental ethic that addresses actual environmental concern must be holistic.

This view of nature leads to the next question of how the relationship between culture and nature can be understood in ways other than the hegemonic dualism of culture-nature, and thus provide conceptual tools for analyzing the ways in which environmental degradation can be understood and prevented. The challenge is to understand how to bridge the gap separating nature and culture and how conceptually to link nature and culture to ensure an understanding of how the destruction of nature also affects humanity. According to Morten Toennessen (2010), there is a counter trend of interdisciplinary research that seeks to synthesize

2 See for example White (2007: 41–4) where he discusses conflicts over rights: environmental and ecological rights, social and human rights.

nature and culture. He refers to Amos Henry Hawley (1986) and the term *human ecology*, that is, the study of humans' collective interplay with their environment and nature. A basic assumption in human ecology is that a human ecosystem is a demographic response to the need to maintain a working relationship with nature.

Naess (1974, 1989) claims that it is possible to achieve change through a feeling of the positive cohesion between all life on earth – an ecological understanding of the world – including the place of human beings in ecological systems. The deep ecological movement calls "... for critical examination of the man-nature relation and basic changes which would affect every aspect of human life' (Naess 1989: 163). How to create the moral communion between nature and culture necessary to prevent the exploitation of nature? We need other ways to understand communion other than division into species, Lars Risan (1998: 7) says, drawing upon Gregory Bateson's (1972) term *ecological network*. An ecological network means a moral communion between nature and society, transcending the dualism of nature-culture. The *purity* of humanism is replaced by *impure* networks. Respect for networks takes precedence over species discrimination and biological and hierarchical classifications, and this means respecting the quasi-subjectivity of human as well as non-human actors. Both Naess's term ecological wisdom and Risnes's term ecological network, as well as the term human ecology, match the understanding of the interconnectedness of nature and culture that must be central to eco-global criminology. These terms may contribute to clarifying the need to analyze the interdependence of nature and culture so as to change the hegemonic view of nature as human property, and of humans having the right to exploite the biosphere. A potential challenge to the co-option of this philosophic sensibility lies in the capacity of jurisprudence, law and criminology to adapt their traditional humanistic philosophic approach to a human ecology perspective.

The Idea of Ecological Justice

The topics of eco-global research have a wide scope: they include legal and illegal abuse of animals, harm to ecosystems and biodiversity, climate change and the consequences of all these to people and societies. What primarily distinguishes eco-global criminology from other areas of criminology is the topic of research. The study of eco-global crime is not limited to the relationship between humans and society, but extends to the inter-connectivity of *culture* and *nature*: to society's use of and damage to nature, including non-human animals, and to how nature impinges on the societal and the cultural.

According to White (2008: 14–23), there are three main approaches for studying damage to nature: one is based on the idea of *environmental justice*, another has its base in the idea of *species justice* and a third is based on the idea of *ecological justice*. White (2007: 41) also uses the concept of *ecological citizenship* which '[...] incorporates the key concerns of both environmental justice and ecological justice.'

White's idea of ecological justice and the concept of ecological citizenship are in conflict with the hegemonic vision which perceives the cultural as separated from the natural. There is a correspondence between ecological justice and a need to abolish the socially constructed dualism of culture-nature; in fact, ecological justice presupposes the transcending of the distinction between culture and nature. Culture and nature are linked together in a common destiny. The idea of ecological justice is well suited to ensuring the holistic relationship of culture-nature – that is of the societal or the cultural and the natural – and to protecting the health of the biosphere. It provides a useful analytical tool for understanding the interaction and interdependency between all parts of ecosystems. The human being is perceived as just one among many parts of complex ecosystems. Human interaction with nature is assessed in terms of how we (ab)use the resources of nature and the biosphere in general. With this approach, human beings and other species have equal value as parts of an ecological whole. All parts of the system – the environment and non-human animals, as well as the human species – may be the victims of exploitation and the abuse of nature.

My interpretation of the concept of ecological justice is that it includes an emphasis on environmental and species justice. The term includes the interplay between all parts within ecosystems, interplay being understood as the *interdependency* of all kinds of life on the planet, whether life is part of culture or nature. Perhaps this understanding of the term conflicts with White's tripartite description of justice: I believe that there must be a commitment to achieving coherence in understanding the unequal relationship between different species, the unequal effects of environmental hazards to different countries, ethnic groups and genders and the destruction by humans of ecosystems. Ecological justice presupposes both environmental justice and species justice. My interpretation of ecological justice matches Lars Risan's (1998) term, ecological network: a moral communion between nature and culture that transcends the dualism of nature-culture, cf. page above. The unfair and destructive treatment of environments, ecosystems and all species – humans as well as other animals – is linked together by the ideological dualism of culture-nature that help to legitimize the capitalist exploitation of nature. This fundamental dichotomy is of course also underpinned and sustained by the focus of dichotomous categorization in human discourse, cf. page above. Humans are perceived as part of culture and, as such, separated and alienated from other animals and nature.

Conceptual Tools in Practice

The application of the ideas of ecological justice and of ecological network as an analytical tool – understood in accordance with an abolition of the constructed dualism of culture-nature – has not been common in research on exploitation of nature. Generally, research projects on environmental damage, animal cruelty and climate change reflect to some extent the traditional 'boxes' of scientific disciplines. Studies of environmental damage, the destruction of biodiversity and their consequences for the climate traditionally belong to natural science, while ethical analyses of attitudes to and uses of nature and animals have traditionally been the philosopher's domain (among other Naess 1974, 1989, Singer 2002, Regan 1999, 2004, Ryder 1989). In recent decades social science has contributed to this literature with research in which the societal dimension is added to studies of animal abuse (among others Nibert 2002, 2003, Noske 1989, Donovan 1996, Larsen 2003). Nevertheless, some of these studies of speciesism and animal cruelty are still subjects of separate projects, as in the case of research on climate change and environmental damage, and to a lesser extent, analyses of the interaction and interdependence of nature and culture. In this way, through the power of diciplinary practice, much of research still reflects the dualism of culture-nature. However, a growing demand for interdisciplinary research is a response to this fragmentation of knowledge, cf. research in the field of human ecology) (Hawley 1986, Toennessen 2010). Eco-global criminology is also an example of an interdisciplinary direction of research that analyses damage to humans, animals and the environment in context from a critical global perspective.

In the footsteps of the hegemonic dichotomy of culture – nature follows a constructed division of our conceptualization of nature – the separation between environment, animals and humans. This separation is not peculiar to science. The very same split is found in politics: there are separate NGOs for environmental protection, for animal protection/animal rights and for human rights.[3] Both national and international legislation divide nature into separate parts. The fragmentation of scientific knowledge and similar fragmentation in the political and the legal spheres make it difficult to comprehend the relationship and interdependence between environmental harm, animal abuse, climate change and damage to humans and societies. This fragmentation is in many ways helpful to political and economic elites, but harmful to those people around the world who struggle against environmental damage, climate change and deterioration of their living conditions.

Overcoming Problems with Eco-global Criminology

While eco-global criminology addresses issues of nature and culture adequately, there are still some areas that need to be developed in order to move toward a common understanding of environmental damage and harm. The lack of clarification of the notion of harm within eco-global criminology must be explored in more detail. Three areas that are examined here are definition of harm, the global critical perspective and crime definition in the context of power.

3 See for example Brulle and Pellow (2005) and their discussion of the environmental justice movement and Carroll and Hannan's (2004) work on density dependence of corporations and industries which is starting to be applied to NGOs when they operate to capture their markets and resources and may specialize in some particular niche in order to do this.

Definitions of Harm

The term harm, whether environmental, green or ecological appears to be neutral. The concept of harm is also interdisciplinary in nature and not specifically criminological. Whether the issue is social harm or environmental harm, criminology's use of the concept harm is vague and causes problems because it serves to obscure the extent of the greatest threats to ecosystems, biodiversity and climate caused by legal activities, and to obscure who is responsible for them. These legal activities systematically – though not intentionally – destroy nature, torture animals and contribute to the climate crisis, which has an impact on humans and society as well as, in the long term, all life on the planet. With political strategy in mind, it makes sense to distinguish conceptually between different types of harm, noting whether it is criminalized or not, and how severe the harm is.

In White's latest book, *Transnational Environmental Crime* (2011), he specifically defines the meaning of *transnational environmental crime* by incorporating '[...] different, albeit inter-related notions of harm', including legal concepts of harm as well as considerations of ecological wellbeing and justice concepts of harm. White distinguishes between three approaches to conceptualizing environmental harm: conventional criminology, ecological concepts and green criminology. He defines illegal harm as the topic of the *conventional* criminology approach. Investigation of problems with climate change, waste and pollution and biodiversity belongs to his second approach, *ecological concepts*. His third approach, *green criminology*, considers rights and justice concepts: environmental rights and environmental justice, ecological citizenship and ecological justice, animal rights and species justice (see White, this volume). Admittedly, White notes that the approaches 'incorporate at times competing yet overlapping notions of harm.' As I understand him, conceptions of harm focused on justice – environmental justice, ecological justice and species justice – are more appropriate to eco-global criminology than is the use of the different concepts for legal and illegal harm. I agree that it is important to use justice concepts to understand damage to nature, but I disagree with the separation of justice concepts and legal concepts in their respective approaches. I perceive justice as an overarching term that conveys a moral view of events and actions regardless of whether they are legal or illegal. To perceive justice concepts, ecological concepts and legal concepts as belonging to different approaches makes it difficult to analyse the comprehensive exploitation of nature in accordance with my understanding of the idea of ecological justice.

White's fragmentation of approaches conflicts with an analytical approach that is based on the interaction and mutual dependence of nature and culture. My concern is to try to integrate these different conceptual approaches into a unifying approach, not to distinguish between the approaches of 'conventional' and 'green criminology' and not to isolate ecological concepts into a separate approach.

As I see it, ecological justice is an overall or key concept for analyzing destruction of the nature-culture unit; a way of bridging the socially constructed gap between nature and culture cf. the term ecological network and human ecology. Nevertheless, in analyzing destruction in this way I find it useful to stick to criminological tradition to make a conceptual distinction between legal and illegal activities. The crime concept in penal law does not include legal destruction, regardless of the extent of the damage, and the concept of harm provides no understanding of the seriousness of the destructive activities. I am not arguing for the necessity of reaching consensus on the conceptualization of different types of harm. However, distinguishing between the legal and illegal concept of harm will hopefully clarify what we are dealing with: that is, the difference between the kind of damage power elites find it necessary to criminalize, and the kind of destruction they want to protect from criminalization. In my opinion, that difference matters. Global damage to nature and climate is very much a product of the global structure of power and transnational economic interests. They represent the very same systems that are responsible for the most serious destruction – making destruction into a legal activity – and have a vested interest in keeping things as they are. In analysing global hazards to nature I think it is of paramount importance to include in the analysis the reasons why destructive activities are considered legal. This is crucial knowledge; it tells the story of why national governments and international bodies protect corporate interests and their exploitation of nature.

Critical Global Perspective

According to White (2009, 2011) eco-global criminology refers to a criminological approach that examines transgressions against ecosystems, humans and animals from a critical global perspective concerned with questions of justice. Environmental harm, as described originally by Lynch (1990), emphasizes the context of the domination of capitalism over nature. However, as White suggests, many other types of harm exist. These harms may be *social* as well as environmental harm and can be analyzed in the context of power structures and social control, at local and global levels. For me, these structures have names: imperialism and economic exploitation. Here it is relevant to refer to the 94-year-old Stephane Hessel's petition pamphlet Time for Outrage![4] (2011): *the current dictatorship of the financial markets* is his excellent definition of what constitutes the greatest threat to peace and democracy. Threats to the environment, animals and climate could be added to the list, since transgressions against nature pose a threat to peace and stability for the world's people. Economic globalization helps to increase the exploitation of nature, for example through the industrialized food production and global free trade.[5]

White states (2008: 3) that the purpose of eco-global criminology is to expand the scope of *mainstream criminology* by including themes of global importance,

4 This is the translation of the original French pamphlet *Indignez vous!*

5 See for example Naomi Klein's (2007) discussion of economic globalization's importance for natural disasters, wars, terrorist attacks or economic turmoils.

and at the same time employing the knowledge from *conventional criminology* to shed light on ways to understand and react to harms against nature.

Themes of global importance are consistent with previous research in criminology, and therefore it would be misleading to interpret eco-global criminology as renewal of criminology. The critical global perspective is not an innovation of researchers within eco-global criminology. Analysing all kind of harms – social as well as environmental – from global power structures has been well anchored in criminological topics since the 1970s, when criminology loosened its formal ties with the penal law. At least this was the case in Norway when criminology was established in 1966 as a separate discipline in social science and detached from the legal discipline. In the early period of criminology as social science, one example of research that has a critical global perspective is Cecilie Høigård's (1971) analysis of imperialistic trade policy using criminological theories and ways of understanding.

Other exsamples of long-standing fields of research are transnational economic crime and organised crime (for example, Braithwaite 1984, 1993) and analysis of 'Crime Control as Industry' (Christie 2000) in an international context. Likewise, studies of border control of migration, of the development of transnational surveillance systems and of human rights violations constitute a large part of international criminological research that has critical global perspectives (for example, Aas 2007, Aas, Gundhus and Lomell 2010).

Høigård's (1971) analysis of structural violence caused by a global political and economic system is relevant to this view. However, like Sleeping Beauty, this critical global perspective has almost been asleep for a long time. Most criminologists have analysed crimes in terms of the penal law – with the exception of researchers in eco-global criminology – without taking into consideration the serious harm done to humans and societies through structural violence perpetrated by nation-states, and by global political and economic systems.

Ståle Eskeland (2011) has recently resumed a similar perspective to Høigård. He claims that actions defined as crime by the penal law can be seen as less serious for human beings than the pain and violence caused by wars forced upon innocent civilians by agreements between nation-states, NATO or resolutions in the UN Security Council. According to Eskeland, these actions violate the principles of crime against humanity and genocide in International Law. My contention is that the current worldwide practice of destroying the climate, the environment and the life of animals could well be defined as a crime according to the International Convention of Biological Diversity. I will return to this idea below.

Another example of the analysis of globalization processes in criminology is the work of Baillet and Aas (2011). They employ the concept *cosmopolitan justice* to analyse how globalization resulted in a deepening of unequal power relations – ills produced by neo-liberalism. Since cosmopolitan justice is an analytical concept aimed at transcending national boundaries and nationalist views of societies and justice, it could be perceived as a parallel to the concept of ecological justice. However, cosmopolitan justice adds to the constructed dualism of nature and culture; justice being reserved for understanding and analyzing relationships between humans and between humans and society. Cosmopolitan justice is an anthropocentric concept, unlike ecological justice that focuses on the interplay between all species on earth. Thus, eco-global criminology must not ignore the research of the critical global perspective in a field of research that has criticized the concept of crime in national penal laws. These studies are, however, based on an anthropocentric view. The introduction of an ecocentric view in eco-global criminology represents new perspectives and topics in criminology.

The Crime Concept in a Context of Power

How can the global critical perspective be connected to a definition of crime? The discourse concerning the concept of crime is relevant to discussion about the use of approaches and concepts in eco-global criminology. Cecilie Høigård (2002) argues that the concept of crime is saturated with power. She argues that actions disliked by the power elite will be naturalized as crime, and as a final result, this will reproduce the social order and its power relations.

My concern is that *the opposite* position has the same implications: seriously harmful activities and the infliction of pain, which the power elite *do not* want to criminalize, also contribute to the reproduction of social, economic and political power relations. The contrast between the range of actions naturalized as crime and the infliction of harm which is not criminalized, sheds light on how the power base of society is maintained and reproduced both through the range of actions which are criminalized and the selection of harms which remain legal.

Studies of recorded crime and the life situation of offenders highlight the reproduction of a poor underclass by the penal system (Finstad 2000, Høigård 2002). This outcome may also be illuminated by studying destructive activities the penal system *does not* have the task of controlling: the reproduction of the power basis responsible for environmental degradation. This is quite obvious when lawful injury has more extensive consequences than actions currently penalized by the legal regime: injury that finally results in climate change.

Damage arising from legal activities may also be defined as *structural violence* or *structural damage*. These actions and activities are *not intended* to inflict damage, and are justified out of consideration for the economic interests of societies: economic growth, regional or agricultural interests and global free trade. However, when the *consequences* of legal activities are documented as causing large-scale destruction, they should be considered as criminal either in terms of legislation or criminal in the moral sense. The idea of the negation of the penal system's reproduction of power means that atrocities which are not criminalized – not defined as crime in penal laws – can be defined as crime as regards their *moral* significance, which is a way of trying to reveal the way the criminal system is interwoven with the interests of the power elite and why some atrocities are legal activities. Eco-global criminology needs a clear conceptual distinction between legal and illegal harm to expose and analyse how the penal system and the existing concept of crime represent a barrier to understanding what is the most serious threat to the planet. When studying the basis for eco-genocide, important issues are the penal system's failure to define as crime the destruction caused by the global economic system and the fact that the existing concept of crime legitimizes this praxis.

Towards a Definition of Eco-genocide

How should one conceptualize the difference between legal and illegal harm as well as between the most serious harm and less severe harm, as criminological concepts? And how to conceptualize destruction that affects the nature-culture unit? If the idea of the opposite/negation of the penal system's reproduction of power is a starting point, it might be helpful to find concepts that reveal the power elite's destructive legal activities. One first step to arriving at a conceptual clarification is to classify harm according to whether or not the damage is judicially defined. Harm may be divided into three types: illegal harm; harm in the judicially grey area between legal and illegal harm; and legal harm.

1. The first type of harm is judicially defined as such and I divide it into two subgroups:
    a. Harm defined as illegal in the criminal/penal law. Norwegian penal law governs the use of the environment and of animals only to a small extent, but the law has a general clause concerning environmental crime, with a maximum penalty of 15 years for the worst cases of pollution, destruction of our cultural heritage and crimes against the fauna.
    b. Harm defined by national environmental laws, international environmental law and international conventions. International environmental law is a relatively new jurisdiction and is not a legal field in its own right, but part of the International Law. The Convention on Biodiversity and the Bern Convention on Species Diversity are among the relevant international conventions. In Norway we have among other legislation, laws regulating pollution and the 2009 Law on Biodiversity. Animal protection is dealt with by the Animal Welfare law and the Wildlife Act.

2. The second type of harm is located in a judicially grey area between legal and illegal activity: the purpose and aims of legislation to protect biological diversity, ecological systems and the sustainable use of nature are not safeguarded in the design of specific individual clauses. Basically, if the ideal objectives and intentions stated in environmental legislations and international conventions were considered as the basis for how laws should be put into practice, most damage to nature falls within the official definition of

environmental degradation, perceived as illegal activities qualifying for legal penalties.

One example of far-reaching intentions and targets is the recent Norwegian law on animal welfare that protects animals on an individual level. The main clause of the law states that animals have intrinsic value. The specific provisions of the law do not, however, reflect the intrinsic value of animals. Crime as understood by the law is imprecisely defined and reported animal cruelty is always subject to discretion or vague interpretation (Larsen 2003). If the content of the main clause was actually applied, animals would certainly have much better legal protection than is currently the case. In my view most present day use of animals in Norway would be illegal if the statement of animal's intrinsic value in the main clause was supposed to be the basis for animals' living conditions.

Another example is the Norwegian law on biodiversity. This law sets out to provide systemic protection of ecosystems. Its aim is to safeguard ecological processes by protecting the diversity of species and ensuring a sustainable use of nature that maintains biological and geological diversity, and diversity of landscape. The aims of this law find official expression in – for example – the Planning and Building Act, that is, human society and nature are considered in relationship to each other. The land use of the municipality should always be assessed with the aim of protecting biodiversity.

The intention stated in international environmental law is also to provide a regulatory regime for sustainable development, that is, for safeguarding ecosystems. As is well known, the intentions and ideal goals of laws are rarely realized.

I choose to define both illegal harms as well as harms in legal grey areas as *eco-crime* since the harms are judicially defined – either as violations of individual clauses in laws or violations of the intentions and goals of legislation. Most damage to the environment and climate would be considered as illegal if the intentions and goals of international environmental law were actually put into practice (see examples of eco-crime in Dybing's chapter, this volume).

3. The third type of harm – legal harm – differs from the two other types because they are not defined in legislation as a judicial category of environmental degradation that is open to proscecution. Although legal harm may have enormous global consequences –and has long been the greatest threat to ecosystems, to the climate and to humankind – it is still perceived as legal activity and not as the most serious of crimes.

   What is perceived as legal harm may also be considered as eco-crime if such actions are results of violations of the goals and intentions of environmental legislation, but no damage done intentionally. However, this means a return to the confusion of concepts in eco-global criminology, with no distinction between the official definition of illegal and legal destructive use of nature.

Possible examples of legal environmental degradation are the activities of coal, oil and gas industries with their emission of harmful greenhouse gases. These industries are perfectly legal, though emissions of harmful gases are limited and regulated by laws. The fact remains that emissions of these gases now constitute the main threat to the climate.

How may legal harm – often non-intentional harm – be defined as a criminological concept and how can the severity of environmental degradation be indicated? The aim of such activities is not to inflict harm, but rather to contribute to economic growth, job-creation and profit. However, they are consequences of the deliberate policy of nation-states, and of the strategies of transnational corporations.

If the point of reference is the term *ecological justice*, signifying the interdependency between nature and culture, and the aim is to conceptualize legal harm against nature as a criminological concept, one solution is to introduce a non-judicial, but *moral category*: *ecocide*. By ecocide I mean violations of ecological justice which as such constitute a moral category of crime, that is, destructive activities which destroy ecosystems and biodiversity. Ecocide is not recognized as a judicial category and is not yet part of International Law, but the term clearly indicates what kind of emerging catastrophe we might be facing and should try to prevent.

The term ecocide is used by several researchers in eco-global criminology. Boekhout van Solinge (2008: 26) refers to Mark Allan Gray (1996) and his argument that ecocide is derivable from principles of International Law. 'Ecocide can be established on the basis of two fundamental human rights: the right to life and the right to health', Gray argues, as quoted by van Solinge. Polly Higgins (2010) argues that ecocide should be recognized by the United Nations as a fifth crime against peace.[6] The use of the term ecocide can be interpreted as if it only relates to harm to humans. However, to prevent ecocide is not just an instrument to prevent genocide and war crimes. It is not an anthropocentric term, but an ecocentric one.

Nigel South (2010: 230) refers to the concept of ecocide, saying that we have not yet '[...] passed a catastrophic "point of no return"'. Nevertheless, as South argues, our task as scientists is '[...] to raise awareness of prevalent late-modern tendencies to ecocidal behaviour [...]'.

Understanding ecocide as a moral category of crime and a violation of ecological justice is contrary to traditional and accepted definitions of crime and the concept of crime in penal law. However, it corresponds to an analysis of the negation of the penal system's reproduction of existing power relations: the power elite has vested interests in not criminalizing ecocide. Laws are based on an anthropocentric point of view. The aims of laws are human safety and social protection; the protection of nature is an instrument to benefit humans.

6 The other four international crimes against peace are genocide, crimes against humanity, war crimes and crimes of aggression.

> My concept of crime is derived from an ecocentric view; it runs counter to the human-centric position in the legal definitions of harm. From an ecocentric perspective, ecocide is a crime.

In writing this, I am indebted to Rob White (2007, 2011) who uses this perspective to understand why some types of harm are criminalized and others are not. *Illegal* environmental and ecological harm mostly reflect an anthropocentric perspective, he argues. When ecological harm is criminalized, it is not out of concern for nature and animals, but out of consideration for – and in the interests of – humans and society. I would add, indeed, that ecological damage prevailing as *legal harm* reflects the same human-chauvinist point of view and reproduces the hegemony of the human centric perspective: considerations of societal and economic interests take precedence over concerns for animals and nature. The paradox is that by harming nature and animals, we are damaging ourselves.

Is it possible to conceptually summarize all types of hazards to the culture-nature unit (damaging one part of the unit may cause damage to the other part), legal as well as illegal and crime both as a judicial and moral category? I reiterate my reference to the term ecological justice. The concept of ecological justice includes humans defined in a different way from the hegemonically constructed dualism nature-culture that separates humans from nature. The interconnectivity of nature-culture in my view indicates how human damage to nature backfires on humanity and societies. Both legal and illegal destruction are in my opinion violations of ecological justice and therefore criminal in the moral sense, not just in the judicial sense.

International Law separates genocide and environmental crimes (the term ecocide does not exist in International Law), isolating humans from nature. How to conceptualize destruction that affects the culture-nature unit? Can the use of a concept help to illuminate the enormous impact ecocide and genocide has for all life on earth?

I choose to use the concept of *eco-genocide* as a unifying category for both illegal and legal damage which causes destruction to the culture-nature unit: the societal, the environment, humans and other animals and the climate. Eco-genocide I define as destruction of the culture-nature unit. Eco-genocide, in my opinion, is a useful analytical tool to reveal the justice system's weakness in combating the most serious crime currently being committed because of its close connection with the global power elite. The term also helps to recognize how the fate of humankind, the condition of ecosystems, animals and climate change are interwoven. Eco-genocide, as a unifying concept, binds together all species on earth in a common destiny, and also recognizes the interaction between crimes against peace (crimes against humanity, genocide, war crimes, crimes of aggression) and environmental crime in International Law.

Eco-genocide should be added to the list of *the most serious crimes* since these crimes have already caused catastrophe for some communities and people in poor countries in the South and have the future potential to destroy nature and climate and thus decide the destiny of all species on planet earth.

To summarize:

The unifying category *eco-genocide* I divide into one judicial and one moral category in order to clarify the status and severity of transgressions against nature:

- *Eco-crime and genocide* as *judicial* categories
- *Ecocide* as a moral category.

The judicial concept eco-crime I divide into three sub-categories:

- Harm defined as environmental crime by penal law
- Harm defined as environmental crime by environmental laws, either of national legislations or of international environmental law
- Environmental damage in a legal grey area.

Criminological Contributions of Eco-genocide

How can criminology contribute to research into, and to perceptions of, eco-genocide, both as a judicial and a moral category? Does criminology have specific expertise in a field that goes beyond analyses of crime and the penal system, deviance and social control?

Criminologists are not typically climate or nature researchers. Criminology needs to find its own place within eco-global research and certainly has a role in developing interdisciplinary studies of the interconnectivity between nature and culture, for example by applying empirical data from natural science to analysis of the social implications of environmental crisis. Criminology can elucidate the interdependency of nature and culture; it can contribute to clarifying how societal structures inflict damage on nature and how this rebounds on society. Social conflicts, wars, migration, poverty and oppression are concomitants of environmental damage and climate changes (cf. White, this volume).

Research within eco-global criminology is expanding. Several important empirical studies of activities destructive of nature and animals have been published during recent decades – studies of both legal and illegal destruction – from different parts of the world.[7] Not all of these studies clarify what kind of harm is legal and what is illegal, and do not analyse why some actions are criminalized and others are not.

What I would consider worthwhile would be to develop research into the interest of the governing institutions in preserving the well-established concept of crime and in justifying this, as well as the hegemonic praxis of the control systems. Specific and targeted research tasks for criminologists could be to analyse why certain acts are defined as a crimes and others are defined as legal activities and

7 See for example *Issues in Green Criminology* (2007), *Global Harms: Ecological Crime and Speciesism* (2008) and *Environmental Crime: A Reader* (2009).

why the most serious crime – eco-genocide – is not on the political agenda. Such research would also illuminate the *negation* of the penal system's reproduction of power: the power base for *the unwillingness* to criminalize the most serious and threatening type of destruction and pain: *eco-genocide*.

Studies using such a perspective should analyse ecocide as well as eco-genocide as a moral category: possible studies could examine the consequences of industrialized food production for biodiversity, humans and other animals, the social and environmental consequences of global free trade and of emissions of harmful greenhouse gases. Also needed are more empirical studies demonstrating that socially inflicted abuse of animals, the environment, the climate and humans is interwoven – is all of one piece – and that it should be recognized as precisely that.

Numerous studies of eco-genocide could be conducted. Here are a few of the questions that research on eco-genocide would need to address. Who and what suffer from the consequences of eco-crime and ecocide? In what way do they suffer? What are the reasons and who is responsible for the activities that cause eco-genocide? How to operationalize eco-genocide to conduct empirical research projects showing the interdependence of nature and culture and how damage to nature causes damage to humans and society, and vice versa? What are the interests and power relations protecting the legal status of eco-genocide? How is eco-crime regulated and controlled? Any analysis would have to focus on existing laws regulating the field, as well as control mechanisms and efforts to prevent eco-genocide and eco-crime and analyses of the weaknesses of legal strategies.[8]

In such studies, the connection between sociology of law, environmental law and criminology is obvious. It is, however, equally necessary to take knowledge from natural science and other disciplines such as philology and philosophy. The question of judicialization to fight eco-genocide could be a very promising field of research. Also, what importance is attributed to legal strategies and what is the role of counter-power strategies? Much more knowledge is needed; eco-global criminology is still in its early stages.

Eco-global Criminology's Role in Fighting Eco-genocide

Do legal strategies have credibility in the future battle to save the climate, biodiversity and all species: non-human animals as well as humans?

The ambiguous principle of the sovereignty of nation-states is discussed by Nicolai Nyland (2009) in his doctoral thesis on traditional and new ways of viewing the legal relations between states in the context of environmental questions. A central aim of International Law is to ensure the survival of states and

8 The debate about the use of legal strategies has, at least in the Nordic context, been concerned about the advantages and disadvantages for social movements, political lobbying groups and non-governmental organizations in using judicial (legal) means (legal arguments, legal institutions and so on) as strategic efforts to promote their political aims.

humans. However, according to Nyland, that same principle of sovereignty is now beginning to threaten the existence of humanity.

International Law based on the nation-state is the point of reference. The question is how trans-border environmental damage and climate change can be controlled and regulated within a system where the nation-state has sovereign power to determine how to handle environmental damage within its own territory even though transgression also has global effects? Nation-states are often themselves responsible for damage, and economic interests are usually involved.

The universal desire of national authorities for economic growth and development within their own country encourages isolated solutions rather than involvement in tackling global climate problems that affect other countries and peoples, as well as their own country. Under the current regime of International Law, states can refuse to cooperate to solve global environmental and climate problems. An illustrative example is the failure to obtain legally binding climate agreements between states.

According to Nyland, 'the principle of sovereign self-determination over one's own environment can not extend so far that states have the right to decide the environmental quality of other states' (2009: 9, my translation). Environmental problems must still be resolved within the framework of International Law, Nyland claims, but the rooting of International Law in the nation-state must be changed. In his opinion a new interpretation may change the main clause stating states' freedom to environmental interventions and 'form a legal basis for better protection of the environment'. He refers to 'the growing norms of environmental rights'. Perhaps he is here thinking of the constitution of Ecuador as one example of how nature has been given rights of its own. And Bolivia is set to pass laws granting nature equal rights to humans (Guardian 10.04.2011). If nature obtains rights – not just on paper – what does it mean for our use and exploitation of nature and animals?

Nyland also refers to a growing recognition of how harm to the environment may become a threat to international peace and security, the right of nations and people to survive and the principle of sustainable environment (ibid.: 10). One might regard him as having come close to the concept of eco-genocide in his analyses of the threat to climate, environment, peace and survival of the people of the world.

The issue of the weakness of legal strategies to prevent environmental catastrophe – both on the national and global level – has to be discussed (cf. Ellefsen, this volume). It seems reasonable to conclude that legal strategies have failed despite existing legislation. Examples from Norway illustrate the negative tendencies: the Norwegian partly state-owned oil company, Statoil, has more influence on the global climate and environment than Norwegian politicians and even the majority of the shareholders – the Norwegian government. Among other international initiatives, this company is involved in an oil and gas project in Canada (North American Oil Sands), extracting oil from tar sands. This activity causes extremely high emissions of CO2, and does harm to the environment and to the indigenous people of the region. Statoil has been reported for 19 violations of water law in Canada. When confronted with this, the snappy answer from the Norwegian Prime Minister, Jens Stoltenberg, was: 'Emissions in Canada are the responsibility of Canada' (Aftenposten 29.08.2009). He is of course right. He has International Law on his side, but what about his moral responsibility to the environment and the climate?

Lately there has been a fierce political debate in Norway as to whether or not the oil industry should be allowed to extract oil in the Barents Ocean and off the northern coast of Norway. The main issue is the impact oil drilling could have on marine ecosystems and on the fish stocks near the coast. Climate changes caused by the oil industry and various uses of oil and oil products[9] are hardly mentioned, not even by the political opponents of oil drilling. Both for the Norwegian Cabinet and other politicians, economic development and local employment in the oil industry is more important than protecting marine biodiversity, local inshore fishing and the global climate.

The Norwegian Cabinet is trying to build an image of being something of a global hero in saving the climate, and seeks to act as a moral agent in international forums. The Cabinet has, however, a contradictory position in the matter of global climate change and environmental damage: it wishes to be perceived as a moral pioneer in the struggle to prevent climate change by donating billions of Norwegian kroner for the protection of the world's rainforests, while at the same time the government-owned Oil Fund invests even more billions in oil companies in Peru which destroy the very same rainforests they seek to protect. In one way the Cabinet is morally paralyzed, while in another, political rhetoric seeks to conceal moral decay.

Some dilemmas must be mentioned. Oil has been found off Greenland, with the possibility of its being extracted. On the one hand, income from the oil industry could be a blessing to the poor society of Greenland and to the Inuit people. The Inuit communities are characterized by a high unemployment, poverty, social problems and high rate of violence. The economy is at present totally in the hands of the colonial power, Denmark. Income from the oil industry could mean economic and political independence from Denmark (cf. Myrup, this volume). The same dilemma may also exist in other poor countries in the South.

International environmental law differs from other jurisdictions in that it is impossible to govern nature – nature has its own internal laws. It is the *(ab)use* of nature which can be regulated and controlled. Laws of nature set the limit for how nature can be exploited or used. Both interventions in nature and protection of biodiversity build on an instrumental view of nature. Is it politically possible to change laws from being human-centric to ecocentric, and in this way define eco-genocide as a judicial category – as well as getting political approval for eco-genocide being the most serious crime? Or do we have to rely on global popular

9 See for example Shiva (2008) *Soil Not Oil. Climate Change, Peak Oil, and Food Insecurity*. Zed Books.

movements fighting against eco-genocide? This too could be a research question for eco-global criminology.

Final Questions

Finally a cruel question needs to be posed: how can ecological justice or the rights of Nature be secured? Is it by securing the *individual* rights of all species or by giving *systemic* rights for the survival of ecosystems with all their biological diversity, cf. Callicott's environmental ethic? (1989).

If the main aim is perceived to be saving the climate and preserving the diversity of life on earth and ecological networks, one may claim that a rational environmental policy would be to ensure the subordination of special national and global economic interests to the universal interests of the peoples of the world in a systemic protection of ecosystems. Since the greatest threats to the diversity of life on planet earth come from human activities, it may be reasonable to give precedence to ecological justice rather than to economic growth in rich countries and 'the current dictatorship of the financial markets', cf. Stephane Hessel (2011).

The notions of ecological network (Risan 1998), ecological citizenship (White 2007), ecological wisdom (Naess 1989) and human ecology (Hawley 1986) are also useful in a discussion of how to reconcile the rights of humans, other species and ecosystems. According to White (2007: 50), the idea of ecological citizenship is that humans, as central actors in shaping environments, '[...] must act in accordance with their universal human interests and govern their actions so as to ensure the well-being of the ecosystem as a whole'. To establish *eco-human rights* as a legal notion and as a clue for future practice may be a way to reconcile conflicts of rights. Recognizing a kinship between the ideas of cosmopolitan justice and ecological justice may similarly promote an understanding of the ways in which human justice and natural justice are interwoven and interdependent.

A way of ensuring a moral communion of nature-culture, or ecological citizenship, may be to negotiate an equitable relationship and interaction between humans and nature – to find a fair balance between cosmopolitan justice and ecological justice. As James Lowlock (2006: 233) expresses it, '[...] to be able to survive with our civilization intact, we must conclude a fair peace with Gaia before we are reduced to a defeated bunch of seedy hooligans on the road to extinction'.

The best solution for the survival of humanity is thus to subordinate the interests of humans in exploiting nature to the legitimate right of Nature or Gaia. Gaia has the ability to recover – to heal itself from destruction – humans and other animals have not. Perhaps the best way to prevent humans from destroying biodiversity, diversity of species and the global climate is to strengthen popular resistance: that is, people's ability to fight back against the power elite's destruction of nature?

I do not have answers to these large and seemingly insoluble questions. What I do know is that eco-global criminology has a significant role to play in contributing knowledge and understanding as a basis for political changes necessary to prevent eco-genocide. The use of a diversity of perspectives and theories from different disciplines helps to generate new knowledge. To return to my starting point: my many names for my dog Singa are an expression of love and concern in the same way that the diverse theoretical approaches used in eco-global criminology convey the importance of the subject.

References

Aas, K.F. 2007. *Globalization & Crime*. London: Sage Publications.

Aas, K.F., Gundhus, H.O. and Lomell, H.M. (eds) 2010. *Technologies of InSecurity. The Surveillance of Everyday Life*. Abingdon: Routledge-Cavendish.

Bailliet, C.M., Aas, K.F. (eds) 2011. *Cosmopolitan Justice and its Discontents*. Abingdon: Routledge, a GlassHouse Book.

Beirne, P. 1999. For a Non-speciesist Criminology: Animal Abuse as an Object of Study, in *Criminology: An Interdisciplinary Journal. The Official Publication of the American Society of Criminology*, 37(1), 117–48.

Beirne, P. and South, N. (eds) 2007. *Issues in Green Criminology. Confronting Harms Against Environments, Humanity and other Animals*. Collumpton: Willan Publishing.

Braithwaite, J. 1984. *Corporate Crime in the Pharmaceutical Industry*. London: Routledge & Kegan Paul.

Braithwaite, J. 1993. 'Shame and Modernity', in *British Journal of Criminology*. UK: Oxford University Press, 33(1), 1–18.

Boekhout van Solinge, T. 2008. Crime, Conflicts and Ecology in Africa, in *Global Harms: Ecological Crime and Speciesism*, edited by R. Sollund. New York: Nova Science Publishers, 13–34.

Brulle, R.J. and Pellow, D.N. 2005. *Power, Justice, and the Environment: A Critical Appraisal of the Environmental justice Movement*. The MIT Press.

Callicot, J.B. 1989. *In Defence of the Land Ethic: Essays in Environmental Philosophy*. Albany: State University of New York Press.

Carroll, G.R. and Hannan, M.T. 2004. *The Demography of Corporations and Industries*. Princeton University Press.

Christie, N. 2000. *Crime Control as Industry: Towards Gulags, Western Style*. London: Routledge.

Donovan, J. 1996. Sympathy as a Basis for Ethical Treatment of Animals in *Beyond Animal Rights*, edited by J. Donovan and C.J. Adams. New York: The Continuum Publishing Company.

Eskeland, S. 2011. *De mest alvorlige forbrytelser [The Most Serious Crimes]*. Oslo: Cappelen Damm Akademisk.

Finstad, L. 2000. *Politiblikket* [*The Police's Glance*]. Oslo: Pax forlag.

Gibbs, C.E., Gore, M.L., McGarrell, E.F. and Rivers, L. 2009. Introducing Conservation Criminology: Towards Interdisciplinary Scholarship on Environmental Crimes and Risks, in *British Journal of Criminology*. UK: Oxford University Press, 50(1), 124–44.

Gray, M.A. 1996. The International Crime of Ecocide, *26 Californian Western International Law Journal*, (215), 258–9.

Greer, J. and Bruno, K. 1996. *Greenwash: The Reality Behind Corporate Environmentalism*. Penang, Malaysia: The Third World Network.

Hawley, A.H. 1986. *Human Ecology: A Theorethical Essay*. Chicago: University of Chicago Press.

Herbig, F.J.W. and Joubert, S.J. 2006. Criminological Semantics: Conservation Criminology – Vision or Vagary?, in *Environmental Crime: A Reader* (2009), edited by R. White. UK: Willan Publishing, 50–63.

Hessel, S. 2011. *Time for Outrage!* [Translation of the original French pamphlet 'Cry out! Indignez vous!']. UK: Quartet Books; pamphlet. edition.

Hessen, D.O. 2000. Empatiens evolusjon, ekspansjon og den 'dype økologi' [Empathy's Evolution, Expansion and the 'Deep Ecology'], in Oslo: *Materialisten* no. 3.

Hessen, D.O. 2008. Angsten for Darwin (The Fear of Darwin), in *Darwin. Verdenble aldri den samme* [Darwin. The World was Never the Same], Hessen et al. (eds). Oslo: Gyldendal Norske Forlag A/S.

Higgins, P. 2010. *Eradicating Ecocide: Laws and Governance to Prevent the Destruction of our Planet*. London: Shepheard-Walwyn.

Høigård, C. 1971. *Norsk kriminologi – idyll og ideologi* [Norwegian Criminology – Idyll and Ideology]. Oslo: Institutt for kriminologi og strafferett, UiO.

Høigård, C. 2002. *Gategallerier* [*Street Galleries*]. Oslo: Pax Forlag.

Klein, Naomi. 2007. *The Shock Doctrine – The Rise of Disaster Capitalism*. Metropolitan Books.

Larsen, G. 2003. *Dyrevern eller samfunnsvern? Dyremishandling som lovbrudd og lovlydig handling* [*Animal Protection Or Social Protection? Animal Abuse as Crime and as Legal Activity*]. Oslo: Unipub forlag.

Lynch, M.J. 1990. The Greening of Criminology: A Perspective for the 1990s, *The Critical Criminologist*, 2, 11–12.

Lynch, M.J. and Stretesky, P.B. 2003. The Meaning of Green: Towards a Clarification of the Term Green and its Meaning for the Developement of a Green Criminology, *Theoretical Criminology*, 7(2), 217–38.

Lovelock, J. 2006. *Gaias hevn* [*The Revenge of Gaia*]. Oslo: Spartacus Forlag.

Naerstad, A. 2011. Landbruk og 'grønn økonomi' [*Agriculture and 'Green Economy'*]. Oslo: U-nytt no. 2, Utviklingsfondet.

Naess, A. 1989. *Ecology, Community and Lifestyle*. Cambridge University Press.

Naess, A. 1974. Økologi, samfunn og livsstil [*Ecology, Society and Lifestyle*]. Oslo-Bergen-0Tromsø: Universitetsforlaget.

Nibert, D. 2002. *Animal Rights Human Rights*. Oxford: Rowman and Littlefield Publisher.

Nibert, D. 2003. Humans and Other Animals: Sociology's Moral and Intellectual Challenge, *International Journal of Sociology and Social Policy*, 23(3), 5–25.

Noske, B. 1989. *Humans and other Animals: Beyond the Boundaries of Anthropology*. London: Pluto press.

Nyland, N. 2009. Folkeretten truer det globale miljøet [International Law is Threatening the Global Environment], interview in *Apollon*, Forskningsmagasin fra Universitetet i Oslo, no 4.
Risan, L. 1998. Grenser for det menneskelige? [Limits of the Human?], in *Samtiden*, no 1, 56–64.
Regan, T. 1999. *Djurenes rettigheter, en filosofisk argumentasjon* [*The Case of Animal Rights*]. Forlaget Nye Doxa.
Regan, T. 2004. *Empty the Cages. Facing the Challenge of Animal Rights*. Lanham: Rowman & Littlefield Publishers.
Ryder, R. 1989. *Animal Revolution. Changing Attitudes towards Speciesism*. Oxford: Basil Blackwell.
Shiva, V. 2008. *Soil Not Oil. Climate Change, Peak Oil, and Food Insecurity*. London: Zed Books.
Singer, P. 2002. *Dyrenes frigjøring* [*Animal Liberation*]. Oslo: Spartacus Forlag.
Sollund, R. (ed.) 2008. *Global Harms. Ecological Crime and Speciesism*. New York: NOVA Science Publishers.
South, N. 2004. The Greening of Criminology, in *Criminology: A Sociological Introduction*, Carrabine et al. (eds). London and New York: Routledge.
South, N. 2010. The Ecocidal Tendencies of Late Modernity: Transnational Crime, Social Exclusion, Victims and Rights, in *Global Environmental Harm: Criminological Perspectives*, edited by R. White. Cullompton: Willan Publishing.
Toennessen, M. 2010. The Global Species, in *New formations: A Journal of Culture/Politics*, no. 69 (special number Imperial Ecologies, ed. A. Dawson), 98–110.
White, R. 2007. Green Criminology and the Pursuit of Social and Ecological Justice, in *Issues in Green Criminology: Confronting Harms against Environment, Humanity and other Animals*, edited by P. Beirne and N. South. Cullompton: Willan Publishing.
White, R. 2008. *Crimes against Nature. Environmental Criminology and Ecological Justice*. Cullompton: Willan Publishing.
White, R. 2009. *Environmental Crime: A Reader*, edited by R. White. Cullompton: Willan Publishing.
White, R. 2010. *Global Environmental Harm: Criminological Perspectives*. Cullompton: Willan Publishing.
White, R. 2011. *Transnational Environmental Crime. Towards an Eco-global Criminology*. Abingdon: Routledge.

Chapter 4
Constructing a Meta-history of Eco-global Criminology: On Brute Criminologists, Mortified Bunnies, Nature and its Discontent

Per Jørgen Ystehede

When should a proper history of green, or environmental, eco-global or conservationist criminology[1] commence? Perhaps its origins should be considered to be part of the rise of the scientific study of crime in the nineteenth century? The objective of this article is to propose a meta-historical framework for eco-global criminology. By creating a genealogy of eco-global criminological research spanning 150 years, this study suggests that the history of eco-global criminology may be divided into three main intellectual developments, or stages, which can be seen as partly shadowing the history of the science of criminology in general. These three stages all represent shifts in thinking about eco-global criminology, and they might be said to be cumulative, adding elements to the current discourse on eco-global criminology. Although eco-global criminology is often thought of as a fashionable new term for 'environmental criminology', this article will raise the question whether it might also be seen as part of criminology's renewed interest in biology.

These suggestions might seem somewhat surprising, given that most people would argue that the terms green/environmental/eco-global/conservationist criminology were coined in the late twentieth century. However, as this chapter will suggest, it might be quite useful to consider current research as the third phase, or

1 I have chosen to focus on the part of the eco-global intellectual tradition within the broader field of the history of the science of Criminology, which has discussed human–animal relationships; in this chapter I will use the umbrella term 'eco-global criminology' as academic short hand. In this article I define eco-global criminology as criminological research on harms against nature, harms against animals and harms against the eco-system. I understand eco-global criminology as the study of crimes against nature, of criminogenic human–animal relationships and the study of crimes against ecological systems. In addition, eco-global criminology addresses harmful actions that are not covered by the legal definition of crime. For an in-depth discussion, see Guri Larsens' chapter in this volume. I would like to thank the editors of this volume, Guri Larsen, Ragnhild Sollund and Rune Ellefsen, University of Oslo, for making valuable comments to this article – and also Nicole Rafter, Northeastern University.

period, in a long scientific tradition wherein criminologists have attempted to study and develop theories about the relationship between crime and nature. In other words, I consider eco-global criminology as part of a criminological continuum in which criminologists have studied the interrelationship between crime, animals, humans and nature. In this article I will try to provide an outline for how it might be useful to place green criminology within the larger framework of the history of criminology and the criminal sciences.

The first two stages of eco-global criminology, which more or less overlapped each other, may be dated from approximately the 1850s to the 1960s. In the first period, the main focus was on the study of the criminality of the eco-system, of plants, rodents and other animals – as well as on conducting comparative research on the criminality of humans and animals. This latter research was heavily influenced by the ventures by eighteenth-century men of letters into comparisons between moral temperament, and the physiognomy of humans and animals. This was a period marked by a blurring of the distinctions between man and brute, though at the same time there was a project to redraw and establish the differences demarcating humanity from what was considered 'baser' life forms. The main focus of attention then shifted to the study of sexual crimes: bestiality or zoophilia as it was termed by Richard von Krafft-Ebing (1840–1902) in his seminal work of 1885, *Psychopatia Sexualis*. The focus on bestiality reflected the main concern of criminological research at the time: the study of sexual deviance. In this period one also sees the development of a criminological discourse focusing on the city as a natural habitat and/or natural organism. The third and current phase, in which the research focus has shifted to crimes against animals, and to ecological justice, is heavily informed by the rise of the Green movement. Also of importance is the emphasis on animals and nature as victims. As in the nineteenth century discourse, one sees a questioning of and, arguably, a radical deconstruction of categories and old binary distinctions, especially regarding the concept of crime and its relation to nature.

The final part of this article will attempt to discuss what may be some of the consequences of deconstructing a human-centered perspective in criminology. Should eco-global criminology be seen as 'rethink[ing] the social and the natural universe, to reconceptualise the relationships between humans and nature in ways that accord greater weight to the nonhuman when it comes to issues such as environmental harm'? (White 2008: 10). Or is the resurgence of Social Darwinism in the criminological tradition 'disguised' under the mantle of eco-justice socio-politics?[2]

2 Social Darwinism is to many a contentious term, associated with popular catchphrases such as 'survival of the fittest' and so on. In fact, Darwinian thought and the Darwinian tradition influenced and interrelated with a number of broad social movements (other than the infamous eugenic and Fascist movement) such as anarchism, socialism, imperialism, liberalism, Fabianism and the Green movement. These are both democratic and anti-democratic intellectual movements. For further discussion, see Mike Hawkins (1997) *Social Darwinism in European and American Thought 1860–1945. Nature as Model and Nature as Threat*. Cambridge University Press: Cambridge.

Within the limitations of a book chapter, it is impossible to furnish a comprehensive account of the history and development of eco-global criminology over time and in different national criminological debates.[3] I will therefore restrict my argument to a brief outline, suggesting a meta-framework for the major intellectual frameworks and shifts of thinking in eco-global criminological discourse. Thus, I hope to frame some central tropes and discuss some examples of scholarly work that belong to the genealogy of eco-global criminology within criminological discourse. I briefly sketch eco-global criminology's historical development over 150 years – but one should be cautious about making comparisons between different texts and discourses from these different periods, since they of course belong to their specific historical and material contexts. Nevertheless, as this chapter will argue, some of the discussions may echo current theoretical endeavors in a way that is worthy of a passing note. In her excellent edited volume of extracts from key texts from *The origins of criminology*, Nicole Rafter quotes Ekatarina Botchkovar in her introduction: 'There is no science without a history of science' (Rafter 2009: xxiii). Criminology needs histories of its science, and perhaps this short outline may stimulate both practitioners in the field of eco-global criminology and its sceptics to take a closer look at their history, by showing how rich, varied and vigorous (eco-global) criminological research has been, and how it may continue to prosper and evolve in the future.

The Rise of the Scientific Study of the Crimes of Animals and Plants

Piers Beirne, in his essay of 1994, *The Law is an Ass*, reviews E.P. Evans's book of 1906 *The Criminal Prosecution and Capital Punishment of Animals* which traces (non-human) animal trials from the Bronze Age in ancient Mesopotamia to the early 1900s, focusing particularly on the animal trials of the Middle Ages. Evans's work is not, as Beirne suggests, only important as one of the earliest modern scholarly books advocating animal rights. Despite the fact that one may question Evans's historical methods and analysis, his *work* is not only a thorough documentation of the long and ambivalent relationship between man and animals cohabiting in society, but also an examination of the place of animals and nature in the Criminal Justice Process. Furthermore, Evans's work may also be read as quite an astute polemic against the new science of crime – criminal anthropology. According to Evans:

> A striking and significant indication of the remarkable change that has come over the spirit of legislation, and more especially of criminal jurisprudence, in comparatively recent times, is the fact that whereas, a few generations ago, lawgivers and courts of justice still continued to treat brutes as men responsible for their misdeeds, and to punish them capitally as malefactors, the tendency nowadays is to regard men as brutes (Evans 1906: 193).

3 Please also see footnote 1.

Among the new sciences on man and nature, Evans was especially disdainful and critical of the Italian School of Criminal Anthropology, and what he saw as this line of reasoning's flawed logic and potentially harmful consequences:

> If these statements be correct, why should not animals be penally responsible for their conduct as well as human beings? There are men apparently less intelligent than apes. Why then should the man be capitally punished and the ape not brought to trial ... In other words, does evolutionary criminology justify the judicial proceedings instituted by mediaeval courts against animals or regard the typical human criminal as having in this respect no supremacy over the beast? Does modern science takes us back to the barbarities of the middle Ages in matters of penal legislation, and in abolishing judicial procedure [...] (Evans 1906: 236–7).

As well as being an advocate for animals, Evans shows himself to be equally interested in addressing the new criminal sciences of those schooled in the classical Beccarian tradition, asking what would be the consequences if man was not only hedonistic and rational by nature, but also essentially *criminal*. Evans's critique was not far from the mark. For instance, in the third edition of *L'uomo Delinquente* (*Criminal Man)*, the most influential criminological text of the nineteenth century, Cesare Lombroso (1835–1909)[4] writes:

> Is crime the correct label for organized theft among monkeys, domestic theft among cats and monkeys, abduction of minors among ants and child abandonment among cuckoos who lay their eggs in other birds' nests? Are these actions crimes or simply the necessary effects of heredity – an organic structure imposed by competition for survival, by sexual selection, by the social necessity to quell disorder, or by the need for food among voracious animals? These examples underline the absurdity of a concept of justice based on free will and explain why we find criminal tendencies among all creatures, even within the most civilized races. Ancient people were probably right to convict and punish animals that behaved dangerously or mutilated sacred objects (Lombroso 2006: 170–171).

In *Criminal Man*, Lombroso even claims that zoology was the basis for the new science of crime (ibid: 168) and his work may very well be read as an attempt to trace and study crime in the animal kingdom from ancient to modern times – a kind of criminological equivalent to St Thomas Aquinas's *Summa Theologica* – *Criminal Man* might just has well been entitled *Summa Criminalis*.

---

4 Cesare Lombroso was, and still is, a somewhat controversial and often ridiculed figure in the history of criminology. However, this view of Lombroso is about to change. The work of Mary Gibson and Nicole Rafter in particular, as well as that of a number of criminological revisionist historians has painstakingly managed to nuance previous uninformed views of this early criminological thinker. See also P. Knepper and P.J. Ystehede, eds, *The Cesare Lombroso Handbook* (forthcoming 2012) Routledge.

For Lombroso, crime was to be understood as a natural phenomenon, so he deduced that its roots could be traced to the immoral behaviour of animals, for instance the murderous instincts of insects and even carnivorous plants. According to Lombroso:

> Impulsive crimes among animals, as among humans, are frequently prompted by love. Usually prudent, elephants in love can become enraged over the tiniest matter. Among polygamous fowl, the need to reproduce so overwhelms other needs and feelings that they seem to become deaf and blind, and even attack men ... even adultery is not absent in the animal realm, where it is often followed by the murder of the original mate. The apparently innocent female dove is often adulterous, jealous, and cruel to her mate [...] (ibid.: 171).

Lombroso was by no means the only scientist studying the criminality of animals and plants. In *Criminal Man* there is a wealth of references to contemporary research on the criminality of the animal kingdom by French, German, British and Italian scientists (Lombroso 2006). For example, Lombroso's Italian colleague and, at times severe critic, Alfredo Niceforo (1876–1960) studied the shape of the noses of convicted murderers and 'normal men', and found similarities between the noses of the murderers and the muzzles of Arabian horses. The Arab horse was considered the crudest and most murderous of the horse breeds. Thus his study asserted not only the criminal nature of murder, but also the fact that crime was a natural phenomenon. Plenty of similar examples are to be found, and not solely from the Italian School of Criminal Anthropology, but also in the French School of Criminology. For instance, Alexandré Lacassagne (1843–1924), the father of French Criminology, classified six types of crime as the most common among man, animals and plants (Evans 1906).

In the late nineteenth century while Cesare Lombroso was pioneering criminal anthropology with discourses on evolution, degeneration, heredity, medicine, psychiatry and sexology, inquiry in these and related areas forced a rethink of traditional ideas about human beings' bodies, nature and relationships with other forms of life. The new sciences demolished the old, comfortable anthropocentrism and also problematized the relation between external appearances and internal reality, most notably in the case of the human body. 'The human being was not the distinctive creature that it appeared to be on the surface: its lowly origins could be traced by the zoologist, who dissected to find internal structural similarities between human and animal bone' (Rafter and Ystehede 2009: 273). Perhaps the two most important intellectual movements to influence and shape the nineteenth century's scientific discourse on crime was, on the one hand, the rise to prominence and professionalism of the natural sciences – of 'Darwinism'; and on the other hand, the intellectual movement of Romanticism. The studies on human–animal and human-nature relationships by Lombroso, Lacassagne et al. were all forms of romantic scientific research, since it was a science informed by Romantic tropes. Given the growing focus on crime as somehow embedded in the nature of things, and on the horror of criminal deeds, their ideas were more specifically influenced by the Gothic strand of the Romantic imagination, and its iconography:

'The Darwinian narrative of the evolution of species', writes Kelly Hurley (1996: 6), 'was a narrative within which any combination of morphic traits, any transfiguration of bodily form, was possible; species integrity was undone.' Moreover, 'besides positing a too intimate continuity between humans and the "lower" species', Hurley continues (ibid.: 10), 'Darwinism described the natural order as a disorder, within which species identity was characterized by admixture and flux rather than integrity and fixity'. Evolutionism encouraged criminologists to elaborate explanatory schemes involving atavisms and other quasi-humans such as the born criminal. 'Natural selection', Hurley (1996: 60) concludes, 'authenticated the fantastic' (ibid.: 273).

Thus in the earliest periods of the history of eco-global criminology one arguably sees the most radical scientific deconstruction of human–animal and human-nature relationships. At the end of the nineteenth century and in the twentieth this was followed by what some might consider more sober criminological scientific explorations. There persisted, however, a form of eco-global criminology inheriting the older intellectual legacy, and belief that crime was part of (human) nature.

The Brute Criminologist and the Mortified Bunny

> A. is convicted of having committed masturbation and sodomy on dogs and rabbits. When twelve years old he saw how boys masturbated a dog. He imitated it, and thereafter could not keep from abusing dogs, cats and rabbits in this vile manner. Much more frequently, however, he committed sodomy on female rabbits – the only animal that had a charm for him. At dusk he was accustomed to repair his master's rabbit-pen, in order to satisfy his vile desire … A. states that, in such a condition if called upon to choose between a woman and a female rabbit, he could make choice only of the latter (Krafft-Ebing 1885: 103).

> When animals do appear in criminology, they are almost always passive, insentient objects acted on by humans (Beirne 2009: 3).

The new paradigmatic narrative form of the second period in the history of eco-global criminology focused on sexual crimes, bestiality or zoophilia as it was termed by Richard von Krafft-Ebing (1840–1902) in *Psychopatia Sexualis*. Human-animal sexual relations were seen as the mark of the degenerate criminal *par excellence*.[5]

In the earliest period of eco-global criminology there was a shift in the understanding of the criminal from *made* to *naturally born* and the establishment

5 This is not to suggest that the main focus in criminological theory *per se* in this period (1885–1960) was sex crimes. More specifically, I am here referring to criminological literature and studies pertaining to eco-global criminology.

of humans and animals on an evolutionary and biological continuum, and this created both a history of evil in nature and a natural history of evil. Later, however, criminologists were no longer interested in the study of the *crimes of nature per se*. Instead, as Beirne notes, animals and nature became an Object where the human's actions in relation to the animal was of criminological interest. Now the main focus was *crimes against nature*. However, how *crimes against nature* should be viewed became somewhat of an intellectual conundrum, since crime was now also thought to be part of nature. After the establishment of a discourse in which crime was understood as a natural phenomenon, one sees the development of a contradictory discourse in the aftermath of Lombroso, Darwin et al. which sought on the one hand to uphold the biological uniqueness of (at least) the bourgeois part of humankind, while on the other hand asserting that certain types of human beings may somehow be more closely linked to animal nature.

What particularly differentiated this discourse from the earliest stage of eco-global criminology was first of all a stronger sense of morally conservative anthropocentrism, and secondly the emphasis on human–animal sexual contact as a sign of criminality and degeneracy. In Lombroso's view, and this is a noteworthy development, atavism or animal faculties expressed in the human species should not by definition be defined as a bad or evil faculty, whereas for Krafft-Ebing, and later Sigmund Freud (1856–1939), humanity was achieved by repressing, rationalizing and disciplining the brute within. Lombroso at times saw instincts as something to be embraced, but instincts were now to be controlled and feared.

Another important development in this period was the *ecologization of the city* in which theories on crime and urban development were developed from biological/ecological theories of plant life by criminologists such as McKenzie (1924), Park (1925) and Shaw and McKay (1942). For instance, according to Park:

> The city is a state of mind, a body of customs and traditions, and of organized attitudes and sentiments that inhere in this tradition. The city is not, in other words, merely a physical mechanism and an artificial construction. It is involved in the vital processes of the people who compose it, it is a product of nature and particularly of human nature (Park in Gelder 2005: 25).

By viewing the city as an organism and studying human ecology, these researchers were not just using analogies and metaphors from biology to describe phenomena, but were in fact naturalizing and animating urban space. They did not merely employ biology as a metaphor, but used biology as a mode of structuring their thoughts about the city and the language they used to express them. This, in effect, made the city, in criminological research, part of a biological continuum believed to affect man.

Eco-politics and the Ascent of Species

The most important historical event to shape twentieth century criminological discourse was the Second World War (1939–45) (Ystehede 2008). The majority of the criminological literature written after it, one may argue, has the World War as an intellectual point of reference – though it is not always explicitly stated. Of decisive importance to eco-global criminology was the invention of the Atomic bomb. Post-Oppenheimer, human beings were not merely at the top of the food chain. Now there was also a growing awareness that humanity possessed the will and the power to destroy life on earth. Another important intellectual context associated with this was the rise of the Green movement. The technological and industrial developments of the Cold War fuelled a new environmental concern that went way beyond saving forests and establishing national parks. Here one also finds an important meeting point between the eco-global criminological tradition and the tradition of critical criminology with its studies on environmental crime, corruption and so on. Especially from the late 1970s onwards, one has seen the rise and institutionalization of groups advocating radical environmentalism and animal rights.

One of the most important influences on the strands within contemporary eco-global criminology that focus on animal rights and species justice, which can be seen in this volume, was the work of the Australian philosopher Peter Singer (1946–). His work on animal liberation (1975) and against speciesism was of particular importance. Piers Beirne, who is one of those seemingly influenced by Singer's book, argues that eco-global criminology now requires a shift away from humanist notions of life and justice (2009). The concept of eco-justice – which would give species judicial rights, with some also arguing for rights for non-human subjects – has become a topic of growing importance. However, the practical, scientific, ethical and philosophical consequences that would follow from such a shift away from humanist notions of life and justice are not altogether clear. Is one merely seeing criminologists arguing for a balance of power, or a levelling of the playing field when it comes to human–animals relationships – where humans have had, and still have the upper hand OR is what one sees 'disguised' under the mantle of eco-justice socio-politics actually a resurgence of a form of social Darwinism? In contemporary eco-global criminology one sees a reappraisal and re-addressing of evolutionary biology among social scientists – something traditionally considered the property of researchers in the criminological tradition who are more inclined towards psychology or psychiatry. An aspect of 'anti-speciesist thought' is the notion that humanism might be considered anthropocentric. This raises the question whether such a line of reasoning may lead to various anti-humanist stances. In other words, may the eco-global criminological project give birth to a denigration of human worth – and replace humanism with forms of what might be termed neo-Darwinist thought? Again, may this also be seen as part of the revitalization of the idea of crime as somehow a natural phenomenon? Thus is there a danger that, instead of deconstructing traditional notions of crime, which is what Larsen (this volume), for example, argues for, the eco-global criminological project may in effect be a form of epistemological net-widening, echoing in modernistic form ideas already found among criminological thinkers of the nineteenth century? If this is the case, one is tempted to ask if perchance E.P. Evans's critique should also be revisited.

Why Construct a Meta-history of Eco-global Criminology?

In lieu of the more traditional descriptions of the history of the science of criminology, this article has tried to place the history of eco-global criminology at centre-stage, by taking just a few examples from the history of criminology where the relationship between humans, animals and (more broadly speaking) nature has been the focus of criminological analysis. Obviously, there are important distinctions that must be taken into consideration when looking at contemporary eco-global criminological literature and earlier criminological writings. However, as this article implicitly suggests, one also needs to avoid falling prey to a 'myopia-of-the-present'. Take, for instance, Beirne's view, already quoted above: 'When animals do appear in criminology, they are almost always passive, insentient objects acted on by humans' (Beirne 2009: 3). When we consider the history of the science of criminology, this is a 'truth' that is not universal. Certainly, this mode of representation was dominant in twentieth century criminological discourse – but arguably not in that of the nineteenth century.

Even though, not much research in criminology has focused on human–animal relations, crimes against the environment and so on – yet, as this article suggests, arguably more research has been conducted in the area of eco-global criminology than is generally believed. Furthermore, as this article has suggested, some of the concerns of contemporary eco-global criminology could be seen as not 'new', but already under consideration at the very beginning of the criminological enterprise. Obviously this is not to say that one should over-emphasize similarities of themes found, for instance in the mid-nineteenth century and in the present. There are of course important differences between the evolutionary biological discourse of the nineteenth century and that, for instance, of speciesism and of eco-justice. However, I think it would be both erroneous and problematic to ignore the strong historical tradition of human–animal research in criminology when considering current research going on in eco-global criminology. It is important to recognize that the medicalized culture of the late twentieth and early twenty-first centuries mirrors in important respects the biologism of late nineteenth-century culture. Though there may be a recognition of the cultural productions of meaning with regard to nature, one does not need to scratch deep below the surface to find the positivist desire haunting the greater part of the Western criminological and social scientific tradition.

Hopefully this somewhat sweeping account and construction of a meta-history of eco-global criminological research will be modified in due course by more in-depth empirical research. Nevertheless, despite the limitations of this historical narrative, I would argue that it's possible importance lies in *thinking historically* about the theoretical tradition of eco-global criminology – in particular, *thinking historically* about the history of this scientific endeavor. I believe it is important for the field of eco-global criminology to have a 'historical horizon' or narrative framework within to situate its research. As Rafter has argued:

> Whatever its explanation, criminologists' disdain for memory condemns us to operate with one hand – maybe two – tied behind our backs. We lack a sense of our work as part of a project in time. Large chunks of our memory have fallen away, leaving us, like victims of Alzheimer's disease, stripped of our identity. We have to function not only without a past but also without a sense of criminology's possible futures. When we allow our past to atrophy and disappear, we lose track of who we are, where we come from, and where we are going (Zerubavel 2003). We become scientistic, pretending to resemble hard scientists, and we have to struggle along without the sustenance of traditions and without a sense of the field's identity. History, on the other hand, molds individual and collective identities (Rafter 2010: 3).

Arguably, eco-global criminology is still seen as a marginal part of the criminological enterprise. It is often considered as merely a new term for traditional environmental criminology or research on organized crime. However, by revisiting criminology's history, re-reading and deciphering criminological theories found, for instance in the context of the discourse on evolutionary biology, one will soon discover that eco-global criminology is neither 'new' nor 'estranged' from the criminological scientific tradition, though one might have believed this at first glance. Thus, creating meta-histories may enrich our understanding and reposition eco-global criminology. Such exercises may throw light on interpretive disputes and on possible pitfalls as well as perhaps clearing the way to potential new areas for criminological research and criminological thought in general – and eco-global criminological discourse in particular.

References

Beirne, P. 1994. The Law is an Ass: Reading E.P. Evans' The Medieval Prosecution and Capital Punishment of Animals, in *Society and Animals*, 2(1), 27–46.

Beirne, P. 2009. *Confronting Animal Abuse. Law, Criminology and Human-animal Relationships*. USA: Rowman & Littlefield Publishers.

Evans, E.P. 1906. *The Criminal Prosecution and Capital Punishment of Animals*. London: William Heinemann.

Hawkins, M. 1997. *Social Darwinism in European and American Thought 1860–1945: Nature as Model and Nature as Threat*. Cambridge: Cambridge University Press.

Knepper, P. and Ystehede, P.J. (eds). Forthcoming 2012. *The Cesare Lombroso Handbook*. Routledge.

Krafft-Ebing, R. 1892. Pathological Sexuality, in *The Origins of Criminology: A Reader*, edited by N. Rafter (2009). USA: Routledge, 65–73.

Lombroso, C. 2006. *Criminal Man*. Translated and with a new introduction by M. Gibson and N. Rafter. USA: Duke University Press.

McKenzie, R.D. 1924. The Ecological Approach to the Study of the Human Community, in *American Journal of Sociology*, 30(3), 287–301.

Park, R. 1925. The City: Suggestions for the Study of Human Behavior in the Urban Environment, in *The Subcultures Reader*, edited by K. Gelder (2005). Great Britain: Routledge, 25–34.

Rafter, N. 2010. Silence and Memory in Criminology, in *Criminology*, 48(2), 339–55.

Rafter, N. and Ystehede, P.J. 2009. Here Be Dragons: Lombroso, the Gothic and Social Control, in *Popular Culture, Crime and Social Control*. Sociology of Crime Law and Deviance series, vol. 14, edited by M. Deflem. Emerald/JAI Press: Bingley, 263–84.

Shaw, C.R. and McKay, H.D. 1942. *Juvenile Delinquency in Urban Areas*. Chicago: University Press.

Singer, P. 1975. *Animal Liberation: A New Ethics for our Treatment of Animals*. Random House: New York.

White, R. 2008. *Crimes Against Nature. Environmental Criminology and Ecological Justice*. Willan Publishing: UK.

Ystehede, P.J. 2008. *In the Twilight of Good and Evil. Cesare Lombroso and the Rise of the Criminological Scientific Imagination*. Saarbrücken: VDM Verlag Dr. Mueller e.K.

Part II
Speciesism, Animal Abuse and Social Movements

Chapter 5

The Rhetorical Making of a Crime Called Speciesism: The Reception of 'Animal Liberation'

Kristian Bjørkdahl

If a book could start a revolution, would we not want to know *how*? More specifically, if a book gained a reputation for having readjusted our moral imaginations towards inclusion of previously neglected living things, would we not be interested – perhaps even obliged – to find out how mere words on a page could have such an extraordinary effect?

In this chapter, I study the impact of Peter Singer's book *Animal Liberation* on the modern animal movement. My focus is on how that book contributed to the rhetorical making of the crime called 'speciesism', which Singer himself defines as 'a prejudice or attitude of bias in favor of the interests of members of one's own species and against those of members of other species' (Singer 1975: 7). Although Singer's book is often referred to as 'the book that started a revolution' (see Singer 2009), speciesism is not yet an established crime, but rather a crime in the making, and the quest to include non-human animals in our moral sphere an unfinished project. The word 'speciesism' still tends to prompt requests for explanation and justification, and the burden of proof still lies with those who use the term in all seriousness. 'Speciesism' still requires those quote marks. But precisely because it is a crime in the making, it can be taken to exemplify the process whereby a particular course of action comes to be designated as right or wrong, prescribed or proscribed, virtue or vice.

My initial assumption in the following is that, until a certain vocabulary associated with the idea of speciesism gained traction, the phrase 'discrimination against animals' was a misnomer. There could be no such thing – 'discrimination' was not a word that made much sense when applied to animals. The notion that something called speciesism ought to be considered a moral offense – perhaps even a criminal one – came into being with the diffusion of a certain vocabulary, in which words and phrases like 'interests', 'sentience', 'capacity for suffering', 'subject-of-a-life', 'cruelty' and so on were brought to the fore, and where, more generally, animals were redescribed as appropriate objects of moral concern, as beings to whom our traditional moral logic applied.

The diffusion of this vocabulary took place at many sites. Here, I focus exclusively on *Animal Liberation* – the self-styled 'definitive classic of the animal movement' (Singer 2009). By studying readers' letters to the author and editors of the book, I seek to understand how, from the interface between the author, his readers and their respective social positions, a discursive frame emerged in which 'speciesism' would appear to be a crime, and 'discrimination against animals' a phrase that made sense – at least to some people.

Making Right and Wrong

By referring to speciesism as a crime in the making, I want to emphasize not the word 'crime', which I take to mean simply an action or practice that is associated with penalties or castigation of a certain order, and which I use roughly as a synonym for 'wrongness' – whether moral *or* legal. Instead, I want to highlight the word 'making', which I use to signal a rhetorical attitude to understanding norms. In the following, I thus assume a view of normativity where actions or dispositions are made right or wrong by nothing other than rhetorical discourse. Three points can be adduced to explain that statement.

The first is that, on this view, moral rightness and wrongness are understood as functions of conventional uses of language within particular communities. There is no appeal to arguments that purport to anchor our moral beliefs in transhistorical fields or circumstances, nor is there any perceived need for such appeals. In fact, there is no mention of anything that stands beyond or above the dealings of concrete groupings of people on earth. There are only multifarious discursive practices and their placement in historical time, as well as suggestions about how to change those practices.

Those suggestions lead to a second point, which is that there is an aspect of persuasion involved in the process of making right and wrong with language. At least in theory, a community may at any time start employing a different vocabulary with which to conceive of its moral universe. As Richard Rorty says, '[A]nything [can] be made to look good or bad, important or unimportant, useful or useless, by being redescribed' (Rorty 1989: 7). This possibility gives rise to attempts to (re)articulate the moral universe of the community in question. These attempts are struggles, in the sense that each articulation serves certain purposes while foreclosing others, and in the sense that each articulation competes with every other in a game for attention and approval.

This leads to a third point, which is that all articulations are not equal. By virtue of commanding the power of definition, certain authors and certain texts have longer lives and leave greater traces on the community than others. The long-term reception history of a text rests, to appropriate the vocabulary of Pierre Bourdieu, at least in part on the species and amounts of capital that can be (and are) harnessed in its favour, in whatever field the text has found its way into (Bourdieu and Wacquant 1992). Power thus structures the fate of texts. This is important, because, as Jane Tompkins says, 'When discourse is responsible for reality and not merely a reflection of it, then whose discourse prevails makes all the difference' (Tompkins 1980: xxv).

From these points, some interesting questions suggest themselves. How, when and why have the moral universes of different communities been rhetorically redescribed? How have new moral vocabularies been created? In other words, the question of how historical changes in language use have created new conceptions of particular moral communities and their concerns becomes a pressing object of research.

Writing Readers' Letters, Reading Letter Writers

In order to begin answering those questions in the case of *Animal Liberation*, I have studied letters from readers that were sent to Singer in the first few years following the publication of his book.[1]

I have found these letters to be a rich source, in several respects. The number of letters is in itself quite substantial, and as such the letters lay claim to being more than oddities. The collection contains letters from many different sorts of people (many of whom identify their gender, age, education and occupation, as well as other interests and concerns), and they are written in a variety of styles. One widely shared characteristic of the material is that most letter writers approach the reader response letter as a genre that invites honesty, directness and even disclosure of personal – not to say intimate – details. Most of the letters come across as quite frank; there is occasional formality, but little posturing, and most letters are marked by the writers' desire to convey sincerely and openly what reading this book has done for them.

Because the collection of letters has not been selected by a principle imposed on the material, it arguably approximates a 'natural kind', and cannot be criticized as being arbitrary. Of course, with 'natural' selections comes the danger of 'natural' bias, in this case, not least the fact that different people may be differently inclined towards writing a reader response letter in the first place. However, since my concern here is to understand how *Animal Liberation* moved people into thinking differently about animals, I would note that this collection of letters traces a group of readers who were at least so moved as to write a letter. To study comprehensively if and how readers of texts are persuaded to readjust their moral beliefs, one would be obliged to study, in equal measure, readers who were *not* so moved. However, I lay no claim to comprehensiveness in this chapter, and readily admit that by focusing almost exclusively on these letters, I am charting only a tiny

1 Several hundred such letters are archived at the National Library of Australia, in Canberra, in the collection *Papers of Peter Singer*. Not all letters came in response to the actual book; some of them comment on an extract from the book in a newspaper or journal, some on newspaper interviews with Singer or on one of his op-ed pieces, some on his appearances on TV or radio. I have deliberately *not* filtered out these responses, because I view them as part of the wider reception of *Animal Liberation*. In fact, some letter writers admit to not having read the book, while having been greatly moved by its arguments.

piece of the reception of Singer's book, and an even smaller part of the 'making of the rhetorical crime called speciesism'.

The Impact of Animal Liberation

Jean-Paul Sartre once wrote:

> Words wreak havoc when they happen to name something that is experienced but has not yet been named: they revive a complicit reflection by proposing a meaning for something when that meaning is, in fact, only a hypothesis of the future, only an extrapolation which cannot be accepted reflexively except by a vow (Sartre 1987: 127–8).[2]

That quote conveniently illustrates the reception of *Animal Liberation*, because the book not only wreaked havoc, it did so primarily because it supplied its readers with a coherent and authoritative vocabulary with which to speak of our obligations towards animals. It *named something that was experienced but had yet to be named.*

Since its first publication in 1975, the book has gained legendary status in animal protection circles, and is routinely called 'the Bible of the animal liberation movement', 'the definitive classic of the animal movement' or 'the book that started a revolution'. It is generally credited with launching and creating an impetus for the modern animal movement, especially in North America, Britain and Australia, but also elsewhere in the Western world. Singer's fellow philosopher Thomas Nagel recently summed up the importance of the book in an essay in the *New York Review of Books*:

---

2 I take Sartre to be saying that words or phrases from time to time drop into our language, and thus into our universe of meaning, and have the (unintended) consequence of highlighting how our ways of seeing, understanding and speaking stand in relation to the world we operate in. To say that such words offer a meaning for something as 'a hypothesis of the future', is to say that that particular thing does not *now* have a meaning – it is, strictly speaking, *meaningless*. This is to 'revive a complicit reflection' in that it opens up the potential abyss that is the contingency of our relation to the world. They 'wreak havoc' for the same reason: to force people to reflect about meaninglessness is to force a certain *unease* on them. In contrast to words whose meaning is well established, and which we for that reason can place trust in and be committed to, the new words Sartre talks about 'cannot be accepted reflexively'; there is no tradition, or established practice, that allows us to find the proposed meaning meaningful, as it were. These new words we can accept only 'by a vow', that is, not without an element of risk. We don't quite know whether accepting the meaning those words offer will work out in practice – we have to take it on trust. Sometimes some of us are willing to do that, however, precisely because they 'happen to name something that is experienced but has not yet been named'.

> [Singer has] had a larger practical impact on the world than any other philosopher of our time. His 1975 book, *Animal Liberation*, led to effective movements to reduce the suffering of animals in factory farming, scientific experiments, and the testing of commercial products such as cosmetics, and it has persuaded many people to become vegetarians to one degree or another (Nagel 2010).

While one cannot deny the practical effects of Singer's book, Nagel might be seen to overstate its importance. The practices targeted by the book (such as animal testing and industrial rearing of animals) have persisted, and in the latter case at least, even grown considerably since 1975. In addition, the book and its author eventually became objects of quite severe criticisms from within academic philosophy, from other emerging strands in the animal movement and from the industries targeted by Singer.

However, the immediate reception of the book, which is what concerns me here, was overwhelmingly positive. The book appears to have done precisely what Sartre talked about: it named and gave form to something many readers had felt themselves. A surprising number of those who wrote to Singer about the book testified to having had the experience of something like 'speciesism', while lacking the name and attendant vocabulary with which to express it. The significance of Singer's book was thus not to come up with a new way of seeing or treating animals – as if from scratch – but to collect, consolidate and give coherent form to experiences and perceptions that were already widespread.

That is not to say that the apparent success of Singer's book can be explained solely by the fact that Singer supplied his readers with the tag 'speciesism'. In fact, Singer did not come up with that term – Richard Ryder did – and, in any case, the majority of his readers seem to place no great importance on the term itself. Rather, the hullabaloo surrounding the book is more plausibly explained by the fact that an unprecedented type of capital was brought to bear on a topic that previously had been the domain of 'cranks' and 'old ladies in tennis sneakers', as one letter writer put it. Peter Singer, in his capacity as a credentialed university philosopher, and *Animal Liberation*, as a well worked-out philosophical statement and defense of the animal cause, were able to convert capital that had previously been applied predominantly in the philosophical field into valid currency in the field of politics. In that respect, *Animal Liberation* was an example – though undoubtedly the most prominent one – of the ambitions of the emerging discipline of 'applied ethics', the application of the tools of moral philosophy to controversial issues of the day.

The Prehistory of *Animal Liberation*

In a story he has told on numerous occasions, Singer describes his conversion to the animal cause – and to a standpoint where it appeared pertinent to consider 'all animals as equals' – as a quite sudden result of logical reflection. It happened, so this story goes, while Singer was a graduate student at Oxford in the early 1970s, as a result of his reading the work of some of his friends, Stanley and Roslind Godlovitch and John Harris. That work was the edited volume *Animals, Men, and Morals* released in 1971 (Godlovitch et al. 1971). Disappointed by the fact that 'that book essentially failed to attract any attention after its publication in England',[3] Singer decided he could help promote the book and its cause, which he now felt was an urgent one; he therefore submitted a review of the book to *The New York Review of Books*, that – as is the custom at NYRB – was imbued with the reviewer's own opinions on the matter.

Singer himself may well have felt the arguments he encountered in *Animals, Men, and Morals* to be the driver for his own conversion, but historically we must also note a set of contextual factors. The period in which Singer was at Oxford came on the heels of the radicalization of the public sphere in the late 1960s. The civil rights movement in the United States had brought black liberation to the forefront of public life; women's liberation had started to gain momentum for its modern incarnation (helped by books like Betty Friedan's *The Feminine Mystique* (1963), Germaine Greer's *The Female Eunuch* (1971) and Kate Millett's *Sexual Politics* (1970);[4] and there were constant protests against the Vietnam war. Singer wrote his dissertation on the ethics of civil disobedience (later published as *Democracy and Disobedience*). He took part in a 'Radical Philosophy Group' at Oxford, and was generally part of an environment within (moral) philosophy that was looking to make a difference in the world. One of the papers he wrote in this period, for instance, was entitled 'Must Philosophy Be Academic?': Singer did not think it had to be.

At this time, there was no such thing, properly speaking, as 'applied ethics'; Singer's dissertation of 1971, published in book form in 1973, may be seen as an early contribution to carving out such a field. Singer's mentor at Oxford was R.M. Hare, a philosopher who greatly influenced Singer. According to Dale Jamieson, one of Singer's later collaborators, Singer was at this time 'acting as Hare's bulldog', that is, as someone who took the gist of Hare's work as a framework within which to work with acute public issues.[5] Convinced that *something like* Hare's 'universal prescriptivism' was the appropriate way of understanding ethics on a metalevel, and convinced also (as was Hare himself) that *some type of* utilitarianism was the appropriate vessel, as it were, for Hare's theory, Singer and his fellow graduate students turned to the burning issues of the day. Given both the political climate of the early 1970s, and the particular academic milieu Singer found himself in at this time, the ethics of civil disobedience was an obvious choice for a thesis topic. What better way to radically engage with current affairs? Singer's famous article 'Famine, Affluence, and Morality' (Singer 1972), a classic statement of the duties of

3 Unless otherwise noted, I quote from an interview with Singer.

4 In an interview Singer said he had been directly influenced by Greer's book especially.

5 From interview with Jamieson.

the world's rich towards the poor, is another telling example of his desire to turn the tools of philosophy to topics that could be seen as urgent even by the general public.

In this context, the choice of animals as a research topic may seem an unlikely career move for someone like Singer, but one can easily see why it appealed to him. Not only did other main forms of discrimination – against blacks, against women – already have statements somewhat similar to the one Singer would produce for animals, but as a white male he was not the most obvious person to speak out on such issues – not, at least, with any authority.

Also, in the early 1970s there was no such thing as radical animal activism – or to the extent that there was, it had neither a principled philosophical platform to work from, nor the practical-political muscle power that could bring it over the threshold of the public's attention. Rather, the animal cause was largely championed by quite moderate societies for the prevention of cruelty to animals, like the British Royal Society for the Prevention of Cruelty to Animals, the American Society for the Prevention of Cruelty to Animals and the Humane Society of the United States. Many of these societies were run by the types Singer (1975: preface) described in his book as 'animal-lovers', the kind of people who would express shock at animal abuse and then have a ham sandwich. One letter writer summed up the state of the animal movement at this time by opining that it consisted mostly of 'shopping bag ladies'.

In this context, Singer saw the need for a radical, principled statement of our abuse of animals, and a defense of their rights *vis-à-vis* human needs. In a 'Statement of the intent of the proposed book', effectively a book proposal (that Singer first presented to Simon & Schuster, and later to editor Bob Silvers at the *New York Review of Books*, which eventually published the book), Singer wrote:

> The idea of the book is to present a coherent, consistent case for the kind of revolutionary change in human attitudes to other species that may be summed up in the phrase 'Animal Liberation'. The book would differ from *Animals, Men and Morals* … in that it would be consistently and consciously directed towards the goal of animal liberation. With AM&M, only some of the many contributors were arguing for a revolutionary change, and the number of short pieces that made up the book resulted in superficial treatment of some issues, and differing views on others. My book would be written from a single, explicitly stated position, and would cover the whole range of issues raised by our relations with other animals.

Already at the stage of planning the book, then, Singer seemed convinced that a more definitive account of our attitude to animals could be written, that such an account had to be written from a 'single, explicitly stated position', and that it would benefit from being 'consistently and consciously directed towards the goal of animal liberation'. He saw this kind of statement quite explicitly as a weapon in a struggle for a particular articulation of our moral universe, and appears to have thought that a strongly argued philosophical case for animal liberation was essential to 'the kind of revolutionary change in human attitudes to other species' that he envisioned. He was to echo this conviction in the preface to the book, where he wrote, 'I do not think anyone who reads [*Animal Liberation*] to the end will ever again think that the only problems that merit time and energy are problems concerning humans'. Referring to his own opening paragraph, where he compares tyranny over non-human animals to the tyranny of whites over blacks, he placed a bet with his reader: 'I do not ask you to believe my opening paragraph now. All I ask is that you reserve your judgment until you have read the book' (Singer 1975: preface).

While he clearly believed that to rigorously apply the tools of philosophy to current issues was a key to moving things along, Singer was equally aware that those tools had to be phrased in an idiom that could appeal to audiences beyond the seminar rooms at Oxford. In the original preface to the book – which incidentally reads almost like the book's 'user's manual' – Singer told his reader: 'The basic principles of Animal Liberation are very simple. I have tried to write a book that is clear and easy to understand, requiring no expertise of any kind'. To unaccustomed readers who found the first, philosophical chapter too challenging, Singer said reassuringly: 'Don't be put off. In the next chapters we get down to the little-known details of how our species oppresses others under our control. There is nothing abstract about this oppression, or about the chapters that describe it'.

In an interview, Singer spoke of his desire to address 'every reasonably intelligent person', and to appeal to the 'the general, educated reader'. He explained his choice of writing style thus:

> I was writing a book that … I really wanted to change the world, right? … You know, I mean … by this stage, I was convinced that there was a widespread and continuing atrocity, that humans were treating billions of animals in horrific ways, that were completely unjustifiable. And I wanted to stop that, and now I wasn't going to stop that by writing for other philosophers.

At the heart of *Animal Liberation* was thus a combination of convictions, which to some extent was also characteristic of applied ethics in general: first, the belief that the tools of philosophy were not just useful, but to some extent necessary, for dealing properly with controversial, moral-political issues; second, a belief that those tools, in order to be meaningful, had to be applied beyond the discipline itself, and address a larger audience.

To the extent *Animal Liberation* can be understood as a touchstone of applied ethics, Singer's book was a showcase of how to strike an effective balance between the two central concerns of that discipline.

Reading *Animal Liberation*

Among the readers' letters Singer received in the first few years after *Animal Liberation* was published, all but a very few were extremely positive. In a collection of several hundred letters, I have come across only one that is outright hostile, and a certain number that, while appreciative, want to supplement, adjust or correct Singer in some respect. The overwhelming majority of letters, however, hail Singer's effort.

A number of readers wrote to Singer simply to thank him for taking up the issue, and for bringing previously hidden facts to the public's attention: 'I have always loved; that is, respected animals. But I was never fully aware of the gross exploitation and mistreatment they undergo for my "gratification"', writes one reader, 'I innocently assumed that all farm animals really lived on a farm, not in a factory'. In a letter addressed to the publisher, another reader writes: '[Y]ou and the author must be congratulated in having produced such a work; particularly as the general public, myself included, is plainly unaware of the true nature of intensive farming and much research work currently being performed on animals'. Readers who admit ignorance of animal abuse, and who therefore praise Singer for bringing it to their attention, are in the minority, however. Far more numerous (and significant) are those who display familiarity both with the fact of animal abuse and with Singer's project of extending moral concern to include animals. However, readers in both categories report being moved to some sort of conversion by reading *Animal Liberation*, most often that from meat eating to lacto-ovo vegetarianism.

'Dear Dr. Singer; You're darn right', writes a reader from Massachusetts, USA, 'Presentation impeccable, argument incontrovertible. I became a convert to respect of animal rights immediately, and will try to spread the ideas'. A reader from Virginia, USA, writes: 'Prior to this past Christmas, I had always told myself that one day I will become a vegetarian – but my love for meat kept me from doing so. Well reading your book has been enough to firmly convince me I can never go back to an omnivorous diet again'. In some letters, readers tell of their passing the book on to friends and family after reading; in some such cases, something approaching mass conversion appears to have taken place:

> You might be interested in knowing what a tremendous influence your book *Animal Liberation* has had on me and, subsequently, on others, since I first picked it up in the public library in June of this year. Just about halfway through it, I stopped eating meat. In the last few years I've tried to give up meat on several different occasions but always succumbed to my favorites. The good example of my son, now 14, who stopped eating meat at age 5 when he learned it was derived from dead animals, wasn't enough. Your book, however, produced pangs of conscience of sufficient depth to force me into vegetarianism. Since then, I've recommended *Animal Liberation* to a good friend of mine who, coincidentally, was just on the verge of vegetarianism. Your book provided the final nudge. She then recommended it to another woman friend of hers who also promptly stopped eating meat.

Such conversions took place even in people who presumably were well acquainted with the plight of animals. One representative of the American animal organization

Fund for Animals writes, for instance: 'You finally convinced me that I must become a vegetarian, and so I am. Thank you for leading me in the right direction'.

The apparent frequency revealed by the material of such conversions to vegetarianism is impressive. What is more interesting, however, are readers' attempts to describe precisely what it was about Singer's book that could have such an effect. And this is where a great mass of responding readers express reactions similar to the one described by Sartre above. As if prompted by the argument and the vocabulary supplied in Singer's book, many readers appear to be re-reading and re-evaluating their own previous thoughts on the matter, seeing them now as encapsulated in a steadier and more convincing form. A reader from Virginia, USA, writes: 'I'd been struggling for over 2 years to cease consuming animals, and your book provided the final snap. The book is a very logical, rational presentation of the humane ethic which I, for one, had taken as a given for a long time, but was unable to put into words as clearly as you'. Another writes, simply: 'For many years, I have felt the same as you do about animals, but have not been able to express myself as coherently and cogently as you do, in "Animal Liberation"'.

Some letter writers look back on their own previous thinking on the matter depreciatively after reading Singer's book. One American reader writes:

> Dear Peter [sic] … [I] really believe that you did a beautiful job in doing and saying what you said. Your use of the term speciesism and theme throughout the book of equal consideration for all creatures was something, as a fellow non-flesheating friend says, we've been looking for someone to say for a long time. Not only because it is time but also because it puts into words the very way my brother, friend and I have been thinking but have not been able to find a way to express.

Commenting on Singer's appearance on the Australian TV show *Monday Conference*, a reader from Adelaide, Australia, writes:

> As I had not heard about your book prior to tonight's programme, I had the sensation of hearing my very thoughts put in a way that I could never hope to do. Mine have been half-baked ideas that I have put down to being 'over-sensitive'. After tonight, however, I feel I will no longer bury my head in the sand but do what I can. Thank you!

For many readers, the point was not just – or not even primarily – that *Animal Liberation* supplied the formal philosophical tools with which to justify vegetarianism or animal activism, it was simply the realization that such tools did in fact exist and that they could be successfully applied to the animal cause. One practical outcome of this realization seems to have been an increased degree of confidence in people's own, previously 'half-baked' ideas, about animals. As a result of reading the book, many readers whose thoughts about animals had always been similar to Singer's, seem to have found the courage of their convictions, and ceased to be afraid to be frank about their stance on animals to other people.

One long-time vegetarian from New South Wales, Australia, writes: 'I have been inquisitioned more times than I can remember – and cowardly-like when travelling or visiting people I eat whatever they give me – but your book has given me some extra backbone and I shall dig my heels in in the future'. One American reader writes that her boyfriend is vegetarian, and that she respects his convictions, but that she has never had the courage to become one herself:

> One of my reasons (and a very petty one at that) was that people will ask me my reasons & I won't be able to intelligently articulate them. They would then figure I had no logical reason and would consider me another 'fanatic'. And then most of my opinions would be viewed in that light. But you have so effectively and intelligently argued my case for me I no longer have any excuse.

But if many letter writers express first of all a *personal* gratitude to Singer for 'the rational thought that will help so many humans to sort their own ideas out' – as one reader put it – many also expressed how Singer's intervention had helped them explode their latent dissatisfaction with the *political* state of the animal cause. In other words, readers carried out re-readings not only of their own thoughts about animals, but of the previous shape of the animal movement as well. Generally readers expressed the view that Singer with his intervention had transcended the old animal movement in a way that exposed its inefficiency and consequent inadequacy. This reading strategy arguably helped readers perceive the contrast of the old and the new way of thinking about animals, and to establish the book as a major event in the history of the animal movement.

What most readers focused on in this connection was not generally the actual content of Singer's book. Very few took up his use of the term speciesism, and not many actually commented concretely on his argument. Instead, a large portion of letter writers fastened on the book's *form* as its essential aspect. Among other descriptions, readers called the book 'horrifying', 'informative and realistic' and a 'terse vessel of facts and ideas' that was 'as stimulating as it was informative'. They expressed appreciation of its 'clear and undisputable line of reasoning', its 'solid and cogent stance' and its 'logical, detached and rational approach'. One reader was happy that 'the subject of Animal Liberation (or equal consideration of interest for other animals) has at last been raised from the undercurrent of social conscience and presented boldly as a concise issue'.

It is significant, in my view, that readers typically connected the form of the book – and the subsequent impact they envisioned that form would have in creating a more powerful animal movement – with Singer's position as a philosophy professor. The reason the book was so impressive, a lot of Singer's readers appeared to think, was the authority, intelligence and skills of its author – qualities that were seen as functions of Singer's formal training and position.

A reader from Sydney, Australia, writes: 'I am glad that someone has come forward in yourself, as you are a person of professional standing and are in a position to influence people to seriously consider that facts you present'. A reader from Virginia, USA, writes: 'Dear Mr. Singer ... You have very expertly, with strong data, clear reasoning, and irrefutable logic made a powerful case for a more humane treatment of all animals'. Another reader, from New South Wales, Australia, says: 'I feel it is very wonderful & a great step forward when people such as yourself ... speak out boldly on a subject, hitherto more or less taboo'.

A letter writer who saw Singer defend his views on *Monday Conference* writes: 'It was very interesting & you answered the questions so well as only a person well informed and in your position could'. Another letter writer, who watched the same program, wrote Singer:

> Dear Sir, On seeing you for the second time on television, on Monday Conference I want to congratulate you on your wonderful effort and achievement. How wonderful it is that at last there is such a learned person fighting so hard and so well for animal welfare.
>
> I am Vice Pres. of the 5th [?] Div. of R.S.P.C.A in Tasmania & care so very much about what you are striving for. I get discouraged so often because our [?] R.S.P.C.A seems so ineffective. Our inspectors do a tremendous job but the laws are so poor in so many cases & people charged with the worst kind of cruelty one are fined such meagre amounts it makes our cause seem so insignificant. Prevention is of course the answer but putting this into practice!
>
> I am not a very bright person Mr. Singer and doubt that I shall ever be able to do much more for the animal world than the possition [sic] I hold now. To make any significant change for the better we need to talk to the people who make the decisions and you have the ability and the knowledge to do this well.
>
> Thank you Mr. Singer, you are an answer to a prayer. I would like to wish you every success for your future and the future of the ones you are helping.

This letter voices a sentiment echoed by many of Singer's letter writers, namely an appreciation that someone with authority is now speaking out on this issue. The reader has obviously found the book important and well argued, but what she primarily focuses on is the capacity of Singer as author to get the message across more effectively, to potentially serve the cause with more success, than the traditional animal organizations. It reveals a feeling, in someone who is herself involved in an animal organization, of the marginalization of the animal cause. 'How wonderful it is that at last there is such a learned person fighting so hard and so well for animal welfare', implicitly indicates that, hitherto, the movement could not boast many people of this type. The letter writer's view of herself as 'not a very bright person ...' contrasts strongly with her estimation of Singer as 'such a learned person' and 'an answer to a prayer' who 'ha[s] the ability and the knowledge to do this well'. Her prayer, presumably, was for someone to plead the animals' cause more eloquently, that is, more forcefully, with more 'knowledge and ability' than she, and the existing animal movement, had been capable of accomplishing.

A reader from South Yarra, Australia, expresses a similar reaction. He writes that Singer's intervention is a response to a movement 'urgently in need of a leader to back them, show the way, in the apparently hopeless fight for some sanity in our attitude to other creatures'. The fight for animals had apparently seemed hopeless to many, and what Singer did was to give a promise that the animal movement could gain new momentum. A letter writer from Victoria, Australia, says: 'I am just a housewife and feel helpless to do anything except join Anti-Vivisection, but one feels heartened when thousands of people can be reached on TV by someone in your position who cares'.

In the previous era of the animal movement, many readers hinted, the cause had been struggling through neglect, public indifference and marginalization. They felt that Singer's contribution remade and professionalized the animal issue. One important thing they felt Singer had done – or contributed to doing – was to lend authority to an issue that had been associated with cranks and crackpots. The following letter, from a reader in New York, is telling:

> Dear Mr. Singer, Your *Animal Liberation* is the finest non-fiction I've read in years and easily the best book on vegetarianism yet published. With your thoroughly rational, yet easy-to-read approach, you devastate every argument the flesh-eaters raise. ... Occasionally some aspect of the movement troubles me. The leading one revolves around the point that *Animal Liberation* mentions; that many non-vegetarians will consider vegetarians to be cranks. Unfortunately, many followers of the non-flesh diet do indeed act and look like cranks. The views of the movement might go over better with the general public if more 'straight' people would actively propagate its beliefs. I recently attended a meeting of the NY Vegetarians at 1133 Broadway to see what was going on. The majority of the audience were 'shopping-bag ladies', little women in tennis sneakers (though I don't think they wear these sneakers to protest shoe leather), strange-looking guys, and a speaker who continually referred to vegetarianism as a religion and spoke in an old-fashioned, hell-and-damnation oratory. When there is a meeting of the World Vegetarian Congress such as was held in Maine last summer, the periodicals emphasize the guru-types from India and the advocates of sprout-growing. Surely the movement would profit more from magazine articles by vegetarians such as Paul Newman, Jeanne Woodward and especially from ordinary-looking people they can identify with.

The letter writer's frustration is clearly that the animal cause had been championed by the wrong types, within the wrong discursive frames, with the wrong types of arguments. Against that background, Singer's coming is seen to signal a new start for animal activism, where it can be freed from its old image, and where it can therefore reach out to 'the general public'. A similar sentiment, this time couched in gendered terms, is expressed by the reader from South Yarra, Australia, cited above:

> I do not think the Australian male is any more cruel than other males ... but there is the stigma that he 'hides behind his women-folk' in matters relating to help for animals. It is more pleasant to spend spare time at the hotel with the boys, that's all, I think. (He is more lazy?). The animal welfare groups seem to be comprised of ladies only, just an odd husband brought along here and there. True, some men have taken the initiative, but have been generally rather truculent. The calm, determined man who means business has been elsewhere! It was so good to note your reaction, you were so relaxed and unemotional, that you impressed all who viewed the session.

The same letter writer notes incidentally that his local RSPCA – which we understand is dominated by women – 'has always had a very bad name and in all my years of discussion over animals I have never heard one word in appreciation of anything good the society had done, but really enough to fill a book on its failings'. What the animal cause needs, in other words is 'the calm, determined man who means business' – someone who can spearhead the animal cause as something other than a feminized, humanitarian concern. One is left wondering whether anyone could fit this bill better than Peter Singer.

It is hard to gauge just how important the gender issue was to the reception of Singer's book. What can be said is that, at first, both men and women readers expressed admiration for the stereotypical 'male' qualities of Singer's book – it is 'calm', 'determined', 'rational', 'detached', 'unemotional' – while they expressed disdain for the stereotypical 'female' qualities that they saw in themselves or in the old animal movement – 'neurotic', 'half-baked', 'sentimental', 'over-sensitive', 'fanatic'. In the preface to the original edition, Singer implicitly emphasized this traditional distinction between men and women, when he said that the type of concern for animals that he wanted to profess was *not* sentimental, it was not about 'loving animals'. Author and audience thus seemed to agree that animal activism in the sentimental mode, which they both associated with women, had by now proved ineffectual. In order for animal activists to stand their ground in the rough landscape of real politics, another – more rational and determined – mode was called for. Later, these gendered assumptions were challenged, not least by Carol J. Adams's *The Sexual Politics of Meat: A Feminist-Vegetarian Critical Theory* (1990) and by the development of the feminist care tradition within animal ethics (see Donovan and Adams 2007).

Warm Welcome, Aggressive Aftermath

What I hope to have shown is how readers, in the climate of opinion and debate around animal ethics issues in the mid-to-late 1970s, reacted to Singer's book. That should not be taken to mean that the reception of *Animal Liberation* has remained unchanged in the ensuing decades. If the book had a warm welcome in 1975 and immediately thereafter, its later reception and afterlife has been far more troubled. Here I will do no more than to suggest some points that a further reception history of the book would have to encompass.

First of all, only a few years after the publication of Singer's book, other philosophers and writers came along with their own takes on our obligations to animals. Richard Ryder's book *Victims of Science* also came out in 1975, but did not create anywhere near the same stir as did Singer's book. More interest was aroused by philosopher Tom Regan and his book *The Case for Animal Rights* (1983), which provided a rights-based approach to animal ethics, to balance Singer's utilitarianism. That book was soon followed by many others, most notably Mary Midgley's *Animals and Why They Matter* (1983) and Josephine Donovan and Carol J. Adams's *Animals and Women* (1995). In many ways, these books can be understood as supplementing Singer's book, and contributing to the creation of further momentum for the animal cause. However, in the longer term, it seems quite clear that their most significant consequence was to make problematic, and to some extent even discredit, Singer and his theoretical take on animal ethics.

Even occasional collaborators like Singer and Regan sometimes found themselves in open confrontational debate, as in the so-called lifeboat exchange in the *New York Review of Books*. Regardless of what readers thought of the opposing arguments exchanged in these debates, one apparent conclusion to be drawn from them was that the animal movement no longer presented a united front. (In addition, other books were to challenge not just the framework of Singer's argument, but also his conclusions, among them Michael P.T. Leahy's *Against Liberation* (1991), Peter Carruthers's *The Animals Issue* (1992) and Roger Scruton's *Animal Rights and Wrongs* (1996)). The main development in later decades, then, was a theoretical explosion within or around thinking about animal ethics, one important consequence of which was a relative marginalization of Singer's utilitarianism, which in the 1970s ruled supreme. In my estimation, this theoretical division has only become more pronounced over the years. The main controversy of course is whether animals (or indeed any sentient being) have inviolable rights that cannot be entered into utilitarian calculus. Instances of this divide within the movement have come to the surface regularly since at least the 1980s, and most recently, the question of Singer's defense of animal experimentation led to angry accusations against Singer on the part of animal rights supporters.

Another aspect of *Animal Liberation*'s afterlife is the emergence of strong, radical animal organizations, most notably through the work of animal activist and campaign organizer Henry Spira, and what is now the world's largest animal organization, People for the Ethical Treatment of Animals (PETA). It has been well documented that Singer's book and subsequent involvement in the animal cause was the catalyst for the establishments of these organizations. However, the wider consequence seems to have been, once more, a kind of marginalization of Singer. It was not so much that Singer was no longer considered important, but that, with the coming of large, powerful animal organizations, it was clear that there were now other players in the field, who – at least some of the time – had agendas that differed from Singer's.

Thirdly, it did not take long for the full consequences of Singer's theoretical framework to become more apparent to his readers. One early expression of this was the reader response letters Singer received after the publication of his article 'Sanctity of Life or Quality of Life?' in the journal *Pediatrics*, in 1983: whereas the reaction to *Animal Liberation*, as we have seen, was overwhelmingly positive, readers of his 'Sanctity of Life …' article – in which he questioned the notion of the sanctity of life – responded with disbelief, wild criticisms and accusations of inhumanity. Singer, of course, had not changed his mind about anything much, certainly not about his utilitarianism. Something had become clearer, however, to his readers. It is tempting to suggest that the full implications of Singer's theory were not well understood when *Animal Liberation* appeared, perhaps because euphoria over finding someone who could apply *some* authoritative philosophy – of any kind – to this issue was so widespread. With his article for *Pediatrics*, and with his many subsequent books and articles on controversial bioethics issues, Singer's insistence on the authority of theory – which is what was so effective in the case of *Animal Liberation* – seems to have become a liability. Singer was no longer praised for his ability to challenge long-standing moral intuitions; he was criticized for doing precisely that.

Conclusion

In this chapter, I have argued that what it took to redefine the animal issue as a serious one in the mid-1970s, was the ethos of a serious philosophy professor – one who could demonstrate that he had not just taken up a controversial stance in order to sell lots of books, but who was willing to go on national television and defend that stance, cogently and seriously – coupled with a philosophical framework that without any fuss would acknowledge the interests of any 'sentient' being. Scores of readers revealed that they had considered views similar to those Singer presents in *Animal Liberation*, but had found them half-baked, sentimental, even neurotic. The result of having someone like Peter Singer put the philosophical stamp of approval, as it were, on their half-baked ideas, was to provide a new impetus for the animal movement, in fact, to suggest a new type of animal movement altogether – one not made up of 'cranks' and 'old ladies in tennis sneakers', and supported by a well-reasoned, fact-checked book by a serious philosophy professor (an expert, in the eyes of most letter writers).

In other words, one of the most significant things Singer did with *Animal Liberation*, in rhetorical terms, was to create a paradigmatic example of applying philosophy to the issues of the day, and by doing so, establishing the authority of the applied philosopher as expert. The interesting aspect of *Animal Liberation*'s reception history, then, is not simply that Singer said out loud what many people had been thinking, but that he, with that book, created a new and more active public role for the philosopher. He accomplished this by updating and consolidating a literary genre – we can call it 'the applied ethics polemic' – that let philosophers engage in controversial, political issues. In the person of Peter Singer, the philosopher thus became someone who, by virtue of his knowledge, seriousness and argumentative skill, implicitly demanded an audience and a following. This reading is contextualized by the fact that Singer himself came to function as something of an oracle on animal matters. People would approach him, as an expert, with all sorts of questions, for all types of help and advice.

The success of the book was in no small measure due to the perceived character of its author. It is no wonder, then, that when Singer came under heavier fire, his critics targeted his character. The same qualities he had demonstrated with *Animal Liberation* – knowledge, seriousness and argumentative skill – were now portrayed as inhumane. Peter Singer may have his *argumentatio* in the right place, his later critics seemed to say, but the man has no *heart*.

In this chapter, I have not made many pronouncements – I believe, none whatsoever – about what constitutes moral or criminal harm in our relations with other living creatures. In fact, it was not my concern to have an opinion about what we *should* consider such a harm. Rather, I have wanted to show empirically how pronouncements about harms, or about crimes, have a prehistory that can profitably be brought to light. More specifically, I have demonstrated that norms about how to treat animals are not only influenced, but in some sense *made*, by rhetorical attempts to introduce certain words – as well as certain *uses* of words – into the course of history.

Of what use, then, is a study like this for green criminology? That obviously depends on many things, not least on the individual criminologist's academic and moral-political stance. In any case, I appeal to Piers Beirne's 'Animal Rights, Animal Abuse and Green Criminology' to find something like a blessing for my approach. He writes:

> If violations of animals' rights are to be central concepts in green criminology, then we could profitably begin by examining why, just like some harms to the environment, some harms to animals are defined as criminal, others as abusive but not criminal and still others as neither criminal nor abusive (Bierne 2007: 77–8).

I believe I have submitted here one such examination, although I am under no illusion that this is the type of study that Beirne envisioned. As said, I have made my examination from a rhetorical assumption about norms, which says that right and wrong are not timeless, free-floating entities that we have somehow to discover, but instead the temporary outcomes of rhetorical (and thereby political) struggles that will go on as far as anyone can see. In studying the rhetorical making of a norm, we display the contingencies of what, at a particular time, is counted as 'harm', 'crime' and the like. What in turn provides a rationale for this way of seeing is illustrated by Richard Rorty's figure, the ironist, who is someone who 'thinks nothing has an intrinsic nature, a real essence' (Rorty 1989: 74). Rorty explains that, while the ironist is conscious of the contingency of her beliefs, she is still committed them. However, the presence of contingency creates an uncertainty about the ultimate status of those beliefs:

> The ironist spends her time worrying about the possibility that she has been initiated into the wrong tribe, taught to play the wrong language game. She worries that the process of socialization which turned her into a human being by giving her a language may have given her the wrong language, and so turned her into the wrong kind of human being (Rorty 1989: 74).

I think and hope that by unearthing the processes that have caused us to hold certain beliefs and make certain judgments, we can become less certain in our convictions, and more open to those who hold different beliefs and make different judgments. Ideally, I believe that we by studying such processes can adjust ourselves away from a mode of judgment towards one of dialogue – however vague that might sound.

References

Adams, C.J. 1990. *The Sexual Politics of Meat: A Feminist-Vegetarian Critical Theory*. New York: Continuum.

Adams, C.J. and Donovan, J. (eds) 1995. *Animals and Women: Feminist Theoretical Explorations*. Durham: Duke University Press.

Beirne, P. 2007. Animal Rights, Animal Abuse and Green Criminology, in *Issues in Green Criminology: Confronting Harms against Environments, Humanity and Other Animals*, edited by P. Beirne and N. South. Devon: Willan, 55–79.

Bourdieu, P. and Wacquant, L.J.D. 1992. *An Invitation to Reflexive Sociology*. Chicago: The University of Chicago Press.

Carruthers, P. 1992. *The Animals Issue: Moral Theory in Practice*. Cambridge: Cambridge University Press.

Donovan, J. and Adams, C.J. (eds.) 2007. *The Feminist Care Tradition in Animal Ethics*. New York: Columbia University Press.

Friedan, B. 1963. *The Feminine Mystique*. New York: W.W. Norton & Co.

Godlovitch, S., Godlovitch, R. and Harris, J. (eds.) 1971. *Animals, Men and Morals*. London: Gollancz.

Greer, G. 1971. *The Female Eunuch*. London: Paladin Grafton.

Leahy, M.P.T. 1991. *Against Liberation: Putting Animals in Perspective*. New York: Routledge.

Midgley, M. 1983. *Animals and Why They Matter*. Athens: The University of Georgia Press.

Millett, K. 1970. *Sexual Politics*. New York: Doubleday.

Nagel, T. 2010. What Peter Singer Wants of You, New York Review of Books.

Regan, T. 1983. *The Case for Animal Rights*. Berkeley: University of California Press.

Rorty, R. 1989. *Contingency, Irony, and Solidarity*. Cambridge: Cambridge University Press.
Ryder, R. 1975. *Victims of Science: The Use of Animals in Research*. London: Davis-Poynter.
Sartre, J.-P. 1987. *The Family Idiot: Gustave Flaubert, 1821–1857*, volume 2. Chicago: The University of Chicago Press.
Scruton, R. 1996. *Animal Rights and Wrongs*. London: Demos.
Singer, P. 1972. Famine, Affluence, and Morality. *Philosophy and Public Affairs*, 1, 229–43.
Singer, P. 1975. *Animal Liberation: A New Ethics for Our Treatment of Animals*. New York: New York Review of Books.
Singer, P. 1983. Sanctity of Life or Quality of Life? *Pediatrics*, 72(1), 128–29.
Singer, P. 2009. *Animal Liberation: The Definitive Classic of the Animal Movement*. New York: Harper Perennial.
Skinner, Q. 1998. *Liberty before Liberalism*. Cambridge: Cambridge University Press.
Skinner, Q. 2002. *Visions of Politics*, 3 volumes. Cambridge: Cambridge University Press.
Tompkins, J.P. 1980. An Introduction to Reader-Response Criticism, in *Reader-Response Criticism: From Formalism to Post-Structuralism*, edited by J.P. Tompkins. Baltimore: The Johns Hopkins University Press, ix-xxvi.

Chapter 6
Speciesism as Doxic Practice Versus Valuing Difference and Plurality[1]

Ragnhild Aslaug Sollund

Introduction

The topic of animal[2] abuse and speciesism was made relevant for (green) criminology, foremost by Piers Beirne (1995, 1999, 2008), Robert Agnew (1998) and Geertrui Cazaux (1998, 1999). Beirne (1999) argues that the study of animal abuse is a legitimate field of study for criminology because of the extensive harm which victimizes so many animals. Having their work in mind, in this chapter I discuss speciesism as a doxic practice (Bourdieu 1995) and see whether an analysis of techniques of neutralisation (Sykes and Matza 1957) and denial (Cohen 2001) can help develop a broader understanding of the reasons why animals are not given victim status even when they are gravely mistreated, or killed. Speciesism and the construction of animals as 'others' is based on assumed and actual differences between humans and other animals on a number of dimensions (Sollund 2008). This, in turn, is the consequence of, and part and parcel of, the dualism and constructed polarization between men and women, humans and animals, culture and nature, to mention a few of the assumed dichotomies, that are deeply rooted in the patriarchal mindset (for example, Gaard 1993, Noske 1989, Collard and Contrucci 1989, Birkeland 1993, Donovan 1996, Adams 1993, 1996). The polarization is also hierarchic, placing men (white men) at the top, with women, children, animals and nature beneath, in that order (ibid. Gålmark 2008). Such polarization and the consequent construction of supposed contradicting interests

1 I am grateful to Guri Larsen and Paul Stretesky for comments to this chapter.

2 The term animal can be criticized for implying that all animals other than humans are the same, while only humans are unique, and not to be regarded as animals. Authors arguing for non-speciesist language have solved this difficulty in different ways, for example by using the term 'non-human animal' and 'animals other than humans' (for example, Nibert 2003:23, Beirne 1999: 118). As observed by Beirne, this still leaves us with the 'othering' of non-human animals, categorizing them as *one* kind which in important ways differ from human animals, rather than emphasizing the huge variation of animal species of which humans is one. However, for stylistic reasons I will continue to use the term animal when referring to animals other than humans, trusting that my readers acknowledge that I respect humans and other species share basic properties, such as the capacity to think and plan, enjoy pleasure and suffer from pain and deprivations (Regan 1983).

is doxic, in the sense that the practices that cherish and elevate this polarization are far too little questioned in daily practice. However, the last 20 years have shown signs that there can be a change in doxa, as is exemplified by the increased prominence of the animal rights movement (Beirne 2008), that had its starting point in Peter Singer's *Animal Liberation*, first published in 1975 (see Bjørkdal, this volume). As this movement and its ideas spread to, and gain acceptance in, wider circles including academia, there emerges an increased need to justify the damaging results of the doxic practices of using animals. I will therefore attempt to investigate what characterizes the human–animal relationship and the ways in which exploitation is supported by techniques of neutralization, in what may be a time of transition for the position of animals in relation to humans. I suggest that speciesism is more than 'prejudice' that may affect the ways in which some prejudiced people act towards animals. Rather, speciesism is just one aspect of the patriarchal ideological system in which the use of physical power and the act of killing is glorified through warfare and hunting (Birkeland 1993, Collard 1989, Noske 1989). In this system women also have to fight continually to achieve or preserve a position of equality with men, and these patterns of oppression are mutually supportive and interdependent (for example, Gaard 1993, Adams 1993, 1996, Birkeland 1993, Vance 1993, Collard 1989).

The differences between humans and other animals can account for the reason that many humans fail to involve other animals in their 'empathic universe'. However, I argue that the view that the similarity between humans and other animals is the reason that animals should being given equal concern may also be problematic, and imply speciesist prejudice. Philosophers such as Peter Singer and Tom Regan have played an important role in establishing the similarities between humans and animals, and the logic of equal concerns and rights that follow from these similarities. However, I also find it useful to discuss whether choosing another path could contribute to the reduction of speciesism, understood as an institution, as prejudice and as part of doxa.

If different properties, capacities and interests are unacknowledged, or –under-communicated, this may mean that individuals with these interests and properties are not accorded value of their own kind, and this will lead to speciesism. Therefore, one should not only argue for equal rights because other animals have the same capacity as humans to experience pain, suffering and joy; one should also argue for *different* interests, the evaluation of different capacities and equal, or even more respect precisely for this reason – this would be the appraisal of plurality. By arguing for the valuing of difference, I also argue for the cherishing of plurality and heterogeneity, key characteristics of the world.

The Human–animal Relationship

'They were treated worse than animals!' This common expression goes to the core of the human–animal relationship. It emphasizes that the humans in question

have been treated badly, but even more it underlines the fact that bad treatment is routine for other animals. It further legitimates this by implying that such treatment of animals is normal, in contrast to the treatment that should be given to humans. It also contrasts animals to humans, and creates a division that makes animal abuse acceptable, unlike the maltreatment of humans. Thus, humans have rights which can be violated, animals do not.

The relationship humans have to other animals is also characterized by ambivalence, and is paradoxical (Sollund 2009). A multitude of different emotions and approaches exist in humans' treatment of animals, from ignorance and lack of interest to warm affection, fascination, terror and respect. What often determines the position on the spectrum of the human emotional attachment to the animal, or whether it is totally lacking, is the value accorded to the animal by humans. A main division is that between those individuals to whom humans accord *social value* and those who are objectified through the *material interest* they hold for humans. In all aspects of the relationship it is important to note that humans are at the centre, and have the interest in the relationship, not the animals. Even though a dog may be happy in the company of her owner, many dogs and other 'companion animals' are victims of maltreatment and neglect (for example, Beirne 1999, Flynn 1999, Larsen 2003, Vermeulen and Odendaal 1993) and all those animals who have been domesticated over generations to cater to humans' needs would probably have been better off had they remained in their 'wild' state.

Whether an animal is destined to become meat, clothes, a lab tool, a so-called pet or provide some form of entertainment in zoos, circuses and dog or cock fights, the central element of the human–animal relationship is the uneven distribution of power. Through power and physical force humans appropriate animals and deny them basic rights, such as the right to freedom, movement, a social life, food which is good for them and the right to live a life that is not prematurely and violently disrupted in order to turn the animal into a product for human consumption.

Speciesism

Speciesism is central to explaining this uneven relationship and its consequences. Speciesism, when understood as an ideology, serves to legitimate animal abuse, and consequently to foster animal abuse and exploitation. The term speciesism was introduced by Richard Ryder in 1970,[3] and has since been expanded and defined in various ways. Most often and most importantly it is understood as a prejudice or biased attitude favouring the interests of the members' own species as against those of members of another species (Beirne and Cazaux 2006: 11). If animals of species other than the human give priority to their own species' interests, this will hardly have the consequences we witness when humans prioritize *their* own interests. If a rabbit, a parrot, or a pig prioritize their own interests, this would not affect humans in the way animals are affected when humans imprison and

3 http://www.richardryder.co.uk/speciesism.html.

kill rabbits in industrial complexes for their fur, when they catch, abduct, trade and imprison a parrot for use as a 'pet' or as a decoration in a restaurant or when they imprison and kill the pig for meat. As is the case with other 'isms', such as sexism and racism, speciesism is based on domination and subordination (Nibert 2002, 2003), is rooted in patriarchal ideology and is based on the fact that other species are not human. Similarly, women are seen as different to men (for example, generally physically weaker), and have been, and[4] are still, often oppressed in relation to men (for example, Donovan 1990, Birkeland 1993, Gruen 1993, Vance 1993, Adams 1993, 1996, 2011).

The most important point as regarding prejudice is that it may be turned into practice. A prejudice may be conscious or unconscious, passive or active. It may be subject to reflection when consciously realized and either activated or, if rejected through this reflection, disciplined and not translated into practical action (Sollund 2008). For example, racism may not translate into racist acts if prejudiced individuals find themselves in a social environment where such acts are perceived as unacceptable. In that case, their racist prejudices will not have much significance because informal and/or formal social control will prohibit them from coming out into the open. In the case of speciesism, prejudice in the form of abusive acts and exploitative practice is *upheld* by ideology and is thus legitimated, as is argued by David Nibert (2003: 8) and Per-Anders Svärd (2008, this volume, see also Kheel 1993, 1996, Adams 1993, 1996, 2011, Donovan and Adams 1996, Noske 1989, Collard 1989, Birkeland 1993). Strong actors, such as the meat industry, medical science and state authorities, which have an interest in supporting speciesism as doxa, will contribute to the formation of this ideology by spreading propagandistic distortions of reality, such as 'happy cows grazing' (Hallsworth 2008), and the achievements of animal experimentation (Regan 2004). According to Nibert, speciesism (like racism, sexism, and classism) is a set of widely shared beliefs that result from, and support, oppressive social arrangements. Speciesism may also be defined primarily as an institution: that is a network of specific modes and practices of materialization that reproduce the objectification of the other on the grounds of species affiliation (Wolfe, here in Pedersen 2008).

If speciesism as prejudice and speciesism as practice are separated, a statement such as: '*I love lamb*' when pronounced by a person eating a lamb who simultaneously defines him/herself as 'an animal lover', becomes logical, though inherently contradictory. The acceptance of the lamb as 'meat' (Adams 1993, 2011, Gålmark 2008) does not necessarily contradict the person's self-perception as one who respects and cares for animals (Singer 2002: IX). This is for a number of reasons connected to culturally and religiously conditioned practices and denial

4 Evidently this is culturally dependent and women for example in Norway, Yemen and Saudi Arabia live under totally different regimes. In Yemen and Saudi Arabia women are sold as brides as children according to Wikileaks and do not even enjoy basic rights such as the right to freedom. In many countries, for example Pakistan and Sudan, women are stoned for adultery after rape.

(Sollund 2008) together with habitus and doxa, phenomena to which I shall return. These make it impossible for the lamb to achieve victim status and transgress the borders set by the concept of 'meat' (Adams 1993, 2011, Gålmark 2008). As stated by Donovan and Adams:

> In fact, the reduction of animals to 'its' is at the root of most animal abuse. The attribution of deadness to what is alive, conscious, and sensitive involves a psychology of denial that conveniently facilitates the interests of the powerful. Such denial unquestionably has allowed the great human atrocities of the century to occur, and such denials continues to allow unspeakable animal suffering to proceed as a commonplace norm (Donovan and Adams 1995, quoted in Cazaux 1999: 121).

Through this objectification of animals one conceals the fact that animals are individuals with individual desires and needs, as well as a sex.

When we consider the treatment of animals who become 'meat', it is unlike the love and care lavished on many dogs. However, the perceptions of harm differs, depending on the social status of the victim the harm is inflicted upon: '[...] some harms are defined as criminal, others as abusive, but not criminal, and still others as neither criminal nor abusive' (Beirne 2009: 200). It thus becomes easier not to reflect upon practice, and speciesism holds sway, even without any conscious prejudice implying the direct deliberate belittling of others. It is rather the outcome of a *lack* of reflection upon practice, the result of passivity and is therefore not questioned. However, *not* to take a stand is also to *take* a stand, for example by refusing to reflect upon the consequences of one's actions. One example of this is when feminists argue in favour of eating meat in conferences so as not to offend other feminists with minority backgrounds by criticizing 'their culture', and thereby accept the oppression of animals. They thus indirectly accept the oppression directed at themselves as women, as systems of oppression are mutually interrelated and interdependent (for example, Adams 1993, 2011, Donovan 1996, Kheel 1993, Vance 1003, Birkeland 1993, Noske 1989, Collard 1989). Such refusal to reflect on the consequences of one's actions may be caused by the pain produced by these reflections and also for that reason be connected to various forms of denial, not the least *cultural denial*, in which whole societies partake in collective denial of atrocities (Cohen 2001: 11).

Speciesism can thus be defined either as ideology or practice(s) – or as the two in tandem. Specieisism is supported by discourse that polices – and maintains – the human-non-human boundary by creating animals as objects, or as 'the other'. (MacKay in Pedersen 2008, Cazaux 1999). There are, for example, numerous derogatory expressions involving animals. In Norway people say 'stupid as a hen', 'stupid cow', 'sly as a wolf', 'fat as a pig' or 'old dirty pig' when referring to an old male human with an appetite for young girls. Terms are often sexist, thus combining prejudice against animals and female humans, like 'bitch' (for example, Beirne 2007: 63, Cazaux 1998: 385). The association of animals with women has been particularly evident in pornography, and has links to the portrayal of black women as animals, thus facilitating denigration (Collins in Adams 1993: 204) and thereby attaching women more closely to 'nature' in contrast to male ('culture'). Derogatory terms serve not only to denigrate the individual they are directed at, but also to prepare the ground for the use, abuse and objectification of this individual and of others of the same kind, and to make this legitimate (Cohen 2001, Sollund 2008).

Speciesism as Doxic Practice – or Times of Transition?

The practices of animal (ab)use are so extensive – so culturally diverse and widespread – that they are part of doxa (Bourdieu 1995). Bourdieu (1984) explains doxa as that which is self-evident and related to systems of classification determining what is and what is not interesting, that which is unspoken of, as there is no *reflection* connected to it (Bourdieu 1984: 96). Using animals, especially eating their 'meat', is consequently part of habitus for the majority of people on earth (Adams 1993, 1996, Gålmark 2008). This implies that exploiting animals is: part of a system of dispositions in which the socialised body and the social field where the socialised body operates together establish a subconscious physical harmony determining the actions of the individual, depending on his/her biographical experience (Bourdieu 1984: 48, 89). To simplify Bourdieu: what we are socialized to do become 'natural' acts which the individuals leave unquestioned when they are together with their social group doing the same. As stated by Bourdieu: 'Habitus is the principle behind life styles' (1991: 205). This also implies that as a 'style' it is as also a matter of choice, and choices and priorities can change, thus habitus can also refer to the *inertia* of change (but still change). Change of habitus has implications for the repertoire of actions for a person in the present tense, and also for this person's understanding of previous actions, for example, those related to food practices, which will accompany a change of habitus (Sollund 1999). However, as Birkeland (1993) observes in relation to the lack of effects of spirituality and belief systems on actual behaviour, these do not necessarily improve individual behaviour: 'This is because behaviour is not solely a product of either rationality or beliefs. Behaviour patterns are so deeply encoded that we often do not perceive them. Ways of acting and relating are ingrained from earliest childhood, a product of habit, role-modeling, social reinforcement and institutions' (Birkeland 1993: 47). Consequently, though habitus may change, the process will be slow, and it will take time for this to have an effect on doxa.

These practices include regarding animals as 'resources to be harvested' rather than as individuals, as can be seen, for example, in the fishing industry and in the wording of the CITES convention[5] which seeks to control the trade of animals and other species. As observed by (Lynch and Stretesky 2007: 263) '[...] Humans

5 CITES convention. Available at: http://www.cites.org/eng/disc/text.shtml [Accessed 7 January 2011].

view their needs as paramount and superior to all others. [...] human use of the environment as a resource for human pleasure and consumption is dictated by the nature of political-economical arrangements.' Thus, when CITES seeks to control the trade, it is not because individuals of other species that are involved have rights or intrinsic value, but in order to keep the trade in animals viable (Sollund 2011, in print). Human (ab)use of animals further includes the extensive imprisoning of animals in cages, both private and public (zoos), in industrial complexes and research laboratories, as well as keeping them on leads, as is the case with dogs, or putting saddles on them, as is the case with horses (see for example, Collard 1989, Noske 1989, Singer 1992 and Regan 1983). These practices are ingrained and naturalised, and this of course makes them harder to resist and to break – breaking them – and change one set of practices for another – may incur disapproval.

Breaking them also implies a breach with hegemonic denials and a challenge to deeply grounded andro/anthropocentric power structures, especially economic and political ones, such as the military (Birkeland 1993), and the meat industry (Adams 1993, 2011). By hegemonic denials, I mean denials that are so widespread and ingrained that they are doxic and part of habitus. Such denials are not necessarily translated into actions, but may be exercised passively by those who silently, and therefore consentingly, drift with those who find it opportune to actively deny the content and outcome of harmful actions. One example is when the agro-industrial (and therefore heavily biased and financially state supported) *Information Office for Eggs and Meat*[6] in Norway which advocates increased consumption of meat. In so doing they induce people to believe that this is both healthy and ethical, for example by claiming to pay attention to 'animal welfare' (see Svärd this volume).

The industrialisation of meat production is increasing, meat consumption in the industrialised Western world having grown fivefold since 1950 (Jokkala and Strindlund 2003). On average, every Norwegian now eats a quarter of a kilo of meat *per day* (Aftenposten 4.5.10). This is a fact which is incompatible with animal rights or even animal welfare, in the etymological meaning of the word,[7] for the so-called 'production animals'. For example, in Norway, it was recently revealed that a farm for chicken meat production delivered 17,000 chickens to slaughter when they were one month old, and overgrown (with the implications this fast growth has for their health), who were all injured with burning blisters on legs, feet and body.[8]

By speaking about and advocating for animal rights, one risks being ridiculed (for example, Larsen 2003), or shamed (Riise, this volume) or even labelled as

6 Opplysningskontoret for egg og kjøtt.

7 O.E. *wel faran* 'condition of being or doing well', from *wel* (see *well* (adv.)) and *faran* 'get along' (see *fare* (v.)). Available at: http://www.etymonline.com/index.php?search=welfare&searchmode=none [Accessed 3 January 2011].

8 The case was presented on the state Norwegian radio/TV station's website, including a video of the production site and photos of the chickens. Available at: http://www.nrk.no/nyheter/1.6849961 [Accessed February 15 2011].

troublemakers or terrorists (Ellefsen, this volume, Aaltola, this volume, Yates 2007, Regan 2004). Just the simple choice of refusing meat may often lead to a heated debate in which a variety of defences for animal consumption and exploitation will be offered (Adams 1993, 2011). It may be because ethical vegetarianism/veganism challenges the *implicatory denial* (Cohen 2001: 22) (as mentioned above) through which the *significance* of a fact is denied – the emotional and moral implications of animal exploitation, not just what actually happens: as if one could say, 'yes billions of animals are killed, but they do not suffer'. I wonder whether such reactions indicate that many people start to feel the need to defend such practices, and thus seek their legitimacy, because animal rights and animal welfare are topics that are increasingly debated both in academia and in the mass media. The question mentioned in the introduction thus arises: are we living in a time of transition concerning animal rights and may doxic practices actually cease being doxic? Piers Beirne (2009), for example, points out in the introduction to his book *Confronting Animal Abuse* that: 'the support for animal rights has grown into a large-scale, well publicized, and theoretically informed social movement', and claims that 'the movement's gains seem to have been extraordinary' (Beirne 2009: 1). However, when challenged, those who gain by animal exploitation will feel even more pressured to defend and preserve the practice. 'It is the critical breach with doxa that forces the dominators to speak and develop a defence – a thought that expresses the conservatism from the right wing and that struggles to re-establish the silent adherents to doxa' (Bourdieu 1991: 129). In this way – maybe – protests also work counteractively, a point to which I return.

Refusing to consume meat may create a complicated social situation where attention is focused on the suffering and death associated with the food people gather around: it brings out the 'elephant in the room'. As Lisa Gålmark (2008) says: 'Someone has been killed, and no one speaks of it.' Focusing attention on death by refusing to eat meat constitutes a breach of the hegemonic norm, what Gålmark refers to as *meatism.* A breach of meatism can be morally reprehensible because of its unpleasant implications (see Adams, 1993, 2011). An eloquent example of this is suggested by Marti Kheel, who contemplates the consequences of saying not 'pass me the meat', but 'could you slice off her wing for me' or 'could you pass me one of her ribs, please?' (Vance 1993: 136).

From an early age, humans worldwide are socialised into accepting that some animals are food (Gålmark 2008), others are 'wild'[9] and thus a threat and others are for our pure entertainment in circuses, zoos and so on. Over time, the number of areas where animals are used has increased and one has to be very determined and watchful to totally avoid the direct or indirect consumption of animals. Eating is a frequent practice, an innate practice producing, and produced by, likes and dislikes. Eating larva is a daily practice in some countries, but would be disgusting

9 I dislike the connotations of 'wild' and its othering effect. Animals in their habitats do what they are born to do, and will, if left alone, not constitute a danger to humans, as the term 'wild' implies.

in others; however as practice is learnt it becomes habitus (Bourdieu 1977). Eating animals becomes ingrained and naturalised in ways that prevent most people[10] from questioning the practice or looking for alternatives. Consequently, even when people are sufficiently informed to realise the destructive consequences of such habits as meat eating, they will continue this practice, as in the case of the 'lamb-eating animal lover' mentioned in the introduction. People are fully able to act contrary to their beliefs and ethics, because they do not want to make the effort of changing habit(u)s.

The non-meat eaters in the Western world may be challenged morally and practically more often to defend their choice not to eat meat, than meat eaters are challenged to defend their consumption of animals. By rejecting practices involving the abuse of animals, for example meatism (Gålmark 2008) or vivisection, one challenges passive, doxic speciesism, and makes the outcomes of such practices something requiring either to be morally defended or morally rejected (see Cohen and Regan 2001) by taking an active stand. To *re-act* implies to break with habitus, with doxa, with widespread external and internal practices supported by powerful institutions, culture and ideology. Despite the naturalised character of animal objectification and exploitation – the dematerialisation of the individual animals (for example, Adams 1993, 1996, 2011, Vance 1993, Gålmark 2008) – many people still feel the need to justify it, as closeness to individuals of other species may be more natural than the alienation the dematerialisation implies: 'Animal exploitation thrives not because people don't care but in spite of the fact that they do care' (Luke 1996: 86). Justifications may alleviate the pain produced by this fact, but also contribute to the perpetuation of animal exploitation.

Developments in the ways in which animals are perceived, inspired, for example, by research documenting their intelligence and cognitive skills (for example, Børresen 2006, 2007, Noske 1989), may also mean that humans, consciously and/or unconsciously, feel more need to legitimate their exploitative habits. Those who have a taken-for-granted (doxic) attitude to the use of animals are probably least likely to search for techniques of neutralisation, while consciousness of the implications of animal exploitation may produce moral concern and lead people to abstain from animal use, as the growing number of vegetarians worldwide[11] may indicate. However, for many people their own practices constitute a paradox:

10 This does not mean that people may not go vegetarian/vegan for ethical reasons, and for about 50 per cent of vegetarians this is the reason. Still vegetarians/vegans are in minority in the Western world, in contrast to Hindu India. Typically; many teenagers will go vegetarian when they start realizing the conditions the animals they eat live and die under. About 3.2 per cent of the American population are vegetarians according to a study, while only 2 per cent of Norwegians are vegetarians. See, http://www.usatoday.com/news/health/2007-10-14-veggie-kids_N.html. And http://www.vegetariantimes.com/features/archive_of_editorial/667. [Accessed February 24 2011].

11 See Wikipedia: http://en.wikipedia.org/wiki/Vegetarianism_by_country [Accessed 12 July 2011].

they *do* care, but *continue* their practice, and so they need forms of denial to justify these practices which they – in their heart of hearts – know are morally reprehensible. Below I will examine the techniques of denial which can help them to continue consumerist practices based on the (ab)use of animals, and to uphold speciesism as doxic ideology.

Techniques of Denial as Ways of Preserving Doxic Speciesism

Sykes and Matza (1957) developed their theory of techniques of neutralisation to explore delinquency. Their theory has later been employed in a large body of criminological literature to understand a wide array of crimes and harms. In brief, they provide five ways of reducing the consequences of the acts, and making them seem more defensible. Injury, to paraphrase Sykes and Matza (1957), does not imply an injury. In the present case, *because* the victims are animals, injuring them is insignificant and because of the victims' lack of status, it is not to be regarded as an injury (Beirne 2009). The ways in which non-human animals presumably or actually differ from humans have been used to legitimate abuse (Sollund 2008). Features of difference can be obvious such as superficial physical features, like feathers or fur rather than bare skin, four legs rather than two, or they can be assumed: factual and supposed differences can be interlinked. Because fish are 'coldblooded' they were assumed not to feel pain, and not to have consciousness or intelligence – prejudice which a review of etiological studies on the cognitive skills of fish firmly refutes (Børresen 2007). Such arguments have Cartesian roots (for example, Regan 1983, Cazaux 1998, Donovan 1995, Ryder 1989, Noske 1989, Kheel 1993, Collard 1989), implying that other animals are inferior, that they lack the capacity to think and feel pain, do not have social skills and consequently do not have social needs. However, except in the case of fish, which many still tend to believe do not feel pain, few people today would deny that mammals feel pain. Yet the remnants of such beliefs are still very obvious, for example in research laboratories where rodents are toe-clipped for identification (Cazaux 2008). Without there being an explicit claim that they do not feel pain, the pain of the animals is downplayed, thereby making it possible to use them in pain-producing experiments, and to be confined in 'meat factories'. As in the case of many other types of injury and many other criminal acts, whether illegal or not, this is facilitated by the application of neutralisation techniques. Below I will elaborate on how Sykes' and Matzas' techniques of neutralisation are applied in the prevailing acceptance of animal abuse and exploitation.

The Denial of Injury

Sykes and Matza (1957) make a distinction between crimes which are *mal in se* and those which are *mala prohibita.* The ways in which animals are abused would in my opinion be mal in se, given the pain and death that is often inflicted, not least in factory farming, industrialised killing and vivisection (see, for example, Regan 2004, 2007, Sollund 2008, Noske 1989, Collard 1989). These actions, however, are most often not mala prohibita, which may be one important reason why they can proceed, and why injury can be denied. In fact, legislation is helpful in providing support for systemic animal abuse, operating with concepts such as *animal welfare.*

Animal welfare legislation could be expected to protect animals from abuse and the infliction of harm, but this is not necessarily the case (Svärd 2008, Ellefsen 2009). Beirne (1999, 2009) tracks American animal welfare legislation back to the Massachusetts Bay Colony in 1641. In 1822 the first British legislation against animal abuse was passed and similar legislation has been introduced in most 'technologically advanced societies' (Beirne 1999: 126). Yet, as Beirne proceeds to show, this legislation is still based on the perception that animals are property (Ellefsen 2009, Beirne 1999), and the extensive abuse of animals for the food industry and in experiments seem exempt from the legislation. Thus one can ask, if animals can legally be tortured, confined and killed in billions worldwide every year,[12] what purpose is served by the legislation if it does not protect the animals in the way one would expect?

Being 'property' does not confer rights that give more protection to animals (for example, Regan 1983, 2007). Instead it enforces acceptance of the fact that animals are used as a *means* to achieve a human good (for example, Yates 2007: 147). It does not prohibit the infliction of pain and death, but often operates with terms such as *necessary suffering* and not *too extensive suffering* (Beirne 1999, Sollund 2008). Thus Ellefsen finds that the recently amended Norwegian animal welfare legislation[13] does not relate to animal *rights*, as animals are not regarded as *legal subjects.* The fact that the law is a 'welfare'[14] law, rather than a rights law, explains the judicial limitations it

12 The systemic use of animals in industrial complexes is that which costs most animals suffering and premature death. Approximately 50 billion animals are killed for meat worldwide annually, in the US the numbers are roughly 9 billion, while 100 million animals are killed in experiments annually only in the US (Beirne 1999, Regan 2007). In Norway 724,093 animals were killed in experiments in 2006. The majority were fish, but also 35,524 mice, 12,248 rats, 410 guinea pigs, 476 other rodents, 320 rabbits, 22 dogs, 17 cats and 976 pigs, to mention some species, were also killed. Of these 27,475 animals were killed in pain-producing experiments.

13 http://www.regjeringen.no/en/doc/laws/Acts/animal-welfare-act.html?id=571188 [Accessed 15 August 2011].

14 The word 'welfare' should, as shown, imply to fare well in life, yet despite this, what is defined as 'welfare' in the case of so-called 'production animals' is more related to ideally not being killed without anesthesia and does not prevent them from being locked up in small cages, deprived of a social life and the possibility of breathing fresh air, of light and physical and mental stimulation. When such treatment is attributed to humans, for example in cases of kidnapping, it is referred to in quite different terms although the animals are equally captives. For further discussion of the use of the concept of animal welfare, see Regan (2004: 79) and Riise (this volume).

has in preserving the interests of *animals* (Ellefsen 2009: 111) as against the interests of the human *consumers* of animals.

The legislation, however, has another important effect. Despite its obvious ideological deficiencies and failure to give animals protection from pain, by its very existence, the general public is given the false impression that animals really do enjoy protection from abuse and suffering. The law gives carte blanche to those who most profit from animal abuse: the owners of factory farms, the food chains, abattoirs, producers of 'lab equipment' (such as lab rats and devices that inflict them with electric shocks), the pharmaceutical industry[15] and last, but not least, the consumers of animal products. Only small adjustments are made to meet demands from animal rights/welfare groups. In this way people are misled into thinking that there is no reason to abstain from animal consumption, exploitation is able to continue, unhindered by moral judgment, and the doxic meatism and other exploitation is maintained (Adams 1993, 2011, Gålmark 2008). If consumers question the situation for 'production animals', the law helpfully draws a veil of comforting reassurance before their eyes to prevent them from morally evaluating their actions (Ellefsen 2009: 111–15, Beirne 1999: 129).

When a newspaper covers cases of animal abuse, these are presented as exceptional cases which gives the impression that animals in general are protected: a false image of reality (Svärd, this volume, Hallsworth 2008). This serves to consolidate the common delusion that animals enjoy protection from abuse, and also to perpetuate exploitative practices. The paradox is evident when the next page is full of advertisements for cheap meat, which, of course, is not presented as chopped up dead pig or cow, but rather under an array of camouflaging concepts for different body parts. In the shops these are nicely cut and wrapped up in plastic, disguising the bloodbath from which they were produced.

The Denial of Responsibility

This is also closely linked to Sykes' and Matzas' (1957) first technique of neutralisation, the denial of responsibility. As individuals, we do not *kill* the animals or make them suffer: the responsibility for this act is that of someone else. As consumers, we merely enjoy the 'fruits' of others' killing, thereby freeing ourselves from the consequences of our consumption choices – the driving force for the exploitation: others, not we ourselves, made the conditions for the abuse (Agnew 1998: 190). Consequently, and again to paraphrase Sykes and Matza: the delinquent acts are due to forces *outside* the individual and beyond his control (p. 667). In this, cultural relativism may play a part, as in such arguments as: 'Humans have always been meat eaters', 'All animals (including humans) are predators' and so on, despite the fact that this is only true of

15 See for example: http://laboratoryanimalsciencebuyersguide.com/results.php?category=Animal%20Housing&heading=107&category_id=2804 [Accessed 14 March 2011].

20 per cent of all animals (Adams 1993). Again the normative doxic climate is a key reason why injury and responsibility can be denied, not by individual delinquents, but by the majority of law-abiding citizens. Because 'everybody' partakes in the (ab) use of animals, most people do not take *individual* responsibility for their actions. To dress and eat are natural actions, but *what* we eat and *how* we dress (and with what) are *learnt.* Still, because of the constant need for clothes and food, and also because these practices are ingrained, their results are generally not questioned. For many, it is also more trouble to avoid animal products than to use them, and therefore easier not to do a moral evaluation. This can also be achieved by one of the techniques of denial described by Stan Cohen: *renaming;* not denying that animals are killed, but silently accepting that to be killed is in some mysterious way compatible with the term to 'fare well'[16] – and thus the acts of violence committed against animals are reinterpreted as something else (Cohen 2001: 7).

The Denial of the Victim

The animals who are 'production animals', entertainment or 'wild'[17] are seldom perceived as victims of abuse; the 'wild' ones can even be regarded as 'vermin' or 'pest', thus 'deserving' to be killed (Agnew 1998). Other animals are companions, which elevates their social status so that they have victim status in cases of abuse. These animals are the ones benefitting from animal welfare legislation, as different rules seem to apply, rules not determined by the animals' natural needs, but by their social standing among humans (Hallsworth 2008, Larsen 2003, Sollund 2009).

Violence that would be castigated and prosecuted if the victims were human can go on because the victims are not, in Christie's (1986) term, ideal victims. They are weak, and do not fill Christie's sixth condition for being an ideal victim; they are not sufficiently powerful to make their case known, and successfully claim their status of ideal victims. Animals other than companions are seldom given victim status. This can be paralleled by Sykes' and Matzas' '*denial of the victim*', whereby the injury is not a real injury, or rather, the victim is not accorded status as victim because of speciesist ideology, and can therefore not suffer from injury. As Derrida puts it (quoted in Beirne 1999: 125):

16 To claim this in a case in which a human is killed would, of course, be complete nonsense.

17 The term 'wild' is in itself a way of othering, and disregarding that animals who live free from human dominion also are subject to socialisation by their parents and flock, which also includes the transmittance of knowledge, for example, about where to find the appropriate food, how to crack nuts and so on, just as humans transfer their knowledge between generations.

> An animal can be made to suffer, but we would never say, in a sense considered proper, that it [sic] is a wronged subject, the victim of a crime, of a murder, of a rape or a theft, or a perjury.

Abattoirs or fur farms are places for killing and using animals. The *situation* in which the violence takes place with its alienation and objectification of the animals (Sollund 2008), combined with the very motivations of the places' existence, work together to deprive the animals of victim status. A 'slaughter-pig' is not a victim of incarceration and theriocide[18] (Beirne 2007, 2009): the term 'slaughter-pig' defines his/her purpose in life – to be slaughtered – which is incompatible with victim status. Thus the purpose of the location where the animals are put, coupled with the lack of social status of the animal victim – simply a numbered production unit – also means that violence against animals is *not* defined as violence. For example the killing of foxes in the fur industry by anally and orally electrocuting them is referred to as to 'furring' them (Sollund 2008). They are no one. Hence the *acts* of incarceration and killing are not criminalised. In short, those acts are not seen as criminal and there is no violence or victim associated with the electrocution.

As already mentioned, this is not the case with all animals, as even animals can be ideal victims, depending on the social value attributed to them. For example, an abused golden retriever will be a more ideal victim than an abused pit-bull. Except for breeds which are defined as enemies through dangerous dog acts (Hallsworth 2011), dogs in general have more protection than other companion animals (Larsen 2001), and of course, much more than the fox, who, despite being locked up in a small cage all her short life in order to *be* fur (fur being something she becomes, not something she has) is not regarded as a victim of abuse. Both the golden retriever and the fox will have problems in claiming their status as victims and advocating their case. But the golden retriever will be more likely to have spokesmen who can talk for her, while the fox will not, at least not for her individually. Even when animal activists work for her case, this will be unlikely to be on an individual basis; it will be more principle-based, and as mentioned, animal rights activists are not necessarily good spokesmen, themselves risking stigmatisation for their activism. A golden retriever is *per se* defined as a 'pet' and when abused this will imply wrongdoing against her *owner* as much as against her; if the abuse is done by someone else, and if abused by her owner, witnesses are, according to the Norwegian animal welfare legislation, obliged to act to prevent the abuse.

The Condemnation of the Condemners

The labelling of animal rights activists as terrorists and criminals (see Agnew 1009: 189, Shapiro 1996, Ellefsen this volume, Aaltola, this volume, Yates 2004,

18 Beirne has informed the author in personal communication that he has changed the word to therocide, rather than theriocide.

Regan 2004) is a strategy whereby the spokesmen for animal victims who convey the message about animal abuse are targeted, rather than those responsible for the abuse. One example is when animal rights advocates are presented as extremists who are opposed to humans' well-being, and who should therefore be condemned, for example in the case of animal experimentation (Regan 2007). Attention is directed away from the abuse and the abusers, to the messengers who challenge the order of speciesism. As Sykes and Matza say:

> The delinquent [...] has changed the subject of conversation in the dialogue between his own deviant impulses and the reactions of others; and by attacking others, the wrongfulness of his own behaviour is more easily repressed or lost to view (op.cit 1957: 668).

One recent example took place in the United States (Iowa). Angered by repeated releases of secretly filmed videos showing animal abuse in Iowa's agriculture industry, the industry pushed for legislation that makes it illegal for animal rights activists to produce and distribute images of the maltreatment of farm animals. The bill was approved by The Republican-led House with a majority of 65–27. It must pass the Democratic-controlled Senate and be signed by Republican Governor Terry Branstad to become law. Proposed penalties include fines of up to $7,500 and up to five years in prison.[19] In criminalising the activists, the farms may succeed both in deterring them from filming and in directing attention away from their own violence against the animals in their custody, thus counteracting protests and maintaining the status quo – doxic specieisism. As with any other revolution, a revolution in the human–animal relationship may need a vanguard which is sufficiently strong to carry it through: by being labelled, punished and silenced, the animal rights activists may be prevented from getting into a sufficiently strong position to recruit enough followers to carry the revolution through. As shown in the example above, and as noted by Tom Regan (2004), Tom Yates (2007) and Aaltola and Ellefsen, both this volume, counter-movements to animal protectionism are enjoying some success in campaigning to characterise animal rights activists as extreme and terrorist-like. In this way, counter-movements also deter people from joining the cause for animal rights: who wants to be a terrorist?

The Appeal to Higher Loyalties

Sykes' and Matzas' technique of neutralisation, *the appeal to higher loyalties*, is frequently applied to permit animal abuse in the case of factory farming, vivisection and the production of clothing. The use of animals serves a 'higher

19 See for example: http://www.necn.com/03/17/11/Iowa-House-approves-secret-farm-video-bi/landing_politics.html?&blockID=3&apID=11171fe7e92e43659c6ff52db7dd45b7[Accessed 10 August 2011].

need'. Humans claim that the 'need' for meat, medicine and clothing legitimates exploitation, and downplays the excessiveness of the consumption of meat, with its accompanying diseases and environmental degradation, caused by extensive rearing systems (Beirne 2007: 75). As regards vivisection in particular, one often hears the appeal to higher loyalties in the form of the value the experiments have for humans' lives and health. These arguments, such as those of philosopher Carl Cohen when debating with Tom Regan (Cohen and Regan 2002), conceal the fact that millions of experiments take place to satisfy humans' craving for more luxury cosmetics, and in the production of replica products including medicine (for example, Singer 2002, Regan 2007, Gruen 1993, Collard 1989, Noske 1989). Vivisection advocates also conceal the fact that the majority of the experiments are useless, extremely painful and even harmful to humans. Arguments are put forward which position vivisection and other abuse as a necessity, thereby constructing a divide implying that it is either 'them or us', and that not using 'them' would harm 'us' (Regan 2004, 2007).

Appeals to a higher loyalty find great support in religion and philosophy, for example in the Tenth Commandment which establishes that not only are men superior to their wives and their animals, but that women and animals are also men's property, which is where their value lies. Among the philosophers, Aristotle has been important in establishing social hierarchies in which a distinction is made between those who exist to be of servitude to others, women and animals (and slaves), and those who are free to use them, men (for example, Gålmark 2008, Nussbaum 2006, Noske 1989).

Hierarchisation is also evident among the different animal species. Those at the top of the food chain, the big predators, typically have a higher status in Man's eyes than those at the bottom of the food chain, such as mice, rabbits and so on. For example, in the Scandinavian countries one now speaks of 'ulvedrap' [wolfe assassination] (cf Beirne theriocide and Korsell and Hagstedt, this volume) which is probably also linked to the degree of protection wolves *should* have enjoyed as a protected, endangered species through the Bern Convention protecting 'wildlife'. One never hears of 'cow assassinations', 'cow murders', 'pig homicide' or 'chicken killing', although millions of these animals are killed every year. The place the predators have in the ranking is connected to the hierarchy imposed by patriarchy, in which, as mentioned above, what gives status is the potential power to kill (for example, Birkeland 1993, Adams 1993, Noske 1989, Collard 1989). Those with the capacity to kill consequently 'deserve' more respect than those who are prey.

This is evident in trophy hunting, seen, for example, in 'hunting parks' in South Africa where predominantly white males can boost their egos by killing large predators such as the lion,[20] but it is also one of the motives for the illegal killing of wolves in Sweden (Korsell and Hagstedt, this volume). While they have more respect, this status also means that wolves are perceived as suitable, worthy

---

20 See for example: http://www.africanskyhunting.co.za/trophies/lion-hunting.html [Accessed 8 May 2011].

enemies because they challenge the power of Man, and also because they feed on Man's 'property' – sheep.

The polarisation between humans and animals, and the consequent speciesism produced by the patriarchal normative mindset, is the reason why everyone who differs from the white Male standard is regarded as less worthy (except as trophies, property and so on) (for example, Collard 1989, Birkeland 1993, Adams 1993, Noske 1989). To counteract the construction of dualism, othering and speciesism one must take a totally different approach.

Equal Concerns for Different Species

The denial of the victim and the exploitation of animals are based in their 'failure' – their deficiency – in not being human. Human athletes, for example, are highly respected for physical capacities that make them stand out from the majority: the difference between what *they* achieve physically and what most people achieve physically is what generates respect and appreciation. Why – in addition to the argument above – is this not applied to animals? May the lack of esteem be connected to lack of identification, because the apparent differences are too great (Sollund 2008)? Is it the case that, in order to respect the differences constituted by physical properties which make some stand out, there must first be basic, phenotypical similarities? May simple ignorance explain it? Despite an increasing number of ethological studies, animal behaviour is still a mystery to most people, and knowledge is not widespread as regards, for example, fish (Børresen 2007). Is it the case that because we do not comprehend animals, birds and fish, and what they are capable of, disrespect must follow?

This again will probably be connected to the fact that they and their lives are not part of ours – we do not share the same sphere of experience, and thus we don't feel (sufficient) social nearness to be able to empathize with them. They are in the forest, on the savannah, in the air, in the sea or in captivity – socially and physically invisible to us and therefore also beyond our moral concern (Vialle 1994, Sollund 2008), which may explain also why they may arouse fascination rather than humans' respect and compassion (Hallsworth 2008). This fascination also seems to bring with it a human urge to kill, control and tame the 'wild', (Collard 1989, Noske 1989), for example through physical labelling (Cazaux 2007). Fascination also often turns into a desire to capture and possess these animals' essence through the prejudicial consumption of their body parts in different types of medicine, particularly Far Eastern medicine, which results in the endangering of many species, such as the rhinoceros, tigers and bears which are abducted[21] in the forests and even bred to cover the 'need' (for example, Warchol et al. 2003).

21 See for example: http://www.youtube.com/watch?v=j2ZcCX_R0Go&feature=related [Accessed 17 august 2011].

The fact that animals, to varying degrees and in different ways, are physically different from humans also facilitates an exaggeration and misunderstanding of the *relevance* of specific differences and their implications, thus legitimating abuse (Sollund 2008). One reason is, for example, the fact that when other animals are compared to humans, the anthropocentric viewpoint usually leads to the *belittling* of other animals, because they are not regarded as being 'mothers', 'sentient', 'intelligent' and so on in the way humans are, but rather, as being 'mother-*like*', 'intelligent-*like*' and so on. As observed by Barbara Noske (1989: xiii): 'To define them as human-like individuals, such as ethical philosophers do, and give them rights accordingly, is to do them a disservice – to downplay their otherness and to treat them ahistorically as it were.'

Whether to minimise pain or secure rights, philosophers Peter Singer (2002) and Tom Regan (1983, 2007), as well as other scholars (for example, Sollund 2008, Børresen 2006), argue for animals' rights or for concern about them because of their *similarity* to humans, in such characteristics as the capacity to establish social bonds, to feel pain and to plan their actions. The comparison to humans again makes humans the yardstick by which individuals of other species are measured, and humans are the centre around which other species revolve, rather than being just one of many species.

The comparison of animals to humans does a disservice to animals (birds, fish, reptiles), simply because humans, because of their own physical deficiencies, cannot fully comprehend the uniqueness that other animals' physical and mental abilities represent. How would it be if we upgraded our respect and value for precisely those capacities and skills of animals that *diverge* from those of humans, and foregrounded their value because of their uniqueness? Reflect, for example, upon the navigating skills of migrating birds and mammals travelling huge distances across the globe every year: the physical capacities of Bar-headed geese flying *over* the Himalayas, more than 8,000 metres above sea level, in extreme wind and 50°C below zero; the hunting skills of predators, for example lions and eagles, the speed of the hunting leopard that can accelerate from 0 to over 100km/h in three seconds; the olfactory sense of wolves and dogs; and the capacity of many companion animals to foresee the arrival of their human companions (Sheldrake 1996). Furthermore, what speed, intelligence, skill and cooperation does it take on the part of those animals who are prey to avoid their enemies? To comprehend this could bring respect for *difference*, rather than respect for similarities, which certainly exists between all animals including humans. As Regan also states: 'Each is a unique somebody' (Regan 2007: 131).

By emphasising the uniqueness of each individual, as well as the specific properties of the species the individual belongs to, one could perhaps make a step forward. For this, horizontalism, rather than hierarchy, is essential, given that the construction and 'naturalization' of hierarchies has been one very important aspect of the oppression of women and animals (Gruen 1993: 80). Perhaps humans' respect for animals would increase if we did not always attempt to establish the similarities between humans and other species to create grounds for equal rights and concerns. Such comparisons may have provided arguments for those who oppose animal rights, to claim that other species are somewhat *inadequate* species, because of their (assumed) inferior intellectual capacities, language capacities, social abilities and so on, which can be considered of less value and consequently deserving of deprivation of rights. To establish similarity was definitely necessary when Cartesian ideals prevailed, but unfortunately the strategy seems inadequate. Eco-feminists thus argue for a practice and a theory with a vision of a new way of conceptualising reality, moving away from individualism to encompass a respectful appreciation of difference (Gruen 1993: 81, Kheel 1993, Birkeland 1993, Noske 1989, Vance 1993). In this, however, the appreciation of features of equality should not be neglected, as this similarity also can serve as a bridge of interspecies solidarity.

Animal Rights – a Question of Justice?

Animals should not be considered as having rights because they are human-like, but in their own capacity, because it is just (Nussbaum 2006). Benton says: '[...] there seems to be no good reason why considerations of justice should not apply to animals over that range of goods that they can appreciate – such as freedom from torture' (2007: 17). This is in my view an understatement. Nussbaum starts her argument for justice for other species by citing a verdict in the Kerala high court, which states that circus elephants are entitled to compassion and humane treatment sans torture (Nussbaum 2006: 325). Thus *compassion* for the suffering of others should be what generates justice, respect and freedom from pain inflicted by humans: '[...] the touchstone should be respectful consideration of the species norm of flourishing and a respectful attention to the capacities of the individual' (Nussbaum 2006: 378). Josephine Donovan (1996) argues similarly for ethics, sympathy and compassion as a guide for human treatment of animals (cf. also Adams 1996, Vance 1993, Kheel 1993, 1996). Yet there is not necessarily a conflict between care ethics and rights. Just as humans do, animals should both have rights and be protected by our care, compassion and concern. To look at it from another angel, ask the following question: what would the consequence be if humans were only protected by care, rather having the rights established by international conventions? Would they not risk losing those rights that have been fought for over the last couple of centuries? And what exactly is a proper amount of care and compassion? Are not the consequences of uncertainty and variation in this regard what we see in the animal 'welfare' paradigm? In my view, regardless of human compassion, animals are entitled to rights, simply because they have their place in the world. Humans should be in no position to attribute either rights or the opposite, and should not attempt to. This is a position humans have taken for themselves, which has had devastating, deteriorating consequences, not only for animals, but for the globe as a whole. To believe that the human species is capable of carrying out this responsibility is to overestimate its capacity, not just for compassion, but also for rational action. The roles other species play in the ecosystem are, in contrast to those of the human species, important for its preservation. In an ecological justice perspective, in which humans are only one of many species (White 2007, 2008), individuals of other species should indeed have rights, if the goal is the best for all, not just short-sighted *human* benefits. As we face the sixth (man-made) extinction (Boekhout van Solinge 2008), and extensive systematized theriocide (Beirne 2007: 63, 2009), animals of other species should perhaps not only be accorded equal rights, but *special* rights, to safeguard individuals and to ensure the survival of as many species as possible. For this, a reorientation of prevalent norms, values and practices is essential.

References

Aftenposten 12.04.10 *Rekordhøyt kjøttkonsum i norsk kosthold.*

Ascione, F., Weber, C. and Wood, D. 1997. The abuse of animals and domestic violence, in *Society & Animals*, 5(3), 205–18.

Adams, C. 1993. The feminist traffic in animals, in *Ecofeminism. Women, Animals and Nature*, edited by G. Gaard. Philadelphia: Temple University Press, 195–219.

Adams, C. 1996. Caring about suffering: a feminist exploration, in *Beyond Animal Rights*, edited by J. Donovan and C. Adams. New York: The Continuum Publishing Company, 17–34.

Adams, C. 2011. *The Sexual Politics of Meat.* Reprint. New York: Continuum.

Agnew, R. 1998. Causes for animal abuse. A social-psychological analysis, *TheoreticalCriminology*, 2(2), 177–209.

Collard, A. and Contrucci, J. 1989. *Rape of the Wild. Man's Violence Against Animals and the Earth.* Bloomington: Indiana University Press.

Beirne, P. 1995. The use and abuse of animals in criminiology. A brief history and current review. *Social Justice*, 22(1), 5–31.

Beirne, P. 1999. For a non-speciesist criminology: animal abuse as an object of study, in *Criminology. An Interdisciplinary Journal*. The official publication of the American Society of Criminology, 37(1), 117–147.

Beirne, Piers. 2009. *Confronting Animal Abuse. Law, Criminology, and Human-animal Relationships.* Lanham: Rowman & Littlefield Publishers.

Beirne, P. and Cazaux, G. 2006. Animal abuse, in *The Sage Dictionary of Criminology*, edited by E. McLaughlin and J. Muncie. London: Sage, 10–11.

Birkeland, J. 1993. Ecofeminism: linking theory and practice, in *Ecofeminism. Women, Animals and Nature*, edited by G. Gaard. Philadephia: Temple University Press, 13–60.

Boekhout van Solinge, T. 2008. Crime conflicts and ecology in Africa, in *Global Harms: Ecological Crime and Speciesism*, edited by R. Sollund. New York: Nova Science Publishers, 13–34.

Bourdieu, P. 1995. *Outline of a Theory of Practice.* Cambridge: Cambridge University Press.

Børresen, B. 2007. *Fiskenes ukjente liv* [*The Unknown Life of the Fish*]. Oslo: Transit.
Børresen, B. 2006. *Den ensomme apen. Instinkt på avveie* [*The Lonely Ape. Instinct Array*]. Oslo: Koloritt.
Cazaux, G. 1998. Legitimating the entry of 'the animals issue' into (critical) criminology, in *Humanity and Society*, 22(4), 365–85.
Cazaux, G. 1999. Beauty and the beast: animal abuse from a non-speciesist criminological perspective, in *Crime, Law and Social Change*, 31(2), 105–26.
Cazaux, G. 2008. Labelling animals: non-specieisist criminology and techniques to identify other animals, in *Issues in Green Criminology: Confronting Harms Against Environments. Humanity and Other Animals*, edited by P. Beirne and N. South. Devon: Willan Publishing, 87–114.
Cohen, S. 2001. *States of Denial*. Cambridge: Cambridge Polity Press.
Cohen, C. and Regan, T. 2001. *The Animal Rights Debate.* New York: Rowman & Littlefield Publishers.
Donovan, J. 1990. Animal rights and feminist theory, in *Signs: Journal of Women in Culture and Society*, 15(2), 350–376.
Donovan, J. 1996. Sympathy as a basis for ethical treatment of animals, in *Beyond Animal Rights*, edited by J. Donovan and C.J. Adams. New York: The Continuum Publishing Company, 147–70.
Ellefsen, R. 2009. *Ny dyrelferdslov: Beskytttes dyr eller næring? Interessekonflikt og motstridende syn på dyrs status i lovprosessen forut for dyrelferdsloven.* [New animal welfare legislation: protecting animals or industries? Conflicting interests and views of animals' status within the legal process before passing of the animal welfare law]. MA thesis, University of Oslo, Dept. of Criminology and Sociology of Law.
Flynn, C.P. 1999. Animal abuse in childhood and later support for interpersonal violence in families, in *Society and Animals*, 7(2), 161–172.
Gålmark, L. 2008. Aristotle revisited: anthro-androcentricm and meat normativity, in *Global Harms: Ecological Crime and Speciesism*, edited by R. Sollund. New York: Nova Science Publishers, 87–109.
Gaard, G. 1993. Living connections with animals and nature, in *Ecofeminism. Women, Animals and Nature*, edited by G. Gaard. Philadelphia: Temple University Press, 1–13.
Gruen, L. 1993. Dismantling oppression: an analysis of the connection between women and animal, in *Ecofeminism. Women, Animals, Nature*, edited by G. Gaard. Philadelphia: Temple University Press, pp 60–91.
Haraway, D.J. 2008. *When Species Meet.* Minneapolis: Minneapolis University Press.
Hallsworth, S. 2011. Then they came for the dogs!, in *Crime Law and Social Change*, 55(5), 391–403.
Hallsworth, S. 2008. Imaginary spaces and real relations, in *Global Harms: Ecological Crime and Speciesism*, edited by R. Sollund. New York: Nova Science Publishers, 71–86.
Holm, J. and Jokkala, T. 2007. *Djurindustrin och klimatet.* [*Animal Industry and the Climate*]. Bryssel: GUE/NGL.

Jokkala, T. and Strindlund, P. 2003. *Djurrettt och Socialism*. Lindelövs bokförlag.
Kheel, M. 1993. From heroic to holistic ethics, in *Ecofeminism. Women, Animals and Nature*, edited by G. Gaard. Philadelphia: Temple University Press, 243–72.
Kheel, M. 1996. The liberation of nature. A circular affair, in *Beyond Animal Rights. A Feminist Caring Ethics for the Treatment of Animals*, edited by J. Donovan and C.J. Adams. NewYork: Continuum.
Larsen, G. (2003) *Dyrevern eller samfunnsvern* [*Animal Protection Or Society Protection*]. Oslo: Unipub.
Luke, B. 1996. Justice, caring and animal liberation, in *The Feminist Care Tradition in Animal Ethics*, edited by J. Donovan and C. Adams. New York: Columbia University Press, 125–53.
Lynch, M.J. and Stretesky, P. 2007. Green criminology in the United States, in *Issues in Green Criminology*, edited by P. Beirne and N. South. Devon: Willan Publishing, 248–69.
Nibert, D. 2003. Humans and other animals: Sociology's moral and intellectual challenge, in *International Journal of Sociology and Social Policy*, 23(3), 5–25.
Nibert, D. 2002. *Animal rights. Human rights.* Oxford: Rowman and Littlefield Publishers.
Noske, B. 1989. *Humans and other Animals: Beyond the Boundaries of Anthropology.* London: Pluto Press.
Nussbaum, M.C. 2006. *Frontiers of Justice. Disability, Nationality, Species Membership.* Harvard: The Belknap Press of Harvard University Press.
Pedersen, H. 2008. Learning to measure the value of life? Animal experimentation, pedagogy and (eco)feminist critique, in *Global Harms: Ecological Crime and Speciesism*, edited by R. Sollund. New York: Nova Science Publishers, 109–31.
Regan, T. 1999. *Djurens rettigheter, en filosofisk argumentation.* [*The Case for Animal Rights*]. Sweden: Förlaget Nye Doxa.
Regan, T. 2004. *Empty the Cages. Facing the Challenge of Animal Rights.* Lanham: Rowman & Littlefield Publishers.
Regan, T. 2009. Vivisection: the case for abolition, in *Issues in Green Criminology*, edited by P. Beirne and N. South. Devon: Willan Publishing, 114–39.
Ryder, R.D. 1989. *Animal Revolution. Changing Attitudes towards Speciesism.* Oxford: Basil Blackwell.
Sheldrake, R. 1996. Seven experiments that could change the world, in *Alternative Health Practicioner*, 2(2), 93–100.
Singer, P. 2002. *Dyrenes frigjøring* [*Animal Liberation*]. Oslo: Spartacus forlag.
Sollund, R. 2009. Menneskers paradoksale forhold til dyr. [The paradox in the human–animal relationship], in *Sosiologi i dag*, 39(3), 42–69.
Sollund, R. 2008. Causes for specieisism: difference, distance and denial, in *Global Harms: Ecological Crime and Speciesism*, edited by R. Sollund. New York: Nova Science Publishers, 109–31.
Sollund, R. Fortcoming 2011. Expressions of speciesism: the effects of keeping companion animals on animal abuse, animal trafficking and species decline, in *Criminal Law and Social Change*, forthcoming.

Sollund, R. 2007. *Tatt for en annen. En feltstudie av forholdet mellom politiet og etniske minoriteter* [*Taken for Another. A Field Study of the Relationship between Police and Ethnic Minorities*]. Oslo: Gyldendal akademisk.

Sollund, R. 1999. *Kan vold forklares? En undersøkelse av voldsdømte menn med flyktningbakgrunn.* [*How to Explain Violence? An Inquiry of Male Refugees Convicted for Violent Crimes*]. Oslo: Spartacus.

Svärd, P-A. 2008. Critique of animal welfarism and green ideology, in *Global Harms. Ecological Crime and Speciesism*, edited by R. Sollund. REGAN New York: Nova.

Sykes, G. and Matza, D. 1957. Techniques of neutralization: a theory of delinquency, *American Sociology Review*, 664–60.

Vance, L. 1993. Ecofeminism and the politics of reality, in *Ecofeminism. Women, Animals and Nature*, edited by G. Gaard. Philadelphia: Temple University press, 91–117.

Vermeulen, H. and Odendaal, S.J. 1993. Proposed typology of companion animal abuse, in *Antrozoös*, 6(4), 248–57.

Vialle, N. 1994. *From Animal to Edible.* Paris: Cambridge University Press.

Warchol, G.L., Zupan, L.L. and Clarke, W. 2003. Transnational criminality: an analysis of the illegal wildlife market in Southern Africa, in *International Criminal Justice Review*, 13(1), 1–26.

White, R. 2007. Green criminology and the pursuit of social and ecological justice, in *Issues in Green Criminology*, edited by P. Beirne and N. South. Devon: Willan Publishing, 32–54.

White, R. 2008. *Crimes against Nature: Environmental Criminology and Ecological Justice*. London: Willan Publishing.

Yates, R. 2007. Debating 'animal rights' online: the movement-countermovement dialectic revisited, in *Issues in Green Criminology*, edited by P. Beirne and N. South. Devon: Willan Publishing, 140–160.

Chapter 7
The Ideological Fantasy of Animal Welfare: A Lacanian Perspective on the Reproduction of Speciesism

Per-Anders Svärd

Introduction: Protecting Animals—from What?

These days, *everyone* is in favor of animal welfare. Consumers and corporations, the state and "animal lovers"—they all condemn animal cruelty and praise welfare reform. But if everyone is opposed to animal mistreatment, what or whom are we protecting non-human animals[1] *from*? Where does animal cruelty come from in a society that universally disavows it?

One common answer is that animal cruelty is the work of an "Other." As a rule, it is not "we" who harm animals, it is someone else. Among the usual suspects, we find the socially or psychologically deviant, foreigners with their alien customs and food habits, and the occasional greedy farmer. These phenomena have an interesting feature in common: they are typically framed as anomalies, as deviations from "our" harmonious relations with animals. Within this framework, protecting animals often means protecting them from the excesses of an alien Other, an intrusive force intent on causing harm and suffering.

From the perspective of animal rights philosophy on the other hand, this framing looks more like a cynical attempt to legitimate our own *speciesism*—that is, the systematic but morally arbitrary discrimination against non-human interests (Beirne 1999, 2007, Cazaux 1999, Cazaux and Beirne 2006, Singer 2002, Dunayer 2004, Larsen, Sollund, Bjørkdahl, this volume). Indeed, some theorists have argued that animal welfarism—the view that animals may be used for human purposes as long as we treat them "humanely" and do not cause "unnecessary suffering"—should be regarded as the dominant form of speciesism in our time. On this "abolitionist" view, animal welfarism does not safeguard animal interests so much as lend ideological legitimacy to speciesist practices, for example by manipulating language to frame animal exploitation as something uncontroversial and "natural" (see Dunayer 2004, Francione 1996, 2008, Hall 2006, 2010, Svärd 2008, 2011).[2]

---

1 Hereafter simply "animals."

2 Over recent years this critique has led to extensive debates within the animal advocacy community over strategies for change: is it more effective to attempt to regulate

Critical animal rights theorists have devoted a lot of attention to the ways non-human subordination is produced and reproduced in discourse. In this chapter I want to approach the issue from a different angle. My aim is to investigate how animal welfarism works not only on the discursive level, but also how it "binds" people by way of *affective investment* in a specific worldview. The objective is to account, at least in part, for the remarkable stability and attractiveness of animal welfare discourse as a hegemonic view of the human–animal relationship. What makes animal welfarism "stick" with us as the preferred discourse of animal treatment? How does this discourse manage to retain its hold despite its evident failure to really protect animals? And what is the role of the Other—the "animal abuser"—in this process?

Drawing on post-Marxist discourse theory and Lacanian psychoanalysis, I will argue that animal welfarism not only glosses over the pervasive speciesism of our own (Western) societies, but that it does so by means of *ideological fantasy*. Fantasy, in the Lacanian sense, refers to a psychological support structure that underpins and stabilizes the social construction of reality. The role of fantasy is to produce an imaginary scenario that diverts attention away from the precarious nature of the discursive constructions through which humans experience the world. In the case of animal welfare discourse, fantasy often figures in the production of an "enemy" to harmonious human–animal relations: the pathological/deviant "animal abuser" who must be controlled in order to prevent animal cruelty. What this fantasy enemy stands in for, however, is the traumatic—but repressed—fact that our society was never particularly animal-friendly to begin with.

From this psychoanalytical point of view, the persistence of animal welfarism as a hegemonic discourse does not result mainly from the convincing force of its reality-representation. On the contrary, thanks to media reports and activist outreach efforts, people often see the hollowness of "our" animal friendliness. Instead, the secret of animal welfarism's success lies in the *affective* register, in its ability to manipulate human desire for stable identification. The attraction of animal welfarism is that it can assure us that there is a secure identity for us as "animal friendly." It holds out the promise that any anxiety over animal exploitation may soon be abolished—*if* we can only manage to control, tame, or banish the fantasy enemy. In this way, the utopian vision of animal welfarism can retain the loyalty of

---

away animal oppression by piecemeal political reform (expanding protection by banning one abusive practice at the time), or should animal rights activists focus their energies on raising awareness of speciesism and promoting veganism as a baseline for respecting animals? (The interested reader will find the main positions in this debate expressed in the recently published debate between Gary L. Francione and Robert Garner, 2010, *The Animal Rights Debate: Abolition or Regulation?*) While I side with the abolitionist position, pursuing this argument is not my main objective here. I will simply assume that both sides in this debate find animal welfarism—as a hegemonic public discourse as well as a political paradigm—troubling in its capacity to neutralize animal rights claims by drawing attention away from systemic animal oppression.

its subjects even though its realization is endlessly deferred. And deferred it is, as Gary L. Francione reminds us: "We have had animal welfare, both as a prevailing moral theory and as part of the law, for more than 200 years now, and we are using more nonhuman animals in more horrific ways than at any time in human history" (Francione and Garner 2010: 49). From this point of view, the vision of harm-free animal use seems further away than ever. But animal welfarist fantasy explains this fact away by the production of new enemies to be blamed for the continuation of animal mistreatment. The outcome is to obscure our own complicity and veil the speciesist character of our own society (where billions of non-humans are routinely reduced to the status of property, commodities, "food," and so on).

Discourse, Hegemony and Antagonism

The argument made in this chapter is premised on post-Marxist discourse theory and Lacanian psychoanalysis. *Discourse* or *discourses* here refers to historically specific "systems of meaningful practices that form the identities of objects and subjects" (Howarth and Stavrakakis 2000: 3–4). In short, this is a constructionist view of the social that emphasizes the role of language and other meaning-making practices in mediating human experience and in directing social action. The assumption is that humans never have direct access to the world "as it really is." Instead, we experience the world as it has been constituted in discourse. This, of course, is not to say that the world does not *exist* outside discourse, only that it has no *meaning* outside discourse (Laclau and Mouffe 1991, Burr 2003, McGowan 2006).

As Michel Foucault (2002: 54) put it, discourses are "practices that systematically form the objects about which they speak." To Ernesto Laclau and Chantal Mouffe (1985), this formation of objects is accomplished through *articulation.* Articulation refers to any practice whereby free-floating elements of language are brought together in a specific arrangement and locked down as fixed moments of a particular discourse, in a way that modifies their meaning (p. 105). In animal welfare discourse, for example, terms like "protection," "care," and "humane treatment" are articulated in a way that differs sharply from their articulation in discourses about human rights. In the former context, "caring" about animals does not exclude reducing them to property, and being "humane" to animals is compatible with killing them for trivial purposes like the taste of their flesh.

Importantly, articulation implies some use of force or repression to limit alternative interpretations of the world. Where language in principle is a flux of signification with limitless variations, articulation intervenes "to dominate the flow of meaning, to arrest the flow of differences, to construct a centre" where none is naturally given (Laclau and Mouffe 1985: 112, see also Derrida 2001, ch. 10). To this end, discursive articulation relies on the construction of certain *nodal points*, privileged moments of discourse from which the other moments in a signifying chain take on a metaphorical surplus value (Laclau and Mouffe 1985: 112). "Animal welfare/protection" works as such a nodal point, in relation to which numerous practices of systematic violence toward non-humans can assume the garb of "humaneness," "care," "respect," "progressiveness," "enlightenment," and so on.

This indicates the political importance of discourse. Control over meaning means not only control over human worldviews, but also over human identities and human action. Therefore, discourse is always a site of struggle between different forces contending for *hegemony*—that is, the institution of their own worldview as the "natural" or "objective" one. Hegemony, in this sense, can be seen as the privileging of a certain version of reality over a multitude of possible alternatives (Winther Jørgensen and Phillips 2002: 36–7). Such a hegemonic "reality" offers itself as a *social objectivity*—a horizon of intelligibility within which the rules are set for what can be legitimately thought, said, and done. Simply put, hegemony defines the "common sense" of a culture or period.

In the Western world today, it is no exaggeration to say that animal welfare discourse enjoys hegemony. Most of us have been raised to see animal cruelty as something evil. It is common sense to be kind to companion animals and the like. But at the same time, it is equally taken for granted that we are free to use animals for food and other purposes, as long as we treat them "humanely." The stability of this particular articulation of appropriate human–animal relations is remarkable. Yet, it should be noted that the stability offered by a hegemonic discourse can at most be historical and relative. Given that hegemony is premised on the repression of possible alternatives and the denial of discursive precariousness, the social realm is always haunted by the *antagonism* created by the exclusion of alternative meaning. The repressed possibilities always threaten to return and undermine hegemonic stability. What makes hegemony possible is therefore also what makes it *im*possible (Laclau and Mouffe 1985: 125–6).

Symbolic Critique—and Beyond

In the case of animal welfare discourse, its hegemonic status relies on its capacity to pass itself off as a final symbolization of the human–animal relationship—that is, as the "common sense" of animal treatment. But this is precisely what has been challenged by the counter-hegemonic critique of animal rights philosophy and the animal rights movement over the last four decades. Academics and activists alike have devoted much energy to the critique of oppressive language. The aim has been to show how animals are routinely devalued and subordinated in and through discursive practices. Joan Dunayer (2001), for example, has shown how everyday vocabulary and syntax serve to naturalize non-human subordination and obfuscate human complicity in routinized violence. Similarly, feminist animal rights advocates have demonstrated how gendered and speciesist discourses intersect to denigrate women as well as animals (Adams 1990, Birke 1994, Dunayer 1995, Gålmark 2005, 2008). Others have drawn parallels between the language of slavery and racism on the one hand, and the language of animal exploitation on the other (Spiegel 1989, Patterson 2002, Strindlund 2011). Finally, efforts have been made to spell out the capitalist interest in sustaining ideologies that facilitate the transformation of sentient creatures into property and commodities (Nibert 2002, Jokkala and Strindlund 2003, Torres 2007).

Critiques like these have been invaluable to our understanding of the construction of human–animal (and human–human) relations. But while we have learnt much about how hegemonic discourses spin their web of meaning, one question has often gone unanswered—namely, why do people get entangled in the web of animal welfarist discourse? What makes this particular articulation "stick" with us, rather than any other? Or, to turn the question around, what is it with *us* that makes welfarist discourse stick? It is here, in the interface between individual and social discourse, that the Lacanian notion of the subject can help us understand the reproduction of the speciesist social order.

Lacan and the Subject of Lack

In everyday language the notion of "the subject" refers to the individual's experience of being a self-conscious "I"—that is, a stable entity that persists over time and is the source of its own thoughts and actions. In the psychoanalytic theory of Jacques Lacan (1901–1981), however, the subject has a different meaning. Here, the subject manifests itself as "split," "barred," or "castrated"—as a *subject of "lack"* (Fink 1995, Stavrakakis 1999, ch. 1). According to Lacan, the subject is constituted as already lacking from the human infant's first attempts to develop an individual identity. Characteristically, the infant attempts to obtain an identity by identifying with its own mirror image (or "imago"). But this identification is fraught with difficulty since the infant cannot reconcile the wholeness of the imago with its own experiences of bodily fragmentation. The mirror image is said to be the child's "I" but the child observes the discrepancy between the imago and its own self-experiences and is unable to close the gap between them. The mirror image cannot fully capture the infant's existence, and therefore it ultimately alienates the child (Lacan 2007: 75-81, Lapsley 2006: 72-6).

The basic paradox here is that the child's identity must come from the outside, from identification with something else. But this other thing, obviously, can never be the child itself. This dilemma reappears in the second stage of alienation, alienation in language (or "the symbolic order" as Lacan says, a concept that lies close to what we have called "discourse"). When entering language, the child finds itself thrown into a world already constituted in discourse. Here, a range of possible identities await the child in the form of signifiers that the child can take on as its own. The child may, for example, seek a consistent identity as being a "boy" or a "girl," "nice" or "obedient," "strong" or "cute." But this identification too is marred by alienation, since the child must *subject itself* to the signifier. If the child, for example, identifies as a "boy," it must disavow its "girlish" impulses and repress all drives that are incompatible with the binary gender division. It is in this sense that subjection to the signifier represents "castration"; becoming a subject in language entails losing part of oneself, having something precious at the core of one's being cut away (Fink 1995: 99–100).

What is at work here is Lacan's concept of the *real*. The real should not be confused with *reality*—in Lacan's view the latter is always a social construction. Rather, the real is what is left over when the signifier has been attached to some piece of the world in order to constitute (social) reality. The real is the remainder that language fails to capture, that which remains beyond the grasp of signification yet always threatens to return and subvert meaning (Bailly 2009: 222, Daly 1999). It is this failure of the signifier to master the real of human existence that causes alienation in language. The signifiers defined in language seem to be immortal and objective, but it is for this reason that they are unfitted to express the finite, particular, and subjective experiences of the individual (Lacan 1993: 179–80). The price for the subject's insertion in language, philosopher Slavoj Žižek writes, "is the irretrievable *loss* of the subject's self-identity; the verbal sign that stands for the subject, that is, in which the subject posits itself as self-identical, bears the mark of an irreducible dissonance; it never 'fits' the subject" (Žižek 1997: 43, emphasis original).

This fundamental mismatch between real human life and the immortal network of the signifier can never be fully eliminated. This leaves the subject with a sense of incompleteness, a kind of "identity deficit," if you will. As subjects of *lack*, we feel that something precious has been lost to us, and it is the hope of recovering this lost *enjoyment*—that Lacan calls *jouissance*—that drives us to search for new signifiers with which to identify.

Desire and Political Identification

The force that drives the subject to retrieve its lost *jouissance* or enjoyment is called *desire* by Lacan. Desire should not be confused with need. Needs can be satisfied—if I am hungry I can eat, if I am cold I can put on warm clothes, and so on. But desire is insatiable because it tries to eliminate something that cannot be eliminated—the lack of the subject. The world of commerce and consumption provides a good example of this. Through advertising we are constantly offered new products which promise to fulfill our desires. Advertising thus often speaks to human desire rather than to any essential need. As Lionel Bailly (2008: 113) puts it, "one *needs* water, but one *desires* a Gucci handbag." But once the product is bought, it turns out that it does not really contain the mysterious missing object the subject was looking for (Lacan calls this *objet petit a*—the object-cause of desire). The *jouissance* obtained is always less than the *jouissance* expected (Lacan 1998: 111). The product is unable to abolish human lack, but this just means that advertising can turn the consumer's attention to another *objet petit a*—and so the wheel of consumption can continue to spin (see Stavrakakis 2007, ch. 7).

The wider significance of this logic of lack and desire becomes apparent when we turn to political identifications. As pointed out by Slavoj Žižek, Yannis

Stavrakakis, and other Lacanian political theorists the desire for a stable identity figures prominently in making ideologies attractive. The lure of the "grand narratives" (like the nation, religion, the market, revolution, science, and—I will argue—animal welfarism) lies in the promise they hold out of securing a safe place for human identity. The psychoanalytical answer to the question why some discourses fare better than others—why they become stronger candidates for hegemony—is precisely that they offer to eliminate the subject's lack by restoring its lost enjoyment. The problem, of course, is that these political discourses too are contingent historical constructions, and as such they remain unstable. In Lacanian terms, the subject seeks its truth in the *Big Other* of discourse, but this Other in turn has no Other to guarantee its stability (Lacan 2006: 688). The lack from which the subject tries to escape is thus reintroduced at the level of discourse. This means that the subject faces a double lack—first, in terms of the original castration in language, and second in the failure of discourse to fully master the real and constitute itself as a place where the subject's full enjoyment can be recovered (Stavrakakis 1999: 41).

Ideological Fantasy

Constitutive lack thus is part of the subject as well as the discourses it inhabits. Even the grand political narratives will therefore ultimately fail to deliver the completeness desired by the subject (Lacan 2006: 688, 693). This is where *fantasy* enters the picture. In Lacanian theory, fantasy is a feature of the psyche that *stimulates desire by promising to eliminate the lack in the symbolic order*.

How does this work? Sociologist Glyn Daly (1999) offers an analogy. Think of a computer hacker who tries to break into a computer system. The hacker knows that the system contains valuable data, but it is password protected. Now, what is the worst case scenario for the hacker? It would be the message "Access Impossible" on the screen. This would mean the end of the hacker's hope to obtain the data. However, if the screen flashes "Access Denied," it means that the secret is in principle accessible and that whatever force is blocking the data is ultimately *vincible*. In this latter scenario the hacker's desire for his goal can be sustained by the conviction that the secret is really *obtainable*, and that it is only *temporarily blocked* by someone/something (Daly 1999: 221–22).

This is also how ideological fantasy works. Instead of a computer hacker we have the subject in search of a stable identity. The ultimate horror for the subject would be to find that completeness of identity is impossible because there is a lack in the discourse itself ("Access Impossible"). But if the subject can recast the *permanent* blockage of stable identity as a mere *temporary* blockage ("Access Denied"), then desire can be sustained and the quest for the final lacking signifier may continue. The ideological "work" performed by fantasy is thus *to produce a scenario in which the precious identity remains obtainable if only some temporary, contingent obstacle is removed.*[3]

The Fantasy Enemy

How does ideological fantasy work in the world of politics? Žižek gives the example of anti-Semitism in the Third Reich. Nazi ideology promoted the vision of one country, one state, one people—that is to say, a corporatist notion of a harmonious *Volksgemeinschaft*. This Nazi Utopia, however, was contradicted by the pervasive crisis of the Weimar Republic after World War I. So how could the utopian vision of the united German people be squared with the experience of social and economic turmoil?

> The answer is, of course, the Jew: an external element, a foreign body introducing corruption into the sound social fabric. In short, "Jew" is a fetish which simultaneously denies and embodies the structural impossibility of "Society": it is as if in the figure of the Jew this impossibility had acquired a positive, palpable existence—and that is why it marks the eruption of enjoyment into the social field (Žižek 2008: 142).

Thanks to this fantasy scapegoat, critical questions about German society itself could be evaded; if there were any visible problems they could simply be attributed to the "Jewish conspiracy."

The demonization of the Jews relied on two important discursive moves: *displacement* and *condensation*. First, all the problematic features of society were displaced onto the Jews as the source of society's corruption. Instead of a society disfigured by *immanent* antagonism, the fantasy scenario set up an antagonism between sound German society on one side, and the pathological Jew on the other. Unable to grasp the logic of capitalist development, Nazi anti-Semitism dreamt up a division between "organic" German class cooperation on one side and exploitation of the productive classes by "parasitic" Jewish merchants and bankers on the other (Žižek 2008: 141).

Second, this displacement was supported by condensation, whereby the Jew was seen as embodying all the negative and unpleasant traits associated with both the upper and lower classes. The enemy figure was invested with a whole series

---

3 It should be noted that fantasy, as conceived by Lacan and Žižek, is not a mechanism that is activated only on occasion. Rather, it is present as an ideological support structure of *all* reality-experience. On this view, fantasy works as a defense against castration in language. When the failure of discourse threatens to throw us face to face with the traumatic real, fantasy intervenes and offers us socially constructed "reality" as a bearable substitute. Fantasy covers over the antagonistic fissure on which the discourse is founded, so that we can convince ourselves that a stable identity remains possible (Žižek 2008: 45).

of "heterogeneous antagonisms: economic (Jew as a profiteer), political (Jew as schemer, retainer of secret power), moral-religious (Jew as corrupt anti-Christian), sexual (Jew as seducer of our innocent girls)" (Žižek 2008: 141).

Symbolic displacement and condensation, however, cannot fully account for the "stickiness effect" of Nazi anti-Semitism. This effect must rather be located in a particular *affective* bond—that is, the desire to overcome castration and recover lost *jouissance*. And this is exactly what the fantasy of the enemy-Jew offered the subjects of Nazi discourse. Thus, instead of looking for causes of social disharmony in the constitution of society itself—such as for example capitalism's recurrent crises, its structural need for unemployment, its inevitable class conflict, or its incentives for imperialist war—Nazi ideology produced one single *positive* explanation: our misfortune is all because of the malicious Jew who is intent on destroying our precious community! As Žižek points out, it is in fact typical of ideological fantasy to attribute to the Other an alien form of *jouissance*. The Other seems to have access to a perverse enjoyment that manifests itself in a will to sabotage that which is ours or rob us of some precious "national-Thing" we believe to have in our possession.[4]

In the real world, of course, the Jews had nothing to do with the social crisis:

> Society is not prevented from achieving its full identity because of Jews: it is prevented by its own antagonistic nature, by its own immanent blockage, and it "projects" this internal negativity into the figure of the "Jew." In other words, what is excluded from the Symbolic (from the frame of the corporatist socio-symbolic order) returns in the Real as a paranoid construction of the "Jew" (Žižek 2008: 143).

The point here is that the figure of the intrusive Jew actually allowed the Nazi discourse to be sustained. It may seem paradoxical that totalitarian utopianism was stimulated by the same phenomenon that was said to undermine it, but as Žižek points out "*fantasy is a means for an ideology to take its own failure into account in advance*" (Žižek 2008: 142, emphasis original). In a sense then, fascism "knew" that it would ultimately fail to fully hegemonize the discursive field—but thanks to ideological fantasy it never had to perform this impossible feat.

Žižek's interpretation of ideological fantasy can be applied to many other real-world episodes. Consider, for example, Stalin's show trials of "enemies of

4 Modern racism, Žižek says, imputes to the enemy "an excessive enjoyment: he wants to steal our enjoyment (by ruining our way of life) and/or he has access to some secret, perverse enjoyment. In short, what really bothers us about the 'other' is the peculiar way he organizes his enjoyment, precisely the surplus, the 'excess' that pertains to this way: the smell of 'their' food, 'their' noisy songs and dances, 'their' strange manners, 'their' attitude to work. To the racist, the 'other' is either a workaholic stealing our jobs or an idler living on our labor, and it is quite amusing to notice the haste with which one passes from reproaching the other with a refusal to work to reproaching him for the theft of work." (Žižek 1993: 203)

socialism," or the "red scare" in McCarthyist America. In past eras, we can trace similar fantasies in the Roman oppression of Christians, as well as in the Christian church's own persecution of heretics and the witch-hunts (see Stavrakakis 1999: 101–7). And currently, it is quite apparent that European right-wing populism feeds on the fantasy of the intrusive "immigrant" in general, and the "Muslim" in particular. In all these cases, Žižek affirms, the task of the critique of ideology must be to invert the causality identified by the reactionary gaze. Today's "immigrant" bears no more responsibility for the current social and economic malaise than the "Jew" did in the Weimar Republic. On the contrary, the "immigrant" is only a *symptom*—the point where society's immanent negativity takes on a positive form in fantasy. According to Žižek then, the task is to identify the moment of a discourse that expresses its own constitutive impossibility—that is to say, the phenomenon that is identified as the prime obstacle to the realization of social harmony. Within the framework of fantasy, this phenomenon often takes the shape of an enemy who is perceived as the positive cause of social disorder. Consequently, the elimination of the enemy will seem necessary to obtain or retrieve a lost harmony. But if we follow the Lacanian advice to "identify" with the symptom and "go through the fantasy" we might just find that there is simply nothing there and that the problems we experience—inequality, unemployment, crime, powerlessness, poverty, war, and so on—are nothing but the *normal products of our own social organization* (Žižek 2008: 144).

The Ideological Fantasy of Animal Welfare

Based on the discussion above, I suggest the following schematization of the ideological operation that makes discourses "stick" with the subject:

1. Human subjects are castrated in language and hence suffer from an irreducible lack that is experienced as a loss of *jouissance* (enjoyment).
2. The subject attempts to fill this lack and retrieve the lost enjoyment by identification with collective objects and identities made available in discourse.
3. Discourse (the symbolic order, the Big Other) also suffers from lack in the form of constitutive social antagonism. There is no transcendental center that can guarantee the stability of a discursive formation.
4. Ideological fantasy conceals the lack in the discourse by—
   a. displacing the cause of social disharmony from society's immanent antagonism onto an external or internal enemy-obstacle;
   b. condensing heterogeneous social problems into the enemy-obstacle; and
   c. promising the achievement of future harmony, or the restoration of a previously existing but lost stability, if only the enemy-obstacle can be eliminated.
5. By framing social harmony as blocked by a contingent force and not constitutively impossible, fantasy sustains desire and secures loyalty to the discourse.

My argument is that animal welfare discourse fits very well into this schema. Moreover, the fantasmatic aspect of animal welfarism is important because it may account for much of the historical stability of speciesist practices and attitudes.

Hegemony, we have seen, is historical and relative. It has no final guarantee and cannot eliminate all cracks in the social facade. This is true also for the hegemony of animal welfare discourse. While this discourse is hegemonic in the sense that a very large majority subscribes to its worldview, it is also traversed by inconsistent and contradictory norms. Here in the Western world, for example, eating cows is considered "normal," while eating dogs or cats is anathema. Similarly, within our own culture, we make great moral distinctions between different animals like, say, the family dog and the industry pig. Moreover, few people are completely unaware of the ill-treatment of animals going on in the animal industries. When issues like these are brought up in conversation, people often express bewilderment over the great cultural differences and they are very ready to condemn the excesses of industrial animal husbandry. While the hegemonic animal welfare discourse—fuelled by corporate and political propaganda—tries to smooth over these contradictions, hypocrisy is still detectable by many people, even those who have not spent much time studying animal rights philosophy.

This means that the discourses governing the human–animal relationship are not fully fixed in our time (if they ever were). While it is true that speciesist practices continue to go on as usual on a gargantuan scale, it is also true that only very few people can escape all sense of anxiety regarding their involvement in animal exploitation. Therefore, the stability of speciesist practices over time can neither be attributed to total ignorance about the treatment of non-human animals, nor to the elegant coherence of a convincing but mystifying discourse ("false consciousness"). The opposite is often the case. People *do* know—and feel—that "the right thing to do" is to care about animals. People *do* know that animals are often mistreated. People *do* know that our norms regarding animal treatment are jumbled and contradictory. People *do* know that we say one thing and do another.

Now, it is hardly news that humans are proficient in rationalizing their behavior, filtering out disturbing information, and denying the implications of their actions (see Milgram 1974, Agnew 1998, Cohen 2001, Sollund 2008 and this volume). Therefore, it will come as no surprise that the answer to the problem of animal mistreatment under the regime of welfarism is nearly always—more welfarism. The assumption seems to be that more state regulation or more corporate responsibility is all that is needed to overcome the perceived problems (this is perhaps especially so in countries with high trust in official institutions). The converse of this assumption is that animal mistreatment is hardly ever seen as a consequence of the everyday consumption of animal products. Transferring responsibility to the state and bringing in animal protection legislation as a proxy for individual responsibility thus appears as a clever solution that allows the consumer to love animals and eat them too.

An interpretation along these lines is in fact typical for the abolitionist animal rights position. But while this analysis goes some way toward explaining the attractiveness of welfarist discourse, it also leaves out some crucial aspects of the ideological process which may be clarified with the help of psychoanalytical theory.

If we look at the issue from the Lacanian standpoint outlined above, we could argue, first, that animal mistreatment lays bare a lack at the level of the subject. We have all been socialized to believe in kindness to animals and to abhor animal cruelty. But this idealized self-image is tarnished by unavoidable knowledge about the treatment of animals, and the troubling feeling that we are implicated in it ourselves.

Second, this lack on the subjective level is not eliminated—it is only redoubled—when the subject turns to the official discourse on how animals ought to be treated. Here, it is often apparent that when it comes to animals, our society says one thing and does another. Under these conditions, how does animal welfarism manage to sustain itself as desirable object for the subject's identification?

The answer, we could speculate, is ideological fantasy. As we have seen, fantasy stabilizes a discursive formation by restaging its immanent antagonism as a contingent and eliminable obstacle. Thus, the promise of an obtainable social harmony can be sustained and the desire to identify with the hegemonic discourse can be upheld. In the context of animal welfarism, fantasy holds out the promise of ethically unproblematic relations between humans and animals. This promise is typically envisioned as a future improvement of animal husbandry that will soon be realized by welfare reform. Alternatively, the promise is envisioned as the return to a lost "Golden Age" of idyllic, small-scale farming practices characterized by organic relations between humans, animals, and nature in general (see Riise, this volume). In both cases, the fantasy scenario offers to abolish all anxiety pertaining to our treatment of animals.

Unfortunately, in the real world this Utopia of non-controversial animal use seems infinitely delayed. As mentioned above, even after two centuries of animal protection efforts—including the adoption of animal welfare ideology by the state, the animal industrial complex, and the public—more animals than ever before are used under conditions that are, most probably, worse than ever. In ideological fantasy, however, these problems are not perceived as immanent to our speciesist society. Rather, fantasy offers a scenario where harmonious human–animal relations are potentially possible—even close at hand—but at the same time perpetually deferred. There is always some contingent obstacle blocking the full realization of our animal-friendly intentions. And as in racist discourse, this obstacle tends to be produced by displacement and condensation.

Displacement and Condensation of Animal Abuse

The pattern of displacement is well known to many frustrated animal advocates. Whenever a problem arises from institutionalized animal use—for example, when journalists or activists reveal another "animal cruelty scandal"—the typical response is to displace the problem from the system itself to some kind of contingent deviation. When excessive cruelty in a factory farm or at a slaughterhouse grabs public attention, this is usually represented by the industry and its political allies as a mere glitch in otherwise well-oiled machinery. Similarly, when animal abuse is revealed at a farm, the individual farmer is either defended by industry organizations, or—if the charges cannot be denied—denounced as a "bad egg" that is not representative of the business. If these "scandals" ever lead to concrete reform measures, these are usually restricted to commissioning some kind of inquiry or firing a few workers (only to replace them with others so that business can go on). Only rarely is someone prosecuted under the law, and when this occasionally happens, the punishment is unlikely to affect decision-makers at the higher levels of corporate hierarchy.

Moreover, when modern factory farming practices are pointed out as detrimental to animal welfare, the accusations are often directed toward abstract phenomena like "technology" or "economy," rather than toward the concrete actors choosing to invest in intensive rearing systems. Representations like these produce the impression that factory farming is something that simply "happens" to our society and to animals. It is as if we were talking about the fluctuations of the weather rather than the outcome of choices made by real people with a real profit interest in making them. Alternatively, the problem is framed as one of technology "gone too far," rather than as a reflection of a social structure where animals are systematically reduced to the status of property and commodities. Here again, we often hear the call for a return to small-scale, organic animal husbandry as a solution—as if such a return was even a remote possibility in a world characterized by intense market competition and ever-increasing consumption of animal products. (At most, this fantasy has been instrumental in creating a profitable niche for marketing expensive but purportedly "happy" meat to middle-class bohemians—all, of course, without raising critical questions about the moral standing of animals.)

Another common move is to displace the problem of animal cruelty onto socially marginalized, "deviant" individuals. Consider such imaginary personae as the isolated lunatic who kills neighborhood cats; the stereotypical "crazy cat lady" who take on too many strays to keep them fed and healthy; the drunken farmer who cannot tend to his cows; the drug addict who abuses his dog; the sexually perverted zoophile; or the gang of young boys who turn juvenile shenanigans into animal torture, and so on. In animal welfare discourse, "bogeymen" like these tend to excite immense public anger and often figure as targets for legal or police action.

Another recurrent enemy figure in animal welfare discourse is the foreigner or the immigrant/ethnic minority. In the first case, the enemy is located abroad. The major problems with animal mistreatment, we are told, are to be found in other countries and not here among us. Here in Sweden, for example, it is often said that we have the best animal protection legislation in the world. (Unsurprisingly, similar claims are made in many other countries, and to the same general effect; there is no need for change *here*, consumers can feel safe.) This nationalistic pride goes hand in hand with an implicit or explicit deprecation of other countries or people. (In Swedish animal welfare discourse, the typical culprits tend to be Eastern or Southern Europeans, Asians, or people from the Middle East, though our neighbors in Denmark also figure prominently.) Moreover, the domestic animal industries often involve themselves in meat-nationalistic propaganda for protectionist reasons, and politicians tend to follow suit in order to safeguard jobs and maintain economic competitiveness.

Similarly, immigrants and ethnic minorities are sometimes targeted as "enemies within" for their treatment of animals. The best known historical example is probably *shechita*—the ceremonial slaughter of animals without prior stunning to produce *kosher* meat—the vilification of which has often been intertwined with a wish to stigmatize Jewish communities. Today, European right-wing populists seem to prefer Muslim targets, and here again the specter of the Other's inherent animal cruelty—manifested in the production of *halal* meat—is often invoked. The result, of course, is the neutralization and normalization of "our" own slaughter practices. (If ideology is not about producing wrong answers but about asking the wrong questions, then the persistent debates over what kind of slaughter—"ours" or "theirs"—is the most "humane," constitute a prime example of ideology.)

Disproportionate attention to the animal cruelty of the deviant or ethnic Other fits well into discourse theorist Teun van Dijk's "ideological square," a device intended to capture the polarization of in-group and out-group through discursive description (van Dijk 1998: 33). The typical functional moves here are to:

1. Emphasize our good properties/actions
2. Emphasize their bad properties/actions
3. Mitigate our bad properties/actions
4. Mitigate their good properties/actions.

Van Dijk refers mainly to racist and sexist discourse, but nationalist animal welfarism often produces a similar pattern of representations. In short, "our" animal cruelty is represented as *accidental*, whereas "their" animal cruelty is represented as *essential*.

This negative out-group representation brings us to the question of fantasmatic *condensation*. In animal welfare discourse, a whole series of negative and immoral traits tend to be condensed into the problematic Other. Often the enemy figure is seen as having an alien mode of *jouissance*, very different from our own: how can the animal abusers behave like that? Must it not be because they—actually, secretly, perversely—*enjoy* harming animals?

Thus framed in fantasy, the Others are not only perceived as *different* from ourselves, they also represent an active *threat* to something we hold dear—in this case our society's love for animals.[5] And when this mindset of disgusted fascination

5 Something similar is involved in the common suspicion directed at the motives of animal rights advocates: where does their enjoyment of weird vegan food come from? And why do they want to ruin our enjoyment of meat? Must it not be because they enjoy

takes hold, regulating and disciplining the Other's actions tend to take priority over systemic critique. We zealously defend our national-Thing, the *cosa nostra* of animal friendliness, oblivious to the fact that we never truly possessed this Thing to begin with. The enemy is charged with theft/sabotage of something that never existed. Yet this is precisely why the enemy is needed—to keep the *real* of the human–animal relationship at bay. The presence of the animal abuser sustains the illusion that harmonious human–animal relations can be achieved, and thus stimulates our desire to identify with animal welfarism. At the same time, however, this enemy cannot be fully eliminated without the traumatic acknowledgement that animal cruelty is everywhere—*that it is a perfectly normal product of a society like ours*. This means that even if one bogeyman is neutralized, new culprits will always be in demand to explain the continued absence of harmony (Daly 1999). The fantasmatic restaging of speciesist society as a basically animal-friendly place that is, unfortunately, sabotaged by a small animal-abusing minority, is simply animal welfarism's way of taking its own failure into account in advance (see Žižek 2008: 142).

Above all, the ideological fantasy of animal welfare ensures that the atrocities of speciesism are never located within the framework of our "normal" social processes. Whatever animals need protection from, it is not from "us," the everyday consumers of meat, milk, and eggs, even though it is the normality of these food habits that fuel the entire system. Everyone agrees that "animals need protection," but no one adds "from me." When the consumer occasionally figures in animal welfare discourse, it tends to be only as a "victim" in one of the recurrent "food scandals" (the consumer has unwittingly bought animal-derived products produced using cruel methods). In short, "we" never harm animals, only "they" do.

Conclusions

In hegemonic animal welfare discourse, the promise is held out that all anxiety-inducing aspects of the human–animal relationship may be purged once and for all. In Lacanian terms, animal welfarism offers the lacking subject a secure identity in being "animal friendly," thus relieving it of guilt over complicity in animal exploitation. This stable identity, however, can only be obtained if the contradictions of the speciesist social order are masked or covered over. This is where fantasy intervenes to produce an enemy-obstacle which serves as an explanation of the lack in the social structure. In the context of animal welfare discourse, the enemy often takes the form of a deviant or racialized animal abuser,

---

acting morally superior and taking pleasure in sabotaging our way of life? Consider also the eruption of *jouissance* in the case of Swedish wolf hunting, as discussed by Korsell and Hagstedt (this volume), where heated feelings are aroused among many hunters over what is perceived as attempts by national and EU authorities to rob them of their enjoyment and ruin their lifestyle.

or, more abstractly, figures as the threat of impersonal technological or economic development. By the twin maneuvers of displacement and condensation, the culpability for animal abuse is transferred from "us" onto this enemy-obstacle. Consequently, animal welfarism can continue to interpellate us as loyal subjects even though its efficacy is challenged by empirical experience.

Much of the stability of animal welfare as a hegemonic discourse thus lies in its fantasy support, in its ability to manipulate a kernel of *jouissance*, enjoyment, in its subjects. It is in this sense that animal welfarism *needs* the animal abuser to play the role of a blockage to the subject's fulfillment. As Nietzsche once wrote: "Anyone who lives for the sake of battling an enemy, has an interest in keeping that enemy alive" (1995: 271). But the real blockage does not lie in the enemy figure. It is immanent to speciesist society itself, which is incapable of reconciling ethical principles and empathic intuitions with systemic violence and killing. A critical theory of speciesism would therefore take note of the animal abuser as a *symptom*—that is to say, as a fantasmatic positivization of the social antagonism, a condensation point for the immanent negativity which has to be repressed for the discourse of animal welfare to constitute itself to begin with. If we "traverse the fantasy" in this way, we will likely find that there was nothing there—except for the normal, everyday functioning of our own speciesist society.

References

Adams, C.J. 1990. *The Sexual Politics of Meat: A Feminist-Vegetarian Critique*. Cambridge: Polity Press.

Agnew, R. 1998. The causes of animal abuse: a social-psychological analysis. *Theoretical Criminology*, 2, 177–209.

Bailly, L. 2009. *Lacan. A Beginner's Guide*. Oxford: Oneworld Publications.

Beirne, P. 1999. For a non-speciesist criminology: animal abuse as an object of study. *Criminology*, 37, 117–47.

Beirne, P. 2007. Animal rights, animal abuse and green criminology, in *Issues in Green Criminology: Confronting Harms against Environments, Humanity and Other Animals*, edited by P. Beirne and N. South. Portland, OR: Willan Publishing, 32–54.

Birke, L. 1994. *Feminism, Animals and Science: The Naming of the Shrew*. Buckingham: Open University Press.

Burr, V. 2003. *Social Constructionism*. 2nd Edition. London: Routledge.

Cazaux, G. 1999. Beauty and the beast: animal abuse from a nonspeciesist criminological perspective. *Crime, Law and Social Change*, 31, 105–26.

Cazaux, G. and Beirne, P. 2006. *Animal abuse, in The Sage Dictionary of Criminology*, edited by E. McLaughlin and J. Munice. London: Sage, 10–11.

Cohen, S. 2001. *States of Denial: Knowing about Atrocities and Suffering*. Cambridge: Polity.

Daly, G. 1999. Ideology and its paradoxes: dimensions of fantasy and enjoyment. *Journal of Political Ideologies*, 4(2), 219–38.

Derrida, J. 2001. *Writing and Difference*. Reprint. London: Routledge.

Descartes, R. 1641. *Meditations (II)*. 2008 Edition. New York: Cosimo.

Dunayer, J. 1995. Sexist words, speciesist roots, in *Animals & Women: Feminist Theoretical Explorations*, edited by C.J. Adams and J. Donovan. Durham, NC: Duke.

Dunayer, J. 2001. *Animal Equality: Language and Liberation*. Derwood, MD: Ryce Publishers.

Dunayer, J. 2004. *Speciesism*. Derwood, MD: Ryce Publishers.

Fink, B. 1995. *The Lacanian Subject: Between Language and Jouissance*. Princeton, NJ: Princeton University Press.

Foucault, M. [1969] 2002. *The Archaeology of Knowledge*. London: Routledge.

Francione, G.L. 1996. *Rain Without Thunder: The Ideology of the Animal Rights Movement*. Philadelphia: Temple University Press.

Francione, G.L. 2008. *Animals as Persons: Essays on the Abolition of Animal Exploitation*. New York: Columbia University Press.

Francione, G.L. and Garner, R. 2010. *The Animal Rights Debate: Abolition or Regulation?* New York: Columbia University Press.

Gålmark, L. 2005. *Skönheter och odjur. En feministisk kritik av djur-människa-relationen*. [Beauties and Beasts: A Feminist Critique of the Human-Animal Relationship]. Stockholm: Makadam.

Gålmark, L. 2008. Aristotle revisited: anthro-androcentrism and meat normativity, in *Global Harms: Ecological Crime and Speciesism*, edited by R. Sollund. New York: Nova, 87–108.

Hall, L. 2006. *Capers in the Churchyard: Animal Rights Advocacy in the Age of Terror*. Darien, CT: Nectar Bat Press.

Hall, L. 2010. *On Their Own Terms: Bringing Animal-Rights Philosophy Down to Earth*. Darien, CT: Nectar Bat Press.

Howarth, D. and Stavrakakis, Y. 2000. Introducing discourse theory and political analysis, in *Discourse Theory and Political Analysis*, edited by D. Howarth, A. Norval, and Y. Stavrakakis. Manchester: Manchester University Press.

Jokkala, T. and Strindlund, P. 2003. *Djurrätt och socialism* [Animal Rights and Socialism]. Gothenburg: Lindelöws förlag.

Lacan, J. 1993. *The Seminar. Book III. The Psychoses 1955–1956*, edited by J.-A. Miller. London: Routledge.

Lacan, J. 1998. *The Seminar. Book XX. Encore, On Feminine Sexuality, The Limits of Love and Knowledge, 1972–1973*, edited by J.-A. Miller. London and New York: Norton.

Lacan, J. Écrits. *The First Complete Edition in English*. London and New York: Norton.

Laclau, E. and Mouffe, C. 1985. *Hegemony and Socialist Strategy: Toward a Radical Democratic Politics*. London: Verso Books.

Laclau, E. and Mouffe, C. 1991. Port-Marxism without Apologies, in *New Reflections on the Revolution of Our Time*, edited by E. Laclau. London: Verso Books.
Lapsley, R. 2006. Psychoanalytic criticism, in *The Routledge Companion to Critical Theory*, edited by S. Malpas and P. Wake. London: Routledge.
McGowan, K. 2006. Structuralism and semiotics, in *The Routledge Companion to Critical Theory*, edited by S. Malpas and P. Wake. London: Routledge.
Milgram, S. 1974. *Obedience to Authority: An Experimental View*. New York: Harper & Row.
Nietzsche, F.W. 1995. *Human, All Too Human*. (Part I). Stanford: Stanford University Press.
Nibert, D.A. 2002. *Animal Rights/Human Rights: Entanglements of Oppression and Liberation*. Lanham, MD: Rowman & Littlefield.
Patterson, C. 2002. *Eternal Treblinka: Our Treatment of Animals and the Holocaust*. New York: Lantern Books.
Singer, P. 2002. *Animal Liberation*. New York: Ecco, Harper Collins Publishers.
Sollund, R. 2008. Causes for speciesism: difference, distance and denial, in *Global Harms: Ecological Crime and Speciesism*, edited by R. Sollund. New York: Nova, 109–30.
Spiegel, M. 1989. *The Dreaded Comparison: Human and Animal Slavery*. New York: Mirror Books.
Stavrakakis, Y. 1999. *Lacan and the Political*. New York: Routledge.
Stavrakakis, Y. 2007. *The Lacanian Left: Psychoanalysis, Theory, Politics*. Albany: State University of New York Press.
Strindlund, P. 2011. *Jordens herrar: Slaveri, djurförtryck och våldets försvarare* [Lords of the Earth: Slavery, Animal Oppression and the Defenders of Violence]. Stockholm: Karneval.
Svärd, P.-A. 2008. Protecting the animals? An abolitionist critique of animal welfarism and green ideology, in *Global Harms: Ecological Crime and Speciesism*, edited by R. Sollund. New York: Nova, 167–86.
Svärd, P.-A. 2011. Beyond welfarist morality: an abolitionist reply to Fetissenko. *Journal of Animal Ethics*, 1(2).
Torres, B. 2007. *Making a Killing: The Political Economy of Animal Rights*. Oakland, CA: AK Press.
van Dijk, T.A. 1998. Opinions and ideologies in the press, in *Approaches to Media Discourse*, edited by A. Bell and P. Garrett. Oxford; Malden: Blackwell, 21–63.
Winther Jørgensen, M. and Phillips, L. 2002. *Discourse Analysis as Theory and Method*. London: Sage.
Žižek, S. 1993. *Tarrying With the Negative: Kant, Hegel, and the Critique of Ideology*. Durham: Duke University Press.
Žižek, S. 1997. The abyss of freedom, in *The Abyss of Freedom/Ages of the World*, edited by S. Žižek and F.W.J. Schelling. Ann Arbor: University of Michigan Press.
Žižek, S. 2008. *The Sublime Object of Ideology*. London: Verso Books.

Chapter 8
Natural Exploitation: The Shaping of the Human–animal Relationship through Concepts and Statements

Ingvill H. Riise

Introduction

To be an *animal* in our society means being a *thing* and a possession.[1] It means being both on the inside: to live among humans, and on the outside: outside of the protective ethical boundary that ensures basic rights. Why is it that 'animals'[2] are still regarded as inferior – that they find themselves at the bottom of the social hierarchy? How is it done – which concepts and statements are employed to keep it that way? Despite an increasing focus on 'the welfare of animals' and talk of their 'intrinsic value', non-humans can be exploited for practically any purpose that is defined as 'useful'. This means that they are used in the production of food and clothes, and as instruments in research and education. They are objects of entertainment in circuses, zoos and television programmes. They are sold as pets, used as tools in competitive sports and hunted for recreation. Their own needs and wants are subject to a human agenda.

Here, I will discuss some of the ways in which this power relationship is made to seem *natural*. More specifically, I look at how exploitation is expressed in a

1 There are different kinds of property status 'animals' can be subject to, and what determines which one they will get is to what extent they have been made a part of the human society: while 'domesticated animals' are personal property or the property of institutions, free-living or 'wild' 'animals' are in one respect the property of the state; they are seen as 'resources' that can and should be 'managed' and 'harvested' (see Dunayer 2001: 51–6).

2 The word 'animal' is in itself contributing to the maintenance of a moral divide between 'humans' on one side, and 'animals' on the other. According to this division, humans are not 'animals' even though they are biologically related to the beings in this category. Here I will therefore write 'animals' in quotation marks or use the term 'non-human' – as in 'non-human animals' – or 'other animals'. Though this also divides animals in two groups, it is relevant here to demonstrate that one group has moral and legal rights, and the other does not.

central political document (White Paper) entitled *Proposition to the Storting nr. 12 (2002–2003): Animal Husbandry and Animal Welfare*.[3] I will henceforth refer to it as 'the White Paper'. Today, eight years after its publication, it is still of importance to the way non-humans are being perceived and treated in Norway. As far as the ethical framework is concerned, little – if anything – has changed in those eight years. The White Paper represents the dominant and official view of how humans should relate to 'animals'; though being a specific Norwegian political document, it also represents the current ethical framework and settings for debate in the Western part of the world. It exemplifies the common perception of 'animals' and of their place in the social hierarchy. The concepts and statements confirming their inferior status are similar in many countries.

I aim to show how language is employed by the authorities to shape the human–animal relationship; how the exploitation of non-humans is being upheld through the use of conceptual power. By 'conceptual power' I mean the power of signs and symbols; statements uttered from persons or groups in a position of authority. This form of power is thoroughly described in feminist standpoint theory, by Sandra Harding, Nancy Hartsock and Dorothy Smith, among others (Harding (ed.) 2004). They show how conceptual frameworks in themselves promote specific institutional and cultural interests, and that those have not been the interests of women and other oppressed groups – but rather in conflict with these (Harding 2004). Here I aim to give a glimpse into the concept of 'animal inferiority', and the use of conceptual power; in the form of singular words, sentences and statements. They constitute parts of a whole system of thinking – an anthropocentric view of reality – that is taken for granted.

Since language and action are connected, the discourse produces reality (Neumann 2001: 60). In this case it produces a group – 'animals' – that can be exploited. And it is by the help of certain statements that the exploitation can be made to seem natural. I will therefore analyze statements that are particularly significant – as carriers of a certain view of 'animals', and how one should relate to them. The dominant view of reality must be upheld by continuous repetitions of statements (Neumann 2001: 143), and the White Paper is a good example of this process. Since statements are expressions of different interests and of power, one can say something about their context by analyzing them. An analysis can reveal who has the power to shape the 'official' reality; to determine which are considered 'valid' and 'legitimate' viewpoints, and which are not. Such an analysis can also demonstrate which sanctions are being imposed on holders of 'illegitimate' viewpoints.

Recognizing the role of language as a major means of transmitting normative values, green criminologist Piers Beirne (2007) notes that 'we humans routinely discriminate against non-human animals with our everyday usage of "speciesist language"' (Beirne 2007: 62). Joan Dunayer, linguist and animal rights advocate,

3 In Norwegian the document is called Stortingsmelding nr. 12 (2002–03): Om dyrehold og dyrevelferd.

defines 'speciesism' as 'a failure, in attitude or practice, to accord any nonhuman being equal consideration and respect' (Dunayer 2004: 5). She has thoroughly analysed how speciesism pervades our language; how it both perpetuates and masks the exploitation of non-human animals (Dunayer 2001, see also Adams 1990). As Beirne also notes, the distinction between humans and other animals carries with it a cumbersome cultural baggage, and causes many humans not to see themselves as animals at all. We refer to humans as 'human beings' without hesitation, yet do not use the term 'animal beings' when referring to non-human animals (2007: 62–3).

Because of the role of language in bolstering or challenging conventional power relations, Beirne is among those who call for a radical revision of speciesist terminology (Beirne 2007: 63). White Papers concerning the human–animal relationship can be starting points from which to analyse the role of speciesist language in constructing the notion of other animals as inferior and exploitable beings. White Papers are not only an expression of official values and politics, but also of the everyday use of language as it must be met and accepted by the public. It thus also says something about the common perception of 'animals' in the country of publication.

The Norwegian White Paper is part of a discourse and process of change that is going on in many countries; there is to some degree an ongoing debate about the moral status of non-humans. There is increasing knowledge about the emotional and psychological aspects of the lives of other animals, and of how certain practices influence their physical and emotional wellbeing. These are also important reasons for Geertrui Cazaux (1999, 2007) and Beirne (2007) to call for a non-speciesist criminology. Cazaux points out that:

> 'Speciesism' is understood in the same way as more established concepts in the social sciences, e.g. sexism and racism, respectively referring to discrimination on the basis of animal species, gender and ethnicity (Cazaux 1999: 106).

According to Beirne, the environmentalist-based discourse of green criminology and the animal-centred discourse of animal rights also have much in common (Beirne 2007: 55). He notes that:

> [...] in terms of their ethical perspectives and much of their theoretical assumptions, both movements have an underlying concern with relations of power and inequality and with the elimination of their undesirable effects. These latter include harm, exclusion, injury and suffering (Beirne 2007: 56).

A very important link between animal rights and environmental issues, Beirne points out, is the exploitation of non-humans in the agricultural industry. Intensive rearing regimes are a major cause of global warming and seriously threaten the long-term existence of *all* life on our planet (Beirne 2007: 75). The exploitation of non-humans in the agricultural sector is also an underlying topic for my analysis of the speciesist language in the White Paper.

This chapter examines the role of some ethically significant terms and concepts in the process of legitimization of non-human harm and exploitation. The chapter also examines the ways that society avoids the debate about fundamental ethical questions related to exploitative practices. I will focus on two of the many ways in which 'naturalness' is created:

1. The repetition of statements is supposed to back up existing exploitative practices, and ensure their continuation. These statements are both morally significant and politically powerful, but are nevertheless – or rather because of this – exempt from discussion. I also look at the role of terms such as 'intrinsic value' and 'animal welfare'.
2. How is resistance to the dominant world view met; what is done to 'unwanted' viewpoints, and how are the persons holding them being described.

The White Paper on Animal Husbandry and Animal Welfare

The White Paper was, according to the introduction, written in the light of 'increasing knowledge of the behaviour and needs of animals',[4] and 'increasing consumer interest' (LD 2002–03: 9–10). And with the aim of 'improving the welfare of animals, raising ethical debate and providing a basis for changes in legislation' (LD 2002–03: Reader's guide). It was also written because of what is termed 'structural changes in agriculture'; industrialization and mechanization at the expense of 'animal welfare' (LD 2002–03: 9, 31–47). Interestingly, nothing is said about *who* is responsible for these changes – it seems as though it all 'just happened', and that there was nothing anybody could do about it. As Per-Anders Svärd (this volume) points out, society places the responsibility for non-human suffering on abstract phenomena like 'technology' or 'economy'. It is thus not presented as the result of a power relationship, the interests of industries or of ethical choices. The White Paper exemplifies this technique of neutralization; the denial of individual responsibility (Sollund, this volume).

Being written by the Ministry of Agriculture however, the purpose of the White Paper has everything to do with the interests of certain groups. The Ministry of Agriculture (which is now called the Ministry of Agriculture and Food) is a powerful institution whose main task is to ensure a continued agricultural production; and thus maintain the interests of animal industries. The Ministry is

4 This knowledge concerns the discovery of more and more similarities between humans and other animals regarding all 'morally significant properties'; feelings, consciousness, language, thinking and culture. I have discussed the White Paper's presentation of these scientific discoveries in Riise (2010: 21–45).

also responsible for food policy.[5] At the same time, it is given the responsibility for 'animal welfare' in the agricultural industry; to suggest and implement changes – and thus meant to have a critical function. In that way, it functions both as the main promoter and the main critic of these industries. The Ministry of Agriculture wrote the White Paper in collaboration with The Norwegian Animal Health Authority,[6] and together the two institutions constitute a 'centre of expertise' on 'animals' and 'animal welfare'. The Ministry of Agriculture could thus produce an impressive 185-page thick document written by 'experts', full of statistics and colour illustrations, and with their official stamp on the front page; all of which contributes to giving the document great authority.

As a *White Paper* it is also a document belonging to a specific genre, and as such it is supposed to be harmonizing and coordinating, and meant to give guidelines for the future (LD 2002–03: 150), which indeed it has done: the Norwegian Animal Welfare Act (2009),[7] for instance, arose out of this document. Further to the functions of the White Paper, I would add *some reassurance*. The document describes in detail the suffering of non-humans in today's 'animal husbandry', with the consequence that some readers may be upset by the information. This makes it all the more important for the authorities to present it in a way which makes the reader feel that 'everything is under control'. The focus is directed towards 'improvements' to existing practices through 'animal welfare', and to the industries' own 'plans of action'. The White Paper will simply ensure an 'ethically defendable animal husbandry'. One therefore does not need to *worry*.

Throughout the process of making the document, it was possible for individuals and organizations to present their views and to suggest changes. In the end, however, these contributions – which were in some cases in opposition to the underlying principles of the White Paper – had no direct influence on its fundamental conditions. The document was still presented, both regarding ethics and aims, as an expression of 'the common interest' (LD 2002–03: 150). Having little or no influence on the final conclusions in the document, however, the contributions can be said to function as legitimization: they produce the impression that 'everyone's voice' was heard and taken into consideration in the process. The result of such a process can then be presented as 'objective' and 'neutral' (Trippestad 1999: 203).

Being a central political document, and containing an 'ethical platform' and 'guidelines for the future', the White Paper can be interpreted as a definitive statement about the human–animal relationship – at least at the time of publishing. With this authoritative position comes the power to define the premises for debate about ethical questions which helps determine reality. In this document, as in society in general, that means accepting the exploitation of non-humans as *natural*.

5 See the Ministry of Agriculture and Food's homepage: http://www.regjeringen.no/nb/dep/lmd/dep.html?id=632 [Accessed 2 June 2011].

6 The Norwegian Animal Health Authority is now a part of the Norwegian Food Safety Authority (Mattilsynet).

7 The Animal Welfare Act is a revision of the Animal Protection Act (1974).

The exploitation demands the use of symbolic boundaries that separate 'humans' from 'animals', 'nature' from 'culture' and 'us' from 'them'. It is also necessary to separate 'normal' viewpoints from 'abnormal' or 'divergent' ones. The White Paper thus plays a significant role in the maintenance and protection of these boundaries.

Significant Concepts and Statements – the Process of Legitimization

The White Paper contributes to the process of legitimization of non-human harm and exploitation by advancing the notion of 'animal inferiority', stating reality or describing non-human animals as objects to be used. This section looks at these issues, and also at how the White Paper's use of the terms 'intrinsic value' and 'animal welfare' backs up exploitative practices rather than ends them.

The Concept of Animal Inferiority

By the use of conceptual power, it is possible to foster a deterministic view of the relationship between humans and 'animals'. Hierarchy, dominance and exploitation are presented as *natural* and *unavoidable*. In the White Paper conceptual power is expressed, among other things, as the repetition of statements stressing the 'rightfulness' in exploiting 'animals', based on commonly accepted notions of 'animal inferiority'. This 'inferiority' is described in terms of 'lack of verbal language similar to that of humans' (LD 2002–03: 25), and 'inferior or second-rate cerebral cortex', since humans supposedly have a 'superior, first-rate one' (LD 2002–03: 25). Stressing the 'big size' and 'superiority' of the cerebral cortex is equivalent to stressing 'rationality', since this part of the brain is considered the 'home of rationality'.[8]

This way of categorizing and ranking based on 'scientific measurements' echoes the science of *craniology*. In the nineteenth century this preoccupation with cranial capacity supported sexism and racism by assessing brain size, relative development of different areas of the brain, and thus 'intelligence' itself (Steinem 1992: 133, see also Sollund 2008: 116). These 'findings' were then used to legitimize white male supremacy, and 'prove' the 'lower worth' of women and people of colour. Similarly, today's stressing of selected 'differences' between humans and 'animals' is no coincidence, since they constitute morally significant properties: 'rationality', for instance, is a prerequisite for being considered a 'morally responsible agent'. The possession or lack of these properties thus determine whether or not someone will be granted moral and legal rights.

However, this argument in turn also rests on the notion that these are 'superior' qualities *in themselves*, but this highly questionable assumption is generally seldom discussed, and never mentioned in the White Paper. Nor does it embark

8 I have discussed this in more detail in Riise (2010: 29–30).

on the potentially destabilizing discussion that the criterion of 'rationality' also excludes many humans from the moral community as well (Cavalieri 2001).

The understanding of 'superiority' relies heavily on the discoveries of natural science, and thus the anthropocentric (human-centred) ethics become inseparable. However, the very same science is at the same time 'making discoveries' of more and more similarities between humans and other animals, and is therefore continually pushing and destabilizing the moral boundary separating the two groups.[9] The 'solution' to this contradiction seems to be not to mention its radical implications at all – the ethical discussion continues 'as normal', or is avoided altogether.

Stating Reality

The first chapter in the White Paper referring to ethical issues states that:

> Animals are included as an important part of our society and our culture, and have been so for ages. Humans keep animals to satisfy basic needs for food and clothing, but animals and animal products are also used for a great many other purposes. In today's society we commonly keep animals for companionship, entertainment and sport. The areas of use are continuously expanding (LD 2002–03: 17).[10]

Here, as in the rest of the document, the White Paper employs the term 'use' to describe the way humans relate to other animals. To 'use' someone – as opposed to *exploit* them – is something one 'just does' without further need of explanation. The word 'use' thus describes an interaction that is taken for granted; it is seen as 'natural'. The word 'exploitation', on the other hand, describes a persistent social relationship in which certain individuals or groups are being mistreated or unfairly used for the benefit of others. It involves using others as mere means to an end, with little or no consideration for their wellbeing.[11]

Words like 'our' and 'ours' create the impression that the 'use of animals' is something 'everybody' is a part of, and that 'everybody' wants. The expression 'for ages' is very vague but effective, and serves the purpose of bringing about

9 However, as Ragnhild Sollund (this volume) argues, the weight that is placed on *similarities* between humans and other animals may also be problematic. She says that: 'If different properties, capacities and consequently interests are unacknowledged or under communicated *per se*, this may entail that the individuals with these interests and properties are not accorded value in their own kind, and thus cause speciesism. Consequently; one should not only argue for equal rights because other animals have the same capacities to experience pain, suffering and joy, one should also argue for *different* interests, evaluation of different capacities, and equal, or even more – respect – precisely for this reason' (Sollund, this volume).

10 All quotations from the White Paper have been translated into English by me.

11 For a common definition of 'exploitation', see for example the *Macmillan English Dictionary For Advanced Learners* (2007).

a sense of community and permanence rather than describing a historical fact about the relationship between humans and other animals. The choice of words generates the impression that society always has been that way, that it is *natural* – and *important* – that everything 'continues as normal'.

The relationship with other animals, as being 'included in our culture', appears in the statement above not only as something longlasting, but also *unavoidable*. The statement stresses the 'necessity' of exploiting non-humans for 'food and clothing', without explicitly saying so. It almost sounds like Norwegian people find themselves in a constant struggle for survival; that among racks of clothes in shopping malls and countless shelves of food in grocery stores – they are, *by way of nature*, forced to choose animal products. But do we really live in a society where it is *necessary* to exploit non-humans to satisfy basic needs? A closer examination of the Norwegian society, and countries all over the world, reveals that quite a few people live healthy lives without consuming any animal products whatsoever.

The White Paper notes that vegetarianism and veganism[12] are alternatives to non-human consumption (LD 2002–03: 20). Nevertheless, the White Paper does not acknowledge the issue of consumption in its 'ethical discussion', so as not to draw focus to the contradiction between the alleged necessity of non-human exploitation and the existing practice of veganism. Still – or rather because of this underlying contradiction – the document stresses repeatedly that 'we should continue to keep and use animals', and that it is 'fundamental and important in our society'.[13] By describing the 'use of animals' without problematizing it, one creates an impression of what is '*normal*'. Within this framework, the statement that 'the areas of use are continuously expanding' appears as something positive and desirable.

Similar statements can also be found in the consultation paper to the Animal Welfare Act (LMD 2007: 16). Like in the White Paper, they are presented as so self-evident and natural that they can stand on their own without any need of further explanation. They are thus not objects for discussion as one of several possible standpoints, and any objection will seem absurd because the claims are 'obvious'.

This is typical of the way things are (not) discussed in society in general. Statements such as the one quoted above are meant to confirm that there is nothing wrong with the way things are – that exploitation is 'natural'. This is an argument of 'tradition', which says that something is acceptable – or even good – just because it has been done 'for ages'. This line of reasoning has been applied to many social hierarchies over the ages. For example, it has been used to reject the basic rights

12 'The word "veganism" denotes a philosophy and way of living which seeks to exclude – as far as is possible and practicable – all forms of exploitation of, and cruelty to, animals for food, clothing or any other purpose; and by extension, promotes the development and use of animal-free alternatives for the benefit of humans, animals and the environment. In dietary terms it denotes the practice of dispensing with all products derived wholly or partly from animals' (definition taken from The Vegan Society's homepage: http://www.vegansociety.com/about/articles-of-association.aspx. Accessed 2 June 2011).

13 See for example: LD (2002–03: 17 and 150).

of women. Women have traditionally been thought of as more biological than cultural and thus closer to 'animals' and nature than men. They have simply been considered to be *less human*. Thus, women were not allowed to have equal status to men in all areas of society. Why should one do so, when women are 'biologically different' from men, and men have 'always' been in power? Fortunately, most people do not agree with this, at least not in theory. Though there are some who do so. As far as *animals* are concerned, however, this reasoning is deemed adequate; it is 'common sense' – the understanding of the majority.

The exploitation thus rests on incomplete statements and reasoning, where the underlying ethical principles are seldom, if ever, discussed. The statements are hidden viewpoints – they are presented as unavoidable reality by an all-present invisible voice. This 'voice from nowhere' is the voice of the most powerful group in our society; the one that decides the norms and rules. Feminist standpoint theorists have identified this power strategy of not making one's position visible (Haraway 2004, Harding 2004). The claim of 'neutrality' serves the interests of dominant groups. In this case it serves the interests of those who, in several different ways, benefit from the exploitation of non-human animals.

As some green criminologists have noted, the power to define reality belongs to the dominant group (Kitsuse and Spector 2009), and this power consists, among other things, of 'universal truths'; such as 'what everybody knows' or 'this is how it is and how we've always done it'. This provides the basis for the legitimization of current practices. With the help of such 'universal truths', a dividing line is also constructed between what is 'real' and 'unreal' – what does not fit into reality. Great deviation from the universal truths will therefore not only appear as 'inappropriate', but as *deviation from reality* (Berger and Luckmann 2000). And as long as no one questions this, it remains a matter of course – ensuring the continuation of current practices. And no one *will* seem to question it if their voices are excluded from political debate, the media or other important arenas of discussion.

Intrinsic Value and Animal Welfare

Of importance in the White Paper are also the concepts of 'intrinsic value' and 'animal welfare'. They are the cornerstones of an 'ethical platform' that, according to the description, should be 'guiding our attitude towards, and the keeping of, animals in our society' (LD 2002–03: 148). The Animal Welfare Act (2009) also builds on this platform.

Intrinsic Value

What does having 'intrinsic value' imply? It is reasonable to understand 'intrinsic value' as something every single individual is in possession of, regardless of what others might mean or wish? This is also how it is presented in the Animal Welfare Act:

> Animals have intrinsic value regardless of the utility value they might have to humans (Animal Welfare Act 2009: § 3).

Similarly, one would also say that all *humans* have intrinsic value regardless of the utility value to other humans. But in the case of 'animals', the ethical reflection stops with this statement. How is 'intrinsic value' supposed to be put into practice? The White Paper does not say anything about this.[14] How can an individual's 'intrinsic value' be consistent with the fact that she or he is used as a *means* to an end? 'Intrinsic value' – as it is usually understood – implies that someone is an end in themselves, and cannot simply be sacrificed for the interests of others.[15]

Is it possible for an individual to have both 'intrinsic value' and 'utility value' at the same time? In practice, the worth of non-humans is measured in terms of utility value – it is considered to be the basis for their existence. Many people even consider that they are *producing* them – a common way of speaking about fish in the fish farming industry for example.[16] It is also reflected in terms such as 'breed'. The 'produced animals' will in turn either 'produce' commodities for humans, or become 'end products' themselves, or both. Expressions such as 'animal material' and 'standardization of experimental animals' are also common in scientific research. The words reveal that non-humans are seen as *the opposite* of individuals with intrinsic value – they rather constitute a mass or matter for use in the food industry or scientific research.

The way other animals are described in modern language still clearly expresses a view of them as some sort of *machines*, and they are also treated that way. In scientific experiments they may for instance be used for 'producing' substances and organs (LMD 2007: 30), and in agriculture they are treated both as machines that for instance 'produce' milk and eggs, and afterwards they themselves become 'meat products'. They are called 'production animals', and are being described as having good or poor 'production capacity' and 'feed efficiency'. If they have 'good production capacity', they 'yield' a lot, and their value can be measured in terms of 'output per animal' (LD 2002–03: 33). When they are worn-out, and can no longer 'produce', they are 'discarded' – which means that they are killed. Hens

14 However, a statement from the Minister of Agriculture and Food, Lars Peder Brekk, in the process of writing the Animal Welfare Act (2009), confirms that including the term 'intrinsic value' in the wording is not meant to have any practical consequences for animal welfare, but only be symbolic (Ellefsen 2009: 54).

15 The term 'intrinsic value' originates from non-anthropocentric ethics, where it implies that (animal) individuals have value in themselves, regardless of their utility value to humans. That means they cannot simply be regarded as *means* to human ends. See for example the animal rights philosophy of Tom Regan (1988). Most striking however, is the similarity of the wording in the White Paper and the Animal Welfare Act, to the deep ecology of Arne Næss, Bill Devall and George Sessions (Devall and Sessions 1985: 70, in Ariansen 1994: 197). In deep ecology, the term 'intrinsic value' refers to 'equality in the biosphere', which implies that all living beings have the same moral or intrinsic value.

16 See for example LMD (2007: 30) for the use of the term 'produce'.

are 'discarded' when they are less than 1.5 years old and no longer profitable in 'egg production'. Cows are 'discarded' at 4–5 years of age, when they no longer 'produce enough milk'. Pigs (unless they are 'breeding gilts') are killed when they have 'reached the right slaughter weight', which is at around six months of age (LD 2002–03: 60–88).

After being butchered, their bodies are turned into 'products' that can be sold for market price. The 'experimental animals' are literally thrown in the rubbish bin after having been used in experiments. Both in agriculture and research, non-human animals are nameless and *replaceable*, as part of 'livestock' or 'animal material'. They are regarded as 'things' that can be used and thrown away. The 'experimental animals' can in addition be subject to *reuse.*[17]

What happens to an individual's 'intrinsic value' in a system that treats everyone like 'replaceable resources'? Being a 'unit' in a 'production system' means that one's individual existence is insignificant. The fact that every individual is a unique and irreplaceable being is *denied* in such systems. In practice, the value of non-humans lies in what they can 'produce', or in being dead. Their short lives before this have no value in themselves. This is reflected in common language when one for instance speaks of 'milk cows', 'beef cattle', 'laying hens', 'fur animals', 'slaughter-pigs' and 'experimental animals' or 'laboratory animals'. These words imply that non-humans *are* what humans exploit them as – and not unique individuals – and that they therefore 'rightfully' can be used in this way (Dunayer 2001). The terms simply make it seem *natural.*

It is presumed that it is possible to have both 'intrinsic value' and 'utility value' at the same time; in a situation where the individual's life is without significance – where death is as much, or even *more* worth than life. A non-human's 'intrinsic value' thus does not imply that she or he is entitled to any *rights*, as opposed to the 'intrinsic value' of humans that ensures basic rights. Other animals are neither given the right to life, freedom or personal safety. They have no right not to be incarcerated, to have normal relationships with – or even the company of – others, decide over their own bodies and what is being done to them, choose who they want to have sexual relations with, or to keep their children. They can legally be subjected to any form of violence, as long as it is within the framework of accepted practices such as agriculture, research and sport. In the legal system they are classified as 'things', and as 'things' they also have economic value. As 'property' they can be sold, rented, given away, lost, stolen and put to death (Larsen 2003). How can anyone have 'intrinsic value' and at the same time be someone else's property?

Animal Welfare

'Animal welfare' is an important concept in the White Paper, and later also in the Animal Welfare Act. Even though a 'broad concept of welfare' is being used (LD

17 Forskrift om forsøk med dyr: FOR 1996-01-15 nr 23: § 3. *Definisjoner*. [Norwegian regulations concerning animal testing: FOR 1996-01-15 nr 23: § 3. *Definitions*].

2002–03: 27), it has from the beginning a clear delimitation. '*Animal* welfare' indicates that the term is not meant to cover the 'welfare' of both humans and non-humans. In the same way as the term 'animal ethics' indicates that there exists an ethic for 'animals' separate from that for humans, 'animal welfare' involves a similar delimitation. The *real* ethics, that is, the one we usually associate with ethics and that concerns humans, is thus held separate from 'animal ethics'. The latter becomes a separate ethical phenomenon with separate rules.

The White Paper's understanding of 'animal welfare' involves the fact that 'animals' should 'fare well' – they should be ensured '*good* animal welfare'. Nevertheless, it is almost exclusively the 'coping with the environment' that is discussed. 'Coping with the environment' actually means to what extent the 'animals' have managed to 'adapt to' an environment that is unnatural to them. In the White Paper it says:

> A central question in the welfare debate is therefore whether the animals feel frustration or need if they cannot behave like they would have done in more natural surroundings (LD 2002–03: 27).

Why is not the central question: what fosters joy and wellbeing? To discuss whether 'animals feel frustration or need' when they are being deprived of the possibility to live the way they want, is actually about identifying a *limit of tolerance*. It is taken for granted that 'animals' shall be kept in a certain environment – one that suits human purposes – and then it remains to be seen whether they manage to adapt to it or not. The environment is given, and shaped according to what is seen as 'practical' or 'rational' for the producers. The 'animals' are placed in stalls, sties and cages of a size that is determined by 'profitability' and 'time saving'. Then the question is: *how much can they take*?

One can say that there exists both a concrete, physical limit of tolerance, and an abstract, ethical one. The first concerns how much you can put 'animals' through before they get sick or die, and are thus no longer of 'economic value'. The other is about how much strain can be put on the conscience of society: what is seen as 'acceptable suffering for animals'. This is expressed in the Animal Welfare Act, in the division between what is regarded as 'unnecessary strain' – and thus illegal – and the 'necessary' or 'legitimate' strain. What is seen as 'necessary' and 'unnecessary' suffering is a question of interpretation and of (human) interests, and as such has little to do with how non-humans actually experience their suffering (Larsen 2003).

Since 'animals' are traditionally seen as synonymous with 'nature' – as opposed to humans/culture – the attitudes towards them and towards nature as a whole are intertwined (Noske 1997: 40–80). Speaking of a 'limit of tolerance' for instance, the parallel to the Western perception and treatment of nature is striking: how much 'resources' can be taken out of the land, how much can it be 'worked' or how much pollution can it take before it 'breaks down' and is no longer profitable, or perhaps destroyed for future generations (of humans; other species are usually not the concern)? The term 'sustainable development' is an expression of this reasoning and concerns the question of how far humans can push their interests; where is nature's limit of tolerance? At this point in history – and considering the planet as a whole – it seems like we are about to find out.

The White Paper states that 'most of our domestic animals are adaptable', and that they 'apparently thrive splendidly under conditions that are unnatural to them' (LD 2002–03: 29). Strangely enough, on the same page are also listed a number of ways in which the 'environment' severely damages non-humans both mentally and physically. Examples of how they react to life in captivity are calves developing ulcers after being taken from their mothers immediately after birth, caged budgerigars jumping restlessly back and forth on a perch, horses rocking endlessly from side to side, cows rolling their tongues, pigs biting each other's tails, hens pecking – and even eating – each other. This 'stereotypical behaviour' – which would be termed mental illness in humans – is a result of standard procedure towards non-humans in agriculture, research and 'pet keeping'.

It is thus not altogether clear how 'coping' or 'adaptation' should be understood. The way these terms are used today, they mean, among other things, 'adapting to' being caged in, to isolation or overcrowding, artificial light systems that alter the circadian rhythm, concrete floors, the absence of sunlight, fresh air, earth and grass. 'Coping' involves attempting to live with constant boredom, frustration and need. To be forced to live contrary to one's needs and wishes also means *resigning*; to cease trying to escape and to become passive. Is it then so that someone 'copes with the environment' if she or he does not develop 'stereotypical behaviour'? 'Stereotypical behaviour' can in itself be seen as a form of 'coping', as it is a way of dealing with a desperate situation (LD 2002–03: 29). Furthermore, *enduring* something is very different from *thriving*. What is meant, then, by the statement that 'domestic animals are adaptable and apparently thrive splendidly'?

The word 'adaptation' has several different aspects when used about 'animals'. One form of 'adaptation' concerns operations on every individual's body, another is about 'selective breeding'. Both are done so that the 'animals' will fit into human made systems, and not be a bother to anyone. In the case of 'selective breeding', the 'adaptation to the environment' is so extreme that the body becomes very different from what was natural for the species. Often it is a burden in itself, such as for cows with enormous udders meant to 'produce more milk', the hairless and unnaturally large bodies of pigs that 'shall become meat', and extreme and rapid growth in chickens with the consequence that the skeleton does not develop fast enough to support their body weight – so their legs literally cannot carry them. Within medical research for instance, 'selective breeding' is used with the purpose of *giving* 'animals' certain diseases, for then to use them in experiments. Naked mice that develop cancer is an example of this. Non-humans are within the context of research also 'genetically modified'; in other words, 'modified' to be 'better suited' as tools in experiments.

Weighing Intrinsic Value and Animal Welfare

The higher purpose of the White Paper is 'healthy animals in good environments' (LD 2002–03: 150). Words like 'healthy', 'good', and 'quality of life' – which is also used – contribute to the impression that the conditions can hardly be better than what the document sets up. It seems like, within the framework of 'continued use', one really can speak of 'the good life' for non-humans. 'Animal welfare' thus becomes synonymous with this. At the same time, however, it is clearly stated that 'animal welfare' is something that can be 'weighed':

> Value assessments within a field like animal welfare do not stand isolated, but shall be weighed against other values and considerations, especially when they will be put into practice (LD 2002–03: 22).

This means that, in practice, what is in the interest of non-humans is *not* taken as a starting point. 'Animal welfare' is not a fixed and important principle, but something that must be 'weighed' against the 'utility interests' of humans. It is also evident that 'animal welfare' is something that must 'pay off' financially (LD 2002–03: 154). The 'value assessment' of 'welfare' thus is not done separately, but is part of some sort of exchange, making the 'animals' a 'background material' for the 'assessment'. How much, then, are the wants and needs of non-humans worth? If their worth is rather variable, it can easily turn out to be less than the value of the 'utility interests' – whether in the shape of 'industry', 'science', 'hobby' or 'recreation'. It seems to be acceptable to operate with a *theoretical* form of 'animal welfare' and a *practical* variant. There is thus a huge gap between the wording of the Animal Welfare Act, the focus on 'animal welfare' and 'intrinsic value' and the physical realities and the way non-humans are treated. In practice, 'animal welfare reform' usually centres around 'a little more space', 'improved breeding' and 'better killing methods'. The industries are also given a very long time to implement changes.

The attempt to combine 'good animal welfare' and recognition of 'intrinsic value' with the aim of 'continued use' makes it difficult to draw a line for 'human interests' and 'utility considerations'. It also becomes problematic to set limits on new forms of exploitation, since 'human needs' at all times can be defined as 'more important' than those of non-humans. Neither 'intrinsic value' nor 'animal welfare' can protect non-humans against 'human interests'.

To see whether the concepts of 'intrinsic value' and 'welfare' are well suited for the reality they are meant to describe, one can simply ask whether they might as well be used about *humans*? Does it make sense to talk about 'intrinsic value', 'welfare' and 'quality of life' when humans are treated the same way? In general, the treatment non-humans are subject to would be termed as punishment or torture if done to humans. One would speak of 'abuse' instead of 'use'. Concepts such as 'intrinsic value' and 'animal welfare' are thus a stark contrast to the actual lives and experiences of non-humans. Today people seek to combine the terms with practices that *harm* – and with the intention of keeping and further developing these practices. Used in this way, they are contributing to legitimizing exploitation.

Establishing Normality and Naturalness – How is Resistance Met?

This section looks at how the White Paper establishes 'normality' and 'naturalness' – the 'normal' way of relating to other animals – in order to continue exploiting them. The White Paper is an expression of majority values and practices, and it is the majority that holds the power to define 'normality'. This section also examines how resistance to the dominant or 'normal' world-view is met in the White Paper; what is done to 'unwanted' viewpoints, and how the persons holding them are being described. Specifically, it looks at how master suppression techniques such as the use of stigmatizing terms are employed to categorize and marginalize those presenting the critique of non-human exploitation.

The Power of the Majority

For something to come across as 'natural', it is necessary to somehow 'remove' divergent and unwanted viewpoints. Today, viewpoints that reject 'human superiority' and promote animal equality and rights are being marginalized.[18] A division between 'us' (the majority) and 'them' (persons holding these views) is created. The viewpoints are being excluded from debate by the use of master suppression techniques such as ridicule and shaming, and by making them invisible or 'adjusting' them to the dominant view of reality. Another technique is to focus on, and stigmatize, the *persons* representing the 'divergent ideas', rather than the ideas in themselves. These master suppression techniques are more or less all employed in the White Paper.

It is the privilege of the majority to construct a division between the groups 'we' and 'the others'. This privilege rests on tradition and *what is* at a certain point in time. In the description of the human–animal relationship I have quoted from the White Paper, what is first brought into focus is thus typically *tradition*: 'animals are included as an important part of the society and culture'. Meaning also that 'everybody' is a part of it, since 'everybody' lives in the society. Without explicitly saying so, it is implied that 'everybody does it' and 'everybody wants it'.

As the anthropologist Marianne Gullestad (2002) has pointed out, the numerical majority – being in a privileged position – make their views seem *everlasting*, and more legitimate than the views of the minority. The power of the majority is not perceived as power, but consists of what is *taken for granted*. It rests above all on what is 'natural' (Gullestad 2002: 17). It is also the privilege of the majority to decide the rules of society. However, the hegemony is not secured once and for

18 Though these viewpoints are also progressing compared to the situation 20–30 years ago.

all, but must be maintained by creating agreement in the population about what constitutes the 'natural' and 'normal' (Gullestad 2002: 17).

In the quotation from the White Paper, the 'common' way of treating non-humans – exploiting them – is not questioned. Instead, it is presented that 'this is the way things are', and also implied that 'this is the way it must be'. This consequently also presupposes the existence of a boundary between 'nature' and 'culture', 'humans' and 'animals', even though the text does not explicitly say so. An anthropocentric view of reality that is founded on such hierarchies, is taken for granted. Thus the 'common' moral categories are legitimized through the assertion that they have existed 'for ages'. Even though, as for instance the anthropologist Barbara Noske points out, 'this anthropocentric notion happens to be a fairly recent one in the history of human ideas' (Noske 1997: 41).

When the White Paper speaks of 'our society', it is referring to the Norwegian society. But after this sentence it proceeds to speak of humanity *in general*. It says of 'humans' that they 'keep animals to satisfy basic needs for food and clothing'. Here, the statement involves *everybody*, regardless of where in the world they may be, what sort of society they live in, or what sort of situation they may find themselves in. It is not mentioned whether this 'keeping of animals' is a question of survival, or a matter of 'utility' and 'cosiness'. It says nothing of traditions, various notions of human superiority, the distribution of power or of gender roles.[19] The notion of a 'joint human attitude' towards other animals thus goes beyond the majority of the Norwegian society to include 'the whole world'. It is as though one tries to make a statement about *human nature*, rather than culturally specific practices. First, a particular conception of non-humans is made universal, for then to be used for backing up and legitimizing Norwegian attitudes and practices.

The following statement contributes to a further confirmation of these, and to strengthen the impression of inevitability:

> Even though the starting points are very different, the reality is that animals have been and still are used and exploited to the advantage of humans in all cultures, though to varying degrees (LD 2002–03: 18).

'The reality is', it says about how non-humans are treated. But can the statement be said to be a 'neutral description of facts' and 'reality'? Are there no *interests* involved, and a certain ethical standpoint and view of reality that is taken for granted? Such as the state's interest in maintaining the societal order: both the industries and jobs that are based on non-human usage,[20] and the foundation of our culture built on the the notion of humans as superior beings? It is interesting to look at the same statement when the word 'animals' is being replaced with 'women', and 'use/exploitation' with 'subordination' (even though the words 'use' and 'exploitation' are of course

19 See Adams (1990) and Gålmark (2005) for a discussion of meat-eating and gender.

20 For a further discussion of these interests and what happens when they are threatened, see Ellefsen's article in this volume.

the right terms in many cases). The statement now sounds like this: 'Even though the starting points are very different, the reality is that *women* have been and still are subordinate to men in all cultures, though to varying degrees'. If this statement was situated in a context where different forms of subordination and exploitation of women were described – and where this was seen as both acceptable and wanted – would one call it a 'neutral description of facts'?

The statements about 'animals' and 'women' are both 'true', in the sense that exploitation and subordination is *commonplace* all over the world. One can also say that a hierarchical world-view that places both 'women' and 'animals' below 'men' is very common. But this world-view is undergoing some serious changes however, and in many countries it is now seen as *natural* that women should have the same rights as men – for instance in Norway. It has not always been so, and the rights and relative equality Norwegian women now have are the result of a long political struggle.

Statements such as those I have described above have a certain *function* which can be understood from their context. When information about 'how the world works' is left on its own – without criticism or thorough report – it becomes support for the status quo. It contributes to the legitimization of attitudes and practices that are *common* today.

Marginalization

Generalizations that encompass 'everybody' in Norway, or 'the whole world', also make difference and resistance seem invisible – they *deny* them in some way. Naturalizing statements which decide what is 'normal', create a 'marginal group' of people – the ones that are not included in 'normality'. However, in Norway. as in the rest of the world, there are a lot of people who oppose one, several or all forms of exploitation of non-humans. This resistance is expressed in many different ways; for instance as the boycotting of animal products, contributions to newspapers, book writing, membership in an animal protection or animal rights organization, demonstrations, films, art exhibitions and everyday communication with other people.

Notions of normality also decide what will be perceived as 'acceptable' critique of majority values and practices. There seems to be acceptance of disagreement concerning *certain* forms of exploitation of non-humans, or *the way* it is done. This is reflected, among other things, in the fact that 'animal welfare' is now on the political agenda. Both animal protection and animal rights organizations were invited to make suggestions to the White Paper during the process of writing it. At the same time, the document expresses that 'there is a limit to how far the critique can go'. When the limit of 'acceptable critique' is crossed, it is signalized by the use of stigmatizing terms for the persons presenting the critique. This is clearly shown in the description of the animal rights movement, which in the White Paper is represented by two defenders of, respectively, animal rights: the philosopher Tom Regan, and animal liberation; the philosopher Peter Singer. After a short description of their theories, there is the following statement:

> Many of these viewpoints have sympathy far outside of the more extreme lines (LD 2002–03: 20).

What are 'extreme lines', and who constitute them? The word 'extreme' suggests that something is both unusual and *exaggerated* – it is 'too much' according to a standard of normality. No description of this standard is given however. When an individual or a group is characterized as 'extreme', it is attempted to create as big a distance to them as possible. They are 'far away' from the common, safe and natural. The 'extreme' are people finding themselves far out in one end, while the 'normal' group find themselves in the middle. If one is in the middle, one is 'just suitably concerned about the welfare of animals' – not too little and not too much.

'Extreme' has many negative associations; aggression and violent behaviour among others. The word 'lines' really belongs to military jargon (as in 'enemy lines'), and supports the image of something threatening. I have also heard the word 'camp' being used – as in 'your camp' – by someone assuming that I was speaking on behalf of this 'camp'; and that 'the camp' was one group with one opinion. 'Camp' also has a military ring to it, corresponding with the term 'militant vegans'.[21] The word 'militant' – which is a more explicit version – is used in everyday speech, more like slang, but the words serve the same purpose. 'Militant' is used without any further explanation, and the stigmatized group or individual will have their work cut out for them if they want to free themselves of its associations. The label 'extreme' is even harder to shake off, because it covers a lot of different behaviours, and also just *being* without necessarily *doing* anything. In the case of the White Paper, the use of the label 'extreme lines' is due to the claim that non-humans must have basic rights.

Interestingly, the expression 'militant vegans' draws associates both with something dangerous[22] and ridiculous at the same time, since veganism in itself is often not taken seriously. Plant-eaters are, in a meat-eating culture, not taken as seriously as meat-eaters; meat and violence have a high status while plant-eating and non-violence do not (Adams 1990). The combination of something threatening and something ridiculous seems impossible, *inhuman* in a way: and incidentally, very much like the way 'animals' themselves are often described. Being potentially dangerous, silly and worthless, they can consequently not be taken into account.

But if 'the others', the marginal group, consists of 'extreme individuals', then who and what are '*we*'? The 'we' in 'our culture' must then be 'normal persons' with 'moderate views'. The 'normal' – the norm – is thus to accept the exploitation of non-humans in one form or other, and to consider it 'necessary' and 'natural'. It is 'abnormal' to proclaim that non-humans constitute a suppressed group in society; and that they have integrity, a right to live, and not to serve the interests

---

21 See for example Gjøvik (2003) for the use of the term 'militant vegans'.

22 For a further discussion of what is seen as threatening and dangerous, and the responses to the 'threat', see Ellefsen's article in this volume, and also Sollund's article this volume.

of humans. It is the 'extreme' who find this is a fundamental ethical question. The opponents must show *moderation* in their opposition, otherwise their protests will not be taken into consideration. The critique must simply appear as 'reasonable' by those who are criticized. It is not acceptable to oppose 'everything'; one must operate within 'the plausible'. And what is 'plausible' is always determined by those who hold the majority of power.

Categorization

The categorization and naming of individuals and groups in society is the privilege of the majority; it is about establishing order and exercising control. When the various categories are perceived as 'natural', their *political* property is made invisible (Gullestad 2002: 43). The categories are political in the sense that they are employed to maintain existing boundaries between different groups in society, or to establish new ones. That way, groups with unwanted viewpoints can be marginalized to the outer edges of society. Categorization is also about protecting the interests of certain groups at the expense of others. In the case of 'animals', huge financial interests are also involved – so there are more than symbolic boundaries at stake.

Roughly speaking, one can say that three categories are used in the White Paper to classify different viewpoints:

1. The 'normal' who view the exploitation of 'animals' for human purposes as acceptable, and who are either entirely uncritical of it, or show 'moderation' in their critique.
2. The 'moderate' 'animal protectionists' who are critical of several practices, but not all, or who criticize the *way* 'animals' are exploited – not exploitation in itself. This category is more or less accepted within 'normality'.
3. The 'extreme' 'animal rights activists' who strive to end all forms of exploitation of non-humans, and who consider that they should have rights. (In the White Paper these are wrongly referred to as 'animal protection activists', even though they do not want 'protection of animals', but rights). This category is seen as outside of 'normality', and thus 'deviates from reality'.

The first category is made invisible as a category, and constitutes what is often called 'we' or 'everybody'. Here lies the power to define, and the opportunity to construct the other categories.

Other Master Suppression Techniques and the Avoidance of Ethical Debate

There are also other master suppression techniques employed in the White Paper in addition to the use of labels such as 'extreme'. Such categorizations make viewpoints illegitimate, though at the same time visible. But important ethical considerations are also made *invisible* through 'modification'[23] or by not being included at all. Both in this central political document and in the consultation paper to the Animal Welfare Act (LMD 2007), one is content with only mentioning two early – and male – representatives of the animal rights movement; Peter Singer and Tom Regan. The thousands of other books[24] that have been written on the topic are not mentioned at all, which conceals important contributors such as for instance Lisa Gålmark, Evelyn B. Pluhar, Lori Gruen, Josephine Donovan, Marti Kheel, Paola Cavalieri and Barbara Noske – all of whom had published articles and books before the White Paper was written.

Another technique is about making the resistance seem trivial; arising as a result of the fundamental notion that 'animals' and their interests are so trivial that the issue cannot really be about them. This can explain why the focus is always directed towards the humans pleading their case, and not the ethical issues. The cause being 'trivial', the persons promoting it are often not allowed to speak for themselves, or to control their own opinions (Baker 2001). This way of marginalizing persons and concealing viewpoints finds its academic equivalent in several sociological studies, such as those of Keith Tester (1991), Adrian Franklin (1999) and James M. Jasper and Dorothy Nelkin (1992). There are simply other rules for what the 'extreme activists' are allowed to say and for what can be said about them, than for the 'normal majority'. The sanction or power technique of inflicting shame is especially effective in this context.[25]

Both the use of statements stressing the 'correctness' and 'unavoidability' of exploiting non-humans and the stigmatizing of opponents makes it possible to avoid the entire question of ethics. By making opposing viewpoints illegitimate, and focusing on the persons holding them, one does not have to deal with the arguments and answer them. The White Paper can thus be seen as an example of what happens when individuals and groups start to question society's cultural foundations; the ethical boundary between humans/culture and animals/nature.

The Human–animal Relationship is Changing

The way humans relate to other animals is changing, however; the notion of humans as 'superior beings' is met with opposition, and appears as significantly less obvious to younger generations. An increasing number of people are being upset by information about what happens to non-humans in fur farms, the egg, milk and meat industry, in fish farms and research laboratories. Knowledge of the alternatives to exploiting other animals is growing. The White Paper is also a part and expression of this reform process where 'animals' are becoming increasingly

23 I have discussed this in Riise (2010: 58–61).

24 See Singer (2003), Bekoff (1998) and Magel (1989).

25 Berit Ås identified this and four other master suppression techniques (Ås 1981). See also Gålmark (2005).

'ethically relevant'. As such it is also an expression of the great challenges facing society: it shows how doubt and ambivalence are being generated about its very foundations. The political solution to this problem is trying to 'downplay' or 'bridge' the contrasts. This process makes the conflicting viewpoints 'agree with' the official story of how the relationship with other animals should be.

The attempt to restore order causes several problems however. Considering the authoritative role of natural science, the disparity between existing knowledge and practice becomes especially exaggerated. There is no lack of knowledge concerning the suffering non-humans are subject to, or of how similar they are to humans. This leads to an *ethical* problem: the question of why the insight does not bring about any significant consequences. What is it about 'animals' that makes this acceptable? In the attempt to answer the question, it is argued that 'animals' are a group that 'lack certain qualities', and can therefore be 'rightfully' exploited. However, the same rationale has been employed to deny other groups – like 'women' and 'people of colour' – basic rights. But in relation to these groups this form of logic is no longer considered acceptable.

A *political* problem arises when values such as 'intrinsic value' and 'animal welfare' are emphasized as important, but at the same time as *relative*, and not meant to bring about significant practical consequences. Political responsibility is disclaimed when fundamental ethical questions regarding the group 'animals' – which includes an enormous number of individuals – are not discussed. This group is exploited for the same reasons as other oppressed groups: because it is 'useful' and because 'it is in one's power to do so'.

But values and attitudes are changing, and the ethical debate thus cannot be brushed aside indefinitely. The White Paper is also a sign that existing attitudes and practices have been questioned, it signals *unease* to such an extent that the making of a political document was found necessary. Even though master suppression techniques were employed against viewpoints stressing animal equality and rights, they were not completely ignored – it was found necessary to mention them. As Piers Beirne points out: 'support for animal rights has grown into a large-scale, well-publicized, and theoretically informed social movement' (Beirne 2009: 1). This means that it must somehow be taken into account; one cannot 'go back' and pretend that the idea of human superiority has not been challenged, nor is it possible to ignore the brutality resulting from speciesism: the way non-humans are treated. The way of regarding and treating other animals that was once 'obvious' to everyone, now needs a justification. It needs the repetition of statements confirming its legitimacy. In that way, a document like the White Paper also shows that the relationship between humans and other animals must not be the way it is today, but that it naturally can be changed.

References

Adams, C.J. 1990. *The Sexual Politics of Meat: A Feminist-vegetarian Critical Theory*. New York: Continuum.

Ariansen, P. 1994. *Miljøfilosofi. En innføring* [Environmental Philosophy. An Introduction]. Oslo: Universitetsforlaget.

Baker, S. 2001. *Picturing the Beast: Animals, Identity and Representation*. Illinois: University of Illinois Press.

Beirne, P. 2007. Animal rights, animal abuse and green criminology, in *Issues in Green Criminology: Confronting Harms Against Environments, Humanity and Other Animals*, edited by P. Beirne and N. South. Cullompton: Willan Publishing, 55–83.

Beirne, P. 2009. *Confronting Animal Abuse: Law, Criminology, and Human-Animal Relationships*. Lanham: Rowman & Littlefield Publishers.

Bekoff, M. (ed.) 1998. *Encyclopedia of Animal Rights and Animal Welfare*. Westport Conn.: Greenwood Press.

Berger, P.L. and Luckmann, T. 2000. *Den samfunnsskapte virkelighet* [The Social Construction of Reality]. Bergen: Fagbokforlaget.

Cavalieri, P. 2001. *The Animal Question. Why Non-human Animals Deserve Human Rights*. New York: Oxford University Press.

Cazaux, G. 1999. Beauty and the beast: animal abuse from a non-speciesist criminological perspective, in *Crime, Law & Social Change*, 31, 105–26.

Cazaux, G. 2007. Labelling animals: non-speciesist criminology and techniques to identify other animals, in *Issues in Green Criminology: Confronting Harms Against Environments, Humanity and Other Animals*, edited by P. Beirne and N. South. Cullompton: Willan Publishing, 87–113.

Dunayer, J. 2001. *Animal Equality. Language and Liberation*. Maryland: Ryce Publishing.

Dunayer, J. 2004. *Speciesism*. Maryland: Ryce Publishing.

Ellefsen, R. 2009. *Ny dyrevelferdslov: Beskyttes dyr eller næring? Interessekonflikt og otstridende syn på dyrs status i lovprosessen forut for dyrevelferdsloven*. [New Animal Welfare Act: Protecting animals or agroindustries? Conflicting interests and opposing views on animals' status in the legal process leading up to the new Animal Welfare Act]. MA thesis University of Oslo, department of Criminology and Sociology of Law.

Forskrift om forsøk med dyr. 1996. FOR 1996-01-15 nr 23. [Norwegian regulations concerning animal testing]. Norges Landbruks- og matdepartementet.

Franklin, A. 1999. *Animals and Modern Cultures. A Sociology of Human-Animal Relations in Modernity*. London: Sage.

Gjøvik, J.A. 2003. *Hvitbok for kjøttspisere. Håndbok i etisk argumentasjon for jegere og fiskere*. [White Book for Meat-eaters. Handbook in Ethical Argumentation for Hunters and Anglers]. Trondheim: Dovre Forlag.

Gullestad, M. 2002. *Det norske sett med nye øyne. Kritisk analyse av norsk innvandringsdebatt*. Oslo: Universitetsforlaget. [Parts of this book has been translated into English, and forms a substantial part of a collection of essays:

Marianne Gullestad (2006): Plausible prejudice : everyday experiences and social images of nation, culture and race].

Gålmark, L. 2005. *Skönheter och odjur: en feministisk kritik av djur-människa-relationen* [Beauties and Beasts: A Feminist Critique of the Animal-human Relationship]. Göteborg: Makadam.

Haraway, D. 2004. Situated knowledges: the science question in feminism and the privilege of partial perspective, in *The Feminist Standpoint Theory Reader. Intellectual and Political Controversies*, edited by S. Harding. New York: Routledge.

Harding, S. 2004. Introduction, in *The Feminist Standpoint Theory Reader. Intellectual and Political Controversies*, edited by S. Harding. New York: Routledge.

Jasper, J.M. and Nelkin, D. 1992. *The Animal Rights Crusade: The Growth of a Moral Protest*. New York: Free Press.

Kitsuse, J.I. and Spector, M. 2009. *Constructing Social Problems*. New Brunswick: Transaction Publishers.

Landbruksdepartementet [LD]. 2002–2003. St.meld. nr. 12 (2002–2003): Om dyrehold og dyrevelferd. [Proposition to the Storting nr. 12 (2002–2003): Animal Husbandry and Animal Welfare].

Landbruks- og matdepartementet [LMD]. 2007. Høringsnotat for høring om ny lov om dyrevelferd (16.11.2007) [Consultation paper to the Animal Welfare Act].

Larsen, G. 2003. *Dyrevern eller samfunnsvern? Dyremishandling som lovbrudd og lovlydig handling*. [Protection of Animals Or Protection of Societies? Animal abuse as Violation of the Law and Law-abiding Action]. Oslo: Unipub.

Lov om dyrevelferd. 2009. LOV 2009-06-19 nr 97 [Animal Welfare Act]. Norges Landbruks-og matdepartementet.

Lov om dyrevern. 1974. LOV-1974-12-20-73 [Animal Protection Act]. Landbruksdepartementet.

Macmillan English Dictionary For Advanced Learners. 2007. Second edition. Oxford: Macmillan Education.

Magel, C.R. 1989. *Keyguide to Information Sources in Animal Rights*. London: Mansell.

Neumann, I.B. 2001. *Mening, materialitet, makt: En innføring i diskursanalyse* [Meaning, Materiality, Power: An Introduction to Discourse Analysis]. Bergen: Fagbokforlaget.

Noske, B. 1997. *Beyond Boundaries. Humans and Animals*. Montréal: Black Rose Books.

Regan, T. 1988. *The Case for Animal Rights*. London: Routledge.

Riise, I.H. 2010. *Den selvfølgelige utnyttingen : om formingen av vårt samfunns forhold til dyr: En analyse av Stortingsmelding nr 12 (2002–03): Om dyrehold og dyrevelferd* [Natural Exploitation: The Shaping of Our Society's Relationship to Animals: An Analysis of Proposition to the Storting nr. 12 (2002–03): Animal Husbandry and Animal Welfare]. MA thesis University College Telemark, department of Culture and Humanities.

Singer, P. 2003. Animal Liberation at 30, in *The New York Review of Books*, 50 (8).
Sollund, R. 2008. Causes for speciesism: difference, distance and denial, in *Global Harms: Ecological Crime and Speciesism*, edited by R. Sollund. New York: Nova Science Publishers.
Steinem, G. 1992. *Revolution from Within: A Book of Self-esteem*. Boston: Little, Brown and Co.
Tester, K. 1991. *Animals and Society. The Humanity of Animal Rights*. London: Routledge.
Trippestad, T.A. 1999. *Som man reder, ligger man. Gudmund Hernes som maktutreder og maktutøver, in Normalitet og identitetsmakt i Norge* [Normality and Identity Power in Norway], edited by S. Meyer og T. Sirnes. Oslo: Ad Notam Gyldendal.
Ås, B. 1981. *Kvinner i alle land: håndbok i frigjøring* [Women in All Countries: Handbook in Liberation]. Oslo: Aschehoug.

Chapter 9
Differing Philosophies: Criminalisation and the Stop Huntingdon Animal Cruelty Debate

Elisa Aaltola

Introduction

Particularly in the past two decades, the values and norms attached to non-human animals have emerged as a point of serious interest in societal debate. Next to various cultural and historical factors, this is partly due to the influence of both academic and political developments. On the academic side, animal ethics has put forward arguments, according to which the sentience ('phenomenal consciousness', that is, capacity to experience) of non-human animals means that they or their interests have value in themselves, rather than merely as instruments for human purposes (see Singer 1975, Regan 1983, Midgley 1983, Rowlands 1998, Cavalieri 2001). Also, cognitive ethology has introduced the wider public to various fascinating studies concerning the cognitive abilities of animals, and thus manifested that many animals are altogether something more than blind, biological automata (see for instance Dawkins 1998, Bekoff 2002, Panskepp 1998, Rogers 1997). On the political front, the animal rights movement has gained attention with various forms of political actions carried out in the name of advancing the moral and legal status of animals (see Francione 1996; Best and Nocella 2004).

Although academic discussion has provided an important impetus for exploring the moral status of animals even further, the political front has had a much more concrete effect on how the wider public creates meanings concerning the human–animal relationship. This is most notably because corporations, states and the media have all taken a public stance on activism, and thus created a background for public debate: via 'action' and 'reaction', the status and treatment of animals has become a publically recognised issue. In this debate, 'crime' forms a significant element. On the one hand, activists argue that given forms of animal (ab)use are, or should be, illegal. On the other hand, corporations, states and many within the news media suggest that activists themselves are taking part in acts that are, or should be, illegal. Thus, whereas the academic debate has centered on normative and cognitive reconfigurations of the human–animal relation, the political front is increasingly revolving around different understandings of 'crime'.

The impetus behind this chapter is to explore different representations of the notion of 'crime' in the context of the animal industries: what types of actions are considered a crime in the framework of animal (ab)use? The chapter concentrates on the campaign carried out by Stop Huntingdon Animal Cruelty (SHAC) against Huntingdon Life Sciences (HLS), and brings forward a qualitative analysis[1] of the internet websites of these two parties during perhaps the most heightened time of the campaign (year 2006), together with relevant reports from the state and mainstream news media. Emphasis will be on the United Kingdom, although implications from the Nordic viewpoint will also be discussed.

Before continuing, some background information may be needed. HLS is a large, contractual testing laboratory that tests the toxicity of various chemicals on animals. About 75,000 animals are used each year, ranging from mice to wild-caught primates. As a consequence of various undercover scandals and SHAC activism, HLS has had to fight for its public image and economic profitability. On various occasions it has been hit by very disappointing share figures, and has had to be saved from the brink of ruin by the UK government. Today, HLS carries on with its business activities, whilst maintaining a relatively low profile.

SHAC is a campaign directed at closing HLS down. It was founded in Britain in 1999, and particularly in the first years of 2000 the campaign was very successful. SHAC developed a unique form of activism by putting the onus on affecting economical gains. It concentrated on targeting HLS shareholders, banking facilities and market makers, with an astonishing success rate: after different actions, banks began to avoid HLS, shareholders would quickly sell their shares for pennies and market makers would refuse to facilitate the trading of HLS stock. The most typical form of action was demonstrations outside HLS business partners, which proved very effective – also a wide variety of other actions such as e-mail and phone-in campaigns were utilised. The point of debate has been to what extent SHAC utilised criminal means (see Goodman and Sanders 2011), and this issue has culminated in various acts of criminalisation that have had a hindering effect on the SHAC campaign. Most significantly, the imprisonment of key activists has meant that the campaign has slowed down – however, it is still active.

Criminalisation

Criminology has placed relatively little emphasis on the environment (Gibbs et al. 2010), and arguably even less emphasis on non-human animals. Beirne has argued that, historically, both legislation and criminology, in general, remained uninterested in crime against non-human animals (Beirne 1999, see also Cazaux 1999).This is surprising, particularly when one takes into account the magnitude

1 The chapter makes a broad use of critical discourse analysis, and seeks to map out reoccurring, key themes in the target texts.

and variety of real and potential crimes in the animal context. Here, use of the term 'crime' has particularly two important dimensions.

The first of these has to do with how animals are treated. As has been argued, legislation concerning the treatment of animals tends to remain overly ambiguous and superficial, which has meant that violations of animal welfare are rarely the subject of law enforcement, and that punishments have remained minimal (Silverstein 1996; Rogers and Kaplan 2004; Arluke 2006). Moreover, animals are given only very basic and limited protection against obvious physical pain and discomfort, whereas welfare problems related to psychological issues (such as anxiety and frustration) tend to go unnoted (Beirne 1999). What is more, anti-cruelty clauses tend to implicitly suggest that animal use which does not involve clear, direct and intentional 'cruelty' is morally acceptable, and thus standard, institutionalised forms of animal agriculture are implied to be beyond reprimand or even scrutiny. Also, 'cruelty' is often reduced to acts that are not relevant within a given animal industry, and thus it may be perfectly legal to castrate pigs without any analgesia or keep sows in crates where they cannot turn around. That is: only acts that are financially or practically insignificant for the animal industries are categorised as 'cruelty' (Rogers and Kaplan 2004).

All these aspects of existing legislation point toward an anthropocentric take on non-human animals, wherein human utility is always primary in relation to animal welfare, and wherein duties toward animals remain minimal. Even though welfare laws are often hailed as symptoms of growing concern for non-human animals, they also tend to reflect a morality, within which the normative status of non-human animals is secondary and instrumental. Significantly, besides reflecting anthropocentrism, current welfare legislations may also enforce it in that they render violence toward animals legal: whilst the laws may place some restrictions on animal (ab)use, they also give their official blessing to keeping animals in conditions, which go against their most basic of needs, and to killing animals for utterly secondary gain. This means that the welfare laws may even be 'a major structural and historical mechanism in the consolidation of institutionalized animal abuse' (Beirne 1999: 129). In fact, even the term 'cruelty' can reflect the anthropocentric order, in that its moral potency is very limited in comparison to terms such as 'violence', 'torture', 'murder' or 'atrocity'. Placing emphasis on 'cruelty' may also misdirect attention away from institutional forms of violence, and create an impression, according to which violence toward animals is the handy-work of deranged individuals and thus both rare and easily dealt with (see Svärd in this volume).

The other significant question concerns acts done in order to advance the treatment or status of non-human animals. Whereas within the framework of animal welfare, criminalisation is rather rare (that is, the use of the term 'crime' remains marginal), here criminalisation is increasingly common. There are various reoccurring forms of criminalisation that target the animal rights movement (see also Ellefsen in this volume). One common form involves reading the law in a way that makes it possible for the police to arrest activists for seemingly legal actions (such as holding peaceful demonstrations, displaying pictures of experimentation animals on placards and using the megaphone). Another common form of criminalisation involves arresting and prosecuting activists for illegal acts of a very minor nature (such as street collections, graffiti or minor vandalism) that would usually be ignored by the police. The third form consists of making use of the law in an atypical manner, so as to render activism as difficult as possible. Examples include use of injunctions and restrictions that make, for instance, demonstrations either impossible or very intricate to organise. The most severe variety of criminalisation involves legislative changes that render thus-far legal forms of activism into illegal acts.

Therefore, criminalisation involves: 1) targeting legal actions; 2) targeting minor crimes in an atypical manner; 3) excessively stringent policing or atypical interpretations of the law; and 4) legislative changes. All these forms of criminalisation have been used extensively in relation to SHAC. Wrongful arrests for legal actions, or arrests for minor offences, have been commonplace. Injunctions have been put in force in order to protect businesses against demonstrations, and anti-social behaviour orders have been used in order to curtail individual activists. These measures have coincided with police operations, the scale of which is usually left for high-profile crimes. The most significant of these is the police operation 'Achilles', which spanned over three years, cost £3.5 million and utilised nearly 700 officers around Europe. In 2007, 32 arrests were made in various European countries, which eventually led to a number of court cases. In 2009 and 2010, 12 UK SHAC activists were given prison sentences of up to 11 years (similar trials have taken place in United States, where huge fines have been added to long prison sentences).[2] The main charge has been 'conspiracy to blackmail'. The charge itself is highly ambiguous and has raised debate, as it is not clear whether it renders protest campaigning itself illegal (is the claim 'we will not stop until you stop' blackmail?) (see again also Ellefsen in this volume).

Most importantly, special sections have been added to the British Serious Organised Crime and Police Act 2005 which render campaigns against animal experimentation corporations *de facto* illegal. They are specifically designed to protect animal-testing industries. Section 145 renders it a crime to interfere with animal research organisations with the intent of harming contractual relationships. 'Harm' includes situations where customers of these organisations leave their contract, or where potential customers refuse to enter into a contract. 'Harm' is also understood to cover 'loss or damage of any description' and one is guilty of causing harm, if he/she is 'to prevent or hinder the carrying out by the organisation of any of its activities'. The 'interference' in question need not be illegal, for what suffices is that it is 'tortious', that is, a breach of a civil duty toward a person that is not a 'crime' (examples of torts include negligence and nuisance that lead to economic, emotional or reputational injury). Because the Section 145 is so

2 One activist had already in 2006 been sentenced to serve three years in prison for property damage.

broad in its definitions, and because it, in particular, defines 'harm' to include any sort of hindrance, damage or loss, in practice it opens the door for naming any type of successful activism against HLS illegal. That is, if an activist manages to dissuade a potential customer from doing business with HLS, he/she may be found guilty. This is a significant point: because the section in question refers to not only 'crimes' but also 'torts', it enables the state to pursue activists who have not committed crimes. Thus it potentially means that if a demonstration causes prospective customers of HLS to not enter into contract with them, the activists can be convicted, even when they have not participated in any sort of criminal activity (the possible implications are vast – perhaps the section could even render it illegal to write critical articles about the HLS). Section 146 argues that activists are guilty of 'intimidation' if they threaten a person linked to an animal research organisation with a 'tortious' act that will lead to loss of any description. Again, this opens the door for prosecuting activists for merely telling a worker of a research laboratory that they intend to hold future demonstrations. Maximum sentences for these two sections vary from one to five years (the first prison sentence handed out for these offences was three years).[3]

As is commonly argued, 'crime' as a concept includes political and cultural underpinnings. What is categorised as 'crime' is partly dependent on power-relations and cultural presumptions concerning, for instance, the value of given beings (Lynch and Stretsky 2003). This is obvious also in the context of non-human animals. What is defined as 'crime' in relation to animals is largely dependent on: 1) what type of normative relevance is given to non-human animals; and 2) what type of economical and political gains are at stake for those who hold political power. As seen, welfare legislation is at risk of reflecting deeply anthropocentric understandings of the moral status of animals, and economical considerations are a strong impetus to keep on protecting current animal industries. Together, these factors make it unlikely that welfare laws will be able to challenge, let alone eradicate, institutional violence toward animals. However, the very same factors may enhance criminalisation of animal rights activists. First, the activists' aims are brought under question via reference to anthropocentric values: their assault on anthropocentrism is met with fierce resistance. Second, the bigger the economic losses caused by the activists,

3 It should be noted that criminalisation does not only involve the state and the police, but also the economical elite that are being affected by social movements, and the private investigators that this elite is able to hire. As manifested by Walby and Monaghan (2011), in Canada SHAC has been targeted by private security officers mobilised by the shareholders and other economical instances involved with HLS. The private security officers have surveilled and harassed activists, and worked closely with the local police, who again have clamped down on activists with a very heavy hand. As a result, even information stalls concerning HLS have become *de facto* impossible, as activists are continuously arrested for holding them, and as all their materials are routinely confiscated. As a *post-hoc* excuse for these utterly disproportionate tactics, the state has labelled SHAC activists as 'eco-terrorists'. This manifests the power that the economical elite have in criminalising those that seek to criticise them.

arguably the more stringent the criminalisation. These factors are evident also in the SHAC debate.

Understandings concerning 'crime' are affected by corporative actions and intentions. As Michael Lynch and Paul Stretsky point out, this applies also to notions of 'green crime'. Corporations use the media to advance their own understanding of 'green', which again has had an impact on how the wider society relates to environmental issues. Here, 'green' is de-politicised, non-radical and demands little action, as emphasis is shifted from producers to consumers. As a result, environmental movements have lost a significant portion of their previous influence, as the activist with his/her uncomfortable criticism has been replaced with a belief that the industries are themselves solving and eradicating environmental problems. Corporations have managed this shift via two particular actions. First, they have made small and superficial concessions toward green issues, and second, they have embarked on huge public relations campaigns which advertise their concern for the environment (Lynch and Stretsky 2003, see also Karliner 1997). This phenomenon has – rather famously – been termed 'greenwashing' (Greer and Bruno 1997).

Arguably, a similar trend is happening in relation to non-human animals. States and industries are more eager to emphasise their 'welfare credentials', as the image put forward is that states and industries have the best interests of animals in mind. Here, particularly, reference to 'strict regulation' is common. Various formidable corporations, ranging from McDonalds to Scandinavian fur industries, have argued to follow strict guidelines on animal welfare, and the same claim has been made by numerous states. References to welfare serve as a marketing strategy, via which companies and states can invite individuals to consume even more of those animals that they claim to care about. What is significant is that, as Wahlström and Peterson have pointed out, welfare regulations are also used as a justification for a given practice. Hence, they are a 'pacifying tactic' utilised by corporations and states that seek to justify their own actions toward non-human animals. By asserting that a given practice is legal, different instances claim that the same practice is also moral. The implication is that morality can be reduced to law, and that as long as one follows welfare regulations, everything is morally in order (Wahlström and Peterson 2006). Thus, next to 'green washing', one can talk of 'welfare washing'.

Elements of welfare washing are obvious in the SHAC debate. However, they coincide with a strong emphasis on the anthropocentric world-view. Whereas it can be argued that green washing rarely includes arguments according to which human beings matter the most (on the contrary, holistic notions are often underlined, albeit superficially), in welfare washing such arguments are very common. The motto is: animals matter, but human interests always come first (on the background of this type of thinking, see Sollund in this volume). This serves to render criminalisation less likely in the animal context: current practices related to animal (ab)use are not under risk of becoming illegal, as long as the anthropocentric framework is emphasised. Therefore, what consumers are offered is not any substantial improvement in welfare legislation (for this would require wholesale critique of anthropocentrism), but rather clarity of conscience, as animal (ab)use appears justified. This is a factor that underlines the passive and non-radical nature of corporative welfarism: within such welfarism, nothing much changes.

Huntingdon Life Sciences

The HLS internet website[4] begins with the slogan: 'Working for a Better Future'. The readers are immediately brought to the realm of the anthropocentric calculus, which emphasises human benefit. This theme is present throughout the website. It is maintained that the benefits of experimentation are not only 'enormous', but also 'undoubted' and 'plain to see'. Various 'landmark discoveries' are listed. What emerges is an inherently utilitarian view on animal experimentation: experimentation is justified, because it is useful to human beings. Therefore, animal experimentation is placed within an anthropocentric paradigm, and its claimed benefits are given great prominence (of course, the extent of the benefits can be also questioned, see for instance LaFollette and Shanks 1996).

On the website, various non-medical products (from pesticides to household chemicals and 'food packaging, adhesives, and clothes dyes') are repeatedly listed in order to lure potential customers. However, in sections, where HLS seeks to justify the use of animals, only medical products are mentioned. Thus, there is significant tension between what is told to chemical manufacturers (prospective clients) and what is told to the wider public. As a result of this tension, a company which tests primarily non-medical substances is justifying its actions solely on the basis of medical advancement. In other words, force-feeding or injecting household and industrial chemicals into animals until they get sick or die is given the noble title of 'medical progress'. Here HLS is resting on 'benefit of association', as all animal experimentation is included in the same moral category. Benefit of association is, in fact, repeatedly referenced. The website argues that: 'Animals benefit man in many ways – clothing, food, science, medicine and entertainment', and therefore animal experimentation is put in the broader category of animal use: if the society accepts animal suffering in the context of farming, why should it get upset about animal experimentation?[5] This type of categorisation may be logically flawed, but it is an effective form of persuasion. It helps to support the

4 Available at: http://www.huntingdon.com [Accessed 30 October 2006].

5 Also, it is pointed out that 'dogs and monkeys account for a very small part of the total number of animals involved'. In this way, the website implies that it is only 'pets' and primates that have value significant enough to warrant concern. This stance follows the example of the US welfare legislation relevant to experimentation, which does not include mice and rats (the most common experimentation animals) in the sphere of 'animals' at all (and thereby places no limits on how these creatures ought to be treated).

case for experimentation by tapping on widely shared anthropocentric meanings concerning human benefit and the normative status of non-human animals.

However, HLS does not only bring forward the human angle. It is stated that: 'Many of these applications have also benefited veterinary medicine, which in some small way repays the debt humanity owes to the animals used'. What is significant here are the implications of this sentence: something, indeed, is 'owed' to animals, which suggests that the use of animals is seen to be morally significant, after all. Moreover, not only are animals owed something, but animal suffering is viewed as a weighty moral consideration: 'In a situation without veterinary medicines, animals would suffer and that would clearly be unacceptable'.[6] Thus, HLS suggests that it shares the common belief that animal suffering is a moral evil – what is more, we also learn that HLS actively seeks to alleviate animal suffering, and that this alleviation is its moral duty. Even 'respect' for the animals is mentioned. Interestingly, the moral relevance of animals is suddenly depicted in much the same way that the moral relevance of human beings was depicted earlier. Thus, HLS bring forward both strict anthropocentrism and concern for animals. One interpretation is that HLS is, in its conflicting and contradictory depictions of the normative relevance of animals, simply reflecting the ambiguity of contemporary societal attitudes toward animals: animals both matter and do not matter. However, the more likely interpretation is that HLS is embarking on an advertisement campaign. By paying such high regard for animals and their welfare, HLS is quite evidently taking part in 'welfare washing'. In fact, by emphasising its own role as an agent that actively works to reduce animal suffering, HLS is putting itself forward as a replacement for the animal rights activist. Nothing needs to be done, the consumer need not worry, for HLS is looking after animal welfare.

Following the theme of welfare washing, HLS makes use of the pacifying tactic of referring to welfare guidelines. The website repeatedly states that HLS follows 'stringent welfare laws', and even argues that these laws are the 'best' in the world (which again sparks the impression that HLS is doing the 'best' one can toward animal welfare). In this way, HLS emerges as an instance committed to both passively and actively ensuring animal welfare. The result is a non-radical and very moderate and shallow form of 'animal welfarism', which is incapable of questioning the very processes and structures that lie behind welfare problems. By posing as a welfare-committed instance, HLS is able to further undermine reasons for criminalising practices related to animal experimentation: nothing needs to change. In the meantime, the huge contradictions in HLS's claims for welfare and its actual acts toward animals are by-passed.

The website continues by painting a rather negative image of the critics of animal experimentation. The critics are argued to offer people false information in the form of 'scare stories and myths'. In fact, it is implied that what animal rights activists say is generally unreliable. This further helps to segregate SHAC and

6 In a rather paradoxical twist, animal experimentation is justified on the account that it helps animals – animals are caused suffering and death so that animals may flourish.

pose HLS itself as an authority on animal welfare. Here, HLS becomes the bearer of the 'truth', which immediately gives it a position of power. More importantly, however, it helps to ensure the second type of criminalisation relevant in the animal context: criminalisation of animal rights activists.

Therefore, the HLS website brings forward a clear message: experimentation need not be further criminalised, and if anything, the existing laws mean that animals are treated well. Moreover, HLS is itself a guardian of legality, who seeks to ensure that the welfare of animals is protected. If anything, it ought to be the activist who is criminalised.

Stop Huntingdon Animal Cruelty

In order to counterbalance corporative influence, Lynch and Stretsky emphasise the need for an environmental justice view, which requires 'substantial economical and political reorganisation' (Lynch and Stretsky 2003). Such reorganisation is important partly because corporations and legislative instances tend to have little interest in the welfare of the most oppressed groups of the society: in order to make those with least power heard, we need to be ready for substantial reconfiguring of current practices. This has obvious relevance in the context of non-human animals, who within the anthropocentric society remain a clearly oppressed group, and whose interests are rarely given consideration.

One party that seeks to bring forth such substantial reorganisation is the animal rights movement. It aims to alter what is considered 'a crime' in the context of non-human animals, and argues that animals should not be positioned as instruments for human benefit. The central claim of the movement is that violence toward non-human animals is itself a crime, whereas action in order to alleviate this violence is (*prima facie*) not. The anthropocentric framework is therefore turned on its head: more emphasis should be on criminalising violence toward animals, and less on criminalising acts that seek to prevent such violence.

Understandings of crime can be impacted by 'moral entrepreneurs and moral crusaders', who seek to challenge and alter how different forms of 'crime' are made meaningful (Lynch and Stretsky 2003). Here, political actions themselves can have a significant bearing, ranging from demonstrations to direct action. The political movements behind such actions typically seek to challenge the moral legitimacy of corporations and states, and therefore attempt to replace emphasis on narrow economical self-interest with wider moral reflection (Lynch and Stretsky 2003; Wahlström and Peterson 2006). The animal rights movement can be defined in these terms. It has emerged as a moral entrepreneur that uses various forms of political action (including also illegal direct action) to advance its wholesale criticism of the animal industries. With these actions, animal rights activists invite 'frame transformation', which seeks to confirm, alter or introduce altogether new normative landscapes. According to Wahlström and Peterson, even 'violent attacks' by animal activists can be attempts at frame transformation –

that is, the short-term goal of closing down given businesses may not be the only motivation behind direct action (Wahlström and Peterson 2006, see also Schnurer 2004). SHAC can be depicted in these terms: it is seeking to attack the narrow economical interests of HLS both on the practical and moral level, and to offer an alternative to the type of egoistical utilitarianism endorsed by HLS. In so doing, it poses a radical challenge against the anthropocentric paradigm.

Wahlström and Peterson maintain that animal rights activists and animal industries are 'locked in a cultural struggle' over how issues related to animals and animal use are framed in public discussion (Wahlström and Peterson 2006). This is evident also in the debate between HLS and SHAC, as both are presenting the general public with their own competing views in order to challenge one another and bear an impact on how the society makes sense of the status and treatment of non-human animals. Following suit, the SHAC website offers a very different take on experimentation than HLS.

The SHAC website[7] begins with a quote from *Journal of Life Sciences*: 'No group is more dangerous or determined to end animal testing than the Stop Huntingdon Animal Cruelty'. The front page includes icons of companies that have shares in HLS, with the title: 'Shareholders in Death'. Underneath, tens of news items from the campaign are listed, mainly to do with demonstrations held in various locations. Therefore, the front page has momentum. It states SHAC's aim very clearly and brings forward formidable determination: animal experimenters are immoral due to the violence and death they cause, and SHAC is going to stop them. It becomes immediately apparent that SHAC wants animal experimentation to be made illegal: using animals in, for instance, toxicity tests is a moral wrong, and should be rendered into a crime. Following suit, HLS is repeatedly linked to illegality. Firstly, it is argued that HLS breaks existing welfare laws (for instance, it is claimed that HLS continuously takes part in 'illegal acts', 'falsifying data', 'criminal activities' and 'gross incompetence'), and secondly, it is stated that violence toward animals should be viewed as a crime and is, indeed, something akin to terrorism. The message is clear: HLS is the true criminal.

Moreover, HLS is described as a deceitful and secretive organisation, whereas SHAC is characterised as an organisation that actively attempts to find the truth: 'We have proved HLS to be liars yet again'. Hence, the debate between HLS and SHAC touches on authority over 'truth', as both seek to contest the other one's ability or willingness to offer accurate information to the wider public. In addition, the SHAC website strongly disputes the welfare claims made by HLS. If anything, HLS is argued to cause 'horrific suffering' to animals. It is maintained that HLS is constantly 'killing animals due to neglect', and that it takes part in 'daily cruelty'. What is more, the argument is that it is not welfare but rather money that motivates HLS, as it is characterised as financially greedy, and as economic profit is placed as its main impetus. In this way, the arguments presented by SHAC seek to obliterate the 'welfare washed' image of HLS, and to directly challenge the anthropocentric

---

7 Available at: http://www.shac.net [Accessed 30 October 2006].

framework which HLS relies on. The message is simple: contrary to what is says, HLS does not respect animal welfare, and in fact it relies on an unjustified stance which prioritises financial gain at the expense of sentient life.

Welfare washing is directly attacked also on the practical level. Harrowing descriptions of various undercover operations are offered, ranging from those carried out by British Union Against Vivisection to those implemented by Channel Four, People for the Ethical Treatment of Animals and the *Observer*. Most accounts are very graphic and disturbing. A two year chronic toxicity study on a tranquillizer is described with following words: 'Clinical reports recorded: "rats having fits after dosing for up to one minute"' and 'cages 85, 95 and 100 had large amounts of dark red blood on their trays …' One technician described the animals in this room as: 'rotting but still alive.' It is stated that in the Dog Toxicology Unit, undercover operators have witnessed beagles being 'poisoned with pesticides, dental hygiene products, drugs and food wrapping film …', and one of the operators is quoted as saying: 'Whilst cleaning out the cages, I regularly found blood, vomit and diarrhoea on the floor. Many dogs were very ill. They were extremely thin with their fur standing on end. They were visibly shaking and often so scared they were unable to leave their cages.' It is depicted how primates [wild-caught baboons] died after suffering symptoms such as 'violent spasms, bloody discharges, grinding teeth and uncontrollable, manic eye movements'. Further explicit examples of experimentation are given: 'Dog number 1185 trembling struggling … trembling nervous, 1181 pulling back in sling, struggling … 1179 severe head tremors and whole body shaking … 1187 closing of eyes, drooping of head, head supported by sling, slow deep breathing, staggering in sling, semi consciousness … 1183 shaking of head, unconsciousness …'. Tests on mice are also described: 'paddling of forelimbs, very unsteady, eyes half closed, whole body tremors.' Many accounts are supported with visual evidence, and scenes of sadistic cruelty are displayed (these include instances where young dogs are repeatedly punched on the face when they try to escape the syringe).

These descriptions vividly present HLS as an animal welfare violator rather than an animal welfare agent. Moreover, the very welfare laws that HLS emphasises are placed under doubt, as violence takes place right under the nose of the representatives of the law: '… 32 puppies … are sick as they are being injected … If the puppies wriggle, they are hit or shaken by the scruff of their necks … Walk into my unit and one of my puppies, number 1619, has half a pint of congealed bloody feces around his cage. The vet looks at him and says it is all right to continue with the daily doses.' In fact, government inspectors are claimed to chat with the staff and ignore the animals altogether. Hence, it is suggested that HLS nurtures a culture of disregard, which begins from technicians and goes all the way up to vets, inspectors and scientists. It is also described how: 'In one incident a technician holds a monkey in mid-air as he administers a tuberculin test material into the animal's eyelid. Asked by the undercover investigator if he can do it this way, the vivisector replied: "Nope, not supposed to, never saw it, never did it, can't prove it."' As a consequence, the strict welfare regulations that HLS emphasises are argued to remain cosmetic, as in practice they are not followed or enforced, and even sadistic behaviour is tolerated.

Moreover, it is stated that the government's involvement is 'clear', together with its 'failure' to 'adequately' regulate animal experimentation. Whereas the HLS website seeks to support its case by referring to governmental support, the SHAC website uses a large 2004 exposé by the *Observer* to denounce the government itself as a biased party, utterly unable or unwilling to protect the welfare of animals (the exposé revealed, for instance, that the Home Office was eager to classify extreme experiments on primates as 'moderate' in order to render licenses more easily attainable). This further undermines the notion of welfare regulations, as the very body that creates and enforces those regulations is argued to be non-trustworthy. SHAC is putting forward a clear argument: the laws regarding non-human animals need to be restructured on a basis that prioritises the good of the animals rather than economic gain. That is, what we understand to be 'crime' in relation to animals needs to go through radical reformation.

Therefore, whereas HLS brings forward anthropocentrism and welfare washing, SHAC challenges both. SHAC also approaches the third key factor underlined by HLS – possible benefits of experimentation – in an interesting way. Instead of emphasising, like many animal rights philosophies do, that the benefits are irrelevant, SHAC posits that they rarely exist. The introduction to the website starts with the slogan: 'Huntingdon Life Sciences – Making Life Hell for People and Animals'. It is maintained that: 'HLS are directly responsible for human misery, suffering and death …', and a sub-section 'Drug disasters' lists instances where drugs likely to have been safety tested by HLS have been withdrawn or re-labelled because of serious side-effects. Animal testing is claimed to be scientifically flawed. Most importantly, the purposes of the experiments are brought under question, as it is pointed out that the majority of HLS research indeed concerns chemicals such as pesticides, herbicides and household products – not life-saving medicine. Therefore, the utilitarian calculus offered by HLS is turned upside down: the animal cost is too great, and the human benefit too slim, non-existent or utterly secondary to justify experimentation.

What about the criminalisation of activists? The website seeks to justify different forms of direct action by linking them to intra-human struggles on behalf of the oppressed (such as slaves and women), and by thus confirming existing cultural values. The question concerning legality of these actions is present throughout the website. An injunction against SHAC is laid out on the front page, followed by a claim: 'SHAC does not encourage or incite any illegal activities …'. Therefore, SHAC is presented as group that uses legal methods and which, in fact, is opposed to illegalities. The website also takes a stance on the negative portrayal of activists. It argues that: 'Those who campaign against HLS are often portrayed as misguided and/or terrorists. Nothing could be further from the truth. SHAC is made up of compassionate people from all walks of life …'. However, the issue is nuanced. Elsewhere on the website it is argued that people should get as active as they can, and do whatever it takes to close down HLS – also prisoner lists are brought forward. This suggests a complex relation to law and criminality. Therefore, whilst SHAC are contesting anthropocentrism and contemporary takes on what constitutes a 'crime' against animals, they may also be contesting the notion of 'crime' on behalf of animals.

The British State

When considering the actions of political movements, attention should also be placed on the external, rather than merely the internal, factors that impact the movement's scope and success. Here, for instance the state's capacity for repression is relevant (Wahlström and Peterson 2006, McAdam 1996). This is particularly evident in the context of the animal rights movement and SHAC, which have been hit hard by different forms of criminalisation instigated by various states worldwide (see again Ellefsen in this volume).

How 'crime' is perceived is partly the result of the actions of law enforcement agencies. Here, it is imperative to explore the motives behind the agencies: 'It is important to understand *which* behaviors become the focus of law and *why*' (Lynch and Stretsky 2003). One way to dig deeper is to explore the connections between the state and the economical interests of animal industries. In the context of animals, the links are rather clear, as the economical revenue produced by animal industries is significant. It would seem that the more efficiently a movement attacks the economical interests of the state and corporations, the more vehemently it will be penalised with various forms of criminalisation. Arguably, SHAC acts as one clear example of this phenomenon.

Wahlström and Peterson argue that the repression practiced by the state toward animal rights activists is often discursive, in that it seeks to represent activists as 'illegitimate in their methods and, by association, perhaps also in their grievances' (Wahlström and Peterson 2006). This means that, via the act of criminalisation, the broader morality of activists is brought under question: perhaps the moral framework presented by activists is as illegitimate as the methods that they use. Criminalisation is not the only form of discursive repression. The state is also often eager to find mainstream organisations that comply with its own values in order to marginalise 'the moral radical factions of the animal rights movement' (Wahlström and Peterson 2006). Various other forms of discursive repression are also evident, and will become obvious in the following extracts from official documents produced by the British government during the most heated years of SHAC activity. More importantly, criminalisation can also be more than purely discursive, in that it has a very concrete effect on how both activists and animals are treated.

During the first decade of 2000 the British government issued various reports in support of experimentation. In the reports the utility of experimentation is repeatedly emphasised. For instance a Government Progress Report from 2006 (HM Government: 'Protecting people from animal rights extremists: Progress report'), together with a statement from the Prime Minister, emphasises the benefits of animal research: 'Many millions more will be spared an early death or a life of pain because of the research now under way'. A Home Office White Paper from 2004 ('Animal Welfare – Human Rights') claims that 'extraordinary' breakthroughs are made possible by animal testing, with 'huge contribution' to human welfare. Thus, the state takes part in the type of anthropocentric utilitarianism favoured by HLS. Interestingly, also economical benefit is brought forward. It is pointed out that biosciences have made a 'massive contribution to our economy and prosperity', and that in 2003, pharmaceutical exports were worth £12 billion. The economical gain is, in fact, positioned as a major utility made possible by animal experimentation. This would seem to support the argument, according to which economical factors form one motive for state repression.

The reports also emphasise welfare, often from a rather nationalistic perspective. Thus, the White Paper mentioned above claims that the United Kingdom has a 'proud record on animal welfare' and that 'The UK has in place one of the world's toughest regimes for licensing and controlling animal experiments'. A House of Lords Commission Paper from 2002 (by Select Committee on Animals in Scientific Procedures) talks of the 'best' regulation in the world (this is something which many nations seem to declare – see again Svärd in this volume). Throughout the reports, animal welfare is correlated with existing legislation, and the latter is seen as evidence of the former. This method of legalisation is an effective means of discursively downplaying SHAC, as the state takes authority over 'animal welfare': rather than SHAC, it is the state that recognises the good of the animal. Here, just like HLS before, the state presents itself as an active agent working for animal welfare, and therefore arguably takes part in 'welfare washing'.

The governmental documents also emphasise negative stereotypes of animal rights activists. The White Paper from 2004 describes SHAC as 'a tiny minority of animal rights extremists who are behind an illegal campaign of intimidation and violence'.[8] It is argued that their activity is 'despicable and will not be tolerated' – it is also characterised as 'illegal and violent' and 'totally unacceptable'. In very clear terms, SHAC is rendered into a morally and legally reprehensible party, isolated from the rest of the society. This offers a fertile ground for marginalisation and ensuing criminalisation of SHAC activists. Quite strikingly, the White Paper goes on to claim that: 'Some of the activities of animal rights extremists are often considered to be acts of terrorism.' It states that such terminology is enabled by the Terrorism Act of 2001, which 'widened' the definition of 'terrorism' by linking it to ideological behaviour (therefore, in order to define animal rights 'extremism' as terrorism, it needs to be characterised as an 'ideology'). Rather conveniently, the paper itself then continues to describe animal rights activism as ideological, and thus quite explicitly paves the way for calling it 'terrorism'. The state thus uses the well-known power of discourse and 'naming' in its efforts to castigate and chastise

8 SHAC are not mentioned by name, but all emphasis in the document is on HLS and animal rights activity related to it.

SHAC. Hence, it is not only criminalisation, but criminalisation of the highest order that awaits SHAC activists.

The White Paper also brings forward moderate animal welfare organisations, like the RSPCA, as 'legitimate' and 'well-respected', thereby further pinpointing SHAC as a negative force, and linking the government itself to welfare concerns. Thus, the British government is using two of the discursive forms of repression mentioned above: animal rights activists are labelled as illegitimate in their methods and their aims, and considerably more moderate parties are brought to the fore as the 'respectable' choice.

Most importantly, the UK government also makes explicit its intention to take action against activism. The House of Lords Commission Paper from above argues the following: 'The protests against Huntingdon Life Sciences in particular have proved a focal point in the public debate on animal rights and the use of animals in scientific experimentation. Animal rights protests and the use of both innovative and violent measures have resulted in new legislation'. What is interesting in these sentences is the possible implication that because SHAC has managed to raise wider awareness concerning the animal rights issue, action needs to be taken. The Paper also does not only discuss criminalising violent measures, but 'animal rights protests' themselves. A cynical reading of these lines suggests the following: SHAC has become effective, and therefore needs to be dealt with by the hand of the law.

In the White Paper from 2004 it is maintained that 'The Government, police and courts are stepping up efforts to stamp out this illegal and sometimes violent conduct'. The impetus is to 'stop extremism' completely, and the methods are manifold. 'New measures' will be introduced and the government will 'tighten the law still further'. The document considers in great depth how existing legislation could be used to make otherwise seemingly legal acts illegal. The police and courts are urged to take activism 'extremely seriously' – something the government seeks to make easier by offering them 'new powers to tackle [activism]'. They are asked to be as stringent as possible, to use 'robust enforcement', and to view animal 'extremism' as an aggravating factor. The document also points out that a special police body, *The National Extremism Tactical Co-ordinating Unit* (NETCU), has been set up in order to curtail animal 'extremism'. It trains police officers around the country, advises them to be particularly diligent with animal rights activists, and has, for instance, printed out and disseminated to the police forces handbooks and leaflets on how to curtail activism (these handbooks include lists of all the different laws under which activists can be prosecuted – put simply, they are a guide to 'how to arrest an activist').[9] Legislative changes are also introduced, and it is stated that the government 'shall introduce a number of new offences to fill gaps in the law'. Therefore, emphasis is on making a robust use of existing laws, and criminalising thus far legal acts – moreover, heavy (and arguably in many ways disproportionate) policing is utilised.

9 For an example, see 'Policing Protest – Pocket Legislation Guide'. Available at: http://animalrightscambridge.webs.com/NETCUHandbook.pdf [Accessed 10 January 2011].

It is noteworthy that the scope of actions being criminalised is very vast. In the first instance, they include standard actions like demonstrations, which are without further explication given the prefix 'intimidatory'. Plans of criminalisation even concern thus far legal activities that make use of the internet, which would also render the SHAC website itself illegal. It is stated that: 'The Government is well aware that animal rights extremists use the internet to intimidate or incite others to commit violence', and various options for removing also '*legal* material' (emphasis mine) from the internet are discussed. Most importantly, also causing economical losses to an animal testing facility is criminalised, which – as already pointed out – renders SHAC *de facto* illegal. Serious Organised Crime and Police Act 2005 also renders it 'harassment' to approach two different people from the same organisation just once, rather than to approach the same person on a number of occasions – this, again, will make protesting very difficult (if an activist sees both x and y from HLS, he/she may be guilty of harassment). The significance of these measures cannot be overstated, as key forms of protest, previously legal, are being outlawed.

The British state is taking a clear stance against animal activism, and supports the key-themes emphasised by HLS. There need not be further criminalisation in relation to animals, as welfare laws are already amongst the best in the world. However, the acts of those seeking to better the status of animals do need to be criminalised, particularly when they start to have a broader influence that threatens medical or financial interests. The ensuing legal changes have had a clear impact on the SHAC campaign, particularly in the form of reducing the number of actions, and it can be argued that criminalisation of SHAC offers a palpable contemporary example of how state repression can influence the scope of a movement (albeit it is still too early to say whether SHAC will gain back its momentum).

The News Media

Crime is constructed also socially, and here various forms of popular media (including news media) are relevant (Lynch and Stretsky 2003). In short: the media repeats, affirms and constructs different understandings concerning crime, which have an impact on how the society at large makes sense of crime. This is also evident in the context of 'animal crime'. Thus Wahlström and Peterson argue that the way in which the media depicts the animal rights movement is 'crucial in the formation of public opinion', and also 'decisive in the placement of these issues on the political agenda'" (Wahlström and Peterson 2006).

Much of the mainstream news reporting concerning SHAC from the first decade of 2000 is eager to resort to negative stereotypes. However, there is an interesting shift in the reports. Whereas until around 2006–07, news reporting also included some positive and empathetic views on SHAC activists, this was quick to change toward the end of the decade. It is around the time that the government first began to plan and implement tough policing and legislative changes that – arguably – also the media image turned more negative.[10]

An article from the *Guardian* (Steve Boggan: 'Money talks', 1 June 2006) presents a perhaps surprisingly empathetic picture of SHAC. Greg Avery, one key figure in SHAC, is described as the 'protestor of the future', and afforded the chance to depict his own views on activism. The article mentions how difficult it is 'not to fall back on stereotypes', and the journalist describes how he is expecting Avery to be eccentric and fundamentalist, and how he is surprised that Avery looks like 'a clean cut accountant'. Avery's background is brought to the fore, and Avery is allowed to freely present his own persona and views. His statement that SHAC does not take part in illegal activism is brought to the fore without skepticism. The economic impact that SHAC has had is portrayed as a notable achievement, and even given the aura of a David and Goliath scenario: the economic world is filled with 'greed and self-interest', which the small group of activists is using against it. The reporter argues that the interview was 'candid', thus giving it an aura of realism. Therefore, the interview offers us the following picture: SHAC activists are ordinary people rather than extremists. They seek to use legal means to fight against animal testing, and they are an honest source of information. That is: SHAC activists are reliable, law-abiding and moral. Avery himself is depicted as a person – an individual with his own past and views – rather than an empty stereotype. Most notably, there is something heroic about activism: it is a field of virtue rather than vice.

The same year, *The Independent* offered another chance for the activists to express their viewpoint (Terry Kirby: 'Blair's hard line on animal testing will backfire, say campaigners', 15 May 2006). The article in question begins with a statement from activists, according to which the 'hard-line stance' by the government will only serve to increase violence. The notion that many from the general public oppose animal experimentation is brought to the fore and claims that experimentation does not work are introduced. Prime Minister Tony Blair's explicit support for the experimentation industry is also discussed, and it is described how the industries have asked for governmental protection against 'intimidation and violence'. The overall theme of the news story seems to be the following: in a problematic way, the industry is pressuring the government to adopt overly harsh methods in order to clamp down on animal rights activism. Whereas in the previous news article, the implication is that perhaps animals should be protected with more stringent laws, the implication here is that activists should not be further criminalised. In these two instances, the media are presenting a view very dissimilar from HLS and the state.

A rather more negative image of SHAC activists began to emerge particularly after four SHAC activists were convicted of conspiracy to blackmail HLS

10 The news analyses here are very limited indeed – however, it is hoped that comparisons of different news stories from the same sources during different time spans will be indicative of a broader change.

employees in 2008. *The Independent* (Rober Vervaik: 'Animal rights four guilty of terror spree', 24 December 2008) discusses the case, this time with a wholly different approach. Activists were argued to have led a 'terror campaign', and SHAC was described as 'an extreme direct action protest group'. Crimes such as hoax bombs, accusations of paedophilia and graffiti were listed. The *Guardian*, too, had a change of heart (Sandra Laville: 'Animal rights extremists still targeting lab', 24 December 2008). Here, the campaign against HLS was described as one of 'threats and intimidation', and activists were termed 'extremists'. Smear campaigns and hoax bombs were yet again mentioned. In both, the type of reflective and more nuanced take on activism offered in earlier news stories was missing. The activist was described as a criminal rather than a moral agent, and an empty stereotype rather than a person. Significantly, any reflective critique on the role of financial interest was absent.

It should be noted that, amongst British mainstream newspapers, the *Guardian* and the *Independent* have arguably been the kindest toward activists. The popular tabloids have provided the most direct attacks on SHAC. A typical example is an article from *Daily Mail* (Tom Kelly: 'Guilty: Animal terror gang who raised £1million rattling tins on the high street', 24 December 2008), which began by describing SHAC activists as 'fanatics who pursued a terror campaign', and as 'terrorists'. It also defined Avery as a 'notorious' and 'brutal' activist, who 'groomed' teenagers into joining his 'criminal network'. Terms such as 'extremist' and 'vandalism' were mentioned many times. SHAC was also characterised as a 'cult' and activists as 'disciples' of Avery. The list of tactics included the most extreme forms of methods used during the SHAC campaign: branding workers as paedophiles, graffiti and sending hoax bombs. It is implied that SHAC used 'emotive' pictures of animals in order to gain funds from ordinary people who did not know that their funds would support a 'criminal conspiracy'. A police representative is quoted as saying that SHAC was guilty of 'conspiracy to blackmail' and 'relentless intimidation'. Interestingly, the article quotes information from the *Guardian* interview with Avery, albeit with a negative twist. What in the *Guardian* was a sympathetic take on the background of an activist, in *Daily Mail* turns into a stack of evidence in support of criminalisation.

Therefore, the news media has – at least in these examples – followed the state's progression towards criminalisation. Sympathetic or open-minded news stories on SHAC have been replaced with blunt, one-sided and incriminating news stories. What is significant is that instead of paying critical attention to governmental efforts to brand activists as 'terrorists', the news media have fully participated in such branding by openly endorsing the use of the term, and by concentrating solely on the most criminal aspects of activism. Depictions of the motivations and beliefs of the activists are entirely missing. In this sense, the media have become a voice for corporative and governmental views, whilst the viewpoints of SHAC activists are omitted – put simply, the activists are missing a voice. The news media depictions will bear an enormous impact on how the general public makes sense of the moral status of non-human animals and the character of animal rights activists.

This further strengthens the case for less criminalisation in the field of animal experimentation, and more criminalisation in the context of animal activists.

Differing Philosophies

Behind the different takes on criminalisation in the animal context lie different 'animal philosophies'. On the most obvious level, these philosophies concern the normative status of non-human animals. HLS, the state and many media representatives follow the anthropocentric framework, according to which the moral value of animals is either primarily or merely instrumental. SHAC, on the other hand, emphasises a zoocentric framework, according to which human beings are only one animal amongst many, and which states that all sentient beings have inherent value and cannot be used as mere instruments for the benefit of others.

However, perhaps more interestingly, the debate also concerns ontological differences that have to do with how non-human animals are depicted and made meaningful. HLS, the state and the media bring forward an understanding of animals that overlooks the experiences and viewpoints of those animals. The actual bodily and mental harm suffered by animals is left without mention – or rather, it is replaced with an emphasis on human benefit. In this way, animals are absent from the anthropocentric paradigms concerning experimentation. Carol Adams has famously discussed how animals often remain 'absent referents' in contemporary discourse. Animals are referred to with terms that do not take into account the living, experiencing animal, or which are the complete antithesis of that animal. She uses the example of meat products (Adams 1990), but perhaps absent referents should be understood as a broader phenomenon that concerns the exclusion of the subjectivity of animals from discussion concerning animals.

It is precisely absent referenting that HLS, the British state and the news media are engaged in when they discuss the use of animals in experimentation without any (or very few) allusions to animal experiences. Depictions of medical procedures or breakthroughs and references to welfare laws replace concern for animal subjectivity. Arguably, this comes close to the type of 'expert jargon' that Hannah Arendt talks of in her analysis of the Holocaust, or the 'crisis' that Edmund Husserl discusses in his exploration of modern alienation and loss of phenomenality. Lived experiences are replaced with a clinical terminology that underlines matters such as legislation or scientific validity, and as a consequence the experiences of other beings, and with them the understanding of the moral relevance of the other, are lost. It can be argued that this forms the basis of the pro-experimentation ontology: within it, the animal viewpoint does not exist in any independent sense, and the animal perspective and value are ultimately lost.

Fox and McLean use Martha Nussbaum's term 'moral perception' in order to refer to the need to reflect on moral issues from more than a purely intellectual viewpoint, by taking the viewpoint of the other into account. They argue that knowledge of facts is not enough to comprehend the morality of given events, for empathy and 'seeing with feeling' are necessary in order for one to make just conclusions concerning the treatment of sentient beings. As an example, Fox and McLean discuss a particular experiment on animals, the purpose of which was to produce a state of helplessness in dogs via bombarding them with electric shocks. Intellect, they maintain, tells us to ignore the viewpoint of the animals and urges us to instead turn to utilitarianism in order to justify the infliction of suffering. However, this will render moral perception blurry: 'To look away from the suffering of the dogs, to turn off our perceptual capacities and in essence our feelings is to get only half the moral story, but worse still, to get that half which further serves to cloud our moral insight and numb our sensibilities … we no longer see … the animal's pain and suffering' (Fox and McLean 2008: 165). Fox and McLean go so far as to suggest that the resulting state is psychopathic, as it enables experimenters to cause dogs to 'piss and shit themselves, howl and struggle' to no avail until they are reduced into broken beings, whilst the experimenter her/himself pays attention only to clinical observations rather than morality. It is this moral perception that SHAC seems to be trying to evoke. SHAC is urging us to take a leap from detached utilitarianism toward an empathetic reading process, within which the experiences of every single animal put through experimentation are to have a bearing. Their unbearably graphic descriptions (both textual and visual) serve this function, and manifest how utterly primary the animal viewpoint is. For them, as for McLean and Fox, the experimenter has become a psychopath in her/his attitudes toward animals.

But what does the recognition of the animal perspective imply? The Noble laureate J.M. Coetzee has a literary character, Elizabeth Costello, who is plagued by the horrors met by non-human animals. To her, they are immensely vivid, and the society capable of continuously inflicting them on animals grotesque. Philosopher Cora Diamond has argued that Costello has become a wounded being in her incapacity to make sense of a reality, in which animals are caused horrific suffering and treated as mere instruments. Costello has become 'exposed' to not only what happens to animals, but also her own incapacity to make sense of her own society, and this has left a permanent mark on her. Costello's 'fellow-feeling' toward animals has been evoked, and she no longer can see animals via utility but rather compassion (Diamond 2008). It would seem that SHAC are precisely trying to expose us to what happens to experimentation animals behind all the jargon about welfare legislations and utility. In doing so, they are challenging core societal notions concerning the human–animal relationship, and in particular rendering the animal 'an other' that has a viewpoint. Most importantly, SHAC is urging one to take a leap into 'the difficulty of reality' (a term used by Diamond) by accepting that there are no clear utilitarian calculus one can use in order to solve interest conflicts between humans and other animals. That is, seeing value in animal viewpoints may mean that we have to accept a much more demanding reality than that afforded by the black-and-white utility calculus offered by the pro-experimentation lobby.

Although the debate over animal experimentation is often depicted as something that exclusively concerns morality, it can be argued that it also revolves around ontology (that is, what types of creatures non-human animals are deemed to be), and more broadly metaphysics (how human beings relate to other animals). Whereas for HLS animals are the type of beings who either lack viewpoints, or whose viewpoints lack relevance, and human beings are the type of creatures who can justifiably relate to other beings via detached utility, SHAC claim the exact opposite. It is in this context that 'animal crime' is made meaningful. Whereas the voice of the experimentation industry has gained most attention, perhaps it is time to also listen to the activist.

Derrida argued that the question concerning animals is the most important question of our time, and can unravel anthropocentric metaphysics to the core. He urged us to pay heed to the animal viewpoint, and famously used as an example his own cat who can look at him just as he can look at the cat (Derrida 2004). Although SHAC may be plagued with insurmountable difficulties in their choice of tactic, their challenge to the anthropocentric worldview needs to be taken seriously into account in order to make sense of contemporary animal rights criminology. In SHAC's graphic descriptions there is always an animal that is looking at us, and thus forcing us to reconsider what 'crime' in the animal context means.

Conclusion

Law seeks to represent both those with and without power, and is presumed to bring forward also the interests and wellbeing of the latter (Lynch and Stretsky 2003). Unfortunately, this has applied poorly to non-human animals, legislation concerning whom remains vague and superficial. The animal rights movement, including SHAC, has sought to question the dismal status of animals via the use of different forms of direct action, which – likely due to corporate pressure – again have become increasingly criminalised by different states. The news media has seen tendencies to echo and further strengthen the case for criminalisation.

The type of criminalisation mentioned in this chapter has also been witnessed in Nordic countries. In these countries, particularly, various undercover campaigns (concerning primarily meat and fur farming) have gained corporate, state and media attention, and have paved the way for a rather startling conclusion: instead of looking into how to improve existing laws so that they offer greater protection for animals, particularly state attention has been on how to criminalise the activists who have taken the footage. As a result, activists in different countries (including Denmark, Sweden and Finland) have recently been charged for filming undercover footage of animal abuse.[11] The Finnish state prosecutor charged activists in 2011 for filming footage in pig farms, and demanded an unconditional jail sentence for the activist, who openly admitted to having taken the footage (for others, the prosecution demands conditional jail terms). Charges were also brought against

11 See for instance http://www.ettlivsomgris.se/20110308322/nyheter/tysta-inte-djurens-vittnen [Accessed 1 August 2011].

activists in an organisation that advertised a link to a website on which the footage could be viewed. Proposed damages that the activists would have to pay are 180,000 Euros. In this case, the main charge is 'gross libel': it is point blank argued that the activists have harmed the reputation of the pig farmers, and therefore need to be punished. The undercover footage in question raised considerable media attention, and it is quite evident that the state has opted for taking a harsh stance against activism in order to prevent similarly embarrassing campaigns that damage the profitability of the animal industries (in the meanwhile, as another measure meant to counteract the activists' influence, the Finnish government has given significant sums to advertisement campaigns that are meant to increase the consumption of pig meat). In the United States, various states have proposed legislation that would render the very act of taking undercover footage from within the animal industries a crime.[12] Thus governments are taking very concrete yet ethically dubious measures in order to, via the act of criminalisation, prevent the public from knowing what happens to the animals that they consume.

The type of heavy-handed criminalisation that is taking place deserves more critical attention. This applies for particularly three reasons. First, activists are faced with extraordinarily tough punishments, which are arguably disproportionate in comparison to what they have done (thus, as we speak, SHAC activists are serving very hefty prison sentences for acts that normally would not warrant such severity of punishment). Second, criminalisation today opens the door for wider criminalisation tomorrow, and the fear is that soon any effective grass root activism will face the risk of being labelled 'a crime'. Thirdly, criminalisation of activists prevents the society from concentrating on the much more relevant animal crime: the treatment of the tens of billions of animals bred and killed for food each year in the Western countries alone.

Behind different understandings of 'crime' in the animal context lie differing philosophies concerning the human–animal relationship. Within the anthropocentric philosophy, animal viewpoints are not brought forward or seen as valuable. Within the zoocentric viewpoints, the opposite applies. What the activists are putting forward is a radical claim, according to which we are to become exposed to the animal perspective and phenomenality: rather than actions of the activists, it is violence toward animals that ought to be criminalised.

References

Adams, C.J. 1990. *The Sexual Politics of Meat*. New York: Continuum.

Arluke, A. 2006. *Just a Dog: Understanding Animal Cruelty and Ourselves*. Philadelphia: Temple University Press.

12 See for example http://www.greenisthenewred.com/blog/new-york-bill-undercover-investigators-factory-farms/4918/ [Accessed 1 August2011]. I am grateful to Rune Ellefsen for pointing out to me the two links above.

Beirne, P. 1999. For a Non-speciesist Criminology: Animal Abuse as an Object of Study, in *Criminology*, 37(1), 117–48.

Bekoff, M. 2002. *Minding Animals: Awareness, Emotions, and Heart*. Oxford: Oxford University Press.

Best, S. and Nocella, A. (eds) 2004. *Terrorists or Freedom Fighters? Reflections on the Liberation of Animals*. New York: Lantern Books.

Cazaux, G. 1999. Beauty and the Beast: Animal Abuse from a Non-speciesist Criminological Perspective, in *Crime, Law & Social Change*, 31(2), 105–26.

Cavalieri, P. 2001. *The Animal Question: Why Non-human Animals Deserve Human Rights*. Oxford: Oxford University Press.

Dawkins, M.S. 1998. *Through Our Eyes Only? The Search for Animal Consciousness*. Oxford: Oxford University Press.

Derrida, J. 2004. An Animal That Therefore I Am, in *Animal Philosophy: Essential Readings in Continental Thought*, edited by P. Atterton and M. Calarco. London: Continuum.

Diamond, C. 2008. The Difficulty of Reality and the Difficulty of Philosophy, in *Philosophy & Animal Life*, edited by C. Wolfe et al. New York: Columbia University Press.

Fox, M.A. and McLean, L. 2008. Animals in Moral Space, in *Animal Subjects: An Ethics Reader in a Post-human World*, edited by J. Castricano. Waterloo, CA: Wilfried Laurier University Press.

Francione, G. 1996. *Rain without Thunder: The Ideology of the Animal Rights Movement*. Philadelphia: Temple University Press.

Gibbs, C. and Gore, M. et al. 2010. Introducing Conservation Criminology: Towards Interdisciplinary Scholarship on Environmental Crimes and Risks, in *British Journal of Criminology*, 50(1), 124–44.

Goodman, R. and Sanders, C. 2011. In Favor of Tipping the Balance: Animal Rights Activists' Defense of Residential Picketing, in *Society & Animals*, 19(2), 137–55.

Greer, J. and Bruno, K. 1997. *Greenwash: The Reality behind Corporate Environmentalism*. New York: Apex Press.

Karliner, J. 1997. *Corporate Planet*. San Francisco: Sierra.

LaFollette, H. and Shanks, N. 1996. *Brute Science. Dilemmas of Animal Experimentation*. London: Routledge.

Lynch, M. and Stretsky, P. 2003. The Meaning of Green: Contrasting Criminological Perspectives, in *Theoretical Criminology*, 7(2), 217–38.

Midgley, M. 1983. *Animals and Why They Matter*. Athens: University of Georgia Press.

Panskepp, J. 1998. *Affective Neuroscience: The Foundations of Human and Animal Emotions*. Oxford: Oxford University Press.

Regan, T. 1983. *The Case For Animal Rights*. Berkeley: University of California Press.

Rogers, L. 1997. *Minds of Their Own. Thinking and Awareness in Animals*. Westview Press.

Rogers, L. and Kaplan, G. 2004. All Animals Are Not Equal: The Interface between Scientific Knowledge and Legislation for Animal Rights, in *Animal Rights: Current Debates and New Directions*, edited by C. Sustein and M. Nussbaum. Oxford: Oxford University Press.

Rowlands, M. 1998. *Animal Rights. A Philosophical Defence*. London: MacMillan Press.

Schnurer, M. 2004. At the Gates of Hell: The ALF and the Legacy of Holocaust Resistance, in *Terrorists or Freedom Fighters? Reflections on the Liberation of Animals*, edited by S. Best and A. Nocella. New York: Lantern Books.

Silverstein, H. 1996. *Unleashing Rights: Law, Meaning, and the Animal Rights Movement*. Ann Arbor: University of Michigan Press.

Singer, P. 1975. *Animal Liberation. A New Ethics For Our Treatment of Animals*. New York: Avon Books.

Wahlström, M. and Peterson, A. 2006. Between the State and the Market: Expanding the Concept of 'Political Opportunity Structure', in *Acta Sociologica*, 49(4), 363–77.

Walby, K. and Monaghan, J. 2011. Private Eyes and Public Order: Policing and Surveillance in the Suppression of Animal Rights Activists in Canada, in *Social Movement Studies*, 10(1), 21–37.

Chapter 10
Green Movements as Threats to Order and Economy: Animal Activists Repressed in Austria and Beyond

Rune Ellefsen[1]

Introduction

On 21 May 2008 armed Special Forces (WEGA)[2] of the Austrian police raided and searched 23 apartments, houses and offices across Austria, marking the start of large-scale state sanctions aimed at the Austrian animal rights movement. Ten people were arrested in the operation and accused of forming a 'criminal organization' according to § 278a of the Austrian criminal code (StGB).[3] In this article I investigate this controversial Austrian case, where a national animal rights movement was under suspicion, with anti-mafia law being used to prosecute its social movement organizers as a 'criminal organization'. My purpose is to investigate why these movements are perceived as possible threats, and how this might have caused counter-mobilization by the movements' opponents. I also explore what might have triggered the state repression, as well as the defendants' experiences and interpretations of these recent events. Green criminologists have looked at the role of social movements in influencing the enforcement of environmental laws (for example, Stretesky, Shelley and Crow 2010). But green criminology has not done much to examine how social movements may become targets of state repression. That is the focus of this chapter.

Over the last 15 years a rise in threat assessments that includes environmental and animal rights movements can be observed in reports from American and European state institutions, and from private security firms. Sections of these social movements[4] are increasingly described as security threats both by states,

---

1 I would like to thank Marte Rua, Guri Larsen and Arild Tornes for constructive feedback on draft versions of this chapter.

2 Counter-terrorist unit 'Wiener Einsatzgruppe Alarmabteilung' (WEGA). In English 'Viennese Special Task Force Alarm Section'.

3 Strafgesetzbuch (StGB).

4 A social movement can be defined as '[...] a group of people who are organized for, ideologically motivated by, and committed to a purpose which implements some form of personal or social change, who are actively engaged in recruitment of others, and whose

and by industries that use animals and nature for capital accumulation. What has caused such developments? Is it a result of the movements' achievements which threaten the economic interests of powerful groups? Is it a logical response to illegal practices on the part of green activists? Is it because such movements challenge hegemonic anthropocentrism, and thereby the societal order? Or are there other reasons? And how do current state control trends, which are aimed at risk and threat management, affect the social control and perception of such movements in the Western world?

There are three main reasons why this case study is of importance: firstly, for the first time anti-mafia law (§ 278a of the Austrian penal code) was used to keep large sections of a social movement under surveillance, and to prosecute them. Secondly, the outcomes of the court case have been crucial to all social movements and political dissent in Austria. Lastly, this was a highly controversial and widely debated trial with a clear political edge, which tapped into core questions regarding the connection between law, power and politics.

Green Criminology and Repression

Avi Brisman (2010: 162) raises an important point when arguing that 'green criminology needs to consider not just activities that hurt the environment and that are unregulated and underregulated, but also activities that are proscribed yet benefit the environment.' I support Brisman's argument, but suggest extending it even further; green criminologists should pay attention to these activities (that benefit the environment, humans and animals, yet being proscribed), but also such legal activities being threatened by criminalization or repressive use of existing law, and similar conduct subjected to state repression and/or policing that limits the possibilities of dissent.

Much work of the green movements is beneficial, and when such lawful activism is repressed by state institutions or others it deserves scholarly attention. This involves picking up the themes of 'criminalization associated with conflicts over environmental issues, [...] including the actions of protestors and those who are opposed to protest actions' (White 2008: 28) and '[assessing] the role of green social movements, and their countermovements involved in a backlash' (Carrabine et al. 2004: 328–9). Roger Yates (2007: 140–157) has discussed such dialectics between the animal rights movement and its counter-movements, Rob White (2005, 2008: 271–9) has written about the legal and other strategic means used for stifling environmental dissent and Brian Walters is concerned with similar questions in *Defamation, Developers and Community Activism* (2003). The core issues of this chapter have briefly been discussed in these green criminological writings, but I would argue that such topics should be increasingly integrated into green criminological research.

influence is spreading in opposition to the established order within which it originated' (Munro 2005:17).

Methodological Note

This chapter builds on a qualitative study of limited size and with a limited duration.[5] My empirical data stems from interviews[6] with four of the thirteen Austrian defendants, from text documents such as news stories about the case published in the Austrian media and from various online sources and publications. I interviewed the defendants while the trial was still in progress, and the outcome was unknown. I sent requests for interviews directly to some of the defendants and to the organizations they worked with, as many had published statements on various websites, together with their names and personal details. I established contact with a key contact (defendant) who helped me get in touch with three more defendants. The interviews were carried out by non-encrypted email communication. Before the interviews the Norwegian Social Science Data Services[7] requested an explanation for the fact that the emails were not encrypted. During the trial the use of hard disk and email encryption was portrayed by the prosecutor as an indication that the defendants had something to hide. If the use of regular, legal encryption could incriminate the interviewees in any way it seemed appropriate not to encrypt the interviews. The interviewees also read through a draft version of this chapter and gave additional comments after the trial ended.

The Case: Animal Advocacy or Organized Crime?

The police raids in 2008 against animal advocates marked the culmination of the surveillance and comprehensive two-year investigation of animal activist groups, led by a 35-strong police unit[8] called 'SOKO clothing'. This task force was set up in fall 2006[9] to combat illegal actions against clothing companies selling fur products, in particular the Austrian Kleider Bauer firm. Extensive surveillance

---

5 This study has been made possible by research grants from The Scandinavian Research Council for Criminology.

6 I have partially anonymized the persons interviewed by removing names and sensitive information. Quotes from interviewees might reveal who is saying what, if someone had detailed knowledge of the case and defendants. The interviewees have therefore been given access to the article so that they can approve their quotes, and other information given in interviews.

7 This project is registered and approved by the Norwegian Social Science Data Services (NSSDS). I abide by NSSDS guidelines in regard to data gathering, data storage, and especially as regards issues of research ethics and the protection of informants.

8 Kronen Zeitung (28.02.2010): 'Aufregung wegen Anwendung des "Mafiaparagrafen"' [online]. Available at: http://www.krone.at/krone/object_id__187610/hxcms/ [Accessed: 6 December 2010].

9 Der Standard (26.02.2010): 'Ermittlungen seit vier Jahren' [online]. Available at: http://derstandard.at/1267132164786/Chronologie-Prozess-Ermittlungen-seit-vier-Jahren [Accessed: 6 December 2010].

and investigative measures were conducted by the special unit prior to the raids: tapping of mobile phones, localization of mobile phones, homing devices on cars; months of personal observation; financial investigation into individuals and groups/organizations; bugging of at least one private apartment and an office; the use of two known undercover infiltrators; and the installation of hidden cameras monitoring the front doors of several people (Mackinger 2009: 247). One of the people I interviewed saw the degree of surveillance she underwent as the start of a series of events ending in a trial:

> Police have been listening to my phone calls since March 2007. And since January 2008 plain-clothes police have been following me and observing my every move, around the clock. Then, on 21 May 2008 police broke into my home, searched it and arrested me. Following this I was thrown into prison for three-and-a-half months. Since 2nd March 2010 I've had to stand trial in court in Wiener Neustadt to answer to the accusation of belonging to a criminal organization (Defendant in interview).

At least 40 people have been identified as having been subjected to surveillance before the arrests, plus a number of others (Mackinger 2009: 247). Following the raids and arrests, the case received massive media attention; seven of the arrested began hunger strikes, solidarity groups were established and actions in support of the arrested took place in numerous countries across the world.[10] The arrested activists were held in custody for more than 100 days of pre-trial detention, and a year after their release the charges were made official: most of the original allegations were dropped, but accusations of 'membership of a criminal organization' still remained (ibid.), and the charges were extended to a total of 13 individuals.

The trial itself started 2 March 2010 in the Austrian Court of Wiener Neustadt. In addition to the accusations of forming and being part of a criminal organization, seven of the activists were accused of other offences, such as property damage. There was the possibility of up to five years' imprisonment[11] for the accused, in one of the biggest cases ever heard in the Regional Court of Wiener Neustadt.[12] All the defendants plead not guilty, and maintained that there had never been any such thing as a criminal animal rights organization. Some of the defendants, however, confirmed that they had conducted, and still support, illegal actions in

10 Solidarity group for the defendants 'Antirep: 'The Story So Far: Chronology of events' [online]. Available at:http://antirep2008.org/?page_id=886&lang=en [Accessed: 17 December 2010].

11 Kronen Zeitung (27.02.2010): '13 Tierschützer stehen ab Dienstag vor Gericht' [online]. Available at: http://www.krone.at/Nachrichten/13_Tierschuetzer_stehen_ab_Dienstag_vor_Gericht-Monsterprozess-Story-187528 [Accessed: 6 December 2010].

12 Die Presse (20.03.2010): 'Die Tierschützerin und die Mafia' [online]. Available at: http://diepresse.com/home/panorama/oesterreich/547632/Die-Tierschuetzerin-und-die-Mafia?from=suche.intern.portal [Accessed: 6 December 2010].

the context of what is known as non-violent civil disobedience.[13] This strategy is not to be confused with other types of action breaching the law by anonymous groups such as the underground activists of the Animal Liberation Front. The variations and boundaries between civil disobedience and anonymous sabotage actions are essential for a nuanced understanding of the different strands within the movement. Nevertheless, the defendants were accused of engaging in anonymous illegal actions, also under the banner of the Animal Liberation Front.

After years of intense police investigations and a trial lasting for over 100 days, the verdict was finally announced by the judge on 2 May 2011: the verdict acquitted all the 13 accused of all charges, both of membership of a criminal organization, and of other individual offences, because a lack of evidence to support the charges.[14] The acquittal has been hailed by activists internationally, and there has been a wide political debate on whether the anti-mafia law should be reformed or abolished altogether. Petra Velten, head of the Institute of Criminal Sciences Institute at the Johannes Kepler University in Linz, argues that the mafia paragraph should be totally abolished;[15] 'The mafia paragraph is a dangerous tool: Actually, it was created to combat human trafficking, but it is useful for criminalizing NGOs and is used to neutralize "hostile"-minded troublemakers.' Although the defendants were acquitted, Vetlen describes the process itself (the trial, custody, raids and surveillance) as a form of punishment for the activists, with effects in some ways extending considerably beyond what a conventional punishment could deliver. Christian Pilnacek, of the Criminal Law Section of the Ministry of Justice, says in an interview on 27 May 2011 that the Austrian Ministry of Justice does not intend to reform the mafia paragraph.[16] In the same interview, Pilnacek also emphasizes that the verdict is not the end of the case, and that there still might be further criminal proceedings against the defendants – not on the previous charge of belonging to a criminal organization, but in individual cases where he claims there is evidence of criminal offences.

The case does not seem to be fully closed, and there are still important questions as to whether and how the § 278a can be used in the same way against

13 An action can, according to Persen and Johansen (1998), be termed *civil disobedience* when it meets the five requirements of: 1. Openness; 2. Non-violence; 3. Breaking a law or norm; 4. Serious personal conviction; and 5. Societal and/or ethical objectives [my translation].

14 Der Standard (02.05.2011): 'Ein Freispruch als Rundumschlag' [online]. Available at: http://derstandard.at/1303950774834/Tierschuetzerprozess-Ein-Freispruch-als-Rundumschlag [Accessed: 11 July 2011].

15 Der Standard (02.05.2011):'Das Verfahren selbst war eine Strafe' [online]. Available at: http://derstandard.at/1303950755859/Interview-mit-Petra-Velten-Das-Verfahren-selbst-war-eine-Strafe [Accessed: 12 July 2011]

16 Der Standard (27.05.2011): 'Justizministerin will "Mafia-Paragrafen" nicht reformieren' [online]. Available at: Justizministerin will 'Mafia-Paragrafen' nicht reformieren [Accessed: 11 July 2011].

other dissidents and NGOs in the future. Below I go on to explore how repression was brought to bear, and to examine some of its possible aims and motives.

Repressing a Whole Movement?

The Austrian animal rights movement is known as having achieved some remarkable results. Amongst other things, whole industries, such as fur farming, have been banned, specific uses of animals have been outlawed and progressive animal welfare laws have been pushed through. Progress and success were in danger of being slowed down when the Austrian Ministry of the Interior together with the police applied § 278a of the criminal code for the first time, to prosecute members of various non-governmental organizations. The prosecutor claimed a 'criminal organization' consisting of the 13 persons prosecuted, supported materially by the organizations they work with, were responsible for a huge number of both legal and illegal actions and campaigns that have pressured and affected animal industries and businesses across Austria over the last 20 years.[17]

Paragraph 278a was originally introduced to fight organized crime and money laundering, by making the simple fact of belonging to a 'criminal organization'[18] a crime, regardless of whether the criminal organization or its members had committed any actual crimes. Any activity involving a criminal organization is thereby made criminal, regardless of whether the activity in and of itself is a crime. Thus legal actions could in principle be accused of supporting a criminal organization, and thus become criminal.

17 The prosecutor claims the criminal organization is responsible for various legal and illegal actions dating back to 1988, according to the website Tierschutzprozess.at: 'Chronologie des 278a-Verfahrens' [online]. Available at: http://tierschutzprozess.at/chronologie-des-278a-verfahrens [Accessed: 19 March 2011].

18 Definition of 'criminal organization' in the Austrian criminal code (StGB), §278a: 'Whoever establishes a longer time scale to enterprise-like compound, or a larger number of persons engaged in any such constellations as a member (§ 278 para 3) 1st which, if not exclusively, on the recurring performs or plan to commit serious criminal acts that threaten the life, physical integrity, liberty or property, or serious criminal acts in the field of sexual exploitation of persons, the smuggling and the illicit traffic in connection to munitions, nuclear materials and radioactive substances, hazardous wastes, narcotics or counterfeit currency is, 2nd thereby enrich themselves or strive for a large scale or significant influence on politics or economics and 3rd to corrupt or intimidate others or themselves in a special way to shield against prosecution or investigation shall be punished with imprisonment from six months to five years. § 278 para 4 shall apply accordingly [my translation].' From: Bundeskanzleramt Österreich (2011) [online]. Available at: http://www.ris.bka.gv.at/Dokument.wxe?Abfrage=Bundesnormen&Dokumentnummer=NOR40033827 [Accessed: 25 August 2011].

Differing Defence Strategies

The 13 defendants adopted two different strategies in relation to the prosecutor and the court. Five people decided not to speak in court and not to cooperate with the prosecutor, a position explicitly stated in court. The remaining eight chose a more active and outspoken defence strategy. The differing approaches showed how defendants, connected to different groups in the movement, have quite different views of the possibilities of a defence in court and of the alternatives of cooperating or not. The defendants who chose not to cooperate published their court statements online, explaining their understanding of the court case and why they decided to remain silent. The following is a statement written under the pseudonym 'The 6th defendant':[19]

> Stating one's opinion is used as evidence of being a member of a criminal organization, the assumption of innocence is systematically undermined. This is what we experience here. This whole trial is based on charges which are full of misinterpretations and allegations without any evidence at all. This will be shown during the course of the trial. In this trial § 278a is used to undermine the right to free speech and public assembly, to invade privacy and to criminalize press and media work. Because I do not want to take any part in this, I will from now on make use of my right to remain silent.

The statements of all the non-cooperating defendants point to the 'prosecutor's disregard of the assumption of innocence', and they claim that, in defiance of this basic legal principle, an assumption of guilt was made regarding the defendants. This seems to be a crucial reason for deciding not to cooperate. In another statement 'The 9th defendant says: "I will not actively contribute to this show trial, not least because the presumption of innocence has obviously been disregarded by the public prosecutor. Instead of [the prosecutor] proving our 'guilt', we are told to prove our innocence"'. The interviewees also supported such views of the trial as unjust and clearly political. Criticism of the legal proceedings was reinforced after the disclosure of extensive use of an undercover police investigator, which until then had not been mentioned in court. After the revelation of the existence of the undercover agent, and her testimony in court, many strong reactions appeared in the media.[20] The police infiltrator did not find any evidence of illegal activity

19 Statement published (24.03.2010) on a website supporting the defendant, called 'We are all § 278a – Solidarity with the animal rights activists who are under investigation for § 278a of the Austrian Penal Code' [online]. Available at: http://antirep2008.org/?p=2044&lang=en#more-2044 [Accessed: 7 December 2010].

20 Examples seen in Die Presse (14.01.2011): ,Tierschützer: Justiz unter Druck, Kampf an mehreren Fronten' [online]. Available at: http://diepresse.com/home/panorama/oesterreich/625480/Tierschuetzer_Justiz-unter-Druck?_vl_backlink=%2Fhome%2Fpanorama%2Foesterreich%2Findex.do [Accessed: 17 January 2011], and in Niederösterreichische

during her close surveillance in the midst of the animal activists over 18 months. The use of such an infiltrator was also legally questionable, and Justice Minister Claudia Bandion-Ortner ordered a report on the use of this undercover agent in the SOKO-investigations.[21] Later another police informant, agent 481,[22] was revealed to have also been operating inside the movement. This agent had similarly observed no crimes and no preparation for crimes. One of many critics, the head of the Institute for Criminal Law at Johannes Kepler University in Linz, Petra Velten, clearly expressed her view of the trial. She stated: 'that the defendants are receiving a fair trial can now barely be believed'.[23] On the other hand, the Austrian People's Party (ÖVP)[24] seems to have been the most important supporter amongst the political parties, of the prosecution against the animal advocates. The Austrian Green Party (Die Grünen) was the party in parliament that most actively criticized the prosecution and police operations.

When asked whether the whole animal rights movement was in principle under suspicion and on trial, the interviewees have a quite unanimous view. They see the state sanctions as a politically motivated response to the effects of the movement as a whole. According to the interviewees, all the defendants were people still active in the movement, and had all been involved in organizing animal rights initiatives over the last five years or more: another person says that a thousand people were registered by the undercover police agent, that five groups were targeted for house raids in 2008 and that 40 activists were police suspects. An interviewee also makes some interesting remarks about the general functioning of the § 278a, for both the animal movement as a whole and political dissent in Austria:

> The whole animal rights movement in Austria is accused of being at least a permanent potential member of a criminal organization. But not only that: Any NGO constituting (by definition) an organization aiming for 'significant influence on economy or politics' [section § 278a of the Austrian criminal code] is threatened by this law (Defendant in interview).

Nachrichten (11.01.2011): 'Tierschützer: Ministerium prüft 'Ungleichbehandlung' [online]. Available at: http://www.noen.at/lokales/noe-uebersicht/wiener-neustadt/aktuell/Tierschuetzer-Ministerium-prueft-Ungleichbehandlung;art2575,20096 [Accessed: 17 January 2011].

21 Der Standard (03.01.2011): '"Ungewöhnliche" Ermittlungen' [online]. Available at: http://derstandard.at/1293369827842/Ungewoehnliche-Ermittlungen [Accessed: 17 January 2011].

22 DiePresse.com (19.03.2011): 'Tierschützerprozess: Die Spionin, die nichts weiß' [online]. Available at: http://diepresse.com/home/meinung/kommentare/643101/Gute-Spione-bitte-melden?direct=643113&_vl_backlink=/home/panorama/oesterreich/643113/index.do&selChannel= [Accessed: 19 March 2011].

23 DiePresse (02.01.2011): 'Tierschützer-Prozess: Die gröbsten Fehlentwicklungen' [online]. Available at: http://diepresse.com/home/panorama/oesterreich/622374/TierschuetzerProzess_Die-groebsten-Fehlentwicklungen [Accessed: 17 January 2011].

24 Österreichische Volkspartei.

If any of the defendants had been found guilty of the charges under § 278a, this would undoubtedly have had a wider effect on Austrian grass roots activism and dissent. If the prosecution had been able to put a stop to activism that had previously been legal, by the use of a law originally passed to counter the mafia and racketeering, then the boundaries between legal and illegal methods used by activists would have been dramatically blurred.

Targeting the Underground or the Above Ground?

One interviewee says the police and the state prosecutor had clearly differing approaches as to which groups they targeted: on the police charge sheets there are 16 groups mentioned as suspicious, and about 300 activists described as suspects. But the state prosecutor clearly had a different agenda according to the interviewee: 'he wanted to separate "the goodies from the baddies"', for example by desperately trying to keep the international animal protection organization Four Paws out of the trial, and by instead focusing strongly on only two of the animal organizations that were under suspicion.

What is interesting about the Austrian case, compared to similar repression against animal rights activists in the UK (see Aaltola, this volume), and USA (Potter 2011) is that the police surveilled, raided and suspected such large sections of the movement. The Austrian enforcement efforts targeted all organizations, not just the radical or more controversial groups. Such widespread repression could make for more solidarity within the whole of the movement, which might counter at least some of the potentially destructive effects of repression.[25] The police efforts to engage against large parts of the whole movement, even the more moderate animal welfare groups, at first seems hard to understand from the point of a police strategic view. Author and journalist Will Potter has raised some interesting points about repression against environmental and animal rights movements in the USA. His interpretation might give some basis for understanding the Austrian police strategy. Potter claims that '[...] the government hasn't been able to catch the people actually committing the crimes, so they're going after the visible above ground activists that ideologically support them' (Potter 2009: 678). Potter continues by explaining why this is the case: 'The point is to protect corporate profits by instilling fear in the mainstream animal rights movement [...] – and

25 The effects of political repression are not necessarily predictable and straightforward. They might turn out different from or even opposite to what was intended. The ability of the targets of repression to build solidarity within and across movements and to raise critical public support, as well as the media's portrayal of the group in question, seems crucial for the way repression is able to play out. My interviewees point to the importance of their success in making their stories heard by the public, and also by making the misconduct of the SOKO unit and the use of § 278a itself both visible and debated on a political level. Some of the defendants go as far as claiming they would maybe not even have been let out of pre-trial detention, if critical press coverage and a critical public had not engaged in the way it did.

every other social movement paying attention – and make people think twice before they use their First Amendment rights'. It's not the illegal activists that are the target; it's the legal, above ground activists, according to Potter (2009: 686). Whether this is actually the case in Austria, too, is of course hard to confirm. Anyway, the argument makes sense of the way the repression played out.

The book *In Defense of Animals: The Second Wave*, edited by the well-known philosopher Peter Singer, has one chapter written by one the Austrian defendants, Dr Martin Balluch. In it Balluch (2006: 166) describes how effective legal campaigning in Austria has had great success, and how this strategy has affected animal industries, in comparison to the illegal strategies of anonymous underground groups. He claims that 'no realistic level of guerrilla attacks of the kind carried out by the Animal Liberation Front could have hurt the battery farming industry as much as the new Austrian law does' (ibid.). A law banning a whole industry does far more economic damage to the animal abuse industry than anything else the animal movement could do, writes Balluch (ibid.).

If stricter animal welfare regulations and the banning of certain uses of animals are what inflicted the greatest economic costs on the animal agro-industries – as results of legal animal advocacy – then it is logical that the larger, legal organizations should be perceived as the main threat by its opponents. But what is actually known about the declared and undeclared reasons for political repression? This is the point of departure for the next part of this chapter.

Reasons for Repression

History offers numerous examples of social movements being pressured by state agencies and counter-movements, by legal, extra-legal and illegal means, in attempts to limit their social and political impact. During the last 25 years such counter-reactions as criminalization and counter-mobilization against environmental and animal rights groups have occurred in both Europe and the USA (Lovitz 2010, Helvarg 2004, Rowell 1996, Amster 2006, Moore 2005, Yates 2007: 140–157). As repression has become manifest, the spectre of new criminal laws and control measures has come into being. The declared object of these measures is often the clandestine parts of these movements that use illegal, underground tactics such as property destruction. Yet previous research on social movements and the Austrian case show how whole movements are affected, independently of who breaks the law often to an extent not proportional to the seriousness of offences.

A state's propensity to resort to repression when challenged by a 'domestic threat' is, according to Christian Davenport (Davenport in Boykoff 2007: 208), one of the few relationships in the social sciences that has stood the test of time. In contrast to this, Davenport (2007: 1) claims, it is surprising that so little systematic attention is given to the topic of state repression. Especially when one takes into consideration 'the duration of this practice, the vast numbers of victims, the range of legal, political, and religious restrictions condemning such activity, and the many human rights organizations dedicated to the elimination of such behaviour' (Davenport 2007: 1).

I define the Austrian case as an empirical example of political repression. And by political repression I mean 'a process whereby groups or individuals attempt to diminish dissident action, collective organization, and the mobilization of dissenting opinion by inhibiting collective action either through raising the costs or minimizing the benefits of such actions' (Boykoff 2007: 282–3). As set out here, this definition effectively conveys the impact of the state sanctions recently aimed at Austrian animal advocates. The possible benefits of engaging in animal advocacy were reduced, and the costs greatly increased in Austria, in a way that could have severely diminished such activism. Although the trial ended with an acquittal, the whole process of surveillance, home raids and months in custody and in court has had huge impact on the defendants' personal lives and on the animal movement in general. Since the verdict found the defendants not guilty, and the events had some positive consequences in Austria for the cause of animal rights, and the movement supporting them, the case could more accurately be described as an example of a partially failed political repression.

What might have caused the state repression in the Austrian case? Do these movements threaten important societal interests to do with using animals for production and commerce? Do industry lobbyists and industry-friendly politicians opposed to green movements initiate backlashes and attempts at marginalization? Or is the repression an inevitable consequence of the illegal and anonymous actions taken by sections of these movements? Are there other causes? Below I investigate these questions. To lead the way to possible answers I demonstrate how animal advocates are perceived as threats by their opponents, and give a general outline of the animal rights movements' scope and aims. I also present what the interviewees see as probable reasons for the repression, and discuss the stated aim and practice of the SOKO police unit.

State Response to Criminal Offences?

Both interviewees and media sources[26] confirm that Werner Graf, head of the Austrian clothing chain Kleider Bauer (KB), initiated a meeting with the ministry of internal affairs and the heads of various police institutions before large-scale surveillance started in 2007. The meeting was presumably a response to a paint attack on Graf's private car by unknown activists. At the meeting Graf demanded that the police should intervene against the animal activists that were targeting his business.[27] It was as a result of this meeting that the 'SOKO clothing' police unit

26 Österreichischen Rundfunk: 'Verlangt, dass Polizei tätig wird' [online]. Available at: http://www.orf.at/stories/2034672/2034667/ [Accessed: 24 January 2011].

27 Der Standard: 'Kleider Bauer wünschte eine Soko und bekam sie' [online]. Available at: http://derstandard.at/1293370077141/Tierschuetzer-Prozess-Kleider-Bauer-wuenschte-eine-Soko-und-bekam-sie [Accessed: 24 January 2011].

was established. This is confirmed by the court testimony of the former SOKO-chief and present head of the Vienna State Office for State Protection and Counter Terrorism (LVT),[28] Erich Zwettler.[29] Zwettler also mentioned in court that Graf had provided a file with details of the activities and ideological orientation of these animal activists. The SOKO unit was said to be established specifically to tackle property damage and illegal actions against the KB chain.

These incidents seem to support the idea that repression is a response to illegal activity. But the prosecutor eventually accused the defendants of a wide range of illegal activities, far from solely related to KB. Additionally, the defendants were accused of offences dating back as far as 20 years. So the question is: what happened after the SOKO unit was set up to tackle crimes targeting KB, to widen its scope and direct its attention towards such large parts of the movement? Were more companies, industries or targets of illegal protest action brought in to present problems with animal activists and to affect SOKO's efforts? I have not found evidence that directly supports this idea, but it is hard to know exactly what happened in relation to the SOKO unit, from its establishment in 2007 until the raids and trial. More important is the discrepancy and disproportionality between the stated SOKO aim of stopping property damage against Kleider Bauer, and the eventual surveillance measures taken, the ensuing raids and the legal actions taken under the § 278a. This disproportionality is precisely what makes it mistaken to interpret the repression as primarily, or exclusively, a reaction to criminal offences against KB.

Repression Seen from the Activists' Standpoint

In an open letter[30] entitled 'My Message to the International Animal Rights movement' defendant Martin Balluch raises the fundamental question: 'So, what is behind all this?'. Balluch presents his own understanding of the causes of repression during the events he describes as the most fundamental attack ever on the animal rights movement in the movement's history worldwide:

> Let me explain. About 11 years ago, we embarked on a new type of campaigning in Austria. We used the classic grass roots campaign tactic with media work and civil disobedience actions for legal reforms. And we were very successful indeed. First, we banned fur farms, then wild animal circuses, then battery cages and vivisection on apes, and finally rabbit cage farming. These successes caused a lot of concern to powerful groups in society.

---

28 Wiener Landesamts für Verfassungsschutz und Terrorismusbekämpfung (LVT).

29 Österreichischen Rundfunk: 'Verlangt, dass Polizei tätig wird'[online]. Available at: http://www.orf.at/stories/2034672/2034667/ [Accessed: 24 January 2011].

30 Published 9.06.2008 [online]. Available at: Url: http://www.evana.org/index.php?id=34567&lang=en [Accessed: 4 January 2011].

In his statement Balluch refers to the movement's successes as the reason behind the repression, an interpretation shared by both my interviewees and other defendants. By being effective, Balluch and the movement directly impact their opponents' economic interests. The perception of the animal rights movement as an economic threat to animal industries is also evident in Harold D. Guither's (1998: 197–8) writings. Guither is a professor emeritus of agricultural economics, who has written about the history and scope of the animal rights movement. He claims that 'the animal rights philosophy and its recommended actions threaten markets, income, jobs and livelihood for those who produce animals and animal products, who use animals in research, or depend on animals as part of leisure and entertainment pursuits' (ibid.). The British newspaper *The Sunday Times*[31] in 2004 reported a new risk analysis, according to which 'animal rights extremism' posed 'one of the most serious threats to Britain's economy because of rising intimidation of individual companies'. Such assessments indicate what a radical challenge the animal rights movement may represent to societal order, societal economy and to the movement's opponents.

Threatening the Animal Economy and Societal Interests

The animal rights movement might have economic effects on its opponents and on society for several reasons. Laws requiring stricter welfare regulations which cost the industry money, and bans on certain animal uses that make animals unavailable as economic resources in certain commercial areas are probably what has been most expensive for companies and businesses that profit from animal usage. An interviewee offers another opinion on why their opponents were frightened and therefore pushed for state intervention in the animal movement:

> What scared the shit out of our opponents was the fact that we were able to exert so much pressure that we got laws made that make production much more expensive, just for ethical reasons. The powerful were scared by the fact that grassroots activists were able to change the system from below. Also the fact that we were a smart combination of street power and intellectual presentation. And that we're able to produce such relentless pressure.

The defendant raises an interesting point when mentioning the ability of grass roots activism to achieve political aims through extra-parliamentary means, thus changing the system from below. This power of the grass roots may be seen as an unpredictable and unwanted political element. It may be seen as a threat to the sovereign power of the state and of ruling political parties that usually possess stronger control over such important political and economical changes. When an

31 Published 10.12.2004: 'Extremist animal rights activists pose main threat to economy'[online]. Available at: http://www.timesonline.co.uk/tol/news/uk/article401368.ece [Accessed: 10 January 2011].

interviewee was asked whether she thought the animal rights movement's level of progress and effectiveness regarding the costs of its opponents would affect the level and degree of state repression, she answered: 'Nothing else, in my opinion. You have the right to free speech and free assembly, as long as your speeches and assemblies have no effect. The moment you have an effect, you must be stopped and controlled.' She further claimed that the contents of the police documents and charge sheets, presented by the prosecutor, confirmed her opinion.

The Austrian animal movement has also pressured businesses in other ways: activists have conducted undercover investigations into industrial animal husbandry, revealing breaches of animal welfare regulations. Such investigations and subsequent media work have occasionally damaged the public image of certain animal agribusinesses. Investigations have been publicized through the media, with graphic documentation of illegal animal abuse and questionable legal practices, often unknown to the general public. One of my interviewees spoke about the background of repression that relates to the movement's effect on public opinion: 'In a time of economic depression states feel strong pressures to ensure good market conditions for their national enterprises. The political activism of animal rights advocates, by definition, damages the optimal conditions of the free market, by uncovering hidden product information, which reduces the sales volume of publicly criticized commodities.' Another interviewee tells me that the Austrian animal rights movement is one of the most efficient social movements in Austria, with nearly 1,000 demonstrations every year and an important influence on animal laws. He concludes that the movement really had 'a significant influence on the economy and politics'. In an interview published online,[32] one defendant also points to a direct aim of combating the use of animals by increasing its costs, as this would logically lead to a decrease in animal use:

> Any law that makes it more expensive and difficult for the farmed animal industry, the vivisection industry, the hunting industry, the animal entertainment industry and so forth, is a good thing, much like economic sabotage. In essence, it is economic sabotage. If a capitalist enterprise does its sums and finds that not abusing animals is less expensive, they will stop doing it.

In Ann Reisner's (1992: 46) research on the American animal agribusiness's response to the animal rights movement, she says the publications of these agribusinesses '[...] described the animal rights movement as large, well-funded, and capable of posing a serious threat to agriculture. [...]'. She goes to say that '[t]he farm press also constantly repeated that view that animal rights issues were not going to go away, that animal rights was one of the most important issues of the decade, and that animal advocates posed a serious threat to agriculture' (Reisner

32 The interview with the defendant Dr Martin Balluch is published on the animal rights website 'Abolitionist online' [online]. Available at: http://www.abolitionist-online.com/interview-issue04_bite.back-martin.balluch.shtml [Accessed: 6 November 2011].

1992: 46). She stresses that the movement is portrayed as a very important economic threat by the industry. But equally, the consequences of the activists' ethically founded criticism are described as a threat to the legitimacy of their practices and to the maintenance of consumer trust (ibid.).

Counter-mobilization by the Animal Movement's Opponents

All social movements have their opponents and enemies who often put forth their own counter-strategies in such forms as repression, cooptation, divide and conquer, distraction and diversion of attention, according to Knut Kjelstadli (2010: 92). When a critical mass of organizations feels threatened by a movement, they may organize a counter-movement (Jasper and Poulsen 1993: 643). Jasper and Poulsen (ibid.) write that, for example, professional or trade associations 'can serve as counter-movement organizations, giving aid to targeted individuals and institutions, coordinating their responses, providing resources, and sharing information about effective strategies'. This seems to be the case with the international animal rights movement, and Lyle Munro's research on the movements in the UK, USA and in Australia confirms that '[...] activists tend to see themselves as targets of established industries (e.g. agribusiness) and various counter-movements' (Munro 2005: 17). One such example is the so-called Wise Use Movement, which is mainly a counter-response to the environmental movement, initiated by American industries and its ideologues. Ron Arnold, who first coined the infamous term 'eco-terrorism' and who is a leading figure for the Wise Use adherents, stated that the Wise Use Movement's 'goal is to destroy, to eradicate the environmental movement' (Hall 2006: 94). Opposition to animal rights activism is also very clear within Wise Use adherents (ibid.).

If the political repression in the Austrian case is seen as a result of counter-mobilization against the animal movement, then Jasper and Poulsen's (1993: 655) analysis of backlashes as a consequence of social movement success can offer some partial explanation: 'We can see how success in specific campaigns can hurt longer term success for a protest movement as a whole: In the absence of state repression, a movement may attain early gains. But these may in turn inspire even more rapid and energetic counter-mobilization.' This means that counter-mobilizations might continue and manifest themselves in other ways and in new forms.

Research on counter-movements describes counter-mobilization as the attempt to undo the social changes brought about by social movements, rather than as active opposition to the social movements (Jasper and Poulsen 1993: 644). Counter-mobilization might take the form of intensified lobbying for the criminalization of previously legal dissent, for stricter policing of specific protest campaigns or for other actions. From this perspective, the Austrian repression might be understood as being triggered by an effective counter-mobilization that was attempting to undo the achievements of activists and reduce the animal movement's scope for action, and potential for further achievements. But, as a counter-strategy it seems to have failed.

Challenging the Status Quo and Anthropocentrism

Since the 1970s an important theoretical and ideological development has evolved: through a dialectical relationship between philosophers, scholars and social movement activists, people have formed what is described as the modern social movement for animal rights. Guither (1998: 13) describes how the writings of philosophers and the actions of their converts, since the 1970s, have 'activated the latent support of millions of citizens, stimulated new movements, driven the development of new organizations, and generated intense political activity.' Dedicated individuals and groups are building a new social movement and introducing the concepts of animal liberation, animal rights and animal welfare, as described by Guither (1998: 14).

In Guither's (1998: 197–8) analysis of the animal rights movement, he calls the animal rights position a doctrine that confronts established systems and practices that people accept without question or much critical remark (see also Svärd, this volume). That animals should be treated well is a commonly held idea, but this often presupposes that animals are actually treated well in Western societies. The growing animal rights movement shows that criticism of the current treatment of animals is getting more widespread. But the movement is not only concerned with how animals are treated when alive. Activists also raise fundamental questions about the right of humans to use and kill other species for their own interests.

The animal rights movement resists the logic of humans' perceived superiority over other animals, and they organize to decrease and abolish practices perceived as speciesism and animal abuse; both of which are often seen as direct negative consequences of an anthropocentric[33] value system (Singer 2002, Taylor 1995: 1). When such movements challenge institutionalized practices of production that cause harm to animals, the activists not only oppose an abstract idea of man's relation to nature and animals. The movement also challenges the basic conditions of production by demanding an end to industrialized use of animals as resources. Animal advocates are working to end practices they see as unjust and harmful. This implies that animals should not be so easily available to use for economic or humanocentric ends. Such a scenario implies a huge economic challenge to industries that build their economy on the use of animals as production entities. Animal rights ideology is a fundamental challenge to the societal status of animals as property and commodities – a status which makes both proper legal protection, and an acknowledgement of animals' interest of life, as regards life and absence of suffering, impossible. According to Bob Torres (2007: 58), animals are 'caught in [a] commodity production circuit in contemporary capitalism. [...], where [a]nimals are not only commodities and property themselves, they also produce commodities, and in a sense, serve as either the "raw" inputs or the productive labour power of business.' Changing this instrumental position and status of animals in Western

33 Anthropocentrism is an eco-philosophy or perspective that views nature instrumentally, as a means to satisfy the demands for humans (White 2008: 12).

society implies radical social changes, as domesticated animals are used extensively in meat production for entertainment purposes, medical experiments and in a number of other industries and institutionalized practices. At a deeper level, such societal change will rock the whole human–animal relationship, which is currently dominated by an anthropocentric world-view that assumes humans have a superior right to use nature and animals for any purpose.

So, Why Did It Happen?

So what can be said about what triggered the political repression in Austria? The repression was probably not exclusively a response to illegal actions. Nor need it have been solely a result of the successes of legal campaigns that were at the cost of animal industries. The movement also threatens the anthropocentric order and larger societal economic interests, but more indirectly and in a way that is unlikely to be the direct triggering factor in this specific case.

All these factors, however, make for counter-mobilization against the movement as a whole, but it is hard to say with certainty what was the most important factor in sparking this incidence of political repression. The SOKO unit had the declared goal of preventing illegal behaviour against KB. But, at some point in the investigation process the special unit and police clearly broadened the scope dramatically to include large parts of the whole animal movement. Exactly what reasons lie behind this change of course, and their final strategy and choice of § 278a as the judiciary reaction, are unclear. However, there are probably important political, tactical and judicial factors associated with that repression. No evidence that supported the allegations of an existing criminal organization was offered by the prosecutor. This supports the impression that the case was not about the Austrian state's reaction to criminal conduct. Rather, criminal law seems to have been used untraditionally, in attempts to tackle the organizers of a social movement that represents a 'troublesome' collective actor that challenges power elites and economies built on animal usage. Such use of criminal law is also evident in more widespread state control policies.

Repression and Crime Control Trends in Europe

This chapter's primary concern is the repression of Austrian animal advocates. However, the case has relevance to animal rights movements internationally, as well as to environmental movements which challenge the destruction of nature. The case can be used to illustrate current and emerging patterns in the state control of green movements. As shown earlier in this chapter in the discussion of the economy of animal usage, and as Rob White claims more generally; 'it becomes clear very quickly that political economy is at the heart of the exploitation of animals and environments – that capitalism in particular, demands profitable use of such [property] as a means to assign value' (White 2007: 42). The animal rights and environmental movements face some of the same challenges when opposing the instrumental value and property status of animals and nature. In addition, both movements are likely to be affected by current crime control trends across Europe and the USA.

An International Perspective on Repression and Control

It is a necessity to look beyond the Austrian national boundaries to understand the international developments that affect this kind of repression. It is necessary to grasp the increasing internationalization of police and intelligence cooperation which targets the animal rights, environmental and other movements. Such a transnational perspective differs from many social movement studies, which often focus on the nation-state as the central unit of analysis (della Porta 2008: 224).

Trends in state control measures have changed over the years, and have become particularly concerned with assessing risks and managing both real and imaginary threats. According to Katja Franko Aas (2007: 111) the goal of combating risk, rather than the more positive objective of social justice, has become an important factor affecting the political cultures and strategies for social control in Western nation-states. Risk assessment that involves some parts of the international animal rights movement has been formulated in many European countries in recent years. In 2008[34] the European law enforcement agency, Europol, added international 'animal rights extremism' to the threat assessment in their annual 'EU Terrorism Situation and Trend Report'. The label 'animal rights extremism' has no definite meaning, but can easily be used as a label to discredit legal activism, even if it is often used about illegal non-violent activities. Animal rights theorist Tom Regan (2004) is one of the latest to suggest that the counter-movements to animal protectionism are enjoying some success in their campaign to characterize 'animal rights' as an extremist mobilization and a terroristic idea, according to Roger Yates (2007: 143). He points to Regan's claim that the negative image of animal rights advocates has been created and sustained by the public relations efforts of 'major animal user industries' (ibid.).

In recent years Europol has also organized several international workshops[35] dealing specifically with what they term animal rights extremism. A recent press

34 In reports prior to 2008 Europol writes: 'Politically motivated violent acts and other crimes committed, for instance, by right-wing or animal rights extremists are thus not included in the TE-SAT data collection unless reported as terrorist activities by Member States.' This changes from 2008; from now on illegal animal rights actions (that are not considered terrorism) are also included as data in the reports. This indicates a shift towards an extension of data collecting regarding 'animal rights extremism'. It also reflects an extended focus on such activities in Europol member countries. See: http://www.europol.europa.eu/publications/EU_Terrorism_Situation_and_Trend_Report_TE-SAT/ [Accessed 15 August 2011].

35 John Madigan from the Department of 'domestic extremism' of the British secret service confirmed the participation of SOKO representatives in several Europol conferences. This confirmation was given in his statement before the Austrian court,

release[36] issued by Europol and Eurojust (the EU's judicial cooperation unit) says: 'The phenomenon of increased violence committed by some extremists in the name of animal rights is a growing cause for concern. In a major conference organised by Europol and Eurojust 58 experts from law enforcement and prosecution authorities, plus representatives from 35 private sector organisations, met last week at Europol's new headquarters in The Hague to discuss the issues behind this new trend.' Further on, Europol and Eurojust stress the '[...] need for increased law enforcement coordination at an international level [...]'.

While in the past control of protest tended to be centralized at the national level, the control of transnational protests has brought about increasing collaboration between different national police bodies, with declining transparency, says Donatella della Porta (2008: 225). According to della Porta (ibid.) this process seems more widespread in Europe, and is linked to increasing intervention by the European Union. Globalization processes today affect people across the globe, and animal rights movements also cooperate more frequently across state borders. The same is true for an array of state and police control agencies.[37] As in the Europol terrorism report, 'animal rights extremism' has become a phenomenon that has received the attention of many European nation-states, as well as that of the animal research industry and its corporations, and animal agribusinesses. In addition to this, several private security firms, such as for example Extremist Watch,[38] collects intelligence on animal rights campaigners and campaigns, including the personal details of activists, which they sell through newsletters and advice to corporations and others. Current research also suggests there is increased cooperation between private security firms, economic elites (such as the threatened animal industries) and the state through the sharing of intelligence and other efforts at social control (Walby and Monaghan 2011: 24–5).

This development fits in with wider patterns in current crime control trends: protest movements, together with Muslim fundamentalism, drug trafficking, migration and poverty, are increasingly being assessed as threats to state security by

according to Antirep: 'Der §278a-Prozess – was bisher geschah' [online]. Available at: http://antirep2008.org/?p=3195 [Accessed: 26 January 2011].

36 Press release of 18 July 2011: 'Joint forces against violent animal rights extremists: Europol and Eurojust hold international conference' [online]. Available at: http://www.eurojust.europa.eu/press_releases/2011/18-07-2011.htm [Accessed: 25 August 2011].

37 For example: On 1 May 2007, 700 police officers raided what were termed 'animal rights extremists' at 29 UK addresses as well as three European addresses. This transnational police operation is thought to be the largest ever conduced against animal rights extremists. See the *Guardian*: '30 arrested as raids target animal rights extremists' [online]. Available at: http://www.guardian.co.uk/uk/2007/may/01/animalwelfare.world [Accessed: 15 December 2010].

38 Extremist Watch is a newsletter that appears regularly with up-to-date information on activist groups and their campaigns. Extremist Watch is produced by the private American intelligence firm INA [Information Network Associates], Inc. (Extremist Watch Vol. 4 #33, 2010).

Western defence analysts, according to criminologist Michael Hörnquist (2003: 10). Such threat assessments are characteristics of what Hörnquist terms the 'Western public order policy' (ibid.). The goals of order and security increasingly seem to come into conflict with social justice goals and citizens' right to privacy, freedom of expression and assembly, in addition to other liberties commonly taken for granted in liberal democracies.

The Changing Landscapes of Dissent: Anti-terror, Racketeering and Anti-mafia Laws used Against Activists

Social movements concerned with the protection of nature, the climate, eco-systems and animals operate under certain socio-legal conditions. The viable alternatives available for legal dissent change according to time and place. Just as social norms and laws have changed dramatically in the course of history, so have the judicial boundaries between legal and illegal protest. My case study reveals such a change in Austria: one of my interviewees point to the possibilities of using existing criminal law to blur distinctions between legal and illegal dissent:

> Organization clauses, like the § 278a, in the criminal codes, blur the formerly clear edge between legal and illegal actions. Organization offences, like § 278a, criminalize activities which – in themselves – nobody would name 'illegal'. So it's not possible anymore to distinguish between legal and illegal activities, if police can always suggest that your legal activities are in fact illegal activities, because they support the aims of an alleged criminal organization.

If § 278a makes it possible to narrow the boundaries between legal and illegal behaviour in the way the interviewee mentions, the law will potentially have such a broad reach that it can be abused politically in ways that threaten the legal security of dissenters. As with other criminal laws used in the same manner, the danger is thus that multiple forms of peaceful dissent and legitimate protest will be classed as 'organized crime', 'domestic extremism' or 'terrorism'.

The problems of § 278a have parallels to aspects of anti-terror and racketeering laws. The common problem regarding these laws, and the legal concept of criminal conspiracy, is that they have a broad and vague character, as well as a negative potential for abuse. Philip E. Johnson (1973: 1138) points to extensive discussions of the potential for abuse in conspiracy charges. He uses a well-known case as an illustration to emphasize difficulties which the ordinary defendant may face when charged with conspiracy. Such charges have a clear advantage for the prosecutor and such a serious disadvantage for the defendant that they may lead to unfair punishment unfairly determined (ibid.). This is like the scenario of the Austrian prosecution, when anti-mafia law was used against the 13 advocates. Similarly, both British and US governments have taken legal steps against animal activists by using the concept of conspiracy[39] rather than holding themselves to the traditional legal duty of finding (reactively) the direct perpetrators of crimes.

The broad and unspecific definitions of anti-terror laws also have similarities to the Austrian charges of being connected with an existing criminal organization. Terrorism is generally understood as violence against people, but European and US authorities occasionally use terror-definitions that could potentially cause a wide range of politically motivated crimes to be treated as domestic extremism or even terrorism[40] (Mathiesen 2006, Hall 2006: 77). The same goes for the use of § 278a, where political campaigns which succeed in affecting politics and the economy in a fundamental way risk being defined and penalized as a criminal organization. As with conspiracy charges and anti-terror laws, racketeering laws enable penalization of what are deemed 'crimes of preparation', as part of the legal development into more proactive and pre-emptive measures (O'Reilly 2010, Zedner 2007, Fitzgibbon 2004). Neither crimes of preparation nor conspiracy are crimes in the normal sense of the word. In a common sense understanding, people are prosecuted and punished retrospectively (reactively) for crimes that have already been committed. By contrast, both conspiracy charges, the § 278a and certain anti-terror laws, make possible a prospective approach to crimes that might take place, or they define legal behaviour as supportive of a criminal organization and thereby make it criminal.

What Magnus Hörnquist describes as the problem of the vagueness of anti-terror laws and of the broad definitions of terrorism also applies to the § 278a. He says that 'all forms of political pressure that do not originate in ever-weaker parliaments can be regarded as "inappropriate force" on companies or governments to do something against their will – and thus it may be deemed terrorism [or organized crime, eco-terrorism, domestic extremism etc.]' (Hörnquist 2003: 101, my translation). It is no longer necessary to have breached a clearly stated criminal law to be prosecuted as a criminal or terrorist. Current crime control trends affecting social movements seem to threaten the legal security and democratic rights of dissidents. This was (and still is) the case in Austria, and there are worrying signs of a similar state of affairs in the USA and certain European nations.

---

39 In the UK several activists connected to the campaign Stop Huntingdon Animal Cruelty (SHAC) have been charged for 'Conspiracy to commit blackmail' (criminal conspiracy) and sentenced both to long prison terms and given anti-social behaviour orders that even prohibit people from engaging in otherwise legal activities related to protest and politics. Kent Police: 'Six sentences for conspiracy' [online]. Available at: http://www.kent.police.uk/news/latest_news/animal_rights_sentencing.html [Accessed: 26 January 2011].

40 'Government officials have labeled environmental campaigners extremists and listed them alongside dissident Irish republican groups and terrorists inspired by al-Qaida in internal documents seen by the *Guardian*.' Quote from news story in the *Guardian* (26.01.2010): 'Ministry of Justice lists eco-activists alongside terrorists' [online]. Available at: http://www.guardian.co.uk/environment/2010/jan/26/ministry-justice-environmental-campaigners-terrorism [Accessed: 19 March 2011].

In Spain on 22 June 2011, 12 animal rights activists were arrested in different parts of the country by armed anti-terrorist units from the Spanish Guardia. The 12 activists deny having any part in what they are charged with: letting thousands of mink out of cages on a fur farm in 2007. The activists claim the police persecution is actually a response to their many undercover investigations and other peaceful tactics that have effectively raised public awareness of animal abuse in Spanish agro-industries. At the time of writing it is unclear how the case will evolve, but this is another case that needs closer study.

Conclusion: What is Threatened by Animal Rights Advocacy?

The intention of this chapter is to raise questions about political repression of green movements, by adopting a bottom-up perspective and providing critical viewpoints on state repression seen in the Austrian case. The Austrian case is important because it demonstrates the extent of state power to define crime and how that power can be studied by green criminologists interested in social movements. Specifically I have discussed factors that might have triggered the repression against animal rights advocates, and have presented four different ways of understanding it: firstly, there is the economic cost inflicted upon individual animal industries by the achievements of animal advocates. The negative effect of activism upon businesses causes the industries to see activists as threats. The animal advocates threaten the economics of using animals in various ways: directly by pushing for stricter regulations of animal use, and by achieving bans on certain animal uses. But more indirectly, they affect their profits by occasionally damaging the public image of animal agribusinesses by revealing information about animal products, depressing sales and damaging trust in such companies. Secondly, the role of illegal actions in sparking repression is discussed. The official reason for establishing the SOKO special unit was to tackle illegal action against the fur sales of clothing chain Kleider and Bauer. At first sight this seems to support the assumption that repression is a response to illegal protest actions. But when one looks more closely there is a striking disproportionality between the unit's original aim and its subsequent practice. What caused this important shift, from supposedly targeting only illegal action against KB to targeting a whole movement and its legal campaigners, is a crucial point for understanding the repression. The facts are not easily accessible, but the incident clearly demonstrates the negative potential of such a vaguely formulated law when it opens up such a wide array of drastic control measures: it enables state institutions to assume powers threatening individual citizen's legal security and human rights.

A third factor for understanding the Austrian events is the fact that important societal interests are being challenged by the animal rights movement. At a state level, industries and a wide array of companies, jobs and tax revenue based upon animal usage are seen as a crucial part of the current societal basis. A threat to such interests can be perceived as a challenge to societal order itself and to the national economy. Lastly, and at an even deeper level, animal advocates threaten the role and place of humans on our planet. Challenging the anthropocentric hegemony also threatens the prevailing understanding of relations between humans and nature, and thus challenges assumptions about man's superiority over other species and the rest of nature. Additionally, the movement challenges the human-centered view of nature and animals as mere resources of instrumental value, since animal rights adherents claim the intrinsic value of individual animals. The two latter factors are more abstract and implicit, serving as an important back-drop to understanding the Austrian case in a wider perspective. The first two factors are, however, what stand out as the most visible factors in my empirical data.

The Austrian animal rights movement is now safe from allegations of forming a criminal organization, but it still remains to be seen if § 278a itself will be revised. If not, the same law has potential for similar misuse in future. The whole case reflects a wider trend where animal rights and environmental movements in Europe and the USA are increasingly portrayed as threats, extremists and even eco-terrorists. There is doubtless a level of illegal underground activity connected to these movements, but the policies on crime, the movements' opponents and various threat assessments seem to blur distinctions between legal, semi-legal, open civil disobedience, anonymous sabotage and other tactics of separate groups. Such false overgeneralizations could have negative effects on these movements, affecting public perception of the movements, and giving political repression an appearance of necessity and justification. This would particularly be the case if activists and organizations are unable to respond to allegations and defend themselves. Here the Austrians scored a success when advocates and their allies managed to resist the potential negative effects of the repression by means of an effective media strategy, broad alliances and trans-movement solidarity.

Animal rights and environmental movements should definitely learn from the Austrian experience and similar cases of political repression. Making use of existing knowledge and experience from such incidents could be crucial for these movements' ability to understand, tackle and resist future backlashes and repression.

References

Aas, K.F. 2007. *Globalization & Crime*. London: Sage Publications.

Amster, R. 2006. Perspectives on Eco-terrorism: Catalysts, Conflations, and Casualties, in *Contemporary Justice Review*. New York: Routledge, 9(3), 287–301.

Balluch, M. 2006. How Austria Achieved a Historic Breakthrough for Animals, in *In Defense of Animals: The Second Wave*, edited by P. Singer. USA; UK; Australia: Blackwell Publishing.

Brisman, A. 2010. The Indiscriminate Criminalisation of Environmentally Beneficial Activities, in *Global Environmental Harm*, edited by R. White. USA; Canada: Willan Publishing.

Boykoff, J. 2007. Limiting Dissent: The Mechanisms of State Repression in the USA, in *Social Movement Studies*. London: Routledge, 6(3), 281–310.

Carrabine, E., Lee, M., Plummer, K., South, N. and Iganski, P. 2004. *Criminology: A Sociological Introduction*, 1st edition. London: Routledge.

Davenport, C. 2009. *Media Bias, Perspective, and State Repression*. Cambridge; New York; Melbourne; Madrid: Cape Town; Singapore; Sao Paulo; Delhi; Dubai; Tokyo: Cambridge University Press.

Fitzgibbon, W. 2004. *Pre-emptive Criminalisation: Risk Control and Alternative Futures*. Issues in Community and Criminal Justice Monograph. London: The Trade Union and Professional Association for Family Court and Probation Staff.

Guither, H.D. 1998. *Animal Rights: History and Scope of a Radical Social Movement*. Carbondale: Southern Illinois University Press.

Hall, L. 2006. *Capers in the Churchyard: Animal Rights Advocacy in the Age of Terror*. Connecticut: Nectar Bat Press.

Helvarg, D. 2004. *The War Against the Greens: The 'Wise-Use' Movement, the New Right, and the Browning of America*. 3rd edition. Colorado: Johnson Books.

Hörnqvist, M. 2003. Ordningspolitikens födelse [The birth of order policy], in *Laglöst land: Terroristjakt och rättssäkerhet i Sverige [Lawless Country: Terrorist Hunt and Legal Rights in Sweden]*, edited by J. Flyghed og M. Hörnqvist. Stockholm: Ordfront.

Jasper, J.M. and Poulsen, J. 1993. Fighting Back: Vulnerabilities, Blunders, and Counter-mobilization by the Targets in Three Animal Rights Campaigns, in *Sociological Forum*. New York: Plenum Publishing Corporation, 6(3), 281–310.

Johnson, P.E. 1973. The Unnecessary Crime of Conspiracy, in *California Law Review*. Berkley: UC Berkeley School of Law, 61(5), 11–88.

Kjelstadli, K. 2010. Kollektive bevegelser [Collective movements], in *Historier om motstand: Kollektive bevegelser i det 20. århundret* [Histories about Resistance: Collective Movements in the 20th Century]. Oslo: Abstrakt forlag.

Lovitz, D. 2010. *Muzzling a Movement: The Effects of Anti-Terrorism Law, Money & Politics on Animal Activism*. Brooklyn, NY: Lantern Books.

Mathiesen, T. 2006. Terrorlovgivning på norsk [Terror legislation in Norwegian], in *Kriminalpolitikk.uio.no*, Oslo University, Dept. for Criminology and Sociology of Law.

Mackinger, C. 2009. AETA, paragraph 278 and conspiracy to … Conspiracy laws and the repression of animal liberation activism, in *Interface: a Journal for and about Social Movements*. Online journal: www.interfacejournal.net, 1(2), 244–9.

Moore, A. and Ireland, N. 2005. Caging Animal Advocates' Political Freedoms: The Unconstitutionality of the Animal and Ecological Terrorism Act, in *Animal Law Review*. USA, Michigan: Lewis & Clark Law School, 11, 255–82.

Munro, L. 2005. *Confronting Cruelty – Moral Orthodoxy and the Challenge of the Animal Rights Movement*. Leide: Brill.

O'Reilly, C. 2010. The Transnational Security Consultancy Industry: A Case of State-corporate Symbiosis, in *Theoretical Criminology*. Los Angeles; London; New Dehli; Singapore: Sage Publications, 2010, 14(2), 183–210.

Persen, Å.B. and Johansen, J. 1998. *Den nødvendige ulydigheten*. [The Necessary Disobedience]. Oslo: Folkereisning Mot Krig.

della Porta, D. 2008. Research on Social Movements and Political Violence, in *Qualitative Sociology*. Netherlands: Springer, 31(3), 221–30.

Potter, W. 2009. The Green Scare, in *Vermont Law Review*. Vermont: Vermont Law School, 33(4), 671–687.

Potter, W. 2011. *Green is the New Red: An Insider's Account of a Social Movement Under Siege*. San Francisco: City Lights Books.

Reisner, A. 1992. An Activist Press: The Farm Press's Coverage of the Animal Rights Movement, in *Agriculture and Human Values*. Netherlands: Springer SBM B.V, spring edition 1992, 38–53.

Rowell, A. 1996. *Green Backlash: Global Subversion of the Environmental Movement*. London; New York: Routledge.

Singer, P. 2002. *Dyrenes Frigjøring*. Oslo: Spartacus AS.

Stretesky, P.B., Shelley, T.O. and Crow, M.S. 2010. Do Conservation Organizations Influence the Social Production of Natural Resource Violations?, in *Organization and Environment*. USA: Sage Publications, 23(4), 398–416.

Taylor, B.R. 1995. *Ecological Resistance Movements: The Global Emergence of Radical and Popular Environmentalism*. New York: State University of New York Press.

Torres, B. 2007. *Making A Killing: The Political Economy of Animal Rights*. Oakland: AK Press.

Walby, K. and Monaghan, J. 2011. Private Eyes and Public Order: Policing and Surveillance in the Suppression of Animal Rights Activists in Canada, in *Social Movement Studies*. London: Routledge, 10(1), 21–37.

Walters, B. 2003. *Defamation, Developers and Community Activism*. Sydney: University of New South Wales Press.

White, R. 2005. Stifling Environmental Dissent: On SLAPPS and GUNNS, in *Alternative Law Journal*. Australia: Faculty of Law, Monash University, 30(6), 268–73.

White, R. 2007. Green Criminology and the Pursuit of Social and Ecological Justice, in *Issues in Green Criminology*, edited by P. Beirne and N. South. USA; Canada: Willan Publishing.

White, R. 2008. Crimes Against Nature: Environmental Criminology and Ecological Justice. USA; Canada: Willan.

Yates, R. 2007. Debating 'Animal Rights' Online: The Movement-countermovement Dialectic Revisited, in *Issues in Green Criminology*, edited by P. Beirne and N. South. USA; Canada: Willan Publishing.

Zedner, L. 2007. Pre-crime and Post-criminology? in *Theoretical Criminology*. Los Angeles; London; New Delhi; Singapore; Sage Publications, 11(2), 261–81.

Part III
Biodiversity, Environmental and Species Justice

Chapter 11
Unlawful Hunting of Large Carnivores in Sweden[1]

Johanna Hagstedt and Lars Korsell

Introduction

The presence of wolves, lynx, bears, wolverines and golden eagles is a hotly debated topic in Sweden. Conflicting attitudes towards these carnivores[2] are associated with supporters of biodiversity and endangered species conservationists on one hand and with the social, cultural and economic interests of hunters, reindeer keepers, livestock owners and with some residents of rural areas on the other. Although the causal relationship between these conflicts and the prevalence of the unlawful hunting of predators is unclear, the two debates are closely linked to one another both politically and in the public debate. Although dark figures are substantial, there are reliable indications that a significant number of large carnivores are killed each year by unlawful hunting.

In light of the heated public debate and the absence of empirical studies, the National Council for Crime Prevention received funding to carry out a large study in order to look more closely at the phenomenon of unlawful carnivore hunting in Sweden. The need for evidence-based knowledge is particularly important in an area where there are many different groups, each with its own narratives and claims to knowing 'the truth' about predators.

This chapter is mainly based on the results of this research. The aim here is to provide a description of the unlawful hunting of large predators in Sweden; to what extent, how and why it occurs, who the perpetrators are and on what terms these crimes are investigated. The larger context in which these crimes

---

1 This chapter is in part based on previous studies: *Poaching for large predators – a pilot study* and *Poaching for large predators – conflict in a lawless land?* The studies were conducted at the National Council for Crime Prevention and the reports written by Johan Forsberg, Mikael Pyka, Anette Nyqvist and Therese Monstad as well as the authors of this chapter. The following description is based in part on the data gathered in association with these reports and in part on newly collected data relating to the years 2006–10.

2 The terms large carnivore and predator will be used interchangeably. The species covered by these terms are the Scandinavian 'big five': the wolf, brown bear, lynx, wolverine and golden eagle. It is important to note, however, that the wolf is the most debated species and is therefore often used as an example in the context of this chapter.

occur is also discussed. The chapter illustrates the social and political conflicts that exist between humans and predators, as well as the consequences that these conflicts produce for the predators. The chapter also describes the local, national and international dimensions causing polarized attitudes and conflicts surrounding the much-debated Swedish National Predator Policy, as well as legislative changes and biological concerns regarding inbreeding, and also a number of other recent developments within the field.

The chapter related to green criminology concepts such as anthropocentrism (hunters' views of predators and predator prey as resources for human consumption) and speciesism (the value of for example reindeer meat in contrast to the 'non-value' of wolves), as well as ecological concerns of extinction and right for non-human animals to exist in their natural environments. The chapter also relates to conventional criminology in terms of the distinction between legal and illegal hunting.

Methodology

The results presented in the chapter are based on the data collected for the report *Poaching for large predators – conflict in a lawless land?* (Brå 2007). The data were collected during the years 2006 and 2007. Due to the lack of research in the field of unlawful predator hunting, a large number of methods were used in order to obtain information from a number of different sources, which were chosen to represent different perspectives on unlawful hunting as well as the attitudes that surround the conflict relating to predators.

The following methods and data where used:

1. A literature study, including official government documents.
2. Official crime statistics, for official data on detected cases.
3. Police reports, investigations and sentences relating to all reported cases of unlawful predator hunting between 1995 and 2005 (344 cases in total).
4. Suspected perpetrators were checked against the criminal register and the hunting license database in order to chart previous criminality and ties to the hunting community.
5. Twenty-five in-depth interviews with hunters, reindeer keepers and livestock owners, some with personal experience of unlawful hunting, recruited through informants and snowball sampling.
6. Twenty-three interviews with representatives from different authorities, such as the police and county administrative boards.
7. Four participant observations with hunters and reindeer keepers.
8. A media analysis of how carnivores are portrayed and how unlawful hunting is legitimized in three hunting magazines and ten local newspapers; and
9. A survey measuring attitudes towards carnivores, the National Predator Policy and unlawful hunting, which was distributed to 3,200 hunters in four counties with predator populations.

In addition to the above, a less systematic review has been made of more recent court cases, the media debate and recent developments in the field, including changes made to the National Predator Policy.

Legislation

For many centuries, the population of large carnivores was extensive in Sweden. They caused damage for reindeer keepers and livestock farmers, and from the beginning of the seventeenth century bounties started to be awarded to people who could prove that they had shot a wolf. The populations of all the large carnivores soon decreased, and by the 1960s the wolf was more or less extinct. As biodiversity concerns started to grow in 1966, the wolf became a protected species. The same happened with the wolverine in 1969. The hunting of bear, lynx and golden eagle had long been regulated off and on, based on the current status of the populations. Over recent decades, all five species have started to recover and to repopulate, mainly the northern parts of the country.

Today, predator hunting is strictly regulated. Hunting throughout the year may occur only under exceptional circumstances, for example in order to protect livestock or to prevent other damage. In addition, for the brown bear and the lynx there is a regulated hunting season for which a quota is determined that may not be exceeded. The Swedish hunting legislation states that the Environmental Protection Agency has responsibility for determining the size of hunting quotas and for issuing control orders. Recently, however, locally situated County Administrative Boards have been given responsibility for permitting the shooting of individual problem bears or lynx. Problem individuals are defined by their inclination to look for food in densely populated areas, to kill and cause damage to economically and emotionally valued livestock and property and by having engaged in other behaviours that are regarded as dangerous or threatening to humans.

Unlawful hunting is regulated in the Hunting Act (1987: 259). The penalties have been increased a number of times over the course of the last decade. Aggravated hunting offences[3] should now result in a prison sentence of between six months and four years. There has also been a change in the acts considered to constitute unlawful hunting. It is now, in special circumstances, permissible to shoot an individual predator in order to protect livestock (Hunting Ordinance 1987: 905 § 28). This change came about after a small number of cases in which animal owners had protected their livestock and where the prosecutions were given a lot of media attention.

3 Aggravated hunting offences constitute cases where the hunted species is endangered or rare and therefore particularly worthy of protection – which is always the case for large carnivores, or if hunting methods have been used that are especially painful.

Biological Considerations

In addition to being bound by several pieces of EU legislation, such as the Convention on Biological Diversity and the Species and Habitat Directive, the Swedish Coherent Predator Policy was implemented in 2000. It stipulates that Sweden has the aim of guaranteeing the continued presence in the country of viable populations of wolf, wolverine, lynx, bear and golden eagles (SOU 1999: 146, prop. 2000/01: 57).

Table 11.1 presents the population sizes of each species for the latest year of inventory, together with the national targets. The table shows that wolves are most uncommon although it could be argued that the other populations are not so large either. One important factor, however, is that the distribution of predators across the country is very uneven. The populations are for the most part distributed in the northern parts of the country, with the main concentration of wolves being centered in only two of Sweden's 21 counties.

Table 11.1 Size of the Swedish populations of wolves, wolverines, lynx, bears and golden eagles

Specie	Number of individuals specified in national minimum level targets	Most recent estimation of the number of individuals	Year of inventory
Wolf (Canis lupus)	200 individuals (20 rejuvenations)[4]	172–208 (28 rejuvenations)	2010/2011
Wolverine (Gulo gulo)	550 individuals (90 rejuvenations)	680 (113 rejuvenations)	2010
Lynx (Lynx lynx)	1500 individuals (250 rejuvenations)	1200–1400 (248 rejuvenations)	2010
Bear (Ursus arctos)	1000 individuals (100 rejuvenations)	3200	2010
Golden eagle (Aquila chrysaetos)	600 breeding pairs	500 breeding pairs (221 rejuvenations)	2008

Source: Naturvårdsverket 2011a, Viltskadecenter 2010a, Viltskadecenter 2010b, Kindberg, Svensson and Ericsson 2009, Viltskadecenter 2009

The Swedish wolf population is suffering as a result of inbreeding. The entire population stems from three individuals that appeared in the country during the early 1980s, and as a result of this the individuals are on average more closely related than siblings (Sand et al 2007). The population is also isolated from other populations, for example those in Finland and Russia. The potential for any natural immigration of wolves is therefore low. The occurrence of unlawful hunting is thought to have prevented the few individuals that have made their way into the country from reaching the Swedish population. Primarily as a result of the

4 In addition to the minimum, the government has also set a maximum level. The number of wolves may not exceed 210 individuals.

inbreeding problem, the Swedish Government has given the relevant authorities the task of looking more closely at the possibilities of introducing wolves in order to improve their genetic composition (Miljödepartementet 2010a).

Attitudes and Conflicts

In addition to the data collected by our own survey, studies have been conducted at regular intervals over the last two decades in order to follow the trend in attitudes towards large predators in Sweden. The two most recent opinion polls were conducted in 2004 and 2009. The results show that a majority of the Swedish population supports the existence of large predators, although support for the wolf and bear has decreased. At the national level, a majority of the population (64–73 per cent) appreciates the fact that the country has predator populations. In municipalities with high numbers of predators, however, the figure is slightly lower (56–70 per cent) (Sandström and Ericsson 2009a). In these areas, there are also more people who object to the specified national targets for population sizes. The difference in attitudes between people in urban and rural areas has increased over time.

A large proportion of the population agrees that Sweden should follow international law (91 per cent) and supports the way wildlife management is administered (Sandström and Ericsson 2009b). The support for administrative measures intended to decrease predator-related problems, such as putting up fences, tagging, moving or scaring away predators, has increased to between 75–91 per cent (Sandström and Ericsson 2009b). Hunting is accepted as a method of limiting the number of predators if they start to make their way into densely populated areas (85 per cent), as a means of minimizing the risk of livestock being eaten (67 per cent) and to a lesser extent because people are afraid of them (45 per cent). Less than a third of the respondents thought it was okay to hunt these animals in order to lessen the competition over game that can be hunted by man (Ericsson et al. 2010).

Almost half of all Swedes state that they are afraid of bears and one in four are afraid of wolves. People living in the regions with large predator populations are more afraid (60 per cent of people living in counties with the largest number of bears and 36 per cent in the county with the most wolves) than people living in other parts of the country. No correlation was found, however, between being afraid of the bear or the wolf and not wanting to have these animals present in the area where the respondent lived (Ericsson et al. 2010). Similar results have also been found in equivalent survey data from Norway (Tangeland et al. 2010).

Among people in general, there seems to be little variation in attitudes towards predators. However, it is among smaller 'pro' and 'anti' groups in the population that the predator issue is a source of conflict and great polarization. It is important to note that the wolf is the main source of conflict. Our survey data showed that 30 per cent of hunters in the county with the most wolves considered the wolf to be a threat towards their personal safety. In light of the mandatory education received before taking a hunting license and the fact that nobody has been killed by a wolf in Sweden since 1821 (the circumstances were very special – a domesticated wolf released into the wild went back to the village where it had been raised and killed and ate a large number of children there; Linell and Bjerke 2002), these results are surprising, particularly since two people have died during the past ten years as a result of bear encounters. It would rather be expected that members of the hunting community who know the biological and physical facts would not be afraid of the wolf. Both in the interviews conducted by the National Council for Crime Prevention and in the media, hunters, reindeer keepers and farmers often mention fear and claim that it is widespread amongst women and children:

> People have called me and cried on the phone because they don't dare go out in the woods and pick berries. They have been picking berries in these woods for fifty years but now they don't dare. I usually say that it is not dangerous. But the fear does exist. And for a mother with a couple of small children it is not much fun spending time in the woods now.

We do not know exactly why there is such a level of fear in relation to the wolf. One explanation is that, historically, the wolf has been portrayed as a symbol of evil in stories and folklore (Ekman 2010). One illustration of this fear of the wolf is found in the Nobel Prize winner Selma Lagerlöf's story *Gösta Berling's Saga*, in which a sleigh is pursued by a pack of wolves. Irrespective of the underlying reasons, it is important to recognize the power and role of the wolf's symbolism in carnivore politics (Tönnessen 2010).

Positive attitudes toward predators are found among environmentalists and conservationists, many of who are members of different nature and wildlife organizations. Negative attitudes to predators are found mainly among the Sami people, livestock keepers, parts of the hunting community and among a segment of the population living in predator-dense areas (Brå 2007). Within these groups, predators are considered to constitute a threat to their lifestyle (due to cultural aspects of the indigenous Sami people and because of traditional and alternative methods of animal keeping and hunting), as well as to economic interests and personal safety. For hunters, predators are also competitors over game as well as a risk factor when allowing hunting dogs to run unleashed in the woods. A number of dogs are killed annually (20 dogs in 2010 – Viltskadecenter 2011), and these are of both emotional and economic value to hunters. These ways of viewing predators is an expression of anthropocentrism as well as speciesism. Wild game and the environment are seen as resources for human exploitation and the threat that predators pose towards the human way of life motivates both legal and illegal predator hunting as predators are regarded to be of less use to humans (for more discussion on speciesism see, for example, chapters by Bjørkdahl, Sollund, Svärd and White, this volume). The polarization between these pro- and anti-groups is evident in the media where 'predator haters' are accused of 'spreading their hatred towards predators in every newspaper' and 'predator huggers' are accused of 'becoming hysterical as soon as a really dangerous wolf should be killed to protect both people and animals' (Brå 2007).

In addition to the focus on perceived threats to lifestyle and economic interests and so on, the predator conflict has also come to represent other conflict dimensions in society at large. The predator issue has become a symbol for the conflict between urban and rural areas, between the governed and the representatives of government and between local governance and globalization in the form of EU directives and legislation.

Recent Developments

The conflicts surrounding predators have intensified over recent years. As a result, a new inquiry was established to look more closely at the dynamics between the Coherent Predator Policy and the opinions of those interest groups that they were being steamrollered by the national predator targets. The inquiry resulted in the publication of a Government Official Report on predators and their management (SOU 2007: 89). The solutions presented were largely based on the assumption that, in order for the predators and the Coherent Predator Policy to gain acceptance among the people, the administration and management of the predators must be determined in consultation with local interest groups. In order to meet these demands, the management and decision-making process has been reorganized, with a transfer of decision-making power from the central to the regional level (prop. 2008/09: 210). Another strategy intended to lessen the conflict has been to allow wolf hunting to a limited extent. At the beginning of 2010, permission was granted to shoot 27 wolves (28 were shot) in those regions that host the largest share of the wolf population (Naturvårdsverket 2009). In 2011, 19 wolves were shot (the permitted number was 20). Almost 7,500 wolf hunters were registered before the hunt began and of these, 4,500 are estimated to have participated (Naturvårdsverket 2011b). The hope is that permitting hunting will increase levels of acceptance for wolves. Environmental associations have been critical against this type of reasoning however. They argue there are other, better ways to gain acceptance for the National Predator Policy. The theory that unlawful hunting will decrease as the legitimate possibilities to hunt increase has also been referred to as an argument for permitting wolf hunting. To date there is no evidence to support the truth of this claim, but it is hoped that the question will be given attention in future research. Advocates claim that having the opportunity to hunt wolves legally will demystify wolf hunting and will increase levels of acceptance for the wolf. Conversely, opponents fear that legal hunting will legitimize wolf hunting in general, will encourage those who do not accept wolves and will serve as a guise for unlawful hunting (Tönnessen 2010).

In connection with the Swedish Government deciding to allow controlled wolf hunting at the beginning of 2010, this was reported to the EU by a number of environmentalist groups. It is the opinion of these groups that the government has broken a number of regulations by giving permission to hunt individuals in such a small population of what is considered an endangered species. The EU Environment Commissioner has openly questioned the government's decision to allow wolf hunting and the issue may now end up before the European Court of Justice.

When the decision was taken to allow wolf hunting, it was also decided that around 20 wolves would be introduced into the Swedish fauna. The Board of Agriculture, the Environmental Protection Agency and the National Veterinary Institute were given the task of looking at the possibilities of introducing individual wolves into Sweden in order to improve the genetic base and lessen the level of inbreeding (Miljödepartementet 2010a). Their results were published at the end of 2010 (Naturvårdsverket 2010). The authorities responsible for handling wildlife have suggested introducing a number of individuals, both pups and adults, from the population of wolves primarily shared by Finland and Russia. This was judged to be the best way of securing the genetic input that is much needed. This has raised the topic of how many individuals are actually needed of each predator species in order to guarantee the future existence of healthy populations in the country. This has lead the government to establish yet another inquiry to submit proposals on how large the populations of wolves, lynx, wolverines, bears and golden eagles should be in Sweden. The inquiry, which is to be conducted by the Environmental Protection Agency, is to take into consideration not only how many individuals are needed in order to ensure the populations' long-term survival, but also the people living in areas with large predator populations (Dir. 2010: 65). The report is due in the summer of 2012. The suggestion of importing and/or reintroducing wolves has received a lot of criticism however (Miljödepartementet 2010b). The views of representatives from both hunting as well as environmental organizations are that the predator policy is being put into action too quickly and that it is too soon to start implementing these strategies before they have gained approval. Some authorities have also warned that this will cause an increase in unlawful hunting. One reason for this is that there is even now a false preconception that wolves have already secretly been introduced into the forests (Norlén 2006, Tönnessen 2010). This was confirmed by the results of our survey, which showed that over 56 per cent of the respondents agreed to the claim that authorities have been trying to hide the fact that wolves have been secretly reintroduced. This was also mentioned in our own interviews:

> - We had not had a wolf here in almost one hundred years and then all of a sudden a couple [of wolves] showed up and no one believes that it has gotten there by itself.
>
> - Do you mean that you think it was reintroduced?
>
> - Yes, that is the most likely. The authorities have known about this, but it was ordered by the Environmental Protection Agency … but no one pretends like it happened, but there are many witnesses.

A strategy based on reintroduction as opposed to encouraging individual wolves to wander into the country naturally may therefore be conceived as a part of this conspiracy.

These recent developments show that predators and predator management have become a politically important question and that the prevalence and prevention of unlawful predator hunting has therefore also become politically significant.

The Crimes

The National Council for Crime Prevention has developed a model as an aid to examining and explaining aggravated hunting offences against predators (see Figure 11.1). The model is based on the literature and on a theoretical framework and it has been further developed through the empirical studies conducted at the Council (Brå 2005, 2007).

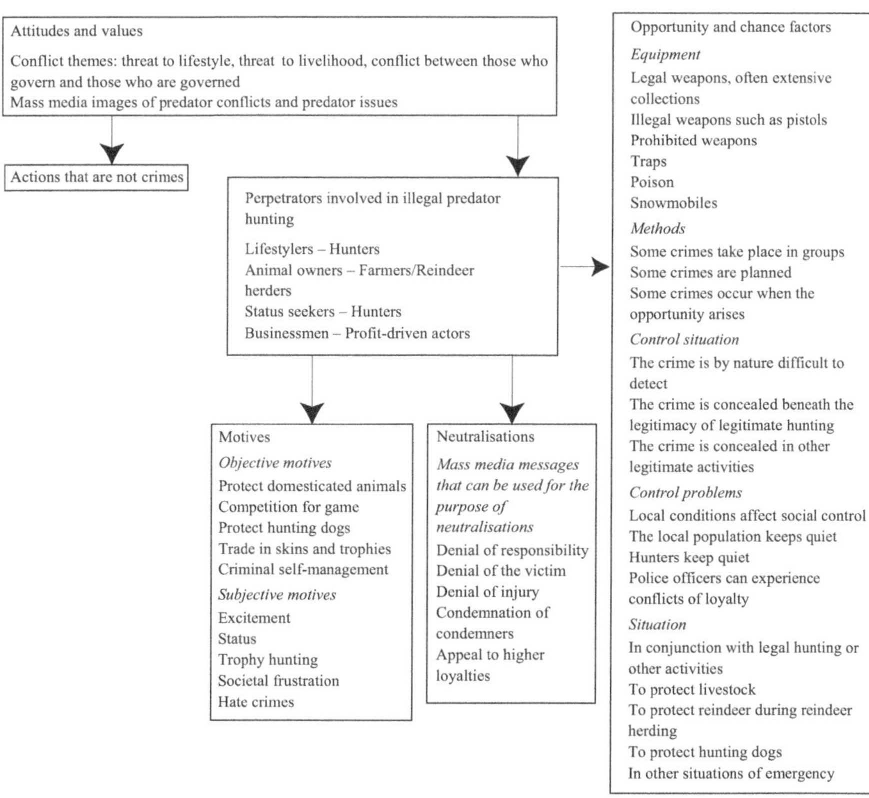

Figure 11.1 Model for analyzing and explaining unlawful hunting

The model begins by focusing attention on the attitudes and values shared by people with negative feelings towards predators. These can largely be traced to the conflicts surrounding the National Predator Policy that have already been discussed. The model then presents the different categories of perpetrators and the different types of motives that exist. It is in part on the basis of the negative attitudes described at the top of the model that objective and subjective motives for unlawful hunting are formulated. The model illustrates that these can be reinforced by the way in which predators are portrayed in the media. The ways in which these negative representations can be used to neutralize unlawful hunting will not be discussed here, however, due to limitations of space. The role played by opportunity and chance factors is noted but not accounted for exhaustively.

Judgments and Reports

Table 11.2 shows the number of reported and cleared cases of aggravated hunting offences for the last five years. The number of reported crimes differs in different parts of the country, mainly in proportion to the number of predators found in different areas.

Table 11.2 The number of reported and cleared unlawful hunting crimes against wolves, bears, lynx, wolverines and golden eagles for the years 2006–10

Year	2006[5]	2007	2008	2009	2010
Number of reported cases	12	54	45	32	59
Overall clearance rate (no. of clearances)	42% (5)	50% (27)	56% (25)	41% (13)	41% (24)
Technical clearances	5	25	19	10	19
Person-based clearances	0	2	6	3	5
Decisions to prosecute	0	0	4	1	1

Between 1995 and 2010, 546 cases of aggravated hunting offences were reported to the police. Of the 344 cases reported to the police during the period 1995–2005, 76 cases were closed because the reports concerned acts that were not considered to be crimes or because there was no reason to believe that a crime had been committed (Brå 2007). In 268 cases, however, there were suspicions that a crime had taken

5 The separate collection of statistics relating to hunting offences of this type was initiated in 2006 (previously these offences were included among all types of hunting offences). The figures for 2006 are therefore probably not representative of the true number of crimes reported and cleared that year.

place. As regards the different species of predator, the reports related to: 52 wolves, 60 lynx, 82 bears, 43 wolverines, 26 golden eagles and 9 unidentified predators. Most of the reports come from counties in the northern regions of Sweden: Norrbotten (75), Dalarna (56), Jämtland (51), Västerbotten (27) and Västernorrland (12).

The clearance rates are also low; especially the number of cases where a person can actually be tied to the crime. Of the 344 reports, only 33 resulted in prosecution and one case concluded with the suspect being served a summary imposition of a fine. In 18 of the 33 cases that were examined by the courts, the crime had initially been reported by the shooter personally or by another person in the hunting party. In six of the nine judgments that were handed down during the period 2006–10, the initial police report was made by one of the individuals involved in the offence. These types of offences mainly occurred in the context of legal bear hunting. Most of the prosecutions were therefore based on self-reporting rather than on the crime having been detected by outsiders. This demonstrates an important difference between the cases of unlawful hunting that are reported and that lead to convictions, which are often self-reported, and those that constitute part of the large dark figure, which occur in other circumstances and are concealed from the authorities.

Unlawful Hunting is Hard to Detect and Difficult to Prove

It is difficult to estimate the extent of unlawful hunting. As has already been noted, the dark figure is very large. One study (Sand et al. 2007) has shown that 9 per cent of the 69 untagged wolves and 50–57 per cent of the 42 tagged wolves that were found dead during the period 1999–2006 were estimated to have been killed as a result of unlawful hunting. Liberg et al. (2008) conclude that every second wolf death is due to unlawful hunting. Another study concludes that 100–150 lynx are killed unlawfully each year, based on the premise that the tagged lynx are representative for the entire lynx population (Liberg and Andrén 2006). More detailed accounts for all the predator species can be found in the Official Governmental Report regarding predators and their management (SOU 2007: 89) and in the National Council's previous study from 2007. The consequences being the populations have not grown at the rate that would be expected.

The fact that these crimes are subject to a large dark figure becomes particularly clear when animals found dead from natural causes, and those killed legitimately in the context of legal hunts, are found to have old injuries and healed wounds from unlawful hunting attempts (Liberg et al. 2008). It is safe to say that the number of cases that become known to the police (see Table 11.2) is nowhere near the actual number of crimes committed each year.

There are a number of circumstances that complicate the investigations of these crimes. They are committed over large, deserted forested areas and Sweden's unique Right of Public Access grants every person the right to be in the woods at any time of year (although not the right to be carrying a weapon unless it is hunting season). In addition, the crime scene may be spread over large distances if the animal has been moved or has been able to move itself some distance from where it was shot/caught/poisoned/run over.

When it comes to proving that a crime has been committed, there are further difficulties. In the police reports studied by the National Council of Crime Prevention, there are signs of deliberate attempts of making the investigation of offences more difficult by cutting off and moving tracking devices that have been attached to the animal, and by trying to dispose of carcasses by burning them or by submerging them in lakes. Among persons with strong anti-predator views and therefore also among the persons who commit these aggravated hunting offences, there is an implicit rule of not cooperating with the police or other investigative authorities. The 'shoot, shovel and shut up' (skjut, gräv och tig) principle is a common mantra, which points to the fact that there are explicit expectations that persons who commit these types of crimes should keep it to themselves. Due to the occurrence of threats and the exertion of unlawful influence (see below), there is also a fear among other people in the community of telling the police what they may know. Peer pressure also plays a role, since expressing positive attitudes towards predators can lead to social exclusion from some groups, and the inclination to report or stand as a witness in relation to these crimes is therefore very small. As one hunter explains:

> There are 30 people in my hunting team and when we are out hunting no one says anything, but when we are in the cabin in the evening … and then it is the most aggressive ones that are heard all the time and the others are quiet … because you're afraid … afraid to voice your opinion … it is easy to think that I'm the only one who has another opinion, but when you speak to the others alone, they may also think that the wolf should be allowed to exist. But no one dares say it. You're afraid of being excluded. The norm says that as a hunter you should be against the wolf and the predator policy.

The result is that when cases of unlawful hunting are detected, the police and other investigative authorities have excessive trouble trying to build cases that will hold up in a court of law.

All of the above mentioned factors contribute to the fact that the proportion of convicted perpetrators, compared to the estimated levels of unlawful hunting, can be counted in the tenths of 1 per cent. And when a person is convicted, the sentences are low. In 2001, the sanction for aggravated hunting offences was increased to imprisonment for at least six months and up to a maximum of four years. However, during the period 1995–2005 nobody has received a more severe sanction than the most lenient specified in the scale – six months in prison. In fact, the sentences awarded are often below the minimum specified in the legislation. In other words, the problems of control are significant and society has obvious difficulties in dealing with unlawful hunting. In practice, the possibilities of detecting and sanctioning unlawful hunting are very low.

Who are the Perpetrators?

Table 11.3 shows the number of persons suspected of aggravated hunting offences committed against large carnivores. We can see that there are very few cases where a perpetrator has been identified; 13 persons in the last five years.

Table 11.3 The number, age and gender of the persons suspected of large carnivore hunting in Sweden for the years 2006–10

Year	Age							Gender		Total
	15–20	21–24	25–29	30–39	40–49	50–59	60+	Male	Female	
2006										0
2007						1		1		1
2008			1	2	1	1	1	6		6
2009					1			1		1
2010	1			1	3			4	1	5

In 18 of the 33 cases that resulted in prosecutions between 1995 and 2005, the suspected perpetrators were active hunters. In 12 cases they were reindeer keepers/owners, in two cases keepers of other animals and in three cases there was no clear link to any of these categories.

The different categories of perpetrators that have been identified are presented under separate headings below.

'Lifestylers'

Lifestylers have a major interest in hunting, and predators are therefore seen as competing with their lifestyle. They feel strongly dissatisfied with the way that the authorities are handling predator issues:

> - Being a hunter is a way of life … and now the authorities are ruining that way of life for a lot of people. Of course people will be angry!
>
> - And that [the authorities] cannot admit when they have made the wrong decision. Instead they claim that it is we hunters who are crazy and that we shoot predators from rage.
>
> - But it isn't really the wolf that we want to shoot.
>
> - No, it isn't the animals we are angry at.

For the lifestylers, hunting is a particularly important feature of their way of life. The unlawful predator hunting carried out by this group can also occur in connection with legal hunting.

The court judgments that have been studied include persons with a significant interest in hunting. In some cases, however, it appears that the motive for the crime was economic rather than being a question of lifestyle. In one judgment, a hunter expresses the view that predators compete with them over game, causing economic losses.

Lifestylers are perhaps the most serious threat to predators, since they have both the will and the means to engage in illegal hunting. That they are also able to conceal the crime as part of their lifestyle is connected to spending time outdoors in areas where there are predators.

Animal Owners

Another perpetrator category consists of farmers who keep domestic animals and reindeer keepers. These people feel economically threatened, but perhaps more emotionally threatened by the predators. The problems posed by predators to owners of domestic animals and reindeer have received a lot of attention in the public debate. One such occasion was when demonstrations were held following the arrest of two Sami reindeer keepers on suspicion of unlawful hunting (Brå 2007). These cases of unlawful hunting where the main purpose has been the protection of other animals have served as a symbol for the unjustness of the National Predator Policy and, as has previously been noted, have contributed to a change in the legislation. This was frequently mentioned in the open answer questions included in the National Council's survey:

> -I think it is bloody awful when livestock keepers are sentenced and punished for shooting predators that have attacked their animals multiple times.

Although the threat that predators pose to domestic animals is a big issue in the public debate, these situations are hardly present in the police reports. Only two reports involved situations where predators had been shot in or in the vicinity of an enclosure. A further two reports that led to convictions related to reindeer keepers who had killed bears or wolverines because, according to their own statements, they were unable to protect their herds in any other way. The predator inquiry of 1999 had already shown that the conflicts involving keepers of domestic animals were not particularly widespread, since animal owners receive financial support in order to take protective measures and are reimbursed when livestock has been killed (SOU 1999: 146).

None of the judgments that were handed down during the period 2006–10 involve cases where owners of domestic animals had been protecting their animals. It is possible that the change in the legislation, allowing predator hunting on a preventative basis in some cases, has made it close to impossible for prosecutors to press charges in such situations.

More commonly, reports involve hunters shooting a predator to protect hunting dogs or themselves. This scenario is found in 41 of the 344 offence reports, and these mainly involve bear attacks. One such case is also found in one of the judgments handed down during the period 2006–10.

Status Seekers

Status seekers are hunters motivated by the prestige associated with shooting a predator. This can happen in conjunction with a legal hunt. These hunters take trophies and spend a lot of money on equipment – something that they presumably have in common with the lifestylers.

An additional group of status seekers is comprised of the members of marginalized groups within certain Sami villages who keep reindeer. Status seekers are not found in the court judgments, but were described in the conducted interviews:

> -If you have low social status in a Sami village, you are prepared to do almost anything to advance socially. And high status can be received in two ways: by owning a lot of reindeer or by being a good hunter … large bounties are paid within the Sami villages along the mountain range, primarily for wolves.

> -We received a serious tip from a hunter in a hunting team who told us about rewards being paid out if you kill a predator.

The presence of status seekers is also supported by the documentation from a number of police investigations, in which trophies had been taken from predators that were found dead.

Businessmen

The businessmen are a small group of people who trade in endangered species. Increased supervision as a result of international conventions, in combination with open borders to Eastern Europe, is assumed to have reduced the businessmen's presence in the Swedish forests. However, the businessmen group also includes perpetrators who conduct professional hunts for invited, paying hunting guests. It can be economically beneficial to invite hunting guests to hunt predators. In addition, predators can be viewed as competitors over game for this group of perpetrators as well.

Only a few businessmen can be found in the police investigations. Five of the judgments involved perpetrators who were deemed to belong to this category.

Levels of Prior Involvement in Crime

Of the 51 persons who were suspected of the unlawful hunting of predators during the years 1995–2005, 43 per cent had previously been convicted of a crime. The people who were only suspected of unlawful hunting, but who were not prosecuted and convicted, had a prior criminal record slightly more often (48 per cent) than those who were prosecuted and sentenced. These figures are not out of the ordinary; 37 per cent of all Swedish men are sentenced at some point in their lifetime, usually for traffic offences (Brå 2000). Consequently, those people identified as suspects or prosecuted for unlawful hunting do not differ to any major extent from the general population with regards to previous criminality. Certain previous crimes indicate however that there are some individuals who have what can be described as a criminal lifestyle (Brå 2000). This applies to persons convicted of crimes such as car theft and theft. Furthermore, there is also an element of economic criminality, with crimes such as tax evasion, false accounting, fraud and falsification of documents. There is also an element of violent crimes and assault, violence against public servants, inflicting bodily harm and unlawful threats.

Possession of Hunting Licenses among the Suspects

Of the 131 persons prosecuted, suspected or mentioned in some other way in the police investigations, 93 had a hunting license issued in 2006/2007. A total of 105 of these persons had had a hunting license at some time during their lives. The conclusion drawn from this is that the people who become known to the authorities as a result of some kind of involvement in unlawful hunting are largely also involved in legal hunting and are thus registered hunters. This is quite understandable, since members of the hunting community are those who have the ability, opportunity and equipment to commit these crimes. For this reason, hunting organizations have been identified as having a responsibility and the opportunity to work preventively to combat unlawful hunting.

As has previously been noted, there are currently expectations at the political level that the licensed hunting of wolves will lead to the wolf becoming more accepted in the hunting community. In this way, the management of predators could become a matter of concern and a responsibility for the hunters, rather than an issue over which they have no control or say. It remains to be seen whether these hopes will materialize. We have seen, however, that the conflict between the supporters and opponents of predators has remained, if not even intensified, during the two years that licensed wolf hunting has been allowed.

Motives

The identified motives have been divided into two categories, objective and subjective. The objective motives are defined as motives related to economic loss or gain directly caused by predators. These are often lifestyle-oriented. The subjective motives are instead emotionally based, such as stress, frustration with society, emotional rewards and status (Eliason 2004, Forsyth and Marckese 1993a, 1993b). Both subjective and objective motives are often likely to lie behind each individual crime. Although the motive or the combination of motives is individual to the particular perpetrator of a crime, several of the motives and arguments regularly appear in the predator debate. This means that there is also a political dimension to these crimes. They cannot be seen as isolated occurrences as they are part of a much larger societal context.

Lifestyle-oriented Economic Motives

Historically, the motive for hunting predators has been that they can attack domestic animals. Whilst it is true that government reimbursement systems exist for reindeer keepers and farmers, the problem is more about protecting domestic animals from suffering. Many hunters have stated in our survey that the reason for unlawful hunting is that predators constitute a threat to the domestic animal industry (Brå 2007).

> -As soon as there is an economic loss, people will start to hunt unlawfully … if the predators take all the game, there will be nothing left to hunt.

> -We found them in the enclosure, a ewe and a lamb, half eaten. Two wolves had been there. But that was the last year, because after that I didn't want to keep wolf food any more … When they interviewed me in the newspaper and I said I was a wolf hater they asked if I could stand by my word on that and I said yes I can. As if that was a terrible thing.

Hunters also express the view that predators compete over game. Additionally, the renewed spread of predators produces problems in relation to hunting with unleashed dogs, of which a number are killed each year.

A less common economic motive is referred to as criminal self-management, whereby landowners and other interested parties pay persons who have killed a predator.

Trophy Hunting and Status

A number of dead predators have been found where the animals have been skinned, or where the eyes, tails, claws and other body parts have been removed. As mentioned above, the reasons are suspected to be both so that a person can show that he has killed predators – in order to receive payment (criminal self-management) – and also as a kind of trophy taking:

> -Some hunting teams have them. There is a gang, you may have heard of them when you were up in [x]. They collect hunting trophies in their cabin. But they'll beat me to death if I take you there.

Hatred of Predatory Animals and Unlawful Hunting in Protest

The report from the previous predator inquiry discussed the hatred of predatory animals as a reason for unlawful hunting (SOU 1999: 146). The police investigations include examples where predators had been hunted using cruel methods and where the animals had suffered a great deal of pain. In a couple of cases, transmitter collars or parts of the dead animal (for example paws) have been sent to the Swedish Environmental Protection Agency or the County Administrative Boards, presumably to demonstrate contempt for the authorities and for the National Predator Policy. One example is found in the following quote from a police investigation:

> A motorist notifies the police that he had seen something strange next to a main road. On the edge of the ditch near a clump of trees lay a headless lynx. The place where the lynx's body was found was arranged much like a burial place. The headless body lay placed on a sheet of plywood, covered with a piece of cloth. In an adjacent tree, someone had nailed up a wooden cross, with the inscription: 'Here lies the lynx cat Nitro hated killed by friends'. The National Veterinary Institute cannot confirm the cause of death, and the police and prosecutors have no ideas for intelligence gathering, and the case has therefore been closed.

There are differing opinions as to the extent to which hatred can be the underlying motive behind unlawful hunting. As has been mentioned, there is in any event a political side to the matter. The renewed expansion of the predator populations is one of the most sensitive political issues in the country. It is true that predators affect conditions for hunting and keeping domestic animals. But the conflict is much larger, and the predatory animals issue has become an arena for far greater conflicts, with some groups of people feeling that the EU and urban politics are steamrollering their lifestyle:

> -No, no one listens to us. No one listens to what we who are living here think. The biggest reason why people breach the hunting legislation is probably because they feel steamrollered by the authorities and the people who make decisions in Stockholm.

Some also feel that many rural parts of the country are in decline, with outward migration, fewer job opportunities and reduced services, and that the large amounts of money set aside for managing predators would be better spent on other things:

> -We have a small school in the village with only 80 kids and they receive no money whatsoever to travel to the public swimming pool that is nine kilometers away. There is no money for that … And then we sit here and look at all these millions! I saw the numbers of the amount they were investing in wolf research myself! And all of a sudden the wolves and lynx and bears are worth more than my sons … And then you get angry. Really pissed off.

There is a widespread mistrust of decision-makers, administrative authorities and the current national predator policy that causes a strong dislike for predators. In view of these circumstances, it is not surprising that people who commit unlawful hunting acts feel they have support for their actions in their surroundings.

Additional Crimes

The conflicts surrounding the predators also give rise to other types of crimes than aggravated hunting offences. Firstly, there are crimes directly connected to hunting offences such as using illegal hunting methods, having weapons on snow scooters, hunting predators from snow scooters or vehicles and using certain weapons and trapping devices.

There are also other types of crimes which are associated with the conflict surrounding predators. Persons that are known to have positive attitudes to predators and persons working in the field of wildlife management, for example, at the county administrative boards or within wildlife preservation organizations, are exposed to threats and unlawful influence:

> -We are always subject to a lot of sabotage and threats; authorities are prey to those who want to cross the line. But sometimes I am afraid they will step too far over the line. Right now they are loosening bolts on car wheels, cutting off cables to boat motors, pouring things in the fuel tanks and putting things in locks and such.

Examples of the type of acts involved include cases of property damage (for example, destroyed mailboxes and punctured tires), harassment (for example, test-firing weapons close by during predator inventories) as well as assaults. Threats have also been directed at hunters for participating in the legal wolf hunt (Tönnessen 2010). The interviews conducted with police also included accounts of encountering resistance to the investigation of hunting offences within the police organization itself:

> -It is difficult investigating unlawful hunting, because we get to hear things from our colleagues who are hunters, who interfere in what we are doing, that don't like it. Especially if you're investigating someone's friend.

This also illustrates the problem of small communities, where people who work with wildlife management, within the legal system or who are hunters, may be neighbours or friends in private, making professional relations and decisions difficult.

What Can Be Expected in the Future?

The results presented in this chapter show that the predator issue in Sweden is a topic that can be further explored through the framework of green criminology. Not least, it suggests that as long as the predators are viewed from an anthropocentric perspective, measures that revalue predators and increase ecological understanding of the benefits of predators should help lessen the conflict. Also, future research concerning the differing perspectives on harm and of rights associated with human and non-human animals would be valuable to further explore in order to understand the many differing perspectives involved.

In a recent article published in one of Sweden's largest daily newspapers, the chairpersons of the Swedish Society for Nature Conservation, the Swedish Carnivore Association and the Directors-General of the World Wildlife Fund for Nature in Sweden and Animal Welfare Sweden voiced their criticism of the political decisions that have been taken regarding the wolf (Karlsson et al. 2011). They are concerned that wolf hunting has been allowed even though the population is currently biologically unsustainable and they look forward to the EU commission reviewing and taking legal action against this. They believe that the lack of approval for predator policy should be of greater concern to the Swedish Government and that every proposed measure should be discussed in light of the polarized climate and the extent to which unlawful predator hunting exists. They are also critical of the fact that so much attention is being given to the minority within the population who have negative attitudes towards carnivores.

As for the government being reported to the EU commission for allowing wolf hunting, the EU commission is in the process of assessing whether there has been a breach of the regulations, which may necessitate a preliminary ruling from the Court of Justice if the case is taken further and a formal infringement procedure is launched against the Swedish Government. An answer should be on the way soon, as should the results of the inquiries being conducted into reintroduction and levels of sustainable populations.

It can be seen from the above that there are a large number of unresolved issues with regard to predators and the politics surrounding them. This suggests that we are in the middle of a conflict that will continue to develop for the foreseeable future: only time will tell what consequences this will continue to have for the occurrence of unlawful hunting. It is plausible that while species conservation arguments are gaining support, there will still be certain groups who are prepared to break the law, and who will continue to find motives, neutralizations and support for their actions in the ongoing debate.

References

Brå. 2000. *Strategiska brott. Vilka brott förutsätter en fortsatt brottskarriär?* [*Strategic Offences. Which Crimes Predict a Continued Criminal Career?*]. Report 2000: 3. Stockholm: Brottsförebyggande rådet.

Brå. 2005. *Illegal jakt på rovdjur. En förstudie* [Poaching for Large Predators. A Pilot Study]. Stockholm: Brottsförebyggande rådet.

Brå. 2007. *Illegal jakt på stora rovdjur. Konflikt i laglöst land?* [*Poaching for Large Predators – Conflict in a Lawless Land?*]. Report 2007: 22. Stockholm: Brottsförebyggande rådet.

Dir. 2010: 65 [Kommittédirektiv]. *Utvärdering av mål för rovdjursstammarnas utveckling* [*Evaluation of aims for the development of predator breeds*]. Kommittédirektiv 10. Miljödepartementet.

Ekman, H. 2010. *Vargen – den jagade jägaren* [*The Wolf – the Hunted Hunter*]. Slovenien: Nordstedts.

Eliason, S.L. 2004. Accounts of Wildlife Law Violators: Motivations and Rationalizations, in *Human Dimensions of Wildlife*, 9(2), 119–31.

Ericsson, G. et al. 2010. *Om svenskars rädsla för stora rovdjur, älg och vildsvin* [*About Swedes' fear of large carnivores, elk and wild boar*]. Rapport 2010: 1. Institutionen för vilt, fisk och miljö. Sveriges Lantbruksuniversitet, Umeå.

Forsyth, C.J. and Marckese, T.A. 1993a. Thrills and Skills: A Sociological Analysis of Poaching, in *Deviant Behavior*, 14(2), 157–72.

Forsyth, C.J. and Marckese, T.A. 1993b. Folk Outlaws: Vocabularies of Motives, in *International Review of Modern Sociology*, 23 (spring), 17–31.

Karlsson, M. et al. 2011. Sverige behöver en ny vargpolitik [Sweden needs a new wolf policy]. *Svenska dagbladet*, [Online, 8 February 2011] Available at: http://www.svd.se/opinion/brannpunkt/sverige-behover-en-ny-vargpolitik_5924207.svd [accessed 11 March 2011].

Kindberg, J., Swenson, J.E. and Ericsson, G. 2009. *Björnstammens storlek i Sverige 2008 – länsvisa uppskattningar och trender* [*Bear population size in Sweden in 2008 – county estimates and trends*]. Rapport 2009: 2. Skandinaviska björnprojektet.

Liberg, O., Sand, H., Wabakken, P. and Pedersen, H.C. 2008. *Dödlighet och illegal jakt i den skandinaviska vargstammen* [*Mortality and illegal hunting in the Scandinavian wolf population*]. Viltskadecenter Rapport nummer 1-2008.

Liberg, O. and Andrén, H. 2006. *Lodjuret – Artfakta. Rapport till rovdjursutredningen 2006* [*Lynx – Species facts. Report for the predator investigation 2006*]. Grimsö Forskningsstation, Institutionen för naturvårdsbiologi, Sveriges Lantbruks universitet.

Linell, J. and Bjerke, T. 2002. *Rädslan för vargen – en tvärvetenskaplig studie*. [*Fear of the Wolf – an Interdisciplinary Study*]. Stiftelsen for naturforskning og kulturminne, Norge och Viltskadecenter, Grimsö.

Miljödepartementet 2010a. *Uppdrag om rutiner för införsel och utplantering av varg i Sverige* [*Assignment of procedures for importation and release of wolves in Sweden*]. Miljödepartementet. 2010-03-04. M2010/1524/Na.

Miljödepartementet 2010b. *Remissmöte den 13 december i riksdagen med anledning av rapporten Genetisk förstärkning av den svenska vargstammen* [Consultation meeting 13 December in Parliament on the report Genetic Enhancement of the Swedish Wolf Population].

Naturvårdsverket 2009. *Beslut om licensjakt efter varg 2010* [*Decision about License Hunting of Wolf 2010*]. Dnr 411-7484-09 Nv. 2009-12-17. Stockholm: Naturvårdsverket.

Naturvårdsverket 2010. *Genetisk förstärkning av den svenska vargstammen. Svar på uppdrag om rutiner för införsel och utplantering av varg i Sverige* [*Genetic Enhancement of the Swedish Wolf Population*]. Naturvårdsverket, Statens Jordbruksverk och Statens veterinärmedicinska anstalt.

Naturvårdsverket 2011a. *Arter* [Species]. [Online, 16 February 2011]. Available at: http://www.naturvardsverket.se/sv/Start/Statistik/Arter/ [accessed 16 June 2011].

Naturvårdsverket 2011b. *Anmälda vargjägare* [*Reported Wolf Hunters*]. [Online, 28 February 2011]. Available at: http://www.naturvardsverket.se/sv/Start/Naturvard/Jakt-rovdjur-och- vilt/Jakt/Jakt-pa-varg/Anmalda-vargjagare/ [accessed 16 June 2011].

Norlén, N. 2006. *Avslöjandet – om vargens återkomst* [*The Revelation - About the Return of the Wolf*]. Estland: Faunaförlaget.

Prop. 2000/01:57. *Sammanhållen rovdjurspolitik* [*Unified Predator Policy*]. Stockholm: Fritzes.

Prop. 2008/09:210. *En ny rovdjursförvaltning* [*A New Predator Management*]. Stockholm: Fritzes.

Rovdjurscentret, de 5 stora, 2003. *Ökade insatser mot jaktbrott* [*Increased response to hunting violations*]. [Online, 17 November 2003]. Available at: http://www.de5stora.se/aktuellt/rovdjursnyheter/detalj.asp?Id=699 [accessed 15 June 2011].

Sand et al. 2007. Vargen – Artfakta. En sammanställning av data från det skandinaviska vargforskningssprojektet SKANDULV 2007 på uppdrag av utredningen om de stora rovdjuren [Wolf - Species facts. A compilation of data from the Scandinavian wolf research project SKANDULV 2007 on behalf of the investigation about the large predators]. Skandulv.

Sandström, C. and Ericsson, G. 2009a. *Om svenskars inställning till rovdjur- och rovdjurspolitik* [*About Swedes' attitude towards carnivores and carnivore policy*]. Rapport 2009:1. Institutionen för vilt, fisk och miljö. Sveriges Lantbruksuniversitet, Umeå.

Sandström, C. and Ericsson, G. 2009b. *Om svenskars inställning till rovdjurförvaltningen* [*About Swedes' attitude towards predators management*]. Rapport 2009:2. Institutionen för vilt, fisk och miljö. Sveriges Lantbruksuniversitet, Umeå.

SOU 1999:146. *Rovdjursutredningen - Slutbetänkande om en sammanhållen rovdjurspolitik* [*Predator investigation - Final report on a coherent policy predators*]. Stockholm: Fritzes.

SOU 2007:89. *Rovdjuren och deras förvaltning* [*Predators and their Management*]. Statens offentliga utredningar (SOU) 4 December 2007. Miljödepartementet. Stockholm: Fritzes.

Tangeland, T., Skogen, K. and Krange, O. 2010. *Om rovdyr på landet og i byen. Den urban-rurale dimensjonen I de norske rovviltkonfliktene* [*About predators in the country and in the city. The urban-rural dimension to the Norwegian predator conflicts*]. NINA rapport 650.

Tönnessen, M. 2010. *The legality and ethical legitimacy of wolf hunting in Scandinavia*. The Scandinavian Council for Criminology: Research seminar report, 52, 65–72.

Viltskadecenter 2009. *Resultat från inventeringar av kungsörn i Sverige 2009. Nationell sammanställning av länstyrelsernas inventeringar* [*Results from surveys of golden eagles in Sweden in 2009*]. Rapport 2009:3. Inventeringsrapport från viltskadecenter.

Viltskadecenter 2010a. *Varg i Sverige vintern 2009/10* [*Wolf in Sweden, winter 2009/10*]. Preliminär statusrapport. Rapport 2010:2. Inventeringsrapport från viltskadecenter.

Viltskadecenter 2010b. *Resultat från inventering av lodjur i Sverige vintern 2009/10 Preliminär nationell sammanställning över länsstyrelsernas resultat av inventeringar av lodjur* [*Results from the census of lynx in Sweden, winter 2009/10*]. Rapport 2010:3. Inventeringsrapport från viltskadecenter.

Viltskadecenter 2011. *Viltskadestatistik 2010. Skador av fredat vilt på tamdjur, hundar och gröda* [*Predator injury statistics 2010*]. Rapport från Viltskadecenter 2011-1.

Chapter 12
Native Nature and Alien Invasions: Battling with Concepts and Plants at Fornebu, Norway

Marte Qvenild

> After the airport [at Fornebu] was closed down in 1998, 50 mills NOK have been spent to create an unwanted botanical garden [...] (Environmentalist).

> I personally think of Fornebu as a symbolic case used to draw attention to the general problem of invasive alien species (Planner).

Following the closedown of the airport at Fornebu, Oslo, 'alien' plant species were used by the Norwegian Directorate of Public Construction and Property (Statsbygg) to reconstruct the former landing strip into a green area neighbouring two nature reserves. During this process the environmental NGO, SABIMA,[1] reported Statsbygg to the police in 2007 for having committed an environmental crime by planting alien invaders. Even though Statsbygg argued to have acted according to agreed upon plans and disputed being labelled environmentally criminal, negative publicity was presented in the media and Statsbygg consequently had to remove several alien plants. A pending question remaining is whether this actually was an environmental crime. Defining environmental crimes are, as we have seen in other chapters of this book, no straightforward task. One of several definitions describes environmental crimes as 'those harms against humanity, against the environment and against non-human animals committed both by powerful institutions (e.g. governments, transnational corporations, military apparatuses) and also by ordinary people' (Beirne and South 2007: xiii). From these large-scale perspectives of harms against humanity and the environment, Fornebu might appear to be a local concern, a lawsuit to be solved and settled. Yet it is so much more. The conflict at Fornebu illustrates how the concepts 'alien' and 'native' species respectively are used by different scientific disciplines, in this case landscape architecture and biology/ecology, in a battle to legitimize their vision of the ideal nature. Defining what is native, alien or even criminal can be seen as political activities that will have implications for people, other species and nature? Consequently, when we use such concepts in specific ways we simultaneously seek to 'impose a particular

1 SABIMA (Samarbeidsrådet for biologisk mangfold) is a national umbrella organization working to preserve biological diversity in Norway. See www.sabima.no.

moral vision on the working of the social world' (Skinner 2002: 182). The battles over concepts and the moral visions related to their uses lay at the core of the global alien species debate, which will be exemplified through the conflict over planted material at Fornebu. The questions this chapter seeks to address, in essence, are the following; is the spread of alien species environmental criminality, and further, what are the consequences of labelling alien species as environmental outcasts?

To deliberately spread invasive, alien species may qualify as an act of environmental crime as such species currently are termed a global threat towards biodiversity (see for example Simberloff 2000a, CBD 2007, European Commission 2011). What complicates the labelling of environmental criminals is, however, the difficult task of distinguishing the aliens from the natives. Interestingly, these are scientifically constructed concepts which appear to emanate from ecological theory and 'desk work' rather than practical experience. Further, humanity depends on the uses of a diverse range of alien species as most agricultural food crops as well as horticultural plants used in gardening are by definition alien. In Norway an illustrative example of the sea is the Red King Crab that has spread from Russia and down along the Norwegian coastline since the 1970s onwards. The crab was considered a resource until around 1992 when large quantities of crabs were caught as by-catch in fishing nets and caused problems and economic losses for fishermen (FKD 2006–07). Today the crab is in fact treated as a commercial resource northeast of the cartographic boarder drawn at 26° east, while it is restricted as an alien species west of this same boarder. Thus, alien species are entangled in economical, cultural and historical practices, and often have a dual status of being simultaneously harmful and valuable resources.

While the damaging consequences of several alien invaders are real enough, defining what is alien and native is a politically loaded activity with real world consequences. Inspired by the British political philosopher Quentin Skinner, I will examine such encounters between linguistic actions and 'the real world' (for example Tully and Skinner 1988, Skinner 2002) exemplified by the Fornebu case. Skinner argues that conceptual changes do not necessarily result in changed *meanings* of a concept, but rather changes of the moral implications attached to the concepts (Skinner 2002: 179). Such moral implications influence how concepts can be rightfully used, and whether for example planting alien roses is considered an acceptable or unacceptable practice. Concepts can thus be seen as rhetorical 'tools' used in negotiating societal 'right-doings' and 'wrong-doings'. With this perspective in mind, I will investigate how the interest groups at Fornebu, representing different types of scientific knowledge, used the same concepts in very dissimilar ways, and with particular moral and material consequences.[2] I will, however, first provide some background explaining the current framing of alien species.

2 I conducted 17 semi-structured interviews during 2009 and 2010. I have categorized the interviewees into three groups; 'the Planners', referring to bureaucrats involved in planning, 'the Landscape Architects', involved at different stages in the Fornebu process

What Make Species Invasive Aliens?

The Japanese Rose (*Rosa rugosa*) was one of the planted alien species the environmentalists reacted against at Fornebu. The Leader of SABIMA compared the rose to rabbits in Australia in a newsbreak on public television (NRK Lørdagsrevyen 2007). Before giving a thorough description of what happened at Fornebu, I will spend some time investigating what makes a Japanese Rose an example of invasive invaders.

Who Are the Aliens?

The Japanese Rose is a sprouting shrub that forms dense thickets in habitats it thrives in. The flowers are big with varying colours from white to dark pink (Weidema 2006). Alien species such as the Japanese Rose are typically referred to as species occurring outside their natural dispersal ranges. They have been brought to locations they could not have reached on their own by the intentional or unintentional help of humans. When they manage to establish and reproduce in the new location for at least ten years, they become naturalized (Richardson and Pyšek 2006). Further, if the plants manage to reproduce in large numbers and spread over considerable geographical distances they become invasive. Naturalization thus does not imply that an alien has become native; it just means that the species managed to 'sustain populations over many life cycles' (ibid.). The Japanese Rose was introduced to Europe from Japan, and the first record is from 1796 (Weidema 2006). The rose was, and is, used as an ornamental plant in gardens and parks throughout Europe. In Norway it was first recorded in a naturalized condition in the 1940s, and it is currently spreading northwards and especially along the coast (ibid.).

Historically, diverse terms have been used to describe such species for example 'introduced', 'non-native', 'exotic', 'new', 'weed', 'pest', 'biological invasion' and 'adventives'. The Secretariat of the 1992 Convention on Biological Diversity (CBD) took on the task of standardizing the terminology in collaboration with other regional and international organizations (Shine et al. 2000). The CBD[3] defines alien species as those which manage to reproduce and survive outside their natural range, while alien invasive species are aliens threatening biodiversity (CBD 2010). Alien species are contrasted to native species which are species '(…) occurring within its natural range (past or present)' (IUCN Council 2000). A problematic aspect that will be further exemplified in the Fornebu case is the lack of a temporal scale specifying how long period of time a species must spend in a location to be considered native.

---

and 'the Environmentalists' who constitute a diverse group of academically skilled and trained people as well as 'lay-experts'.

3 The CBD is currently the only international legally binding instrument addressing the prevention, control and eradication of all kinds of alien species (Article 8 (h)). The CBD obliges the member countries to implement Article 8 h and the associated guiding principles through national strategies and action plans to meet the threats posed by alien species.

In fact, Woods (2001) argues that there is no clear-cut line distinguishing aliens from natives as both concepts have fuzzy boundaries.

The focus on alien species as a global threat against native biodiversity is actually quite recent. In fact, Cadotte claims that early biologists studying alien species in previous centuries were not so concerned with the outcomes of species invasions or their geographical origin, but rather with documenting the occurrence and role of alien species in ecological processes (Cadotte 2006: 22). In 1958 came Charles Elton's classic *The Ecology of Invasions by Animals and Plants*. Elton is often portrayed as the founding father of the field of studying ecological invasions (Ricciardi 2003, Chew 2006, Richardson and Pyšek 2006, Ricciardi and MacIsaac 2008), although there was quite a large interest in the topic among many scientists prior to his book. Elton was apparently the first to bring together three important ecological components; firstly, that plant and animal communities of different continents have become very distinct from one another over millions of years; secondly, that humans are rapidly altering these distinctions; and thirdly, the serious consequences this process have on the conservation of species diversity (Simberloff 2000b: viii). Elton used militaristic metaphors and normative language to describe and warn against what was happening. Since Elton's book, his language and way of framing alien invasions has become highly influential in biological literature, the media and in environmental policymaking such as the CBD framework (see for example Davis 2006, CBD 2010).

How Harmful are Invasive Aliens?

In the first chapter of this book Rob White comments that eco-global criminology pays special attention to ecological considerations of harm. Since I am to discuss whether the spread of alien, invasive species can be considered a crime, it is worth spending some time discussing the harm-aspect of alien invasions. The Japanese Rose mainly invade sandy, gravely or stony seashores (Weidema 2006). If the conditions are favourable it forms dense, shrubby blankets that may cause reduced numbers of native spices as a result of the shading effect (Isermann 2008a, 2008b, Weidema 2006). The reduction of native species may further affect animals depending on these species, for example butterflies laying eggs on certain types of plants (Weidema 2006). Furthermore, as the rose forms such impenetrable, thorny covers it is problematic for landowners and visitors to beaches. Davis (2009) identifies the following ecological impacts of invasive alien species; impacts on populations or biodiversity caused by for example pathogens or predators; impacts on food webs and communities; impacts on biochemical processes or impacts altering the physical structure of the environment (Davis 2009). Another important harm element is of course the economic harm caused by many alien invaders, such as the Colorado beetle that hit potato crops from the 1850s onwards in for example Germany, France and Britain (Elton 1958). It is important to note that some sites are more open to invasions than others, and these are often locations that have been disturbed by human activities such as roadsides, dumps or railroads (McNeely 2005).

Globally, the threat posed by invasive aliens has been termed a homogenization of the world's biodiversity (Brown 1995, McKinney and Lockwood 1999). A central aspect in this 'homogenization' thesis is that alien invasions increase local species' richness while decreasing the world's species' diversity. Thus, the rare species are replaced by more common and widely spread species (Brown and Sax 2004). In addition to the spread of alien species, habitat fragmentation and climate change contribute to this process (Haber 2008). Rahel (2002), Davis (2003), and Sax and Gaines (2003), however, modify the homogenization thesis by showing that it is not very likely that the world will be stripped of its diversity and inhabited by only a few headline invaders. In fact, several international studies illustrate that there are surprisingly few incidents of resident species having been driven to extinction due to competition from alien species (Mooney and Cleland 2001, Davis 2003, Davis 2009). Rodriguez (2006) argues that some alien species actually can have positive impacts on native species, for example pollination and restoration of habitats through the use of alien grass species.

Biorascism? Critique of Invasion Biology

The field of invasion biology is increasingly criticized for the criteria used to distinguish aliens and natives. Several scientists from the fields of for example geography and philosophy emphasize the cultural and political aspect entangled in the biological categorizations of species (see for example Kendle and Rose 2000, Alderman 2004, Head and Muir 2004, Robbins 2004, Foster and Sandberg 2004). Further, biological scientists have been termed 'biological nativists' with xenophobic attitudes towards aliens (Hettinger 2001). Hettinger (2001) writes that in human affairs, nativists are characterized by morally troubling attitudes as they favour native inhabitants over foreigners. In a similar troubling manner, biological nativists are perceived to favour native plants and work against introduction and spread of aliens. Hettinger mentions the American journalist Michael Pollan who in a *New York Times* article compares biological nativism to Nazi ideology (ibid.). In a similar manner, the philosopher Jonah Peretti has argued that conservation biology suffers from nativist trends that reproduce racist and xenophobic attitudes (Peretti 1998). Against these accusations, the biologist Daniel Simberloff (2003) argues that such critics fail to see that invasion biologists are merely concerned with preventing ecological and environmental harm. Moreover, the critics ignore the serious economical and ecological impacts of many invasive species. Following along similar lines of thought, Hettinger (2001) argues that biological nativism in fact can be praiseworthy. As we value the preservation of indigenous peoples and cultures, he finds it admirable to strive towards the preservation of valuable biological diversity that is threatened by being homogenized due to the spread of alien species. While there may be some parallels in the rhetoric used by nationalistic racists and invasion biology, I find this comparison a bit farfetched. One of the simple reasons is that most invasion biologists know perfectly well that many alien species are not harmful at all (as underlined by for example Simberloff

2003), but necessary resources in for example agricultural production. While these debates have received broad attention, less has been written on the issues investigated in this article; whether the spread of alien invasive species can be defined as a crime.

Alien Species and Environmental Crimes

Many invasive alien species cause some type of harm to nature or human societies. *Harm*[4] is, as described in the Beirne and South 2007 definition, an important element related to environmental crimes. In this volume White identifies three notions of harm related to eco-global criminology; legal conceptions (for example laws, rules and international conventions), ecological wellbeing (of for example species and ecosystems) and justice conceptions (related to the intrinsic value of species and ecosystems). Larsen (this volume) notes that transgressions against nature or activities she defines as eco-crime includes legal environmentally harming activities undertaken by, for example, states or businesses. She distinguishes between 'illegal harm, harm in the gray area between legal and illegal harm, and legal harm' (Larsen, this volume) and argues that harms can be criminal not only in the judicial sense but also in a moral sense. A further element related to harm is the notion of *risk* which relates to predictions or expectations of harm. According to White (2008), environmental problems are constructed and negotiated in relation to competing perceptions of risk and harm. Environmental crime is thus a socially contingent concept. Labelling the spread of alien species an environmental crime will imply what Skinner calls rhetorical redescription (2002), where a concept is increasingly being applied to circumstances where it normally would not be used, for example that the planting of alien species has transformed from being a perfectly accepted practice in gardening and landscape architecture into an act of crime. The processes of rhetorical redescription can be exemplified with the proceedings in a court room where the prosecutor and the defence attorney will redescribe the same course of events in ways that best suit their goals. The result is often two quite different descriptions of the same case. The outcome of such linguistic struggles will sometimes result in conceptual change if social consensus about the new uses of the concept is reached (see for example Bjørkdahl this volume). To address whether the spread of alien species is an environmental crime it is necessary to scale down to a physical location in a particular geographical context which in this case is Fornebu, Norway.

---

4 White (this volume) defines harm as 'an actual danger or adverse effect, stemming from direct and indirect social processes that negatively impinge upon the health and wellbeing and ecological integrity of humans, specific biospheres and non-human animals'.

Introducing Fornebu: The Reconstruction of a Former Airport

Since the airport at Fornebu closed down in 1998 the area has been developed into a commercial site for housing, business and recreation. Simultaneously, Fornebu is a location very rich in biological diversity including red listed bird, insect and plant species. Before the 1930s, when the airport was constructed, the landscape at Fornebu was characterized by forests, dry meadows and agricultural fields (Bendiksen 1994), hence a substantial part of both cultural and natural landscapes were cleared and blasted away due to the airport construction. Some wetland areas were, however, preserved and these are currently considered some of the most important biotopes for migrant birds in the country with over 264 different species registered. The areas were protected as nature reserves by royal proclamation in 1992 (Kongelig resolusjon 1992).[5] The landscape architect company which was engaged by Statsbygg to manage the process of reconstructing the green areas at Fornebu were instructed to preserve both natural and cultural fragments of the former landscape (Statsbygg and Oslo Kommune 2000). The landscape plan (2001)[6] provided guidelines for the new Fornebu forest which would consist of native vegetation registered by the botanist Egil Bendiksen in 1994 (Østengen and Bergo 2001). The plan emphasized the construction of a new landscape where elements from Fornebu's historical nature and cultural landscape would be preserved (ibid.).

A rapid establishment of green buffer zones was given high priority in the planning process in order to protect the nature reserves and bird life from the large amount of people who would move into the area. As a result, the buffer zones were intended to consist of fast-growing and impenetrable local species with thorns. The landscape architects found it very challenging to meet the requirement of using native species as these were difficult to get hold of in the commercial market (Statsbygg and Oslo Kommune 2000). As a result of time pressure and lack of experience in the greeneries of producing native non-commercial material, several native species were substituted with similar non-native commercial species (ibid.). In collaboration with soil scientists, a layer of wood chips was distributed on top of the soil to prevent weeds from surfacing and to secure the moisture content of the soil.

When the conflict over the alien planted material and the thick layers of wood chips escalated in 2007, Statsbygg had arranged a guided tour around the planted areas

---

5 The two landowners at Fornebu, which were the municipality of Oslo and the Norwegian State respectively, together with the Municipal Planning Authority of Bærum, shared the wish to conserve the rich natural diversity at Fornebu, however the end-result was highly disputed.

6 The landscape plan is a superior plan for long-term landscape development at Fornebu. It was developed by a Landscape Architect agency and commissioned by Oslo municipality in collaboration with Statsbygg and Bærum municipality. The plan is, however, not a formally binding planning document like the Local Development Plan, yet it laid out the premises for the further regulation and planning activity.

to try to resolve the conflict with the environmentalists. One of the environmentalists told me about an incident which took place during this guided tour:

> I saw a Salix which had come up on its own in the middle of the wood chips. 'Imagine a forest of Salix here instead of your alien species', I told the chief gardener from Stasbygg. Then he grabbed the Salix and pulled it out. 'This is not supposed to be here', he said. It was not on his list. And I was completely paralyzed and lost my speech. He fixed nature in his own way, even though it was Nature itself which had placed the Salix there. That was the only thing we wanted here (Environmentalist).

The type of nature that the environmentalists wanted was a mosaic of natural and cultural elements with, for example, calcareous pine forests, pastures and dry meadows with drought-tolerant, rare species where many red-listed insects thrive. This had been a typical element of the original landscape at Fornebu prior to the airport (Bendiksen 1994). However, other typical elements of the historical landscape were farms, parks and greeneries (Bærum kommune 1994). One of the landscape architects explained that 'From older maps and pictures we can see that this was a very cultivated area. The soil must have been quite nutrient-rich to suit agriculture' (Landscape Architect). Thus, both natural and cultural elements were part of the past landscape at Fornebu. On the 16 October 2007 SABIMA reported Statsbygg to the police for having acted against the § 3 of the Local Development Plan that specify the use of native vegetation. The environmentalists termed the alien plantings a crime against nature. The case was, however, closed down as a result of lacking capacity by the police to investigate it (Asker og Bærum politidistrikt 2007).

'Wrong Plants at Fornebu'

During the airport period, Fornebu had been actively used as a location for bird watching. One of the local bird watchers told me that 'People thought this was just an airport and did not realize its natural qualities. But we knew about it. We, the bird watchers, knew' (Environmentalist). The bird watchers' involvement and views of the processes around the 'new Fornebu' were deeply emotional as several of them had grown up in the area and were using it on a regular basis. They had strong interests in preserving the natural qualities of the area, which had been largely shielded from human activity during the airport period. When the airport closed down, they established a joint committee called KEF[7] consisting of local ornithologists, environmentalists and local welfare organizations to lobby in the planning process to secure a green alternative at Fornebu. In the summer of 2004 they became aware of what they later termed a catastrophe which was taking place

7 Komite for Etterbruk av Fornebu [Committee for the Re Use of Fornebu].

at Fornebu (Environmentalist). The area, which in their opinion should consist of native nature with buffer zones of native species around the nature reserves, was described by one of the environmentalists in Friends of the Earth Norway's membership magazine as 'a sterile park landscape – a gigantic garden of mould with wood chips on top' (Bergan 2009: 5). They discovered that a substantial part of the plants were alien and did not belong in Norwegian flora. The KEF committee realized, however, that they had to liaise with others in order to get heard: 'How were we supposed to get our arguments through? Nobody but bird watchers had been using these areas since 1939, so how were we to make people realize that we had to take care of this area? We needed the national organization SABIMA to take the lead' (Environmentalist). SABIMA realized that the case had a symbolic value which could be transferred to similar cases at a national level (Leader of SABIMA). In 2007 they sent out a number of letters to planners, policymakers and the media.[8] The letters stressed the national value of Fornebu as a unique location for red-listed plants and insect species in addition to the rich bird life. The environmentalists held that:

> Fornebu is the country's most expensive environmental project. From a natural scientific point of view the project is a disaster. Enormous sums have been spent on plantings which do not meet the intentions of restoring the unique nature of the area. At a time where the international attention has been turned towards the control and eradication of alien species through the Rio convention, thousands of non-native species have been planted at Fornebu (NOF AO 2007).

To save the nature at Fornebu they found that more public attention was needed and the leader of SABIMA proved to be an excellent communicator. On the 26 May 2007 a newsbreak called 'Wrong plants at Fornebu' was broadcasted as prime time news. The voiceover reported that 'an environmental disaster is unfolding at Fornebu. A green site costing 35 mill NOK intended to protect the nature reserves in the area has become a zone of plants which can eradicate the natural vegetation in the area […]' (NRK Lørdagsrevyen 2007). Preceding this introduction, the leader of SABIMA was interviewed together with a biologist from the University of Oslo. The biologist stated that: 'The soil is totally lifeless and unfertile. And with all these alien species very little will make it here.' The next clip showed the director of Statsbygg in his office pointing at a map. According to him Fornebu had become a really great area with a varied terrain, nice recreational areas 'where beautiful vegetation will grow.' Back in the park areas, the leader of SABIMA repeated his disappointment: 'Based on the planned intentions, this is a disaster. Nothing of what we wanted can grow here at all'. Returning to the office again, the director of Statsbygg explained that they did not manage to get hold of native

8 Those who received the letters were Statsbygg, Bærum municipality, The County Governor of Oslo and Akershus, the Directorate for Nature Management and the Norwegian Broadcasting Corporation (NRK).

plants in the commercial markets, and he found it a correct decision to use alien plants in order to protect the nature reserves. Against this claim some of the environmentalists countered that: 'This is a crime against the environment', and they required the immediate removal of the alien plants and the thick layer of wood chips (ibid.).

Two more newsbreaks were broadcasted as prime-time news the same year. In addition there were several stories in national and local newspapers emphasizing the threat of the planted alien species and the lifeless and dead landscape of mould and wood chips where nothing would grow except garden plants (Myhr 2007a, Myhr 2007b). Further, accusations of the incompetence of the people involved in constructing the green site at Fornebu is exemplified in quotes such as: 'They have not understood what native plants are, and have used the wrong type of expertise.' (Sæther and Hansen 2007) and: 'This is the worst case I have ever seen. They have done everything wrong.' (ibid.).

The Construction of Environmental Claims

Statsbygg and the landscape architects felt that the case had been blown out of proportion and that important nuances disappeared in the one-sided media coverage of Fornebu (Landscape Architect). They felt that they did not manage to get their perspective through to the media (Planner). The way Fornebu was framed in the media may fit with what Hannigan characterizes as the processes of socially constructing environmental problems, which consist of the following three tasks; assembling, presenting and contesting (Hannigan 2000: 69). Assembling environmental claims means discovering the problem and supporting it with scientific evidence. This includes naming and defining the problem in a manner which overcomes ambiguities and contradictory scientific evidence (White 2008: 36). Next, presenting environmental claims involves catching public attention and legitimating the claim through, for example, the use of mass media. This often requires a skilled communicator, such as the leader of SABIMA, who expresses clear moral messages such as: 'the introduction of alien species is an environmental crime'. The streamlining and simplification of facts becomes particularly visible through the use of verbal metaphors together with visual illustrations. Some examples are metaphors associated with the spread of diseases, for example 'contamination of the nature reserves' (Aakre and Kirkholm 2008) or 'pest species which will destroy the nature reserves' (NRK Lørdagsrevyen 2007). Further, the planted vegetation at Fornebu was described as 'ecological deserts' (Austad and Rydgren 2007) and 'litter' (Budstikka 2007). Militaristic metaphors were also used, for example, 'aggressive, ornamental shrubs', and 'invading species' (Auestad 2008).

Metaphors play a key role in attaching social and moral values to concepts such as alien or native species. As Skinner (2002) argues, the social values associated with a concept may change while the meaning of the concept remains fairly constant over time. Alderman (2004) illustrates how the introduced Kudzu in the

USA changed from being perceived as a 'miracle vine' used as, for example, animal fodder to being a 'pest' and 'menace'. This is an interesting example in parallel to Fornebu as it shows how a famous radio personality, Channing Cope, played an important role in legitimizing the spread of Kudzu through environmental claims. He gave the Kudzu legitimacy as a resource through the use of metaphors such as 'miracle vine' (Alderman 2004: 160). In a similar manner, SABIMA spread environmental claims by using negatively loaded metaphors to describe the alien plants at Fornebu. Alien species was at the time a relatively new topic to the Norwegian public and SABIMA contributed towards portraying Fornebu as an environmental disaster.

Further, SABIMA was trying to move the Fornebu issue onto the political agenda with the aim of influencing legal and political decision-making, a process that Hannigan (2000) calls contesting environmental claims. Rob White comments that networking with like-minded people, getting scientists on board and initiating public rallies is part of this process (White 2008: 36), as was also done by SABIMA. According to Hannigan (2000: 69), the simplification of complex phenomena into understandable terms increases the probability that the environmental problem will stick in the public arena.

The Blacklisting of Aliens

In 2007, the same year as the conflict at Fornebu reached its peak, a Norwegian Black List[9] of alien species was launched and boosted media attention towards alien species previously barely discussed publicly. Such lists of both invasive aliens (black lists) and threatened, vulnerable species (red lists) have become internationally recognized scientific tools applied in decision-making processes within the field of biodiversity conservation (Jørstad and Skogen 2010). Jørstad and Skogen (2010) discuss how planners, scientists and NGOs use such lists rhetorically and strategically in manners that simplify scientific knowledge. In this way a red list or a black list may be used in a public debate to strengthen and legitimate environmental claims related to harm and risk.

Even though the planning stages of the Fornebu project were finished and the reconstruction process started in 2004, the 2007 Norwegian Blacklist was used as a tool with retroactive effect by SABIMA to strengthen their accusations of environmental criminality against Statsbygg. SABIMA managed to create a successful strategy and attract public attention through national and local media, although they did not manage to fulfil Hannigan's third task of contesting their claims to affect the legal or political decision-making. After the police decided to close the case, it was reopened politically by the Bærum city manager. The city

9 In May 2007 the Norwegian Biodiversity Information Centre presented a Norwegian Black List which consisted of ecological risk assessments of alien species. Part of the aim with the Black List was to help the authorities make priorities in their measures against the most invasive of the alien species.

manager went through the legal foundation of the charges and concluded in a report that Statsbygg had acted in accordance with the agreed upon plans and had done nothing wrong (Rådmannen Bærum kommune 2008). The environmentalists, that is SABIMA, did not agree and one of the involved environmentalists stated in an article in the Friend's of the Earth Norway's membership magazine that 'in a time where there is an international focus on the eradication of alien species [...] thousands of non-indigenous plants have been spread all over Fornebu. Red listed species; native plants and insect species, are thereby threatened with extinction [...]' (Bergan 2009).

Was the Spread of Alien Species at Fornebu an Environmental Crime?

Conceptions of what counts as environmental crimes depends not only on judicial or moral definitions of the criminal or legal, but also on the perceived harms and risks attached to the relevant action. I will use White's three notions of harm to evaluate the status of the Fornebu plantings. In terms of *legal conceptions of harm*, jurisdiction and policies to tackle alien invasions are currently implemented internationally as well as on the national and local scales (IUCN 2000, McNeely 2001, Gederaas et al. 2007). Both nationally and internationally, the legal framework related to alien species has been fragmented and mostly focused around economic production sectors such as, for example, agriculture, forestry, fisheries and wildlife management (Shine et al. 2005). As a result, international rules and regulations have been developed in separate, sector-wise areas (Shine et al. 2000: 14). The 1992 Convention on Biological Diversity (CBD) is, in fact, the only legally binding international instrument addressing alien species' introductions and requiring the contracting parties to as far as possible 'prevent the introduction of, control or eradicate those alien species which threaten ecosystems, habitats or species' (Article 8 (h). For the CBD to become operational, however, the individual member countries to the Convention must implement Article 8 h and the associated guiding principles in their national legal frameworks and strategies.

In Norway alien species as a national problem was placed higher on the political agenda as a result of the entering into force of the CBD. As had been the case in other countries, harmful species within a Norwegian context had been treated fragmentarily, both scientifically and legally, according to economic sector or species group. It took over ten years for different ministries to agree on a National Strategy on Invasive Alien Species[10] which was launched in May 2007, the very same year as the Norwegian Black List and the 'peak' of the Fornebu conflict. The

10 A number of ministries have cooperated in drawing up Norway's strategy: the Ministry of Fisheries and Coastal Affairs, the Ministry of Finance, the Ministry of Defence, the Ministry of Health and Care Services, the Ministry of Justice and the Police, the Ministry of Education and Research, the Ministry of Agriculture and Food, the Ministry of Petroleum and Energy, the Ministry of the Environment, the Ministry of Trade and

most recent legal tool, the Norwegian Nature Diversity Act, entered into force in 2009. It provides a coherent set of rules governing introductions of all types of alien species (Sørensen 2010). Imports and introduction of alien species require a special permit and the applicant carries the burden of proof that the species are not harmful or invasive (ibid.). A separate regulation to the act is being prepared on the introduction of alien species but has not yet entered into force.[11] To return to Fornebu, the plantings initiated in 2004 were in line with contemporary rules and regulations, but had the same process taken place in 2009 after the launching of the Nature Diversity Act, it would probably have been a different matter. Ecological restoration is currently a methodology which is receiving increased attention as an important measure preceding nature interventions (Hagen and Skrindo 2010). At the time of the Fornebu project, ecological restoration was not systematically integrated in planning and management statutory frameworks. Fornebu was never intended as an ecological restoration project, but had it been initiated today, it would probably have been framed as one.

Space makes a difference when it comes to legal practice (Blomley 2008) and the moral conflict fought at Fornebu illustrates that while it may be acceptable to plant alien species in private gardens, their presence becomes increasingly problematic the closer they move towards wild and native nature, such as the nature reserve at Fornebu. The fact that the charges against Statsbygg were dropped without any investigation illustrates the deficient experiences with such cases in the legal system. In addition, there was no coherent national legal framework at the time. The battle over plants at Fornebu thus became an example of what Larson (this volume) terms crime as a moral category rather than crime as a judicial category.

Returning to White's second notion of harm; *ecological wellbeing* is closely related to how the different groupings at Fornebu perceived the risk of the alien plants and the potential future damage related to them. As the environmentalists were people with a natural science background and the landscape architects had perspectives rooted in horticulture and gardening, their perceptions of the ecological harms and risks associated with the plantings were quite dissimilar. At Fornebu a rhetorical battle was fought out between scientific disciplines on how to define species and their potential ecological harm. A central aspect of designating harm and risk was associated with defining the species status as alien or native.

Industry and the Ministry of Transport and Communications (Norwegian Ministry of the Environment 2007: 4).

11 The Regulation is sent out on a public hearing and suggests that a list of prohibited species will be based on the 2007 Norwegian Black List (Direktoratet for naturforvaltning 2010). When the regulation on alien species of the act finally enters into force, new standards will be enforced for plantings and uses of alien material.

The Japanese Rose: An Invasive Alien or Harmless Native?

The use of native plants was a specified goal in the reconstruction process of Fornebu, (Bærum kommune Rådmannen 2001, Bærum kommunestyre 2002) and the central planning documents defined native vegetation as vegetation growing in the inner-Oslo fjord. This vague definition left the issue open for discussion and the landscape architects thought that native plants such as for example the Japanese Rose was a good choice at Fornebu as it had been growing in the inner-Oslo Fjord for decades (Bjørbekk and Lindheim 2005). According to one of the Planners at Statsbygg, the landscape architects defined native species as 'Species which today grow at Fornebu and which includes both original, natural species diversity and cultural plants which have become naturalized or are part of the cultural landscape' (Lundetræ 2007). In line with this definition, the Japanese Rose could be considered a native. However, the criterion of *time* was not something the planners and landscape architects had considered when determining what was native early in the Fornebu project. A botanist stated that: 'the Landscape Architects do not care about biogeography. (…) All that has been here before 1750 or 1820 when they really started to introduce plants and animals through agriculture can be called native'. He did, however, admit that even among botanists 'there is no 100% definition' of the native status (Botanist). Another criterion for applying the term native was that of genetic origin. After the debates between Statsbygg and the environmentalists, a plant scientist approached Statsbygg claiming that 'A plant can be characterized as native to an area if it belongs to the wild-growing flora and genetically belongs to the area by originating or having developed there for a long period of time' (Lundetræ 2007).

We see that there were knowledge-debates about the criteria for applying the concept native and thus distinguishing harmless natives from harmful aliens. Skinner refers to such disagreements as rhetorical debates over the criteria for applying a concept (Skinner 2002: 163). This type of debate is typically a part of struggles to redescribe the conventions for how concepts can be used. These disagreements are also linked to Skinner's second level of disagreement concerning which situations the concept can be applied to (Skinner 2002: 165). In the debates between the landscape architects, the planners and the environmentalists there were quite different opinions concerning in which circumstances species should be termed alien or native. One of the environmentalists stated that even though Japanese Roses were found on nearby islands, defining them as native was out of the question: 'Would you say that the Spanish slug is native because it can be found in nearby gardens? Species do not become native for having been planted in gardens a few decades' (Environmentalist). One of the landscape architects on the other hand was not convinced that the Japanese Rose deserved its status as a harmful and ecologically risky plant to use:

> The Japanese Rose was perfectly ok. We have experienced it along the coast as a natural element. It is fast-growing, thorny, and good for the bird life so we used

> it with the best intentions. (…) I am still not sure if the Japanese Rose really is that invasive. I think it is a more quiet plant. I know the Oslo-fjord pretty well and have not observed any spots where the Japanese Rose has been expansive (Landscape Architect).

Thus the environmentalist and the landscape architects disagreed over the definition of native species, as well as over which species fitted the criteria of being alien. Further, the criteria related to the Japanese Rose's invasiveness and thereby its ecological harm potential constituted a particularly heated topic. Not surprisingly, the environmentalists of SABIMA expressed stronger fears of future threats than the planners and landscape architects did. One of the involved planners explained that:

> One of our main arguments of defence has been that all these plants can be found in the nearby gardens. They are already here. Does it make a difference whether some are planted here in addition to all that material surrounding us? Most plants are spread from private gardens (Planner).

Contrary to this, the environmentalists emphasized in interviews that the fear of future environmental harm and the alien species invasiveness was one of the main arguments for acting like they did. While the perceived risk and harm led the environmentalists to take actions to save future nature in general and species at Fornebu in particular, none of my interviewees were able to document that spread of alien plants from the buffer zones actually had taken place 4–5 years after the plantings. As the Japanese Rose has a fringy reputation of being invasive and harmful (Weidema 2006), most of the roses were actually removed by Statsbygg. The environmentalists, however, were still not assured that the roses had been removed in a sufficient way, and were anxious that they would return (Leader of SABIMA). Another aspect is the issue of geography and the fact that the rose may not be invasive in all types of locations, for example while the Japanese Rose may be invasive in coastal areas, it may not be in the inland (Faglig utviklingssenter for grøntanleggssektoren 2010).

While the actual ecological harms of the alien plantings at Fornebu remain an unclear issue, there may have been other concerns at stake in the Fornebu debate. White identifies the *justice conception* of harm as his third notion. For the environmentalists the justice conception can be related to their disappointment and crushed expectation concerning what the Fornebu was going to be like. In their opinion, Fornebu could have been a unique place where rare species and endangered habitats would thrive. Instead the area was developed into a manmade, artificial nature park, and Statsbygg was reported to the police as a last attempt by the environmentalists to try to realize their visions for Fornebu. The landscape architects and planners never intended to recreate the 'original' nature at Fornebu. Rather, their intention from the very beginning was to construct a clearly manmade landscape combined with some elements from the past (Østengen & Bergo 2001).

Labelling Alien Species as Environmental Outcasts

After having discussed White's three notions of harm in relation to the Fornebu case, the alien plantings at the time could not judicially be considered criminal. This does not mean, however, that the spread of invasive alien species elsewhere or even within today's legal framework may not be termed criminal and ecologically harmful. Interestingly, several other issues were at stake in the Fornebu conflict, particularly a rhetorical battle over concepts with material and moral implications. I will now address the second main question I set out to answer; what were the consequences of casting alien species as environmental outcasts in the Fornebu case?

As we have seen throughout this chapter, SABIMA won the 'media-war' and thereby the right to define the 'truth' about the Fornebu case. While Statsbygg was not legally convicted, a moral sentence was passed on them due to the negative media coverage. This sentence has been difficult to shake off, and the leader of SABIMA held that:

> This case has had its effects. Landscape Architects have started to call me because they are scared of getting reported to the police. Many have woken up due to this case and have started to think about what they are actually doing. And I don't think that would have happened without a reporting the case to the police (Leader of SABIMA).

The very different knowledge and perceptions of landscape architects and environmentalists illustrate that the concepts 'alien' and 'native' have not sprung out of practical experiences with nature but have rather been constructed scientifically as political and rhetorical tools. They are, hence, complicated to utilize and grasp. Landscape architecture has long traditions of shaping landscapes for human uses with plants as their tools, while, for example, biologists, botanists and ecologists generally are concerned with the conservation of wild and 'untouched' nature. The planners, on their part, were in need of advice from scientific consultants within different fields in order to lay out their strategies. The tendency of using science as foundation for decision-making is common in all sectors of society and science is used to give political decisions legitimacy (Jasanoff 1995, Jørstad and Skogen 2010). The environmentalist lobby secured a strong focus on the protection of the rich birdlife in the planning process. Several studies were commissioned by Statsbygg to investigate how the birds best could be protected and the diversity of birds be maintained in the face of residential developments (Bærum kommune 1994, Reitan 1996, Statsbygg and Oslo kommune 1996). The wellbeing of the birds was also the main reason why the buffer zones needed to be fast-growing and dense, and there was no time to let nature do the job. The planners and landscape architects thus did their very best to protect the birdlife. A side-effect of the rapid establishment of vegetation consisting of alien plants was the potential harm and spread to the nature reserves.

Importantly, and rather surprisingly, botany was a field largely ignored by both the environmental lobbyists, the planners and the landscape architects although the botanical qualities of the area had been documented by skilled botanists (Bendiksen 1994, Often and Røseng 1998). As we know, the concept native had a much wider interpretation among landscape architects than biologists, ecologists and botanists. What the landscape architects called 'cultural plants' (Statbygg and Oslo kommune 2008) the environmentalists labelled 'alien'. The focus changed from birds during the early planning and construction processes towards botany after the finalization of the project at Fornebu. The botanical interest increased as alien and native species became hot topics on the public agenda in 2007 with the launching of the 2007 Black List. Fornebu thus became a useful national case to define the spread of alien, invasive species as environmental criminality.

The spread of alien, invasive plants as environmental criminality touches upon our perception of the dual role of humans as ill-makers as well as protectors of nature and species. As we have seen, the alien plantings were ill-makings in the eyes of the environmentalists. They wanted natural succession with just a little bit of human help, such as mowing to keep weeds down. An unanswered question is how much human interference would be acceptable and, of equal importance, which types of human action are acceptable in such processes. Bendiksen (1994) claims that most of the dry meadows the environmentalists cherished are in fact cultural landscapes which depend on mowing to not turn into forest. He further notes that these cultural landscapes are probably the most botanically valuable in the whole area and they are in need of human protection and management in order to be maintained (Bendiksen 1994: 22). Thus, while the environmentalists criticized human interventions at Fornebu, they wanted a type of nature and species which are totally dependent on human maintenance. One of the planners from Statsbygg argued that 'The pendulum has swung far out on the alien species side of the scale. Hopefully it will move more towards the centre again. We are hoping for a compromise' (Planner). This illustrates some of the insecurities of how such a case should be best handled and dealt with today and in the future. The conceptual debates over aliens are still going strong between scientific sectors such as biology and horticulture, however both nationally and internationally biological knowledge seem to be the stronger part in paving the way for future management (see for example the Norwegian Nature Diversity Act 2009, CBD 2007). As underlined by White (this volume) a lot depends on who define harm when it comes to measures against environmental crimes and to alien species. The debates at Fornebu turn out to be precisely about different knowledge camps struggling for legitimate positions in decision-making and definitions of the 'right' types of nature and practices.

Conclusion

This chapter has discussed the environmental lawsuit at Fornebu as an example of how legal and moral standards are negotiated with the native-alien dichotomy as a measuring-stick for belonging. As demonstrated, linguistic disputes between rival theories and knowledge are also social disputes (Skinner 2002: 178) with real-world consequences. Interestingly, Fornebu raises questions of what type of environmental problem the introductions of invasive, alien plant species represents and how such actions should be categorized judicially and morally. While the alien plantings at Fornebu did not classify as an environmental crime according to White's three notions of harm at the time, the spread of invasive, alien species remains a judicial and environmental challenge. We may see law suits in the future dealing with the spread of alien animals or plants, but what complicates this matter are at least two aspects. The first is related to the dual roles of many alien species as being harmful threats towards native species and simultaneously ecological, economic or social resources. The second is related to the dual role of human beings as ill-makers and protectors. The ambiguity created by these aspects leave room for rhetorical battles over concepts, and consequently 'alien', 'native' and 'environmental crime' are used as conceptual tools and weapons in ideological debates over environmental problems. Struggles to define and fix concepts in specific moral lights are constantly going on, and as Skinner argues our social world is held in place by the normative vocabularies we use.

References

Aakre, B.G. and Kirkholm, G. 2008. – Miljøkriminalitet! – Statsbygg anmeldt, henlagt av politiet [Environmental crime! – Statsbygg reported, case dropped by the police]. *Aftenposten Aften*, 27. February, 2.

Alderman, D.H. 2004. Channing Cope and the making of a Miracle Vine. *Geographical Review, People, Place, & Invasive Species*, 94(2), 157–77.

Asker og Bærum politidistrikt. 2007. *Anmodning om overtakelse av sak som gjelder mulig muljøødeleggelse på Fornebu* [*Requests for transfer of case involving possible environmental damage at Fornebu*]. Letter to Økokrim. Oslo

Auestad, I. 2008. Hagens uskyld slår sprekker; Høyrisikoplanter; fakta Svartelisten [Hagens innocence is cracking; High risk plants; Blacklist facts]. *Bergens Tidende* [online, 2 June]. Available at: http://www.bt.no/meninger/kronikk/article574774.ece [accessed 18 October 2010].

Austad, I. and Rydgren, K. 2007. Miljøskadelig kunnskapsløshet [Environmentally harmful ignorance]. *Nationen* [online, 9 November]. Available at: http://www.nationen.no/meninger/Kronikk/article3115320.ece [accessed 05 December 2010].

Beirne, P. and South, N. 2007. *Issues in Green Criminology: Confronting Harms Against Environments, Humanity and other Animals*. Cullompton, UK: Willan Publishing.

Bendiksen, E. 1994. *Botaniske undersøkelser på Fornebu. Vurdering av naturområder i forbindelse med endret arealbruk* [*Botanical Surveys at Fornebu*]. Oslo: Norsk institutt for naturforskning, 33.

Bergan, M. 2009. Hva gikk galt på Fornebu? [*What Went Wrong at Fornebu?*]. *Medlemsblad for Naturvernforbundet i Bærum Nøttekråka*, 1(February), 3–9.

Bjørbekk, J. and Lindheim, T. 2005. *Forprosjekt for Sentralparken Fornebu Oslo* [*Pre-Project for Central Park Fornebu, Oslo*]. Oslo: Bjørbekk & Lindheim.

Blomley, N. 2008. Making Space for Law, in *The SAGE Handbook of Political Geography*, edited by K.R. Cox et al. London: Sage, 155–67.

Budstikka 2007. Krever 100.000 planter fjernet [Demand 100,000 plants to be removed]. *Budstikka* [online, 27 September]. Available at: http://www.budstikka.no/nyheter/krever-100-000-planter-fjernet-1.3438921 [accessed 5 January 2011].

Brown, J.H. and Sax, D.F. 2004. An Essay on Some Topics Concerning Invasive Species. *Austral Ecology*, 30, 481–3.

Brown, J.H. 1995. *Macroecology*. Chicago: University of Chicago Press.

Bærum kommune. 1994. *Forstudie av verneinteresser på Fornebu* [*Pre-examination of conservation interests at Fornebu*]. *Dokumentasjonsrapport*, Bærum: Bærum kommune.

Bærum kommune Rådmannen. 2001. *Estetiske retningslinjer for Fornebu* [*Aesthetic guidelines for Fornebu*]. Bærum: Bærum kommune.

Bærum kommunestyre. 2002. *Reguleringsplan for Storøya* [*Regulatory plan for Storøya*]. Bærum: Bærum kommune.

Cadotte, M.W. 2006. Darwin to Elton: Early Ecology and the Problem of Invasive Species, in *Conceptual Ecology and Invasion Biology: Reciprocal Approaches to Nature*, edited by M.W. Cadotte et al. Dordrecht: Springer.

CBD 2010. *What are Invasive Alien Species?* [online, Convention on Biological Diversity]. Available at: http://www.cbd.int/invasive/WhatareIAS.shtml [accessed 3 March 2011].

CBD 2007. *What's the Problem?* [online, Convention on Biological Diversity]. Available at: http://www.cbd.int/invasive/problem.shtml [accessed 3 March 2011].

CBD 1992. *Decision VI/23* of the Conference of the Parties to the CBD, Annex, footnote to the Introduction*, Convention on Biological Diversity.

Chew, M.K. 2006. *Ending with Elton: Preludes to Invasion Biology (Charles Elton, Aldo Leopold)*. Arizona: Arizona State University. Ph.D.

Davis, M.A. 2003. Biotic Globalization: Does Competition from Introduced Species Threaten Biodiversity? *BioScience*, 53(5), 481–9.

Davis, M.A. 2006. Invasion Biology 1958–2005: The Pursuit of Science and Conservation, in *Conceptual Ecology and Invasion Biology: Reciprocal Approaches to Nature*, edited by M.W. Cadotte et al. Dordrecht: Springer, 35–64.

Davis, M.A. 2009. *Invasion Biology*. Oxford: Oxford University Press.
Direktoratet for naturforvaltning. 2010. *Vil forby skadelige arter* [*Wants to ban harmful species*] [online, Direktoratet for naturforvaltning]. Available at: http://www.dirnat.no/content/500040215/Vil-forby-skadelige-arter [accessed 22 February 2011].
Elton, C.S. 1958. *The Ecology of Invasions by Animals and Plants: With a Foreword by Daniel Simberloff* (2000). Chicago: Uversity of Chicago Press.
European Commission 2011. *Invasive Alien Species* [online]. Available at:http://ec.europa.eu/environment/nature/invasivealien/index_en.htm [accessed 13 March 2011].
Faglig utviklingssenter for grøntanleggssektoren 2010. *Høringsuttalelse til forslag til forskrift om utsetting av fremmede organismer* [*Consultation Statement on the proposed regulations on the deliberate release of alien organisms*] [online, Faglig utviklingssenter for grøntanleggssektoren]. Available at: http://fagus.no/nyheter/forskrift-til-naturmangfoldlovens-kapiv-fremmede- organismer [accessed 22 January 2011].
FKD 2006-2007. *St. melding nr. 40. Forvaltning av kongekrabbe* [*Management of the king crab*]. Oslo: Fiskeri-og kystdepartementet.
Foster, J. and Sandberg, L.A. 2004. Friends or Foe? Invasive Species and Public Green Space in Toronto. *Geographical Review, People, Place, & Invasive Species*, 94(2), 178–98.
Gederaas, L., Salvesen, I., and Viken, Å. 2007. Editors. *2007 Norwegian Black List – Ecological Risk Analysis of Alien Species*. Trondheim: Artsdatabanken.
Haber, W. 2008. Biological Diversity – a Concept Going Astray? *GAIA*, 17 (S1), 91–6.
Hagen, D. and Skrindo, A.B.R. (eds) 2010. *Håndbok i økologisk restaurering. Forebygging og rehabilitering av naturskader på vegetasjon og terreng* [*Handbook of Ecological Restoration*]. Trondheim: Forsvarsbygg.
Hannigan, J.A. 2000. *Environmental Sociology. A Social Constructionist Perspective.* London and New York: Routledge.
Head, L. and Muir, P. 2004. Nativeness, Invasiveness, and Nation in Australian Plants. *Geographical Review, People, Place, & Invasive Species*, 94(2), 199–217.
Hettinger, N. 2001. Exotic Species, Naturalisation, and Biological Nativism. *Environmental Values*, 10, 192–224.
Isermann, M. 2008a. Effects of Rosa Rugosa Invasion in Different Coastal Dune Vegetation Types, in *Plant Invasions: Human Perception, Ecological Impacts and Management*, edited by B. Tokarska-Guzik et al., Leiden, The Netherlands: Backhuys Publishers, 289–306.
Isermann, M. 2008b. Expansion of Rosa Rugosa and Hippophaë Rhamnoides in Coastal Grey Dunes: Effects at Different Spatial Scales. *Flora*, 203, 273–80.
IUCN 2000. *IUCN Guidelines for the Prevention of Biodiversity Loss Caused by Alien Invasive Species*. Gland: Switzerland.
IUCN Council 2000. *Guidelines for the Prevention of Biodiversity Loss Caused by Alien Invasive Species.* International Union for Conservation of Nature.

Jasanoff, S. 1995. Procedural Choices in Regulatory Science. *Technology in Society*, 17(3), 279–93.

Jørstad, E. and Skogen, K. 2010. The Norwegian Red List between Science and Policy. *Environmental science & policy*, 13, 115–22.

Kongelig resolusjon 02.10.1992. *Storøykilen og Koksabukta er vernet som naturreservater* [*Storøykilen and Koksabukta are protected as nature reserves*]. Norsk Lovtidend 1992.

Kendle, A.D. and Rose, J.E. 2000. The Aliens have Landed! What are the Justifications for 'Native Only' Policies in Landscape Plantings? *Landscape and Urban Planning*, 47, 19–31.

Lundetræ, V. 2007. *Notat. Definisjon av begrepet 'stedegen vegetasjon'* [*Definition of the term 'native vegetation'*]. Statsbygg: Oslo.

McKinney, M.L. and Lockwood, J.L. 1999. Biotic Homogenization: A Few Winners Replacing Many Losers in the Next Mass Extinction. *Trends Ecol. Evol*, 14, 450–3.

McNeely, J.A. 2005 Human Dimensions of Invasive Alien Species, in *Invasive Alien Species. A New Synthesis*, edited by H.A. Mooney et al. Washington, Covelo, London: SCOPE 63 ISLANDPRESS, 285–309.

McNeely, J.A. 2001. An Introduction to Human Dimnsions of Invasive Alien Species, in *The Great Reshuffling: Human Dimensions of Invasive Alien Species*, edited by. J.A. McNeely. Gland, Switzerland and Cambridge, UK: IUCN, 5–20.

Mooney, H.A. and Cleland, E.E. 2001. The Evolutionary Impact of Invasive Species. *Proceedings of the National Academy of Sciences*, 98, 5446–51.

Myhr, A. 2007a. Beplantning truer unikt mangfold [Planting threatens unique diversity]. *Fornebu og Snarøyposten*, 8 June, 4–5.

Myhr, A. 2007b. Fornebus ugress sprer seg [The weeds of Fornebu are spreading], *Fornebu og Snarøyposten*, 28 September, 8.

Nature Diversity Act 2009. Oslo: Government.no. Available at: http://www.regjeringen.no/en/doc/laws/Acts/nature-diversity-act.html?id=570549 [accessed 25 February 2011].

NOF AO 2007. *Informasjonsbrev vedrørende miljøkriminalitet på Fornebulandet, Bærum* [*Information letter regarding environmental crime on Fornebulandet, Bærum*] [online, Norsk Ornitologisk Forening, avd Oslo og Akershus]. Available at: http://nofoa.no/Fornebu/ [accessed 13 May 2010].

Norwegian Ministry of the Environment 2007. *Strategy on Invasive Alien Species* [online, Norwegian Ministry of the Environment]. Available at: www.tematea.org/files/Doc2_IAS_Strategy.pdf [accessed January 13 2011].

NRK Lørdagsrevyen 2007. Feil planter på Fornebu [Wrong plants at Fornebu]. *NRK Lørdagsrevyen*, 26. May.

Often, A. and Røseng, O. 1998. Plantelivet på Fornebuhalvøya med vekt på Oksenøya, in *Fornebu's unike natur – en dokumentasjon* [*Fornebu's Unique Nature – a Documentation*], edited by Komite for Etterbruk av Fornebu (KEF), Oslo: KEF, 20–28.

Palonen, K. 2003. *Quentin Skinner: History, Politics, Rhetoric*. Cambridge: Polity Press.

Peretti, J. 1998. Nativism and Nature: Rethinking Biological Invasions. *Environmental Values*, 7, 183–192.

Rahel, F.J. 2002. Homogenization of freshwater faunas. *Annual Review of Ecology and Systematics*, 33, 291–315.

Reitan, O. 1996. *Etterbruk av Fornebu: konsekvenser i forhold til fugl i to naturreservater* [*Subsequent Use of Fornebu: Consequences for Birds in Two Nature Reserves*]. Trondheim: Norsk institutt for naturforskning.

Ricciardi, A. 2003. Predicting the Impacts of an Introduced Species from its Invasion History: An Empirical Approach Applied to Zebra Mussel Invasion. *Freshwater Biology*, 48, 972–81.

Ricciardi, A. and MacIsaac, H.J. 2008. In Retrospect: The Book that Began Invasion Ecology. *Nature* [online], 452(34). Available at: http://www.nature.com/nature/journal/v452/n7183/full/452034a.html [accessed 17 January 2011].

Richardson, D.M. and Pyšek, P. 2006. Plant Invasions: Merging the Concepts of Species Invasiveness and Community Invasibility. *Progress in Physical Geography*, 30(3), 409–31.

Robbins, P. 2004. Comparing Invasive Networks: Cultural and Political Biographies of Invasive Species. *Geographical Review, People, Place, & Invasive Species*, 94(2), 139–56.

Rodriguez, L.F. 2006. Can Invasive Species Facilitate Native Species? Evidence of How, When, and Why these Impacts. *Biological Invasions*, 8, 927–39.

Rådmannen Bærum kommune. 2008. *Notat. Vedrørende Storøya – terreng og landskapsarbeider – orientering om beplantning* [*Note. Regarding Storøya – terrain and landscape works – information about planting*]. Bærum: Plan og miljøutvalget Bærum Kommune.

Sax, D.F and Gaines, S.D. 2003. Species Diversity: From Global Decreases to Local Increases. *Trends in Ecology and Evolution*, 18, 561–66.

Shine, C., Williams, N. and Burhenne-Guilmin, F. 2005. Legal and Institutional Frameworks for Invasive Alien Species, in *Invasive Alien Species – A New Synthesis*, edited by H.R. Mooney et al. Washington, Covelo, London: Island Press. SCOPE 63.

Shine, C., Williams, N. and Gündling, L. 2000. *A Guide to Designing Legal and Institutional Frameworks on Alien Invasive Species*. Environmental Policy and Law Paper A: IUCN – The World Conservation Union.

Simberloff, D. 2003. Confronting Introduced Species: A Form of Xenophobia? *Biological Invasions*, 5, 179–92.

Simberloff, D. 2000a. Introduced Species: The Threat to Biodiversity & What Can Be Done. *ActionBioscience.org* [online]. Available at: http://www.actionbioscience.org/biodiversity/simberloff.html [accessed 28 April 2011].

Simberloff, D. 2000b. Foreword, in *The Ecology of Invasions by Animals and Plants*, C.S.Elton. 1958, Chicago and London: The University of Chicago Press, vii–xiv.

Skinner, Q. 2002. *Visions of Politics: Regarding Method, Volume 1*. Cambridge, U.K: Cambridge University Press.

Skogeierforbund, N. 2010. *DN står steilt på sitt forskriftsforslag* [*DN Are Standing Solid By their Regulatory Proposals*] [online, Skogeierforbundet]. Available at: www.skog.no/Modules/Nyheter/article.asp?Data_ID_Article=4103&Data_ID_C hannel=3 [accessed 24 February 2011].

Statbygg and Oslo kommune 2008. *Grøntstruktur Fornebu. Beskrivelse av vegetasjonsbruk Sentralparken – Storøya – Koksa* [*Green structure Fornebu. Description of vegetation use Sentralparken – Storøya – Koksa*]. Oslo: Statsbygg og Oslo kommune.

Statsbygg and Oslo kommune 1996. *Etterbruk av Fornebu. Konsekvensutredning etter plan og byggningslovens § 33* [*Re-development of Fornebu*]. Oslo: Statsbygg og Oslo kommune.

Statsbygg and Oslo Kommune 2000. *Etterbruk Fornebu Grøntstrukturplan*. Oslo: Statsbygg og Oslo Kommune.

Sæther, J.M. and Hansen, S.S.R. 2007. Naturvandaler i Statsbygg [Nature vandals in Statsbygg]. *Dagsavisen*, 23 October.

Sørensen, H. 2010. *The New Approach – The Norwegian Nature Diversity Act* [online, Norwegian Ministry of the Environment]. Available at: http://www.regjeringen.no/nb/dep/md/aktuelt/taler_artikler/politisk_ledelse/statssekretaer-soerensen/2010/the-new-approach--the-norwegian-nature-d.html?id=622807 [accessed 15 February 2011].

Tully, J. and Skinner, Q. 1988. *Meaning and Context. Quentin Skinner and his Critics*. Oxford and Cambridge: Polity Press.

Weidema, I. 2006. *NOBANIS – Invasive Alien Species Fact Sheet –Rosa Rugosa* [online, Database of the North European and Baltic Network on Invasive Alien Species – NOBANIS]. Available at: www.nobanis.org [accessed 5 May 2011].

White, R. 2008. *Crimes Against Nature: Environmental Criminology and Ecological Justice*. Cullompton:Willan Publishing.

Woods, M. (2001). Strangers in a Strange Land: The Problem of Exotic Species. *Environmnetal Values*, 10, 163–91.

Østengen and Bergo 2001. *Landskapsplanen for Fornebu* [*Plan for Fornebu landscaping*]. Oslo: Statsbygg, Oslo kommune og Bærum kommune.

Chapter 13
Industrialising Greenland: Government and Transnational Corporations Versus Civil Society?

Mikkel Myrup

Introduction

This aim of this chapter is not to attempt contributing to the theoretical perspectives on the area of eco-global criminology, but rather to provide this publication with examples of *how things are*. Transboundary environmental harm is taking place in a variety of guises. Some are unintended and accidental and some are government endorsed and/or approved. Rob White describes elsewhere in this publication (Chapter 2) an incident taking place in Hungary in October 2010. Here the dike of a red mud tailings pond failed, killing ten and injuring hundreds of downstream residents. Red mud is the residue left over of from the refining of bauxite into aluminium oxide, also known as alumina, which is ultimately smelted into aluminium. This incident was unintended or accidental, even though it could be argued that the combination of maintenance neglect and failed regulation places the main responsibility with the company and the authorities. The spill reached the Danube River and spread into the neighbouring countries downstream.

Below an example of government-endorsed transboundary environmental harm will be described. It involves the production of one single metal, namely aluminium. Primary aluminium production requires several polluting, heavy industrial processes, which often take place on several continents. In this regard, the concept of 'government as polluter' is but one of many examples. For a variety of elucidating articles on this topic, see for example *Environmental Crimes – A Reader* edited by Rob White (2009). The introduction of heavy industrial activities such as aluminium smelting, mega-mines and oil drilling and the concomitant transnational corporate power in an immensely sparsely populated country with a relatively young democracy not only implies that considerations about environmental harm are needed, but urgently calls for fundamental discussions pertaining to the future state of our fragile democracy.

Historical Background

Greenland is our planet's largest island, spanning some 2,700 kilometres from north to south. Most of the island is covered by a massive ice sheet though, leaving only a narrow strip of habitable land along the coasts. The landmass between the coast and the ice sheet rarely exceeds widths of 100 kilometres and is comprised of deep fjords and alpine terrain.

Greenland has been inhabited almost continuously for 4,500 years. Migrations came from the West, originating in the Bering Strait area. The last of these migrational waves to Greenland from the West was the arrival of the Thule culture in c. 1300 AD. The modern day Greenlanders – the Inuit – are the direct descendants of this culture. The first European colonisation of Greenland began in 985 AD and ended c. 1450 AD. This was Norse farmers coming from Iceland and settling in the two regions of Southwest Greenland called the Western Settlement and the Eastern Settlement. The Inuit-Norse interaction is not very well known, but archaeological research has established that when the two cultures encountered each other – closing the gap of global human expansion – the Norse existence in Greenland did not prosper (for example Arneborg 2005).

Other Europeans influencing the Inuit were the early explorers and whalers. They began appearing on the coasts of Southwest Greenland in relatively large numbers in the sixteenth century and were soon engaging in extensive trading with the Inuit. The historical and archaeological records show that European goods such as glass beads and different types of utensils became frequent in Inuit households during the seventeenth and eighteenth centuries (for example Gulløv 1997).

In the early eighteenth century it was decided, on the church's initiative, that efforts should be made to turn Greenland into a more formal part of the kingdom – a colony. Dutch whalers had become dominant in the trade with the Inuit, much to the Crown's dismay. Concerns about the fate of the Norse were also playing a part. Three centuries had gone by without word from these northern Christians and the 1530s church reformation had left them with their outdated Roman-Catholic beliefs. So, it was thought, efforts should be made to convert any surviving Norse to the Protestant church, as well as incorporating the heathen Inuit into the Christian belief system (cf. Gulløv and Kapel 1979).

This task was undertaken by the Norwegian missionary Hans Egede. In 1721 he took up residence in the Kangeq area on the outer coast archipelago of the Nuuk fjord, not far from the present-day Greenland capital.

Egede never found any Norse survivors, as they had left before 1450. But for the Inuit this marked the advent of Christianity, as well as an economy based on the organised trading of goods. During the eighteenth century several settlements with both clergy and trading facilities were established along the coastal stretch of West Greenland. By the end of the eighteenth century most Inuit were baptised and had become integrated into the Danish system of colonial rule – a system where all positions of significance were naturally held by Danish officials.

This system had a profound effect on the Inuit way of life, causing *inter alia* an alteration in settlement patterns. In pre-colonial Inuit society, people were mobile and shifted locations according to a yearly cycle determined by the hunting seasons of a variety of game animals and fish. In a colonial system, in which trade and the supply of raw materials to the trading station is essential, a more sedentary population was preferable. This led the authorities to 'encourage' a concentration of the population in the settlements established by the Royal Greenlandic Trade Company, that is, the Danish State. One of the effects of this was an increase in dependency on goods that only the trading company – with its monopoly – could provide.

Some of the most diligent Inuit were gradually eased into positions of some power, albeit never on levels allowing them to autonomously decide any form of systemic change. Ultimately, events such as the global post-WWII decolonisation process resulted in the transformation of the Danish colony Greenland into the Danish county (*amt*) Greenland in 1953. The colonial system, with its powerful influence on ordinary people's daily lives, continued *de facto* until the implementation of Home Rule Government in 1979 and the creation of a Greenlandic parliament.

Although research still needs to be done on this subject, it is widely agreed that one significant result of this influence is that it has engendered an exaggerated respect for authority. But has this fairly widespread blind orthodoxy, combined with a generally low level of education, really made it possible for the authorities and corporate power to appease and manipulate the general public as regards environmental matters with only minimal effort?

In May 2009 there was a referendum on whether or not Greenland should obtain status as a self-governing body within the Danish Commonwealth. This status is considered as being the last step before obtaining full independence. Two-thirds of the votes were in favour of self-government. Greenland receives one-quarter of its GDP from the Danish State in the form of a block grant. According to the terms of agreement this block grant is 'frozen', that is, the amount will not increase as more areas of administrational responsibility are moved from Denmark. Another significant aspect of the agreement is that Greenland has obtained full right to its subsoil. This leaves Greenland free to sell off its mineral wealth without having to negotiate terms of revenue sharing with the Danish State in the – now abolished – Dano-Greenlandic 'Mineral Council'.

Shedding the Colonial Yoke?

Greenland's only significant export commodity is seafood – mainly cold water prawn and halibut. The stocks are, however, diminishing, and with plummeting world prices, the earnings forecast is rather gloomy. This has naturally spurred politicians – and civil servants in particular – to an increased effort to attract transnational corporation (TNC) investments mainly in the minerals and hydrocarbon extraction sector. Hydropower potential is also attractive to heavy industry depending on vast amounts of cheap energy, such as primary aluminium-producing TNCs (for example Alcoa Inc).

Reportedly active hydrocarbon systems were identified off the coast of West Greenland in the summer of 2010, and 'Big Oil' is now queuing up to secure exploration licenses. In addition, several mining megaprojects are lined up and each of these will have a considerable negative environmental impact. In spite of this, they are seen by many as inevitable if Greenland is to overcome its fiscal troubles. TNCs with a lengthy history of environmental abuse are now seeking permission to operate in Greenland, assuring politicians, civil servants and the general public that they adhere to the highest of environmental standards, and utilise only the newest, greenest and best available technologies; they say nothing about the inherent destructiveness that characterises the main activities of these corporations.

In parliament, among cabinet members and civil servants, elements which can be labelled as having traits ascribable to a neoliberal mindset, see swift industrialisation with a minimum of regulation and restriction as *the* solution to provide the country with a self-sustaining economy. These elements are promoting industrialisation solely on industry's terms, using industry's language to persuade sceptics in the public sphere, as well as sceptical politicians, to accepting industrialisation without questioning the validity of the basic premises. Industry and government have apparently entered into an 'extrasocietal' partnership, allegedly with the purpose of creating a sustainable economy. But where does this partnership leave the interests of civil society and the environment?

Transnational corporate power has been subjected to increased scrutiny, especially since the global financial crisis hit in 2008. In Greenland this power has become a substantial presence, exercising its influence on society's fundamental institutions as well as on ordinary people's daily lives. The proposed Alcoa smelter has already caused several legislative changes,[1] and is seemingly making political parties forget all about their policy agendas and ethical principles.[2]

In 2006, after initial contact officially were made by Alcoa, the Government of Greenland and the TNC entered into a so-called joint action plan (JAP) and in 2007 a Memorandum of Understanding[3] (MoU) was signed with the purpose of working towards establishing a 350,000 tons/year primary aluminium-producing smelter and the associated 600 MW hydropower plants. The circumstances under which these and subsequent decisions were made are interesting because they have, in reality, forced the government to form policies in reverse order, so to

1 Legislation concerning hydropower and cultural heritage was customised and passed in parliament in 2010.

2 The opposition party *Siumut* changed their view from a negative stance towards imported low-wage (Chinese) labour to accepting it, as soon as Alcoa made it clear that it wants to exploit this possibility.

3 The Greenland Home Rule Government and Alcoa Inc. (2007): Memorandum of Understanding between the Greenland Home Rule Government and Alcoa Inc.

speak, on matters such as industrialisation, rapid social change, greenhouse gas (GHG) emissions and global warming and so on; that is, the government first decided to accept Alcoa's proposal to establish a smelter and then subsequently attempted to formulate strategies on the issues surrounding it. This pattern, where decisions are made first and inconsequential public debate follows, will emerge frequently during this process. Pivotal decisions regarding the project are being taken behind closed doors by cabinet members and civil servants before they are opened to public scrutiny, thus circumventing the democratically founded procedure of decision making (Hansen et al. 2009, Schmitt et al. 2009).

The main official argument for letting Alcoa build an aluminium smelter is the prospect of steady jobs and a much-needed injection of cash into the public purse in the form of income and corporation taxes and revenues. Another important aspect, however, is the environmental cost of the project. The Greenlandic public is becoming increasingly aware of environmental issues and many people have concerns about the possible contamination of living natural resources, as a relatively large part of the Greenlandic diet consists of fish and marine mammals. Reports about smelter emissions have been made public,[4] but Alcoa and government representatives down play the risks and focus almost exclusively on CO2 emissions as they have direct economic implications for the project. But aluminium production also has transboundary social and environmental consequences. Bauxite (aluminium ore) has to be mined and refined into alumina (aluminium oxide) and these are processes that have social and environmental costs (cf. Padel and Das 2010, Brueckner and Ross 2010). How are these aspects taken into consideration regarding the Greenlandic smelter project? As we shall see, the government's interpretation of these issues does not differ from that of the industry. The Greenlandic public and the decision-makers are being taught by the industry and the government that building an aluminium smelter in Greenland will benefit the global environment and have a positive effect on the global climate, because the 'green metal' will be even greener when smelted using *Greenlandic* hydropower. Up until now many of us apparently accept this premise. But why? A simple search on the internet will almost instantly reveal a much murkier picture.

Greenland – One Step Short of Independence

Two-thirds of the votes were in favour of self-government in the referendum held in May 2009. In the Greenlandic-Danish commission's recommendations on self-government (Grønlandsk-dansk selvstyrekommission 2008) two important economic points are made. The people of Greenland have now at last obtained full rights to the country's subsoil, that is, its mineral deposits including hydrocarbons.

4 A Strategic Environmental Assessment (SEA) has been made by the government (all data concerning smelter emissions derive from Alcoa). Availalble at: http://www.smv.gl/index_us.htm [accessed 18 August 2011].

However, the agreement also states that the block grant is frozen once the rest of the areas of administrational responsibility are moved from the Danish State to the Greenlandic self-government, that is, the funding of each administrational area of responsibility that Greenland 'takes home' will be taken out of the existing budget. This has of course induced a sense of urgency regarding the identification of new sources of income.

Since the late 1990s, efforts to steer the Greenlandic economy into the path of deregulation and liberalisation have been persistent. In 1999 an OECD report suggested how the government should carry out these steps (OECD 1999), and during the first decade of the twenty-first century the housing market was deregulated (Poppel 2005) and the uniform price system for utilities, which was formerly based on principles of solidarity, was partially reformed, the main goal being to introduce so-called cost-based prices (Winther 2010).

Iceland – a Role Model?

Greenlanders and Greenlandic politicians often look east to the neighbouring island of Iceland. This young republic has, like Greenland, lived through the yoke of Danish colonial rule. Independence was declared in 1944 and Iceland has long been a role model for many Greenlanders, who envy its self-sustaining economy, though this admiration has cooled down markedly since the financial crash in late 2008 and the following *kreppa*.[5] Up until the crash, Icelandic society had been heavily influenced by neoliberal trends. The three major banks were privatised in the 1990s. Icelandic economics Professor Dr Ivar Jonsson describes the trend thus:

> Following privatization of the state bank sector in Iceland in the 1990s, a kind of mini-keiretzu system developed in which three privatized banks became the core and base of the growth of three closely knitted webs of related companies in the retailing and transport sectors. These companies and the banks built their strong financial position on oligopolstricken markets, which they use to exploit Icelandic consumers in order to collect oligopoly-rents on which they base their investment abroad in their original branches of industry (Jonsson 2010).

There is one particular aspect of the Icelandic economy which is the subject of many Greenlander's interest these days, namely the aluminium industry and its effect on the national economy. Jonsson writes:

> The government allowed the building of one of Europe's largest hydropower plants (Karahnjukavirkjun) in order to foster large increase in inward foreign direct investment (IFDI) in the aluminum industry by transnational companies. In addition, Icelandic bonds have been issued in European financial markets that have appealed to foreign investors due to their high interest rate. These bonds

5 Icelandic term for the crisis as it is felt in daily life.

> have stimulated considerable demand for kronas [Icelandic currency]. However, in the long run this strategy is problematic, as the krona is vulnerable to the consequences of speculation and shifting mood in international bond markets. As the nominal exchange rate of the krona has tended to fall after construction periods in the hydropower and aluminum plant sectors, the central bank had to increase the interest rate level to prevent inflation from rising. The level of interest rates in Iceland is now more than double the rate than in the other Nordic countries. Higher interest rates un-dermine the profitability of investment in domestic production and industries. The result is creeping stagnation in the local economy (Jonsson 2010).

In relation to the proposed Greenlandic aluminium smelter project, Iceland is quite actively being used as a role model, especially the new Alcoa smelter, which went online in 2007 and which has been the object of several visits by Greenlandic delegations. Study trips are organised in close collaboration with Greenland Development Inc. (GD – the Government's aluminium project agency) and Alcoa.[6] Groups of citizens and primary school pupils from Maniitsoq, the town where the planned smelter will be built, have visited East Iceland and the smelter community so as to see with their own eyes what kind of benefits they themselves can look forward to receiving if it is decided to build a smelter in Greenland. These short and well-organised visits, on which the travellers are in the hands of Alcoa employees and members of the smelter community, produce effective ambassadors for the industry when they return to Greenland. They return to their community (and Greenland) with a message of assurance: there is no need to worry about anything and all the concerns that have been voiced are based on groundless rumours. Opponents to the Greenlandic project have gone on one of these trips, but were outnumbered, and outshone by the sheer size of the smelter. They were unable to make their presence felt. On one occasion the visitors also met with Icelanders opposing Alcoa and the aluminium industry, but their messages were drowned in the overwhelming amount of positive information provided by the industry (personal communication with B. Lyberth, chairman of Against Aluminium Smelter in Greenland, 2011). This way of including the opposition is a shrewd method of making a show of an inclusiveness which in reality will have minimal or no influence, and is a mere token of adherence to democratic rule.

Aluminium Dreams

As mentioned above, Alcoa's official approach to the Government of Greenland was made in 2006. A Memorandum of Understanding between the two parties

6 See for example. http://www.aluminium.gl/en/news/student_study_trip_to_iceland and http://www.aluminium.gl/en/news/chairman_of_the_citizen_group_is_satisfied_with_in [Both accessed 15 August 2011].

was signed in 2007. Since then the government has published a number of white papers and reports concerning economic impacts, social impacts, environmental impacts, and so on relating to the aluminium smelter. Some of the first indications in relation to the Greenlandic project on how the environmental aspects of aluminium production is viewed by the industry, and now the Government, can be observed in the MoU:[7]

> The vision of the Government and Alcoa is to examine, and create the conditions for the establishment of a world-class, sustainable aluminum industry in Greenland, utilizing Greenland's abundant and environmentally conscious hydropower potential, coupled with Alcoa's 100+ years of experience in developing and operating aluminum smelters around the world in a manner that is sustainable, safe, sensitive to the environment, and valued by the communities in which Alcoa operates.

As we shall see below, the MoU's statements regarding sustainability, environment and community acceptance are widely challenged. The government, when describing the environmental aspects, put forward an identical rhetoric in its publications.

Aluminium Production

Aluminium makes up 8 per cent of the earth's crust. It is the commonest metal in the soil. But the metallic form of aluminium is hidden in nature through its bonding with oxygen and other elements. The soil type with the highest concentrations of aluminium is called bauxite and is mostly found in the tropical and sub-tropical forests of South America, West Africa, North Australia and East India. These are areas with the most abundant plant growth on earth (Padel and Das 2010: 3–4). Bauxite is also found in Western Australia, here Alcoa operates two bauxite mines and three alumina refineries. The deposits found here are some of the lowest grade bauxite in the world (Brueckner and Ross 2010: 20, 39).

Aluminium production consists of four stages. First stage: strip mining of the bauxite. The bauxite is typically found in lenses under the top soil. The top soil is peeled off, exposing the layer of bauxite. Often this top soil consists of ecosystems rich in biodiversity. In Western Australia the bauxite deposits are mostly covered by native Jarrah forest (Brueckner and Ross 2010: 38). In Odisha, East India, the bauxite is on the mountains that provide perennial streams of water used domestically and for irrigation. Once the bauxite is removed, this source of water ceases to exist. Second stage: the bauxite undergoes a process of calcination, in which it is baked to reduce the water content, which is usually 10–30 per cent. It is then mixed with caustic soda and 'digested' in the Bayer process, which produces sodium aluminate. This is filtered and decanted to separate the alumina from

7 The Greenland Home Rule Government and Alcoa Inc. 2007.

the red mud. The alumina is then precipitated into crystal form over about three days. The bauxite residue, known as red mud, is then placed in a pond near the refinery. It contains iron, silica, titanium, gallium and uranium together with over 40 additional elements present in bauxite, which exist as highly toxic, destabilised heavy metals, which make it radioactive. A refinery uses approximately 2.3 tons of bauxite to produce one ton of alumina powder, leaving over a ton of toxic red mud. This proportion varies with the chemical composition of different bauxite deposits. Third stage: this is the stage where the aluminium is made. You need two tons of alumina to make one ton of aluminium. By passing a huge electric current through the alumina, the element is separated from its molecular bonding with oxygen and is smelted into its metallic form. Fourth stage: here the different aluminium alloys are produced. Particularly polluting to manufacture is the most sophisticated alloy, the lithium range, which is used in the arms and aerospace industries (Padel and Das 2010: 41–3).

In Greenland the proposed Alcoa aluminium smelter will annually emit:

- 4,600 tons of sulphur dioxide
- 110 tons of fluoride
- 180 kg PAH's
- 90 tons of particles (< 10μm)
- 450.000 tons of carbon dioxide
- 7.1 tons of PFC gasses equivalent to 46,000 tons of carbon dioxide.

Additional emissions will consist of the following airborne substances in unknown quantities: nitrogen oxides, carbon monoxide and cyanide. These are all figures derived from a single source, namely Alcoa (SEA 2010: 10).[8] Another by-product of aluminium smelting is spent pot lining (SPL). SPL contains, among other chemical compounds, cyanide and thus falls into the category of hazardous waste and will have to be exported for disposal according to the provisions of the Basel Convention on the Control of Transboundary Movements of Hazardous Wastes and Their Disposal.

Communities and Bauxite

In the East Indian State of Odisha, local tribal communities have been under siege by the giant mining corporation Vedanta for over a decade. This aluminium-producing corporation has been constructing bauxite mining and alumina refining facilities without having obtained permission from the authorities or local inhabitants. The tribal communities have lived through a ten-year battle with the corporation and its hired gangs of hooligans. These clashes have resulted in

8 Available at: http://www.smv.gl/DK/SMV_2010/SMV2010_02_miljo_DK.pdf [accessed 15 August 2011].

several deaths among the tribals. The bauxite-capped hills provide these people with food and water and they are considered sacred according to local beliefs (cf. Padel and Das 2010). An important factor in making this kind of behaviour possible for the mining corporation has been the authorities' inability to interfere. Interest in establishing mining, refining and smelting facilities in Odisha has also been expressed by Alcoa.[9]

The small community of Yarloop in Western Australia also struggles with a neighbouring Alcoa refinery. Emissions consisting of a so-called chemical cocktail from the refinery and dust blown by the wind from the dried out red mud ponds have severely damaged the residents' quality of life. Numerous residents have been struck by a variety of illnesses caused by refinery emissions. Appeals for governmental assistance have fallen on deaf ears. The WA Government is perceived by the victims as being on the side of Alcoa. The town has now been divided into two. Acknowledging that health problems exist, and having plans to expand the refinery, Alcoa has launched a buy-out scheme. People living inside a line drawn through town will get compensation if they move out, while people living outside of that line get nothing (Brueckner and Ross 2010). When one reads the minutes from the WA parliamentary debate on a solution of the matter, it is quite clear that the ruling party puts in quite a lot of effort to emphasise how many jobs Alcoa provides and how much revenue it generates, implying that the politicians should weigh this against the health and wellbeing of the residents.[10]

The Environmental Discourse

In Greenland, the environmental discourse in relation to the proposed aluminium smelter was initiated with the statements made in the MoU between the government and Alcoa. If you have signed a document with formulations like 'world-class, sustainable aluminum industry in Greenland, utilizing Greenland's abundant and environmentally conscious hydropower potential, coupled with Alcoa's 100 plus years of experience in developing and operating aluminum smelters around the world in a manner that is sustainable, safe, sensitive to the environment, and valued by the communities in which Alcoa operates' (The Greenland Home Rule Government and Alcoa Inc. 2007) this does not exactly invite you to adopt a more objective stance regarding the social and environmental track record of a corporation and an industry which may be about to pay billions of dollars in foreign direct investments.

Environmental considerations, especially outside Greenland, have never been taken seriously. In a white paper to the Parliament of Greenland in April 2007 on the subject of energy intensive industry, the following was stated about bauxite

9 See for example: http://www.dnaindia.com/money/report_alcoa-to-set-up-plant-in-orissa_1066696 [accessed 15 August 2011].

10 See for example: http://www.caps6218.org.au/ [accessed 15 August 2011].

mining and the problematic red mud-issue: '[..] the other half is a residue which is put on areas close to the refinery and has turned out to be quite a good soil for planting' [My translation]. This does not sound much like the toxic red mud described above. This author wrote a letter which was printed in two national newspapers, confronting and contradicting the residue-statement (Myrup 2008). It was the director of Greenland Development (GD) himself who wrote the reply. The explanation was that the then minister of industry had visited Alcoa's refinery and smelter facilities in São Luís, Brazil, and had planted a tree in a place that was allegedly a rehabilitated red mud pond. The point was emphasised by a photo showing the minister on his knees planting the tree in park-like surroundings (Drechsel 2008). Subsequently, GD referred to a report on sustainable bauxite mining produced by the International Aluminium Institute[11] (IAI). The IAI is one of several international lobby groups for the industry, coordinating the discourse on environment and corporate social responsibility (CSR), and building aluminium's 'green and friendly' image (Padel and Das 2010: 216).

The GD director positioned himself in relation to industrialisation and hydropower in another letter in a national newspaper. This time it was on the subject of 'Industrial development with a good conscience' (Drechsel 2007). His main point was that if aluminium is smelted using hydropower it would be of benefit to the global climate. The argument was that the hydropower-driven smelter would replace a coal-fired smelter somewhere else on the globe. This is an example of how one externalises the costs of aluminium. Padel and Das (2010):

> [..] the complexity of aluminium economics is in large part a manipulated product – a mask which conceals a pattern of extreme levels of exploitation and destruction of the environment [..]. The essence of this pattern is externality – how the industry externalises its real costs. In other words, aluminium economics does not make economic sense – it is uneconomic.

This practice is repeated in a government commissioned report known as the *Life cycle assessment of aluminium production in new Alcoa smelter in Greenland* or the LCA.[12] Every single piece of data used in the LCA, was provided by Alcoa. The civil servants in the government administration who defined its terms of reference simply limited its scope so that it would exclusively process information on the carbon dioxide aspect of production. This LCA was included in the white paper which in 2010 was voted through parliament. Its function: to document that building a hydropowered aluminium smelter in Greenland will reduce global warming. This is another clear example of externalising aluminium's real costs.

11 International Aluminium Institute – Fourth Sustainable Bauxite Mining Report 2008.

12 Available at: http://www.smv.gl/Baggrundsrapporter/lca_2009.pdf [accessed 15 August 2011].

'Global Order'

Greenland and the Greenlandic society have in recent years become objects of an increased interest, especially transnational corporate interest. Capital is seeking to 'unlock' the hydrocarbon and mineral wealth of the country and this will have a profound effect on every level of Greenlandic society. Like any other country, Greenland has to navigate in a globalised economy, I have already mentioned the concept of neoliberalism a couple of times without providing a definition of the term, but will try to scratch the surface of what it could imply. Jamie Peck has made these points regarding the nature of neoliberalism:

> Perhaps, instead, the closest one can get to understanding the nature of neoliberalism is to follow its movements, and to triangulate between its ideological, ideational, and institutional currents, between philosophy, politics, and practice. And: Neoliberalism, in its various guises, has always been about the capture and reuse of the state, in the interests of shaping a pro-corporate, freer-trading market order, even though this has never been a process of cookie-cutter replication of an unproblematic strategy (Peck 2010: 8–9).

The shaping of a pro-corporate Greenland has begun. One has seen the introduction of CSR Greenland, assisted by the Employers' Association of Greenland, the signing of the UN Global Compact by some of the biggest publicly owned Greenlandic corporations and the introduction of Transparency Greenland, also by the Employers' Association. High-ranking politicians and well-known corporate figures have suggested publicly that we should feel safe adhering to the guidelines of the International Council on Mining and Metals (ICMM) and the Extractive Industries Transparency Initiative (EITI). All seemingly charitable organisations working for the good cause. But looked at more closely, they will reveal the fingerprints of some of the globe's most unscrupulous corporations. As an example, EITI was established in connection with the World Summit on Sustainable Development in Johannesburg in 2002, at which the chairmen of Rio Tinto and other top mining corporations kept close contact with Tony Blair, who subsequently announced the Extractive Industries Transparency Initiative. It has long been the goal of the mining corporations to rid themselves of regulation with external verification. The solution has been 'voluntary self-regulation' under the banner of 'sustainable development'. A key part of the UN Global Compact is the Global Reporting Initiative which allows corporations to supply their own data instead of allowing the aforementioned regulation with external verification (Padel and Das 2010: 201–2).

The organisation Corporate Watch concludes in a report that CSR is of limited use in creating social change and that since CSR is also a vehicle for companies to thwart attempts to control corporate power and to gain access to markets: CSR is a problem not a solution. Efforts to control corporations' destructive impacts must have a critique of corporate power as their goal otherwise they reinforce rather than challenge power structures, and undermine popular struggles for autonomy, democracy, human rights and environmental sustainability (Fauset 2006).

When the Government of Greenland signed the MoU with Alcoa, the corporation was endorsed by the then US ambassador to Denmark, James P. Cain.[13] One cannot underestimate the symbolic value of the world's only superpower backing a corporation with a multi-billion dollar interest in your 56,000 population country.

Concluding Remarks

Greenland has a very young democracy which is still in the process of building its fundamental democratic institutions. There are obvious weaknesses in the way the public and politicians understand concepts such as public participation and dissemination of knowledge. In its eagerness to transform some of the country's riches in the form of energy and minerals into tangible wealth, the administrative system has adopted a stance that is too close to corporate interests, and has thereby induced the political establishment to do the same.

The 'Alcoa process' has revealed that Greenland and its institutions still have to learn how to approach these kinds of megaprojects with a more objective and critical mindset. It is alarming that other companies are standing at Greenland's door, expecting to be received in the same way as Alcoa. The Greenlandic politicians and civil servants should strive to adopt a more holistic stance regarding transboundary pollution and environmental harm. As it is, politicians and the public should at least be made aware of the intrinsic danger of inflicting harm on other people and their environment, should the aluminium smelter project materialise.

We, as a society, need to publicly debate and critically assess how the interaction between government and transnational corporations is taking place. Corporate influence on policy has become a democratic problem which needs increased attention and public scrutiny.

References

Arneborg, J. 2005. Greenland irrigation systems on a west Nordic background: an overview of the evidence of irrigation systems in Norse Greenland c. 980–1450 AD. *Pamatky Archeologicke Supplementum* 17, *Ruralia* (V): 137–45.

Brueckner, M. and Ross, D. 2010. *Under Corporate Skies: A Struggle Between People, Place and Profit*. Fremantle: Fremantle Press.

Chomsky, N. 1999. *Profit Over People: Neoliberalism and Global Order*. New York: Seven Stories Press.

13 See http://denmark.usembassy.gov/policy/partnership-with-greenland/commercial-and-investment-cooperation/alcoa-mou-signing.html [accessed 15 August 2011].

Corporate Watch 2006. *What's wrong with corporate social responsibility?* Oxford: Corporate Watch.

CSR Greenland 2010. Charter – CSR Greenland [online]. Available at: http://www.csr.gl/HvaderCSRGreenland/tabid/57/language/en-US/Default.aspx [accessed 15 August 2011].

Departementet for Erhverv, Arbejdsmarked og Erhvervsuddannelser 2008. Beslutningsgrundlag for etablering af en aluminiumssmelter i Grønland. [Basis for decision on the establishment of an aluminum smelter in Greenland]. Government of Greenland.

Drechsel, F. 2007. Industrial development with a good conscience. Letter in Greenlandic national newspaper [online]. Available at: http://www.aluminium.gl/en/news/industrial_development_with_a_good_conscience [accessed 15 Augugst 2011].

Drechsel, F. 2008. Viden opnås gennem dialog – ikke spekulationer! [Knowledge is achieved through dialogue – not speculation!]. Letter in national Greenlandic newspaper Atuagadliutit/Grønlandsposten [online]. Available at: http://www.aluminium.gl/da/nyheder/viden_opnaas_gennem_dialog__ikke_spekulationer [accessed 15 August 2011].

Erhvervsdirektoratet, Grønlands Hjemmestyre 2007a. Press release: Projekt aluminiumssmelteværk i Grønland: Hjemmestyret indgår samarbejdsaftale med Alcoa. [Project aluminum smelter in Greenland: Home Rule Government signs agreement with Alcoa]. Government of Greenland.

Erhvervsdirektoratet, Grønlands Hjemmestyre 2007b. Redegørelse om energiintensiv industri i Grønland. [A statement on energy-intensive industry in Greenland]. Government of Greenland.

Fauset, C. 2006. *What's Wrong with Corporate Social Responsibility?* Corporate Watch Report 2006. Oxford, England: Corporate Watch.

Greenland Development 2009. Aluminiumsindustri i Grønland. [Aluminium Industry in Greenland]. Greenland Development.

Grønlandsk-dansk selvstyrekommission 2008. Grønlandsk-dansk selvstyrekommissions betænkning om selvstyre i Grønland. [Greenlandic-Danish Self commission's report on self-government in Greenland]. København: Grønlandsk-dansk selvstyrekommission.

Gulløv, H.C. 1997. From middle ages to colonial times: archaeological and ethnohistorical studies of the thule culture in south west Greenland 1300–1800 AD. Meddelelser om Grønland, *Man and Society* 23, pp. 501. Copenhagen, Denmark: The Commission for Scientific Research in Greenland.

Gulløv, H.C. and Hans K. 1979. Haabetz colonie 1721–1728: a historical-archaeological investigation of the Danish–Norwegian colonization of Greenland. *Ethnohistorical Studies of the Meeting of Eskimo and European Cultures*, No. 1. Copenhagen, Denmark: National Museum of Denmark.

Hansen, K.G. et al. 2009. Decision processes, communication and democracy: the aluminium smelter project in Greenland, in *Knowledge-based Tools for Sustainable Governance of Energy and Climate Adaptation in the Nordic*

Periphery (K-Base), edited by J. Hukkinen et al. Nordic Council of Ministers Research Programme Report 7(2009). Stockholm: Nordregio.

Jonsson, I. 2010. The transnational capitalist class and the mini-Keiretzu system in Iceland in *The Political Economy of Northern Regional Development*, vol. 1: Tema Nord, edited by G. Winther. Copenhagen: Nordic Council of Ministers, 147–62.

Kempf, H. 2007. *How the Rich Are Destroying the Earth*. Vermont: Chelsea Green Publishing Company.

Klein, N. 2007. *The Shock Doctrine: The Rise of Disaster Capitalism*. New York: Picador.

Myrup, M. 2008. Mens vi venter på Alcoa. [Waiting for Alcoa]. Letter in national Greenlandic newspapers Sermitsiaq and Ataugagdtliutit/Grønlandsposten [online]. Available at: http://www.aluminium.gl/da/nyheder/mikkel_myrups_indlaeg_i_aviserne_mens_vi_venter_paa [accessed 15 August 2011].

OECD 1999. Grønlands økonomi: En strategi for fremtiden. [Greenland's economy: A strategy for the future]. Landsstyreområdet for Økonomi og Handel Udkast til brug for OECD's komité-møde 17. Maj 1999. OECD.

Padel, F. and Das, S. 2010. *Out of This Earth: East India Adivasis and the Aluminium Cartel*. New Delhi: Orient Blackswan Private Limited.

Peck, J. 2010. *Constructions of Neoliberal Reason*. Oxford: Oxford University Press.

Poppel, B. 2005. Grønlands Hjemmestyre på vej mod selvstændighed? [Greenland's Home Rule Government heading towards independence?], in Geografisk Orientering, 35(6), 280–6.

Schmidt, J.H. and Thrane, M. 2009. Life cycle assessment of aluminium production in new Alcoa smelter in Greenland. Government of Greenland.

Schmitt, P. et al. 2009. The proposed ALCOA aluminium smelter in Greenland: A case study report, in *Knowledge-based Tools for Sustainable Governance of Energy and Climate Adaptation in the Nordic Periphery* (K-Base), edited by J. Hukkinen et al. Nordic Council of Ministers Research Programme Report 7(2009). Stockholm: Nordregio.

The Greenland Home Rule Government and Alcoa Inc. 2007. Memorandum of Understanding between the Greenland Home Rule Government and Alcoa Inc. Government of Greenland.

Winther, G. 2010. A partial reform of the uniform price system and the consequences on households in Greenland settlements, in *The Political Economy of Northern Regional Development*, vol. 1: Tema Nord, edited by G. Winther. Copenhagen: Nordic Council of Ministers, 123–46.

White, R. (ed.) 2009. *Environmental Crime – A Reader*. Portland: Willan Publishing.

Chapter 14
Environmental Harm: Social Causes and Shifting Legislative Dynamics

Sigurd S. Dybing

Pollution has been more or less an integral part of modern industry long before any establishment of solid legislative practice. Over the last 30 years, with various dramatic accidents and scientific warnings, there has been an escalation of risks connected to global economic development and technological progress, all of which affect the conditions of natural resources. Environmental harm has, on a social level therefore, become one of the most acute risks and future threats for the twenty-first century. Herein lies a concern which draws to the surface certain tensions regarding the relationship between protection and exploitation, and highlights the critical fact that most environmental damage is seldom brought into public awareness.

Environmental harm is characterised by a distance between consequences and their causes. In this chapter I will discuss how the development of knowledge may influence the enforcement of law relating to pollution caused by modern industry. The development of knowledge concerns primarily the relationship between humans and nature which has a direct impact upon: a) how pollution affects the environment, b) the relationship between legal and illegal activities and c) how the polluting industries, as well as the control agencies, relate to current legislation. The following three current examples will provide the main empirical framework for the chapter: 1. PCB pollution in the Norwegian fjords, 2. The Deepwater Horizon disaster in the Gulf of Mexico and 3. The Vest Tank explosion in Gulen, Norway. All three cases will exemplify different kinds of pollution which could be described respectively as previously legal pollution which may entail illegal pollution, which may harm the environment; actions that are a disastrous act of omission; and thirdly, actions that are legally defined as environmental crime. The chapter will therefore cover three topics: how we should perceive nature as a part of the modern society, the extent of knowledge and responsibilities of pollution and what strategies are necessary for effective environmental regulation.

Introduction

During the 1970s, scientists and political leaders around the world began to realise that, despite the merits and benefits of certain technological developments, there was also a prospect that the very foundation of human survival could be threatened. However, while political leaders struggled to preserve their national interests within transnational environmental regulations, a number of grassroots movements began to draw attention to the severity and global dimension of the environmental harms coming into existence. This environmental movement was crucial in drawing attention to specific cases through the media, and therefore increasing public awareness of serious environmental catastrophes such as Bhopal, desertification in Africa, the burning of the rain forests, Chernobyl and pollution in general (Benton 1998: 2–3). The early work of the environmental movement in Norway in the late 1980s consisted primarily of civil disobedience, better known as 'barrel-digging'. This involved demonstrations that raised public awareness about how industry tried to hide extremely toxic waste, although industrial leaders denied this was the case.[1]

Before 1970 there were no special agencies that prosecuted environmental polluters in Norway. As a result of increasing pollution during the 1960s and 1970s, several laws designed to control or prohibit particular forms of pollution were introduced. In 1981 these laws were brought together under the 'Norwegian Pollution Law'. This ruled that any form of pollution was illegal unless the necessary permission had been granted. Environmental crime in Norway carries the maximum penalty of 15 years in prison. Violations of the law, however, seldom result in imprisonment or in any prosecution at all. Even if the violations are serious, fines or other sanctions are a much more common regulatory practice. There could be many reasons for this, but the prosecution authorities have rarely considered taking polluters to court (Høviksland, Hansen and Holme 2005).

The consequences of environmental harm could exceed the traditional conception of injurious activities affecting the whole of society. The complexity of tracking pollution makes it difficult to convince the public about the environmental issues at hand (Haagensen and Johansen 1991: 35). This problem is made worse by the fact that the most severe form of environmental harm is caused by normal business activities and is therefore considered 'justified' as a necessary evil of modern society (Beck 2004). The bulk of environmental crime takes place within the framework of legal business activities which makes any kind of supervision much more difficult than in the arena of traditional crime (Høviksland, Hansen and Holme 2005). A fundamental concern within the field of green criminology is how politically, industrially and socially trends harm the environment and how governments tend to protect humans and other species from environmental harm (Lynch 1990: 167). In order to analyse the social causes and legislative dynamics

1 Bellona 2010. About Us [online]. Available at: http://www.bellona.no/Aboutus/Historie [accessed 4 September 2011].

of environmental harm it is therefore useful to 'reappraise traditional notions about what should be seen as serious crimes, offences and injurious behaviours' (South 1998: 441). One approach to this problem as suggested in the green criminology literature by Rob White (2011) is to discuss how environmental pollution actually affects society. White (2011: 32) calls this approach 'horizon scanning' and suggests that it is a suitable method for obtaining insight into potential risks and harms related to environmental pollution. This is insight into the consequences of environmental pollution in both the short term and the long term, thus creating possible opportunities to achieve further developments in much needed areas.

The United Nations Climate Change Conferences have promoted a global awareness about important environmental issues. A massive focus on vague ecological terms such as climate change may, however, lead the discussions into moral dogmatism that is lacking in critical thinking and thus out of keeping with Western notions of secularised democracy (Ferry 1996).

The Norwegian environmental foundation *Bellona* claims that public environmental discussion is too politically fragmented as regards different terms of environmental pollution.[2] How we perceive nature within modern society is crucial to the understanding of how environmental pollution affects society (White 2008). It seems that within the legal system environmental harm is viewed as harm without victims, in the traditional point of view. This means there is a need for green criminologists to work out a new 'victim perspective' capable of reflecting notions of distance regarding the causes and consequences of environmental harm (Haagensen and Johansen 1991: 43, Dybing 2008).

An essential underlying reality is that environmental protection has never been an official central aim for technology and fields related to it. On the contrary, in Western culture the acceptance of environmental damage goes back to the seventeenth century. The belief in technological advancement seemingly set the agenda for society's development, and as an effect, caused long-term damage to the environment (Beck 2004: 81). Nature, it seems, became something abstract, being perceived as an unfamiliar object to be controlled. This created something that could be regarded as non-society (Ferry 1996: 104). This non-society was a waste disposal site for different kinds of environmental poisons. A great deal of the pollution that is causing environmental harm today results from previous business activities.

Perceiving Nature as a Part of Modern Society

The PCB-and Mercury-[3] contaminated fjords around the Norwegian coast-line are an example of damage caused by discharges made in the past when the regulation

2 Interview with Bellona (Dybing 2008: 98).

3 Mercury is a chemical element which often occurs as the toxic mercuric sulphide when disposed of in the environment. Mercury accumulates within organisms and is therefore most dangerous to habitats at the top of a food chain. The most serious effects are

was lenient and there was little experience of the long-term environmental consequences of such toxins.

Today all discharge of PCB is forbidden. Fresh use of PCB was prohibited in 1980 and since then industry has achieved a total discharge reduction of 90 per cent.[4] Even so, all of the larger fjords and port areas in Norway are contaminated with PCB. This toxin is extremely hard to decompose, and when PCB is absorbed by an organism it is almost impossible to dispose of. As we know, within the marine food chains plant plankton is consumed by animal plankton, which is ultimately consumed by bigger fish. As a result of this process the final destination of this toxin is the dinner plate. PCB is omnipresent. A variety of studies have shown that PCBs have significant negative health effects upon humans and animals, including reproductive concerns for women, breast cancer and mortality (Lynch and Stretesky 2003, White 2008). Love Canal, a neighbourhood in Niagara Falls, was completely demolished after numerous incidents of cancer, miscarriages and birth defects. Other cases were also connected to a massive dumping of toxic chemicals that took place one generation earlier. Among these chemicals was PCB (Talmer 1987). Conditions in 17 of the 32 contaminated Norwegian coast areas were so severe that the whole population was dissuaded from consuming any fish liver at all. Further specific advice for each of the areas is given by the Norwegian Food Safety Authority.[5] The Norwegian Food Safety Authority has also introduced general nationwide advice for fish in both salt water and fresh water. Children, women of child-bearing age, pregnant women and breastfeeding mothers are advised against eating fish liver or any fish liver products. The population in general should limit their intake of such food. In particular, they are advised not to eat fish liver from areas that are known to be polluted by PCB. The problem of environmental toxins could be viewed as a heritage from the past, with previous legal and 'safe' activities turning out to have extensive harmful effects. This heritage includes activities that could be disastrous.

On 20 April 2010, BP was responsible for an enormous oil spill in the Gulf of Mexico, along the coast of Florida. One of the companies' leased drilling rigs, Deepwater Horizon, exploded; causing a blow out that poured oil into Gulf for nearly four months. The Deepwater Horizon oil spill exemplifies important

---

damage to the nerve system, damage to the kidneys or allergy. The foetus is at high risk if pregnant women have high levels of mercury. PCB, polychlorinated biphenyls, are a class of organic compounds which are toxic, hard to degrade and bioaccumulating. PCBs have mutagenic effects by interfering with hormones in the body, and may cause several types of cancer and injury to the foetus.

4 Environment 2011. Toxic Chemicals. [State of the environment Norway]. Available at: http://www.miljostatus.no/Tema/Kjemikalier/Noen-farlige-kjemikalier/PCB/#D [accessed 7 December 2011].

5 Environment.no 2007. Fish and Seafood to Avoid. [State of the environment Norway]. Available at: http://www.miljostatus.no/Tema/Hav-og-vann/Pavirkninger-pa-livet-i-vann/Miljogifter_vann/Miljogifter_marint/Kostholdsrad/ [accessed 4 September 2011].

aspects of large-scale environmental harm caused by legal business activities. Environmental harm is more than often caused by legal businesses (Lynch and Stretesky 2003: 517). The Exxon Valdez oil spill off the coast of Alaska or the civil strife and social unrest associated with Shell's operation in Nigeria involve two of the world's biggest oil companies (White 2011: 98). On the other hand, global warming, overfishing, burning of the rainforest and pollution in general do also represent high ecological risks. The imperative for green criminologists should therefore be ecological, not legal (White 2011: 23, Dybing 2008). As the oil spill from the Deepwater Horizon reached the news headlines worldwide, it became clear that BP was facing huge difficulties controlling the blow out. During the weeks and months that followed the explosion, different solutions were tried in order to seal the leak and to reduce the extent of the oil's penetration inland. Due to the depth of the sea, the engineers faced extreme difficulties in closing the leak permanently. The Deepwater Horizon leakage now stands as the worst oil spill accident in history. Until the well was effectively capped in the middle of July, there had been a total of 4.9 million barrels of oil released into the ocean. This disaster resulted in more than 600 miles of oiled shore-line that required cleaning up.[6] Frederic Hauge, the leader of the environmental foundation Bellona, calls the accident the oil industry's Chernobyl, emphasising that it will come to have an effect on people's view of the oil industry, most notably by arousing fears that such accidents will happen again.[7] This statement is borne out by the fact that the social, economic and environmental impact of the BP disaster was used as evidence in the case against test drilling in the vulnerable areas close to the shores in the North of Norway.

The long-term effects of the oil spill are still unknown, and to understand the consequences of this disaster it is essential that we analyse what kinds of actual harm and possible risks that are involved. People living far away from the actual blow out (which happened 5,000 feet below the surface and 80 km from the coast-line) suffered as a result of the explosion.[8] This example of oil that 'disappears' into oceans can be compared with the invisibility of sugar dissolved in a cup of water: even if the oil has apparently disappeared, its presence in effect can still be detected. The oil, even when 'removed', will probably still have serious effects on marine ecosystems. Catastrophes like this illustrate the potential risks connected with the petroleum industry, a realm ordinarily kept away from any public awareness and of which only the social products and benefits are reported

6 Digges C. 2010. US Releases Report on Oil at Sea as Deepwater Horizon Declared Largest Accidental Spill Ever [online]. Available at: http://www.bellona.org/articles/articles_2010/oil_spill_estimates [accessed 4 September 2011].

7 Ask A.O. 2010. Bellona: This is the Oil Industry's Chernobyl Aftenposten [online]. Available at: http://www.aftenposten.no/nyheter/uriks/article3633041.ece [accessed 4 September 2011].

8 Offshore Technology 2010. Macondo Prospect, Gulf of Mexico, *USA* [online]. Available at: http://www.offshore-technology.com/projects/macondoprospect/ [accessed 4 September 2011].

and presented. Accidents could also happen closer to where people live, and could be caused by activities that, while not approved of by the authorities, may not necessarily be viewed as dubious or potentially harmful.

In May 2007 a tank of Cocker Gasoline exploded at Vest Tank in Norway. The gas from the explosion spread through a residential area, resulting in reports of people experiencing dizziness, sickness, headaches and pneumonia weeks after the explosion. In this case it was unclear what was contained in the tank. One year earlier Vest Tank had been hailed by the press as a successful, fast-growing company, known to specialise in the prompt cleansing and processing of waste from the petroleum industry. Ships were standing in line to get their tanks cleaned. The head of the company told the press that they were highly focused on questions of security.[9] In the Vest Tank accident the company gave misleading information about their actual activities. The contents of the tank that exploded are alleged to have been the same material that was dumped in 2006 in the Ivory Coast, causing the deaths of 14 people and injuring upwards of several hundred more. The people living at Gulen were therefore anxious about the effects the gas from Vest Tank would have after the explosion (Lervåg 2010). The Netherland-based company Trafigura, which was responsible for the toxic waste dumping in the Ivory Coast, entered into an agreement with Vest Tank after the dumping, because no other company in the world wanted the toxic waste. Although Vest Tank didn't have authorisation from the Climate and Pollution Agency to deal with this kind of waste, they nonetheless accepted several shiploads of toxic waste in exchange for a sizable profit (Dybing 2008).[10] The Manager of Vest Tank was sentenced to one-and-a-half years' imprisonment, while a consultant in the firm was found not guilty in the Gulating Court of Appeal.[11] Both of the cases were later appealed to the Supreme Court by The Norwegian National Authority for Investigation and Prosecution of Economic and Environmental Crime (ØKOKRIM).[12]

---

9 Klokeide O.E. 2007. Tankers in Line to Vest Tank. *Dagens Næringsliv* [online]. Available at: http://www.dn.no/gasellene/article935399.ece [accessed 4 September 2011].

10 Stensvold T. 2009. Preparing the Vest Tank Case. *Teknisk Ukeblad* [online]. Available at: http://www.tu.no/industri/article223636.ece [accessed 4 September 2011].

11 The manager, a consultant and the owner of Vest Tank were all convicted in The Nordhordland District Court. Both the manager and the owner were sentenced to 18 months' imprisonment, while the consultant was sentenced to 45 days' imprisonment. ØKOKRIM appealed both the acquittal and the sentence of 18 months' imprisonment which they considered was too lenient in such a serious case. The owner got sick so his appeal will come up later.

12 NTB 2011. The Vest Tank Convictions are Appealed in the Supreme Court. *Aftenposten* [online]. Available at: http://www.aftenposten.no/nyheter/iriks/article4145755.ece [accessed 4 September 2011].

KLIF 2011. The Vest Tank Manager is Convicted in the Court of Appeal. [online: Climate and Pollution Agency]. Available at: http://www.klif.no/no/Aktuelt/Nyheter/2011/Mai/Vest-Tank-leder-domt-i-lagmannsretten/ [accessed 4 September 2011].

The Deepwater Horizon and Vest Tank cases exemplify two kinds of sudden discharge of pollution, where one could be described as a disastrous act of omission and the other as a criminal act. Both of the incidents, together with the PCB example, illustrate how environmental harm can appear very differently over time. Everything appears normal until the accidents occur, or new knowledge comes to light. Sudden changes in environmental conditions will always have social repercussions. Toxic spills or oil disasters only serve to reflect how humanity relates to nature and reveals our great dependency upon pure and renewable resources. Communities with limited resources, such as fishing communities, or people living in close proximity to a plant, are in a particularly high-risk group. The aftermath of the Deep Water Horizon disaster meant that many thousands of people whose lives were highly dependent on the sea in one way or another became unemployed almost overnight. There is still much uncertainty around the possibility for future fishing, owing to the long-term effects of such a disaster. Deepwater Horizon exemplifies the economic and other social turbulence environmental harm could cause. BP has so far faced several hundred lawsuits from people that were affected by the accident.[13] Pollution may also have health-related effects upon human beings. The people near Vest Tank became ill of the poisonous gas, and the same substance that exploded in the tank killed and injured several people at the Ivory Coast (White 2008).

Vital to the notion of pollution exposure are the long-term consequences arising from the constant discharge of environmental toxins, and the problem of setting the maximum limits of exposure. Pollution and environmental harm have no national borders and can be transported by humans and by nature itself: when toxic spills 'disappear' into the ocean or into the air they often get absorbed into food chains that will ultimately be consumed by humans. They may be out of sight and out of mind, but still be active. Inuits in Greenland and Canada have a high rate of birth defects owing to seal meat being poisoned with mercury and PCB from the increasing coal and waste burning in Asia.[14] The substance in Vest Tank had been transported from petroleum productions far away from Norway. Different kinds of discharges occurring in one place may affect people and societies miles away from the primary source.

Environmental Harm is Social Harm

Environmental harm illustrates a cultural contradiction where a belief in technological progress is in conflict with nature. This contradiction has encouraged an industrial trend whose consequences could exceed the traditional concept of

---

13 BP Lawsuit 2010. Over 300 BP Lawsuits Filed So Far in Federal Court [online] Available at: http://www.bplawsuit.net/?p=151 [accessed 4 September 2011].

14 Grønli K.S. 2002. A Serious Problem with Pollution in the Arctic [online: Forskning.no] Available at: http://www.forskning.no/Artikler/2002/oktober/1033995081.81 [accessed 4 September 2011].

social destruction (Beck 2004). This notion is supported by the fact that nature has been given an economic utility value (Halsey and White 1998: 211). The potential value of actually protecting the environment has not yet been considered as anything to invest in. An important issue within the environmental debate is therefore the tension between short-term and long-term consequences; that is to say, the question of what we understand by *distance*. In this tug-of-war the certain profit of exploitation disappears because of more general environmental protection. It can be difficult to measure the meaning of environmental harm. However, if environmental protection was given an economic value, perhaps this would simplify the issue of how we regard the relationship between nature and society (White 2008). Earlier environmental protection issues have not been a particularly lucrative proposition. Accordingly, companies have focused their business activities and pursuits in the light of this reality. In addition to the immediate scene of destruction therefore, environmental harm does not only affect animals, plants and trees, but its repercussions can also be detected in the economic value of a region (Beck 2004). The twenty-first century has shown that people do not fully realise the meaning of the fact that resources are finite, and that, most importantly, nature is a vital part of the society. Be it air, water or earth, any changes regarding environmental conditions will have consequences, and the consequences will have an impact upon human beings, other animals and the World's ecosystems. The three examples discussed above have shown that the consequences of environmental harm can be divided into three types of impacts: environmental, social and economic (see also White 2008).

The concept of the 'environmental victim' raises the notions of time and space onto an ecological and environmental level. Nature is inherent to any civilisation, and humans can be perceived as just one component of many complex ecosystems inhabiting the earth (White 2008: 4–23). Despite the fact that some communities and some people will be more vulnerable than others, the general consequences cannot be restricted to certain individuals. Vulnerability to environmental damage is widespread and multifarious with impacts upon biological elements, locations and of course society in which women and children feature particularly as a high-risk group (Beck 2004, Williams 1996). The poorer a country is in terms of economy, legislation or democracy, the greater the impact of environmental problems on the people (White 2008, Beck 2004, Yanitsky 2009). Environmental harm could therefore be boiled down to include a communal view, a global view and a temporal view (White 2008). The environmental issue could be regarded as a universal fate where we may all, somehow, be affected. But the notion of a universal fate does not help to explain the crooked distribution of knowledge and power. This issue will be discussed further in the next section.

This section has demonstrated that nature is a fundamental part of society. Environmental pollution will always affect humans, as is highlighted by the numbers of serious accidents causing sudden health problems and financial loss, at times far away from the actual source of pollution. The real harmful effects, it seems, evolve over time and are not as obvious as the immediate fall out which occurs after such huge accidents. Although the use of certain environmental toxins has stopped, the previous legal use still represents a health risk for both present and future generations. The concept of distance is essential to an understanding of the legislative dynamics of environmental harm, and it is necessary to develop this area of knowledge regarding how modern business activities affect the environment.

The Extent of Knowledge and Responsibilities

Environmental harm is certainly social harm, but the cultural distance between the consequences and causes of the harm actually helps to exclude environmental protection from current political agendas. Small societies with limited sources of food will be more interested in protecting their vital natural resources than modern societies where the relationship to nature is more remote (White 2008, Yanitsky 2009). It could be useful to see how knowledge is distributed through society: knowledge about how pollution and environmental harm could affect society, knowledge about polluting industries and, more important, the government's knowledge *of* and relationship *to* these industries. In this section I discuss how the extent of knowledge affects the regulation of environmental pollution.

Regulation is mainly carried out by control agencies. Industry also provides the control agencies with useful information about their activities (Dybing 2008). The control agencies use marginal values for how much environmental pollution is acceptable (Beck 2004: 72). These marginal values are based on scientific considerations that are unknown to the public and there are often institutional disagreements about interpretations of these levels. The greyness of this legal area and the fact that modern business has a tradition of neglecting rules and regulations means that a traditional legal practice is poorly equipped to handle the complexities surrounding environmental crime. This is what leads to most actions that one would regard as meriting punishment remaining unprosecuted.

The potential risks connected with environmental harm are often hidden, and developed over time. Pollution has different sources, it is discharged differently and pollution is geographically scattered. Health problems can become apparent gradually, often emerging through the generations. For example, although the Norwegian government issues advice on eating seafood, it is difficult to be sure how much poison Norwegian citizens actually consume.

People living near a polluting plant or who are in contact with toxic materials on a regular basis may be aware of the potential health risks, but may not have the power to do anything about their living environment. Public awareness of the consequences of environmental pollution has also increased during the last 20 years. However, potential victims have difficulty in knowing exactly what contaminants are being released, or even how human bodies will react when certain toxins are absorbed. It is almost impossible to know whether companies are genuinely trying to reduce the risks of accidents like Vest Tank and Deepwater Horizon. Here we can see a co-dependent relationship between the potential victims, the legislative authorities, the polluter and science (Beck 2004: 72). The population has to trust that the legislative judgements carried out by the authorities are based on safe scientific considerations. The authorities have to trust that the information provided to them by the companies is correct. A case in point is the Vest Tank case: when a company is dishonest about their activity it makes trustworthy and reasonable regulations even more difficult to establish. The risks with PCB were similarly kept disguised. Despite being aware of the levels of toxicity, the manufacturers of PCB neither informed the paint-manufacturers, the shipyards nor the government about the potential environmental risks involved, knowing well that PCB used in ship painting increases the risk of harm to humans and animals. The environmental danger of PCB was known in 1966 and confirmed in 1967. It was well known even in the 1950s that the product was extremely toxic and very difficult to degrade.[15]

The Complexity of Liability

Further complications can arise when published sources of information about a situation differ radically. The examples of PCB, Deepwater Horizon and Vest Tank have revealed that contradictory information was issued, and that it is unclear where the responsibility lies. It is not unusual for information given by the authorities and information provided by independent scientific institutions to contradict one another. The US authorities claimed that the oil from the Deepwater Horizon was rapidly dispersing. Scientists from Wood Hole Oceanographic Institution, however, claimed that this was not the fact.[16] Furthermore, the long-term ecological effects of chemicals that were used to break down the oil were also under scrutiny, since they had never been applied so extensively before.[17] The Norwegian Society for the Conservation of Nature/Friends of the Earth Norway claims that the toxic level in Norwegian seafood is higher than official state estimates and that the authorities refuse to take into account the fact that humans are exposed to different kinds of toxins at the same time (Dybing 2008: 87). The Norwegian health authorities tried to play down the health-related consequences after the Vest Tank explosion, claiming that the health problems were primary stress related, despite the local doctor having reported numerous occurrences of pneumonia. Soil tests to check for chemical leakage were not carried out until four weeks after the explosion.

15 NSFCFEN 2001. The PCB Cleanup and the Producer Responsibility [online: The Norwegian Society for the Conservation of Nature/Friends of the Earth Norway]. Available at: http://naturvernforbundet.no/imakerdata/f/0/59/29/4_2401_0/rapport.no.pdf [accessed 4 September 2011].

16 Spilde I. 2010. The Oil is Still There [online]. Available at: http://www.forskning.no/artikler/2010/august/257927 [accessed 4 September 2011].

17 Digges C. 2010. US Releases Report on Oil at Sea as Deepwater Horizon Declared Largest Accidental Spill Ever [online]. Available at: http://www.bellona.org/articles/articles_2010/oil_spill_estimates [accessed 4 September 2011].

A comprehensive examination of the health consequences from the chemicals is expected to be completed in 2013. The previous examples identify a tendency among governments to ignore important environmental information about specific incidents. The various authorities responsible for the regulation of Vest Tank have been criticised for a lack of vigour: it has been claimed that the trust in Vest Tank was too extensive both before and after the accident. The Norwegian Coastal Administration, the Norwegian Customs and Excise Department, the Directorate for Civil Protection and Emergency Planning, the Climate and Pollution Agency and the local council at Gulen all cooperated together to perform their various regulatory tasks which were designed to prevent such an accident, or at least reduce the harm it would cause (Lervåg 2010). As one might expect, it is difficult to sort out the responsibilities here as regards environmental protection. In the case of Vest Tank there were many people involved who had different tasks and this made it difficult to assign responsibility, and, furthermore, complicated the distribution of information. Vest Tank was actually breaking the law *before* the explosion occurred but the information about the early investigations show that state environmental oversight is difficult. The responsibilities are divided between different participants over a period of time. Investigations of the Deepwater Horizon accident indicate that even if the actual technical cause of the blow out was a defective valve on the sea-bed, there were several sources suggesting that blame lay more with company structure.[18] BP was the main company responsible for the disaster and in 2010 set up a fund of 50 billion dollars to pay for the clean-up and compensate for the economic loss to the victims.[19] In an attempt to spread the blame, BP sued its partners for billions of dollars.[20] Repudiation of liability is quite common in pollution cases involving several participants and (sometimes conflicting) interests. Politics, business and technology form a complex of connections that make it almost impossible to pursue questions of guilt, even if the environmental consequences are obvious (Beck 2004). In 2003 the government in Oslo filed a 50 million NOK (Norwegian Krone) claim against Bayer AG, Solutia and Kaneka Corporation and demanded that the producers should be held responsible for the environmental harm PCB had caused, and that they should economically contribute to the cleaning up.[21] PCB leaves chemical fingerprints,

18 Takla E. 2011. The Error that Led to the Deepwater Horizon Catastrophe. *Dagens Næringsliv* [online]. Available at: http://www.dn.no/energi/article2109381.ece [accessed 4 September 2011].

19 Bryan V., Carter J.L 2010. BP to Raise $50 Billion for Oil Spill Costs: Report. *Reuters* [online]. Available at: http://www.reuters.com/article/2010/06/20/us-bp-times-idUSTRE65J10G20100620 [accessed 4 September 2011].

20 Ørstavik L.J 2011. BP Files Suits. *Aftenposten* [online]. Available at: http://www.aftenposten.no/okonomi/article4099993.ece [accessed 4 September 2011].

21 MJ 2003. City of Oslo Launches Claim Against PCB Producers [online: *Maritime Journal*]. Available at: http://www.maritimejournal.com/features101/marine-civils/port,-harbour-and-marine-construction/cityof_oslo_launches_claim_against_pcb_producers [accessed 4 September 2011].

meaning that PCB in the environment can be traced back to its initial source. The economic claims established an important principle, directing attention to the idea that producers should be held responsible even if they act within the law.[22] The PCB manufacturers refused the demands and no lawsuit followed. These examples illustrate how difficult it is to hold polluters legally responsible for the environmental damage they may cause.

Since prosecutions are rather rare it is necessary to isolate and analyse what kind of actions actually lead to prosecution.

The Legislative Dynamics

Norwegian control agencies frequently discover irregularities when they carry out inspections. During 2010 the Climate and Pollution Agency in Norway carried out 1,670 inspections. 60 per cent of those inspections found irregularities, defined as anything from an unsigned paper to a chemical discharge. Most often these irregularities are a matter of incorrect procedures. The important point here is that pollution accidents are not inevitable events (De Prez 2000: 398). Criminal corporate actions seldom result in prosecutions or formal complaints (Næss 1993: 75). They are generally subject to economic or administrative sanctions (Nyborg, Telle and Walle 2003).[23]

The three harshest penalties for environmental crime in Norway have similarities worth studying further. In November 2004 the Supreme Court imposed the first of these when two business managers were sentenced to 45 days' imprisonment and a fine of 150,000 NOK each for violation of the pollution law. The company had discharged substantial amounts of copper and heavy metals into a fjord and ammonia into the air, and an area of woods several hundred metres behind the production factory were damaged by the chemical discharges. The second penalty, for an intentional environmental crime, was handed down by the Agder Court of Appeal in 2006, when a business manager was sentenced three years in prison. He was also given a fine of 4 million NOK. The company managed a toxic waste disposal site, and discharged water mixed with chemicals and oil directly into the local sewer, causing the formation of toxic gas. The toxic release forced a school to close down for a period of time. The company was also convicted for fraud against the Climate and Pollution Agency (former SFT) and for swindling some of the company's own customers (Dybing 2008). Third is the Vest Tank accident. The tank exploded close to a populated area and caused serious health problems for many people. The injury associated with the Vest incident makes it the most

22 NRK 2003. Claims for Damages after Discharge of PCB [online]. Available at: http://www.nrk.no/nyheter/distrikt/ostlandssendingen/1.353301 [accessed 4 September 2011].

23 Nyborg K., Telle K., Walle M.A. 2003. Norwegian Companies Violate the Environmental Regulations [online]. Available at: http://www.ssb.no/emner/08/05/10/oa/200302/telle.pdf [accessed 4 September 2011].

comprehensive form of environmental crime and the one that has received the most media attention in Norway.

All three cases mentioned above involve toxic waste disposal. Waste disposal is a lucrative area to make money and for legal businesses to benefit from illegal waste management, by subcontracting (White 2011: 83). This suggests that companies may be able to get rid of toxins in ways that are considered legal, meaning that the companies have no further responsibility for possible environmental consequences. Safe treatment of toxic waste is absolutely necessary for the environment. Aside from the potential harms it can cause, toxic waste is also something from which money can be made. This of course opens up possibilities for corrupt business activities. Unlike traditional forms of illegal activity, this crime carries little risk of 'being caught'. All the three cases mentioned in this chapter involve companies that over a long period of time were responsible for the corrupt management of waste; they avoided the power of the control agencies, and were guilty of breaking several laws.

An important point to reiterate here is that, aside from the actual environmental consequences arising from industries, green criminologists should be aware of the fact that the problem is not the law or the enforcement of powers, it is rather that environmental protection is not built into legal practice (White 2008: 92). The temporal considerations of environmental pollution makes it difficult to perform causal scientific judgments about one minor incident and relate it to the total sum of environmental harms (Beck 2004). It is even harder when violations are often administrative and have not yet led to any serious incidents.

Getting a Raw Deal as Regards Power and Enlightenment?

The media of course is an important source of knowledge about environmental issues. How knowledge about environmental harm is conveyed through the media may determine public awareness and influence how people react to actual social causes. As mentioned earlier it is therefore crucial what terms and descriptions are being used (White 2008: 41). Unfamiliar technical terms and formal language may make environmental issues appear confusing.

Knowledge about the social consequences and causes of waste, pollution and the relationship between humankind and nature are vital. However, the dissemination of knowledge is not helped by scientific disagreements, political and economical contradictions and limited printing space which can lead to fragmented news stories that mislead the public on important social issues (Yanitsky 2009). The media coverage of the accidents at Vest Tank and Deepwater Horizon did indeed highlight important structural weaknesses within modern businesses and publicise the work of the control agencies, and also the potential environmental damages modern business activities may cause. However, it may also be possible that these incidents, where scapegoats are available, could make the causes look unique. This means that only when there is a blatant violation of the law or catastrophic incident, such as the BP incident and Vest Tank, can the media be relied on to give it attention.

This means that more legalised forms of destructive business activities escape question (White 2008: 197). The structural basis of environmental harm remains unchanged and public awareness is reduced by the fact that the consequences are not immediate and by a fragmented distribution of knowledge that affect the relations of power (Beck 2004). It is useful to investigate how the legal industry is actually situated regarding questions about security and regulations.

Traditional Negligence

Despite the fact that some incidents appear exceptional and blatant, there are obvious tendencies among all modern businesses to seek profit by neglecting safety issues (Mintz 1987: 38). Modern industry is generally negligent regarding regulation (Braithwaite 1994: 309). A string of illegal actions become an institutionalised routine throughout various industries (Simon 2000: 172). When decisions are initiated in an operation based on such practices, human beings are reduced to mere digits in an arithmetic problem. This arithmetic problem must be solved with the most rational solution (Dowie 1987: 20). This solution tends to neglect security issues and to stretch the safety regulations. Even if violations discovered by the control agencies are corrected, it is worthwhile for the company to carry on with the violations until they are instructed to make improvements (Walle 2003). There are many and various reasons why environmental laws are violated. The company may not be aware of the existing legislation or may prefer to operate in a grey area (Dimento 1986: 19–22). A country may also be negligent when enforcing transnational environmental directives (Wennerås 2007: 1–2). One approach to this issue is to see if the violation is an isolated case or a part of a larger measure of illegal activity (Dimento 1986: 178).

During the autumn of 2010 Norway's Statoil had to shut down 50 drilling-wells in the Gullfaks field in the North Sea as a safety precaution. Only in February 2011 did Statoil inform the public about the incident. Although the company was not obliged to report the incidents, the Norwegian Petroleum Safety Authority (PSA) claimed that they should have been informed owing to the large number of wells involved.[24] In May 2010 PSA stated that a disaster was only just avoided when another well went out of control, also at the Gullfaks field.[25] After investigating the incident PSA identified certain serious flaws in the company's security systems

24 Harbo H., Barstad S. 2011. 50 Wells Closed at the Gullfaks Field. *Aftenposten* [online]. Available at: http://www.aftenposten.no/okonomi/innland/article4010709.ece [accessed 4 September 2011].

25 PSA 2011. Gullfaks C: A Close Call Downhole [online: Petroleum Safety Agency Norway]. Available at: http://www.ptil.no/nyheter/naere-paa-for-gullfaks-c-article7606-24.html [accessed 4 September 2011].

and thereafter issued a notice of injunction.[26] A notice of injunction will not have any legal effect, unless the company fails to remedy the flaws.

One of the main challenges faced by the field of environmental protection is the fact that harmful actions are often profitable. This means that it is economically beneficial to damage the environment. The economic significance of environmental harm is therefore important as regards the goods that industry provides to society (White 2008). When the economic crisis hit the world in 2007 the Norwegian government poured billions into Norwegian industries. Environmental issues, however, seem to get put onto the back burner. Law enforcement has a political dimension. Everyday enforcement of environmental protection legislation is influenced by the concerns currently occupying society (Dimento 1986: 65). The leader of The Norwegian Confederation of Trade Unions (LO), Roar Flåthen, claimed in June 2011 that the climate agreement in Norway was too expensive and problematic to fulfil.[27] The goal is to reduce two-thirds of Norway's total emission of greenhouse gases, on Norwegian territory, by the end of 2030.[28] The union leader is obviously afraid that possible legislation and its requirements could force companies to register abroad or be less competitive on international business markets, and thus create unemployment in Norway. This example supports a basic premise of green criminology: the considerations of economic development have always been more important than environmental protection (Lynch and Stretesky 2003: 521). Another point is that transnational companies spend a considerable amount of money to influence legislation and political decisions (Simon 2000: 180–181). An even greater problem is the fact that what are at issue are actions that are viewed as accepted behaviour within mainstream society (White 2008).

The previous discussion about the fragmentation of knowledge showed that it is complicated to single out a source of pollution. It is almost impossible for humans to know how exposed they are. Environmental pollution is characterised by an interdependent relationship between politics, science, industry and the public. This interdependence could be seen as reducing the public's power and knowledge because they do not actually know what legislative decisions pollution control agencies rely on. It is incredibly difficult to prosecute those responsible for pollution. The official control agencies have a dual role, because they ought to protect both current and future generations from environmental harm, while providing good conditions in terms of business activities.

26 PSA 2010. Notification of Order to Statoil-Gullfaks C [online: The Petroleum Safety Authority Norway]. Available at:http://www.ptil.no/nyheter/varsel-om-paalegg-til-statoil-gullfaks-c-article7408-24.html [accessed 4 September 2011].

27 Hornburg T.B. 2011. LO: Reducing CO2 is Too Expensive. *Aftenposten* [online]. Available at: http://www.aftenposten.no/nyheter/iriks/article4142335.ece [accessed 4 September 2011].

28 Government.no 2008. A National Climate Agreement [online]. Available at: http://www.regjeringen.no/en/dep/md/pressesenter/pressemeldinger/2008/enighet-om-nasjonal-klimadugnad.html?id=496878 [accessed 4 September 2011].

A Public Legislative Perspective

In the final section I will focus on the purpose of environmental regulation and discuss the possibilities for more effective control. I will also discuss what kind of role the environmental movement should have in future environmental regulations. This latter area is a key component and an area calling for further discussion.

Regulation strategies may be seen as having one of two sets of justifications (Larsson 2002: 39). A structural justification will focus on the social position of the authority, its relation to the company, victims, political support from the government and the relation to other agencies such as the police force. The other form of justification is that of principal, and of the ethical use of sanctions. The basic concern is with how regulations function in relation to public security and with ethical and juridical limitations regarding the regulation (Larsson 2002: 39). In this respect we can see exactly how crucial environmental damage is to the setting of regulations.

Even if sanctions are considered as safeguards for both individuals and the public, an unrestrained use of sanctions could be counter-productive as regards law enforcement (Braithwaite 1984: 290). Companies may respond to the sanctions by using political and legal means and start to resist the authority rather than adapt to the law. The result could be that the legitimacy of the law is put into question (Dimento 1986: 72). The state authorities cannot make activities illegal or tighten regulations without public awareness and support (Lea 2002: 9).

A combination of sanctions, from punishment to suspension of permits, has shown to be an effective way to change structural misbehaviour (Braithwaite and Fisse 1993: 191, Larsson 2002: 51, Ayres and Braithwaite 1992). To suspend permits is a strong measure and could force a company to shut down its activities for a period of time. The success of enforcement should not be measured in formal complaints and prosecutions. Successful law enforcement should actually lead to affirmative changes for the environment (Dimento 1986: 164).

Unlike traditional crime, punishment for corporate misbehaviour is presumed to have preventive results. The presumption is that business managers are law-abiding citizens, and they certainly do not wish to be portrayed as criminals. Punishment could also be a signal from society that a sloppy attitude towards safety is not acceptable, even if the company has a good reputation overall. Corporate cultures have revealed themselves to be open to change, due to the corporate fear of criminal legislation (Braithwaite and Fisse 1993: 161). The general manager of BP, who was responsible for the Deepwater Horizon accident, had to answer all the criticisms and became the public symbol of the company which had caused the enormous damage. After all the incidents in the Gullfaks field PSA took the extraordinary step of calling in Statoil's leader at the Norwegian shelf to personally answer questions about safety. This also received huge media-coverage.[29] The leaders of a huge company are often far away from those who get injured by their decisions.

Employees have publicly criticised a lack of focus on security within Statoil.[30] The environmental foundation Bellona has claimed that there were several points of similarity between the Deepwater Horizon and Gullfaks incidents.[31] One way to regulate exposure limits and to reduce the risk of an accident is to improve the working environment. The Deepwater Horizon explosion killed 11 workers on the oil rig, and in addition to this there have been increasing numbers of cases of poisoning, cancer and death caused by prolonged exposure to, for instance, benzene among the oil workers at the Echofish at the North Sea.[32] Thus, Bellona points out, improving the working environment will have positive effects on the environment outside it. One explanation for this could be that working conditions have always been connected to certain types of risks, meaning that if a working environment is poor, the environment outside it may also be poor (Dybing 2008: 61).

The cases mentioned above demonstrate a general negligence amongst companies as to the observance of strict rules and regulations. Sometimes it takes more than the control agencies to make a company responsible for its actions. By means of a class action several people suffering similar losses or injuries may combine to sue a company; however, big companies often have millions to defend themselves with. Civil actions are therefore frequently seen as the best way to proceed because the plaintiffs have little to worry about regarding financial loss. As corporations grow more massive this could be a good means to redress the structural balance when dealing with a huge and powerful industry (Braithwaite 1994: 347). Even if civil cases are less time-consuming and demand less proof, a reason to take polluters to court is to indicate that the authorities consider environmental crime as a serious offence (Dimento 1986: 50). A cunning part of an effective regulation could be to refuse to inform companies which kind of offences may result in prosecution and which will be dealt with by means of other sanctions (Dimento 1986).

The environmental movement in Norway has for the last two decades fought to get publicity about the way in which modern business culture affects the environment, both in terms of its legal and illegal operations. Part of the movement functions in close connection with the companies to ensure that it can have some influence on the companies' decisions. NGOs can inform companies about the

29 Bjerke E. 2011. Reprimand of a Statoil leader. *Dagens Næringsliv* [online]. Available at: http://www.dn.no/energi/article2109781.ece [accessed 4 September 2011].

30 Hornburg T.B., Foss A.B., Harbo H. 2011. Statoil Employees Turn their Backs to their Own Safety Deputy. *Aftenposten* [online]. Available at: http://www.aftenposten.no/okonomi/innland/article4033453.ece [accessed 4 September 2011]

31 Vargel A. 2010. From the Gulf to the Gullfaks [online: Bellona]. Available at: http://www.bellona.no/nyheter/nyheter_2010/golfen_gullfaks [accessed 4 September 2011].

32 Hansen A. 2005. – I Pressured the Oil Industry. *Dagbladet* [online]. Available at: http://www.dagbladet.no/nyheter/2005/11/08/448719.html [accessed 4 September 2011].

norms and the responsibilities involved in environmental protection systems, and even about ways to become more environmentally sustainable in the future. It is crucial that the government assists such groups as these (Dimento 1986: 182). The government, for instance, could make it easier to communicate and publicise vital environmental information, and eventually allow the environmental movement to contribute to law enforcement.

The environmental movement in Norway possesses expert knowledge about modern industries, their social impact and the controlling agencies. The prosecuting authority state that formal complaints delivered by the environmental movement are mainly professional. The Climate and Pollution Agency possesses official expert knowledge about pollution and influences the prosecution authority's decisions on whether a case should be prosecuted or not. One dilemma concerning the official control agencies is that they have political guidelines requiring them to protect and preserve both society and industry, which is a kind of setting the fox to mind the geese scenario (Dybing 2008). However, a possibility for NGOs to take companies to court could be a solution to this dilemma (Wennerås 2007). People both inside and outside a company should become more motivated to pay attention to the law, and should be supported when they do so (Dimento 1986: 183). However, Braithwaite and Fisse (1993: 163) discuss an extension of criminal liability, and this means going further than the general manager, or the individuals directly responsible for the action. In the case of Vest Tank those responsible for the explosion got prosecuted. If the case is to make internal routines more effective in preventing violations, there needs to be an extension of liability. A case in point is the issue of what responsibility the PCB producers have when they know about the dangers of the material.

Vital Public Information

Even if the state authorities have a wide range of legislative tools, the public ultimately needs to be involved in enforcement. Criminalisation cannot be controlled solely by the state (Lea 2002: 7). Solutions to environmental problems are hard to put into effect without thinking and acting (Ferry 1996: 157). Awareness could therefore be a catalyst for social control. It is, as Rob White (2011: 117–22) points out, crucial whose voices are going to be heard, and what kind of evidence is given credibility. Scientific evidence of environmental harm is often contested. There are a lot of individuals and interests associated with environmental disputes. Real stories and accounts of victims, together with epidemiological data and medical records, and the use of localised knowledge, could gain a public awareness about environmental harm. Consider the 'Good Neighbour Agreements' where local newspapers impart regular news and documentations about local companies (Williams 1996: 326). The environmental movements provide useful information through the internet or their own magazines, but this information does not reach the ordinary public, except when the media sensationalises the situation into disastrous proportions (White 2008).

Society depends entirely upon sound judgements regarding risks in the development of environmental regulations. This development creates a tight bond between industries, science and the legislative power (Beck 2004). The cases that most frequently lead to prosecution are incidents with similarities to traditional crime, or those with an obvious connection between the causes and consequences.

The Cultural Concept of Knowledge and Distance

Environmental harm can cause severe social destruction and individual distress. One of the key differences between environmental harm and harm to human beings relates to the distance from the consequences. This distance has been culturally accepted because of trust in technological progress and because of unawareness of corporate negligence to questions of security and law. The social benefits gained from modern technology have been deemed more advantageous than the potential and intrinsic environmental disadvantages.

Destructive behaviours by industries are actually normal business practice although these sorts of conducts have devastating consequences for the environment, which often prove to have fatal outcomes. Despite such consequences, the enforcement of environmental laws is complicated because it's founded on a traditional concept of justice. A wider environmental competence and a new conception of jurisdiction is required to meet the need for a transnational environmental protection: 'Competence is essential. It is a vast field'.[33] Formerly, the industry and the official control agencies were the suppliers of information used in court and in control practice. The environmental movement has been almost the only provider of independent information in this 'battle'.

To analyse how distance reduces knowledge and empathy in the social consciousness may be a useful approach when attempting to understand public reactions to environmental harm. Bauman (1998) has showed how bureaucratisation in modern societies leads to the alienation of the individual and consequential breakdown of social relations, thus compounding the need for a foundation of moral and empathetic modalities. It is necessary to underline the fact that environmental harm is not an intentional outcome, irrespective of how cynical some isolated events may appear. However, Bauman, in this context, suggests that the distance of consequences explains how people can carry out actions that cause enormous damage to the environment, despite that fact that the likely consequences are obvious.

In this chapter I have discussed the development of knowledge about environmental pollution in terms of power relations and have suggested distance as a useful concept to contextualise the social causes of environmental harm. The concept of distance is the most crucial characteristic of environmental harm which makes it markedly different from traditional understandings of harm. The purpose

33 Interview with The Norwegian Prosecution Authority (Dybing 2008: 78).

of sustainable development is to ensure that environmental regulation meets social needs both economically and existentially. The absence of a balanced focus on the core issues of environmental protection may have real social consequences for humans and other beings, in the present and most certainly in the future. Actions that for decades were viewed as normal business practice are now forbidden. The scope of environmental regulation should therefore also include initiatives to raise public awareness about harmful activities. Arousing public consciousness is vital for effective environmental regulation and protection, and it is important to address these issues from a green criminological perspective.

References

Bauman, Z. 1998. *Moderniteten og Holocaust* [*Modernity and the Holocaust*]. Oslo: Vidarforlagets kulturbibliotek.

Beck, U. 2004. *Risikosamfundet – På vej mod en ny modernitet.* [*Risk Soceity – Towards a New Modernity*]. Copenhagen: Hans Reitzels Forlag A/S. 4th Edition.

Beck, U. 1998. *Risksamhället: På väg mot en annan modernitet.* [*Risk Soceity – Towards a New Modernity*]. Gothenburg: Bokförlaget Daidalos AB.

Benton, T. 1998. Rights and Justice on a Shared Planet: More Rights or New Relations?, in *Theoretical Criminology*, May 1998, vol. 2 (2), 149–75.

Braithwaite, J. 1985. *To Punish or Persuade. Enforcement of Coal Mine Safety.* New York: State University of New York Press, Albany.

Braithwaite, J. 1984. *Corporate Crime in the Pharmaceutical Industry*. London and Boston: Routledge & Kegan, Paul.

Braithwaite, J. and Fisse, B. 1993. *Corporations, Crime and Accountability.* Cambridge: Cambridge University Press.

Christophersen, J.G. and Johansen, P.O. 1991. Forurensing som tradisjon [Pollution as a Tradition], in *Studier i Økonomisk Kriminalitet* [*Studies in Economic Crime*] edited by P.O. Johansen and J.G. Christophersen et al. Oslo: Department of Criminology and Criminal Justice.

Dimento, J.F. 1986. *Environmental Law and American Business: Dilemmas of Compliance*. New York; London: Plenum Press.

Dowie, M. 1987. Pinto Madness, in *Corporate Violence – Injury and Death for Profit*, edited by S.L. Hills. New Jersey: Rowman & Littlefield.

Dybing, S.S. 2008. *Et akseptert skjebnefellesskap. En kriminologisk analyse av miljøfiendtlige handlinger* [*An Accepted Fellowship of Fate. A Criminological Analysis of Environmental Hostile Actions*] Oslo: Department of Criminology and Sociology of Law.

Ferry, L. 1996. *Ny økologisk orden. Treet, dyret og mennesket* [*The New Ecological Order. Trees, Animals and Men*]. Oslo: Tiden Norsk Forlag.

Halsey, M. and White, R. 1998. Crime, Eco-philosophy and Environmental Harm, in *Green Criminology*, edited by N. South and P. Beirne (2006). Hampshire: Ashgate Publishing Limited.

Høviksland, H.T., Hansen, R.B. and Holme, J. 2005. *Hva er miljøkriminalitet? Håndbok i bekjempelse av miljøkriminalitet* [*What is Environmental Crime? A Guide to Combat Environmental Crime*], edited by H.T. Høviksland. Oslo: Økokrim.

Haagensen, K. and Johansen, P.O. 1991. Økonomisk kriminalitet: En innføring. [Economical Crime: An Introduction], in *Studier i Økonomisk Kriminalitet* [Studies in Economical Crime], edited by P.O. Johansen and J.G. Christophersen et al. Oslo: Department of Criminology and Criminal Justice.

Larsson, P. 2002. *Straffe, Veilede eller Overtale? En studie av fire tilsynsmyndigheters reguleringsstrategier* [*To Punish, Supervise or Persuade. A Study of the Regulation Strategies of Four Regulation Authorities*]. Oslo: The Council of Crime Prevention.

Lea, J. 2002. *Crime & Modernity: Continuities in Left realist Criminology*. London: Sage Publications.

Lervåg, K. 2010. *Tilsyn uten ansvar* [*Supervision without Responsibility*]. Bergen: The Stein Rokkan Centre of Multidisciplinary Social Studies.

Lynch, M.J. 1990. The Greening of Criminology: A Perspective on the 1990s, Critical Criminologist, in *Green Criminology*, edited by N. South, and P. Beirne (2006). Hampshire: Ashgate Publishing Limited.

Lynch, M.J. and Stretesky, P. 2003. The Meaning of Green: Contrasting Criminological Perspectives, in *Green Criminology*, edited by N. South, and P. Beirne (2006). Hampshire: Ashgate Publishing Limited.

Mintz, M. 1987. At Any Cost: Corporate Greed, Women, and the Dalkon Shield, in *Corporate Violence – Injury and Death for Profit*, edited by S.L. Hills. New Jersey: Rowman & Littlefield.

Næss, S. 1993. Straff for industriforurensing: Om håndhevelse av den alminnelige *straffebestemmelsen i forurensingsloven* [Penalties for industrial pollution: About enforcement of the general penal provisions of the Pollution Control Act]. Norway: Institute for public and international law, Oslo University.

De Prez, P. 2000. Excuses, Excuses: The Ritual Trivialisation of Environmental Prosecutions, in *Green Criminology*, edited by N. South and P. Beirne (2006). Hampshire: Ashgate Publishing Limited.

Simon, D.R. 2000. Corporate Environmental Crimes and Social Inequality, in *Green Criminology*, edited by N. South and P. Beirne (2006). Hampshire: Ashgate Publishing Limited.

South, N. 1998. A Green Field for Criminology? A Proposal for a Perspective, Theoretical Criminology, in *Green Criminology*, edited by N. South and P. Beirne (2006). Hampshire: Ashgate Publishing Limited.

Talmer, M. 1987. Chemical Dumping as a Corporate Way of Life, in *Corporate Violence – Injury and Death for Profit*, edited by S.L Hills (1987). New Jersey: Rowman & Littlefield.

Walle, M.A. 2003. *Overholder bedriftene i Norge miljøreguleringen?* [*Do Norwegian companies comply with environmental regulation?*] Oslo, Norge: Statistisk Sentralbyrå.

Wennerås, P. 2007. *The Enforcement of EC Environmental Law*. Oxford University Press.

White, R. 2002. Environmental Harm and the Political Economy of Consumption, Theoretical Criminology, in *Green Criminology*, edited by N. South and P. Beirne (2006). Hampshire: Ashgate Publishing Limited.

White, R. 2008. *Crimes Against Nature. Environmental Criminology and Ecological Justice.* Willan Publishing.

White, R. 2011. *Transnational Environmental Crime. Toward an Eco-global Criminology.* London and New York: Routledge. Taylor & Francis Group.

Williams, C. 1996. An Environmental Victimology, Social Justice, in *Green Criminology*, edited by N. South and P. Beirne (2006). Hampshire: Ashgate Publishing Limited.

Yanitsky, O.N. 2009. *The Shift of Environmental Debates in Russia* [online: Current Sociology. SAGE Pub]. Available at: http://csi.sagepub.com/cgi/content/abstract/57/6/747 [accessed 4 September 2011].

Chapter 15

Enacting Human and Non-human Indigenous:[1] Salmon, Sami and Norwegian Natural Resource Management[2]

Gro Birgit Ween

Introduction

> In the last decades, the world-wide population of wild Atlantic salmon has decreased as much as 75 percent. Also the Norwegian Atlantic salmon population has been dramatically reduced. A consequence of the comparatively larger decline in wild Atlantic salmon populations elsewhere however, is that Norway has become a core area for the species. Norway must take a leading part in the efforts to protect what is now a global wild Atlantic salmon resource. Next to the importance of saving wild Atlantic salmon as a species, wild Atlantic salmon is also of great importance to our nation: Wild Atlantic salmon represents recognized national values, as a significant source of income in marginal areas; as a genetic resource for salmon farming industries, a source of recreation, as well as an important element of Sami cultures (St.prp. no. 79 (2001–02) author's translation).

This introduction cited from what later became a Parliamentary Bill (2001) characterizes with precision the conflict that this chapter describes. In recent years, the growing acknowledgement of the importance of biodiversity and the need to protect endangered species, together with awareness of the cumulative consequences of Norway's position as world-leading in salmon farming, has brought recognition of the need to establish legal protection of wild Atlantic salmon. This paper describes a conflict that arose in the spring of 2009, when

1 The term indigenous is used to highlight the subtle but significant variation of Atlantic salmon from different rivers, as a reflection of different genetic strains.

2 This article is written as part of the project Newcomers to the Farm: Atlantic Salmon Between the Wild and the Industrial, funded by the NRC. It could not have been written without the help of Bjarne Johansen, Steinar Pedersen and a number of other sea salmon fishermen in the Tana and Varanger fjords. I would like to thank Marianne Lien, Britt Kramvig, Benedikte V. Lindskog and Einar Eythorsson for valuable comments.

the Directorate of Nature Management (DN) attempted to regulate the access of coastal fishermen on the coast of Finnmark to Atlantic salmon fisheries.

Within the field of green criminology, a number of authors have pointed to the fact that environmental crime affects people disproportionately (Williams 1996, Low and Gleeson 1998, Halsey 2004). Indigenous groups are often vulnerable to such things as pollution, because so many are dependent on the environment for cultural and physical survival (White 2003). This chapter illustrates that these relations with nature also makes indigenous peoples vulnerable to discriminatory treatment by environmental agencies (Ween and Lien, forthcoming). This chapter tells a story of how a particular relation between indigenous humans and indigenous fish were construed in an effort to secure the future of wild Atlantic salmon, perceived as a resource. The case is an example of how, when a nature is placed under protection, specific interests become 'the common good of mankind'. The understanding of 'the common good' employed by environmental agencies is culturally specific, but rarely officially challenged. It is based upon a combination of scientific knowledge and value-based judgment that are both ecocentric and anthropocentric (Halsey and White 1998, see also this volume, Chapter 1). The anthropocentrism, however, is restricted. In the name of sustainability and 'the common good', fishing rights are transferred from coastal Sami fishermen to tourist fly fishermen. In this chapter, this particular bureaucratic event is placed in connection with a worldwide trend where local hunters and fishermen are criminalized as poachers when the resources they depend upon are commodified (Jacoby 2001, for similar perspectives on commodification of nature see White 2003, Halsey 2004).

The bureaucratic process outlined is based upon a view of wild salmon as a resource. There is, however, little room in this article for what White (2007) describes as a third form of green justice, 'species justice'. In this volume, 'species justice' represents the frame of reference in a number of chapters, recognizing that 'nonhuman animals are considered in instrumental terms (as pets, as food, as resources), or that they are categorized in mainly anthropomorphic terms', in such, as natural resource management perspectives (such as 'wildlife', 'fisheries') (see White 2007, Sankoff and White 2009). While this chapter observes the relevance of such a human-non-human animal perspective, the subtext in this article stresses the use of *not* essentializing such categories or their contents in studies of bureaucratic processes (for similar perspectives, see Halsey 2004): here, the situated nature of the involved knowledge practices must be taken *further* than an acknowledgement of hegemonic anthropocentrism (Haraway 1988). This insight is pursued by exploring *how exactly* humans and animals are brought into being in specific knowledge practices. Rather than confirming static categories, it is essential to my argument that knowledge practices are multiple, relational and co-produced (Law and Mol 2008, Asdal 2003).

As exhibited in the citation from the Parliamentary Proposition, the suggested regulation of salmon fisheries that I will describe the making of came towards the end of a bureaucratic process in which Norwegian wild Atlantic salmon had been recognized as a scarce resource. As cited, these documents positioned the Norwegian state in a central position, as the guardian of resources significant not only to many Norwegian groups, but to the world at large. Natural resource management institutions' understanding of sustainability caused efforts to capitalize on the little wild salmon left by prioritizing tourist access over local fishing practices. However, this was made problematic by a concurrent process, undertaken by the Ministry of Fisheries, to consider the rights of coastal fishermen in Finnmark, following the Finnmark Act (2005). This legal commission was started as part of the ongoing work of the Sami Rights Commission, to determine the rights to land and waters in the county of Finnmark, predicting a conflict between these two bureaucratic processes; the Ministry of Environment process (ME), acting on a need to regulate the coastal salmon fishing in Finnmark, and the Ministry of Fisheries process (MF) to protect the rights of indigenous fishermen in Finnmark, led the DN to question the fishermen's indigeneity.

The conflict brought on by the Ministry of Environment (ME) protection process was dramatic. It involved local fishermen, Sami politicians, the Sami Parliament, as well as a number of researchers. In 2009 it became clear that the ME would not follow through with the DNs suggestion: further regulations of sea salmon fisheries in Finnmark were *not* introduced. Following this document trail (Riles 2000) in Norwegian natural resource management, I explore how the indigeneity of fish and humans were enacted in the bureaucratic documents that brought on this conflict. In my efforts to explore the unfolding bureaucratic event, I am moreover interested in the different kinds of agencies and technologies that co-produced this as a narrative.

Analysing Bureaucratic Nature Practices

This chapter describes a bureaucratic process that did *not* achieve its purpose, that is, to instigate a new regulation system through the use of concessions. In my opinion, bureaucratic documents represent an artifact that deserves significant ethnographic interest. It seems, however, to be ignored in a number of social sciences despite the fact that bureaucratic documents, as this case demonstrates, can change our lives in profound ways.

In green criminology, governmental regulation is primarily an issue in discussions of what is sanctioned and what is not (Goff and Geis 1993, Williams 1996, Halsey 1997, Barnett 1999, White 2003, Walters 2010). Other social sciences generally approach bureaucratic documents as sites of discourse analysis. Social scientists are often interested in particular representations (in environmental processes; for example 'biodiversity', 'sustainability' or 'the common good'). Usually, however, such representations are not *localized* in particular bureaucratic processes, nor are they connected to actual documents. In this chapter I am interested in how these documents produced particular narratives, as well as what happened to this narrative when it became a public event.

I speculate that the Ministry of Environment (ME) process examined here was unsuccessful because the documents were unable to construct an *authoritative narrative*: the argumentation produced was never convincing, obvious or uncontested. The historian Cronon (1992) argues that the very authority with which a narrative presents its vision is achieved by obscuring large proportions of reality: narrative foregrounds and backgrounds hide discontinuities and contradictory experiences. A powerful narrative constructs common sense, it makes the contingent seem determined and the artificial seem natural. It obscures the fact that actions are potentially valued in different ways (Cronon 1992). My question is whether the failure of this bureaucratic process could be explained by the failure to hide inherent discontinuities or the presence of other narratives.

Social science approaches to bureaucratic events also rarely take into account that the authority of bureaucratic documents relies on their *materiality*. Science and technology studies scholars such as Latour and Woolgar were both significant inspirations to new efforts to include the materiality of documents to social science research. Inspired by their work, I perceive bureaucratic work as the production and circulation of such inscriptions. Documents, then, are 'immutable, presentable, readable and combinable' artifacts used to mobilize networks of ideas, persons and technologies (Latour 1988 in Riles 2000: 13). It is the *circulation* of documents, the repeating of the known that establishes and confirms order and produces facts (Riles 2000). The authority of a bureaucratic narrative, in other words, is brought about by connecting documents to other documents: the more often a fact is repeated and inscribed in such documents, the truer it becomes.

We should also not forget that the materiality of documents in itself is convincing (Riles 2000). The weight of a bounded document with government logos has an effect; likewise, the way facts are formed, according to particular norms of presentation and particular aesthetics. Numbers play a particular role as an aesthetic and persuasive device. Verran (2010) points to the fact that the use of numbers in bureaucratic nature practices have increased dramatically in recent years. This, she believes, can be attributed to a fantasy of exhaustive accumulation, where the purpose of the audit project is for the common good of mankind (2010: 176, see also Kohler 2006). 'Common good' is, here, a rhetorical device that argues the need for sacrifices; to ensure the future of mankind. 'Common good' as a device also effectively shifts the burden of sacrifice onto minorities, such as indigenous groups. As this bureaucratic history shows, numbers readily become part of assemblages enacting particular 'common good' scenarios. Numbers are, as Asdal (2008) says, formed by instruments, defined through the intervention of professions, disciplines and protocols, distributed in databases and provided with arguments through being enacted as numbers (Latour 2004 in Asdal 2008: 124). Numbers have an inherent flexibility, as Verran (2010) argues; they can become associated with almost any entity. Numbers are easily assembled, simply because they are radically incomplete. As signs they have little meaning in themselves, they must be combined with other entities (Verran 2010). Numbers are therefore inherently unstable. In combination with other actors, numbers may change. As part of bureaucratic assemblages they become active entities (Verran 2010).

In the bureaucratic documents leading up to the ME suggestion of new regulation of coastal salmon fishing, numbers were introduced at several points in the argument. They also had several purposes: they singularized, hid heterogeneity and provided authority to particular narratives. Numbers demonstrated the value of Norwegian wild salmon stock both with reference to national and international concerns. They were connected with economic value to define the most sustainable use. Through numbers, narratives of the need to protect wild salmon were combined with the narratives of the advantages of tourist anglers who fish in rivers, in what is seemingly a non-political bureaucratic process. In this bureaucratic event, numbers obscured access to the understanding of that facts of protection and conservation invariably are polluted by human values, politics, cultures and ways of seeing things (Hinchliffe 2008: 89).

The Prophesized Death of Wild Salmon

According to existing official narratives, inscribed in Norwegian official reports (NOU 1999: 9) and in the history of NASCO (North Atlantic Salmon Conservation Organization), there was already in the 1970s a growing international concern with the rapidly expanding Atlantic salmon fisheries at sea. In 1983 national resolutions and bilateral negotiations led to restrictions in sea fishing and the establishment of an intergovernmental organization (NASCO). NASCO was established as part of a Convention for the Conservation of Atlantic Salmon in the North Atlantic Ocean. The convention created a large protected zone, free of targeted fisheries for Atlantic salmon in most areas beyond 12 nautical miles from the coast. One immediate effect was the cessation of the salmon fishery in the Northern Norwegian Sea that at its peak in 1970 caught almost 1,000 tons of Atlantic salmon. In 1989 salmon drift net fishing was banned inside the 12 mile zone. Next, the use of bend nets in coastal salmon fisheries was forbidden everywhere on the Norwegian coast, except on the Skagerrak coast and in the county of Finnmark (NASCO Fisheries Management Focus Area Report). NASCOs focus on the regulation of bend net fisheries was connected to its efforts to restrict what was called ‘mixed stock fisheries’. The logic in this is simple, but not altogether clear: bend nets are cheaper than alternative fishing nets; they are easier to use and to maintain. Cheaper nets that are easy to use make salmon fisheries commonly available.

Nationally, wild Atlantic stock is governed by the Ministry of Environment (ME), while coastal salmon fishing is governed by the Directorate of Nature Management (DN) (NOU 1999: 9). Efforts to further regulate wild salmon fisheries were followed up in the Ministry of Environment’s Bills to establish and later finalize establishment of the National Salmon Rivers and Salmon Fjords ((St. prp. no. 79 (2001–02) and St.prp. no. 32 (2006–07)). Next to a more concrete and stricter management regime that isolated salmon farming from recognized salmon rivers and fjords, this Bill encouraged more restrictive regulations of salmon fisheries, and particularly those involving what was called 'mixed stock fisheries'.

The term 'mixed stock fisheries' must be placed in context. Since the 1970s and the start of the Norwegian salmon farming success, Norwegian scientists have worked hard to increasingly monitor the state of wild salmon stocks. Currently, the status of the wild salmon populations is monitored by use of scale samples, keeping track of native stocks and phenotypes, through catch statistics, as well as fish counters, video counters, diving and other visual methods, different fish marking techniques, as well as calculations of the wellbeing of particular populations according to spawning capacity measures (NASCO Fisheries Management Focus Area Report). Such surveillance techniques have enabled a precision in the monitoring of wild salmon stocks down to particular river phenotypes. Summing up the conditions of Norwegian indigenous salmon stocks in 2007, DN reported that we are currently left with a quarter of the population that existed in the 1970s. Out of 450 wild stocks, 45 were recognized as extinct, 30 were threatened and 32 near threatened (St.prp. no. 32, (2006–07), NASCO Fisheries Management Focus Area Report 2007). Existing surveillance techniques, in other words, have provided a perception of scientific ability to monitor each salmon stock. Such precise monitoring moreover opens opportunities for differentiated regulations of particular stocks. Such differentiated regulations are, however, only successful if authorities can map and control fisheries of each particular salmon stock. This is why 'mixed stock fisheries' have become considered increasingly problematic. Sea salmon fisheries it is thought, to a larger extent than river fisheries, fish on mixed stock. A river may contain a variety of fish populations indigenous to particular tributaries. The salmon stock caught in a fjord, however, may be indigenous to a variety of rivers. One could potentially fish endangered stock from elsewhere. 'Mixed stock fisheries', in other words, disturb efforts to monitor and control fishing on particular endangered populations. The introduction of the terms such as 'mixed stock fisheries' have contributed to intensify efforts to restrict coastal salmon fisheries, such as shortening of the fishing season and decreasing the number of fishing days per week in the fishing season (Ween, Rapport til Finnmarkskommisjonen 2010).

Following up the NASCO recommendations, the Parliamentary Bill on the protection of wild salmon and so on (St.prp. no. 32 (2006–07)) ordered further reductions of mixed stock fisheries. The Bill stated that such fisheries should only be allowed on stocks that are at full reproductive capacity, according to the 'spawning capacity measures'; that is, the ideal number of spawning fish a river with a particular salmon population can host. With reference to these instructions, the DN in 2009 suggested that further restrictions on coastal fisheries should be introduced through the establishment of a concession system. The concessions system represented a new form of regulation. The rights to fish would, according to this regulation proposal, be evaluated according to economic criteria: only those sea salmon fishermen who could prove that they were professional salmon fishermen with a certain catch and income would be allowed to fish.

The Logic of Sharing

'The common good' in this story is not just descriptive of the need to protect the indigenous salmon population. Rather, 'the common good' here also refers to *how* the management of wild salmon as a resource better benefits a larger society (St. prp no. 32, (2006–07). In line with the current natural resource management ideals (Asdal 2008, Verran 2008, Ween 2009, 2010), managing wild salmon as a resource is suggested according to an economic rationale (St.prp. no. 32, (2006–07). In the Proposition to Parliament (St.prp. no. 32, (2006–07), the Ministry of Environment drew up a comparison between the economic potential of wild salmon tourism and the existing profits from traditional coastal sea salmon fisheries. According to these statistics, in 1999 the profits on wild salmon tourism were 400–500 million NOK. According to calculations undertaken on behalf of tourism organizations[3] the profits from tourism and retail businesses associated with wild salmon angling tourists was estimated to be as much as 1.3 billion NOK annually. The profits from traditional coastal sea salmon fishing were reported to decrease dramatically. Calculated in kroners per kilo, the tourist salmon could be worth more than 800 NOK per kilo, while the Sea Sami fishermen was worth a meagre 60 NOK per kilo. In the proposition, the reader is asked to consider this fact, at the same time as we are made aware of the fact that coastal/Sea Sami fishermen bring out somewhere between 30–40 per cent of the wild salmon caught (St.prp nr 32, (2006–07)). As readers, we are made to conclude that the value of salmon flesh is only a fraction of what each kilo of salmon *could* be worth. There is more money to be made, for 'the common good', if the salmon fisheries were regulated differently.

Introducing the Salmon Versus Human Indigenous

In the narratives drawn up by these documents in the Ministry of Environment process, it is easy to accept that fishing on mixed populations obstructs the common good, enacted as the protection of particular vulnerable salmon indigeneities. Within this narrative framework, the use of numbers comparing the economy in coastal fishing to the economy in tourist fisheries confirms the logic behind a redistribution of resources. Maybe the coastal fishermen should relinquish fishing for the common good? The argument seems logical, apolitical and unavoidable.

The economic rationale is, however, not uncontested. In the same Proposition to Parliament (St.prp. no. 32, (2006–07)) that started this chapter, the Ministry of Environmental (ME) concedes that there is a *cultural* argument to be made: it notes, as the Ministry of Environment also does, in most documents describing wild salmon as a resource (see for example NOU 1999: 9), that wild salmon is considered to have special significance to, for example, vulnerable coastal Sami populations (St.prp. no. 32, (2006–07)). In areas with Sami populations, the

---

3 Norges Skogeierforbund, Innovation Norway and Reiselivsbedriftenes Landforening.

salmon has been central both materially and culturally. The proposition states that the significance of salmon for Sami culture is manifested in linguistic nuances, in fairy tales, songs (joik) and traditional tool traditions (St.prp. no. 32, (2006–07)). The question is, however, if coastal Sami rights should be prioritized in front of potential economic benefits?

About the same time as the Directorate for Nature Management's efforts to further regulate coastal salmon fisheries in Finnmark, the Coastal Fishing Committee (*Kystfiskeutvalget*) (2006) started its work for the Ministry of Fishing, exploring the rights of Sami and other coastal inhabitants of Finnmark to fish in local waters. In the recommendations of the Coastal Fishing Committee, delivered to the Minister Fisheries in 2008, it was suggested that the waters outside Finnmark should be established as a coastal fishing zone, a Finnmark zone (NOU 2008: 5).

In awareness of the work of the Coastal Fishing Committee, the Ministry of Environment (ME), following up its Parliamentary Proposition (St.prp. no. 32, (2006–07)), asked the Directorate of Nature Management (DN) to investigate whether sea salmon fisheries on the coast of Finnmark *could* be re-regulated without consequences for the coastal population and the sea Sami in particular. What were the legal implications of regulating sea salmon fishing through a concession system, instead of being open to everyone with a legal fishing ground?[4] The cultural argument in existing related documents,[5] the growing awareness that the sea Sami in particular could argue their customary or immemorial rights, along with the ongoing legal developments associated with the Finnmark Act, such as the Coastal Fishing Committee, forced the DN to consider the human indigenous. As was also mentioned in the Parliamentary Proposition (no. 32 (2006–07)), the Coastal Fishing Committee, and, as I will return to, other documents produced by the Sami Rights Commission all emphasized the importance of sea salmon fisheries for sea Sami culture. The question that the Ministry of Environment and the DN had to ask was whether this acknowledgement meant that the sea Sami fishermen should receive special mention in the DN's ongoing work to establish how a concession system DN passes this assignment on to a Tromsø based private research institution, NORUT.

As part of this initiative, both representatives from the DN and the ME articulated a need to locate a significant *difference* between sea Sami and other coastal peoples. Their commission to NORUT asked if there were significant differences in the sea Sami approach to salmon fishing in comparison to other coastal populations. As

4 Lakseplass, salmon fishing lot.

5 See NOU 1994:21 Bruken av land og vann i Finnmark i historisk perspektiv [Uses of land and waters in Finnmark in a historical perspective]. NOU 1997:4 Naturgrunnlaget for samisk kultur [The environmental/material foundation of Sami culture]. NOU 2001:34 Samiske sedvaner og rettsoppfatninger [Sami customary law and rights perceptions]. Sjølaksefisket i Finnmark i et historisk perspektiv. Utredning for Finnmarkskommisjonen, 24. June 2010 [Sea salmon fishing in Finnmark in a historical perspective. Inquiry on behalf of the Finnmark Commission] Sámi Allaskuvla and SEG.

signifiers of difference, these two institutions suggested that NORUT should look at uses of technology as a way of assessing cultural difference.[6]

Upon receiving the NORUT report, the DN was able to conclude that it was impossible to find elements that differentiated sea Sami culture from other coastal cultures. All coastal communities in Finnmark employed the same technologies, ongoing acts of reciprocity that in existing literature (Kramvig 2005, Lien 1988) did *not* appear to a larger extent in these groups than in others. On top of everything else, the sea salmon fisheries did *not* appear to have a significant economic influence on people's lives in these communities, as it only represented one of several sources of income (ref. DN webpage).[7]

Indigeneities Enacted

What caused the conflict in the Ministry of Environment's efforts to protect the wild salmon was the Ministry's effort to order human and non-human indigeneity in the same manner: by establishing particular criteria that enabled difference, the separation of one stock from the next. In this exercise, cultural difference was defined according to criteria such as fishing technologies employed and the existence of what is considered Sami reciprocity networks (see Kramvig 2005, Lien 1988). On the basis of these self-constructed criteria of ethnic difference, DN was able to produce an ordered purity that, since it did not exist in real life, legitimized the dissolution of the existing ethnic categories. The NORUT researchers involved did employ the existing anthropological criteria, such as self-ascription, normally considered when defining human ethnicity.

In other words, this document trail, as in document trails in general, co-produced new realities such as nature and indigeneities. Complex assemblages of knowledge were brought together in a narrative that foregrounded one form of indigeneity – the non-human – with consequences for another kind of indigeneity – the human. Such an act of inclusion and exclusion was made possible by the knowledge practices and the values that permeate natural resource management (Lavau 2008: 41).

Observing this process, I often wondered why the natural resource management institutions did not consider acknowledging the existence of the parallel process involving the Coastal Fishing Committee, investigating Finnmark's coastal communities' rights to fish, instigated as part of the Sami Rights Commission and the Finnmark Act (2005) (NOU 2008: 5). When I questioned the involved natural resource bureaucrats about this, I was told that the investigations of the Coastal

6 The DN does not explain how they came up with these two variables, but, reading Eythorsson's (2008) descriptions of bureaucratic approaches to the Sea Sami, it becomes apparent that this is not new.

7 I cannot provide a specific reference to this webpage as it has been taken down in the autumn of 2009, following the controversy that it created.

Fishing Committee were an *entirely* different story to the DNs efforts to regulate sea salmon fishing. The reason stated was that the inquiries of the Coastal Fishing Committee concerned white fish, *not* red fish, such as salmon. The colour of the fish, of course, has nothing to do with the logic of this understanding. However, as salmon and other fish are governed by different ministries,[8] this answer confirms the existence of boundary mechanisms stopping natural resource bureaucrats from seeing the relevance of the other rights or protection processes.

De-indigenized People, Indigenized Salmon

I could stop there, but such a description would not be fair, as it would present natural resource management practitioners in a slightly naive light. Both the Ministry of Environment (ME) and the Directorate of Nature Protection (DN) seemingly approach the human and the non-human indigenous in the same way, as biological species. The environmental bureaucrats involved in the ME process, looked for indicators of that sea Sami populations showed distinctive species behaviour. To illustrate, in my conversations with environmental bureaucrats one narrative repeated itself:

> Sea Sami culture is not old at all! Why not, I would ask. And it (the culture, author's addition) really comes from Scotland! It cannot be compared to the river fishing. River fishing is different. You see, in Tana, fishermen still use the old fishing techniques, trapping the fish, rowing etc. The fishing gear that sea Sami use, on the other hand, is used everywhere on the coast. Sea Sami fishermen are not different from others at all!

In other words, in the eyes of the environmental institutions, human indigeneity, in the same way as salmon hybrids, was too messy (Law 2003). In my opinion, however this problem of indigeneity, brought into being by convergent bureaucratic processes, should *not* be reduced to a biologically speaking difficult ordering exercise. Stated in Mol's (2002) terms, we must remember that the attempt to make what was admittedly a salmon multiple (a subject involved in numerous cultural practices, as described in early official documents (NOU 1999: 9)) into a salmon singular (described in the Parliamentary Proposition (St.prp nr 32, (2006–07)) was the salmon's becoming an economic entity. In this document, numbers as the calculations made on behalf of the tourism industry showing that the value of salmon no longer was in its flesh played a vital part in the transforming of multiplicity into singularity.

Returning to the performance of human and non-human indigenous in these documents, we have observed a process within the Ministry of Environment (ME).

8 The historical context that led Norwegian salmon to be governed by other institutions than the Ministry of Fisheries is described by Treimo (2007).

Here, a document formulating a Ministerial/Parliamentary request to protect wild salmon is passed to the Directorate of Nature Management (DN) with a more concrete order. The original ME documents cited in the beginning of this chapter were relatively open, enacting a salmon multiple that also included cultural salmons. In the DN's interpretation, the more concrete order established a need to find out whether the wild salmon and the coastal Sami were co-constituted: DN asks the questions whether the Sea Sami indigenous depends upon the wild salmon for their enactment. This is translated into an even *more* narrow order, and placed with NORUT, a private research institution: does Sea Sami use the same tools as the rest of the coastal population and does sea salmon represent a significant source of income to the sea Sami? The pre-given answers to these questions are, then, fed back to the ME, relayed through a questionnaire, using predominantly quantitative analysis. This material is transformed into a research report, and fed back to the Directorate. The Directorate in turn, translates this information into a format suitable for a legal framework, and offers this back to the Ministry of Environment.

Progressing along and delineating a particular trail as *natural* (Riles 2000), where human indigeneity was performed in ever-decreasing forms, the institutions were able to conclude that there was no need to enforce particular measures to protect human indigeneity, as we cannot be sure that they exist. The salmon, as the non-human indigeneity, must be protected from the 'messy' human indigeneity. Translations are made that continuously reduce the scope of the human kind of indigeneity.

Coastal Fishing Committee: Messy Indigeneities

I did, however, start out with describing two endangered forms of indigeneity. Parallel to the Ministry of Environment's process to protect the non-human indigenous, the salmon, is the Ministry of Fisheries process to protect the *human* indigenous. Both enactments of indigeneity refer back to international documents and processes that the Norwegian state has committed to.[9] As with the salmon indigenous, the protection of the human indigenous is brought about through the development of indigenous rights legislation in international fora. In the networks dedicated to the protection of human indigeneity, legal and bureaucratic networks co-produce indigenous salmon and indigenous peoples. However, in these documents, national as international, indigeneity is *not* produced as a static, but rather has a fluid form. Definitions of indigeneity as pure and authentic are no longer present in indigenous rights conventions.[10]

9 See ILO 169; Indigenous and Tribal Peoples Convention (1989), UN Declaration on the Rights of Indigenous Peoples (2007), the Biodiversity Convention (1983), and NASCO (1983).

10 In international law, such changes are visible in the adoption of the new ILO 169 in 1989, replacing the ILO 107 from 1957. In anthropological debates as well as in indigenous studies, numerous scholars last put this matter to rest in 2003 (Ween 2010).

In the natural resource management process, international indigenous rights discourse is both present and absent. In the NORUT report, indigenous rights documents were mentioned, but were made irrelevant by the contested nature of Sea Sami indigeneity. In the DN law proposal, there was no reference to the ongoing and long-term work of the Sami Rights Commission.

Superficially one could say that the mandate of the Sami Rights Commission was to establish the grounds for Sami rights in Norway. However, going through the many thick reports that they have produced in the course of the last (almost) 30 years; it becomes apparent that their work had a more complex purpose. The reports of the Sami Rights Commission not only made suggestions as to how indigenous rights legislation could be implemented into Norwegian law and bureaucratic practice, the reports also represented an effort to rewrite Norwegian history to understand the colonizing processes that hardly anyone in the south were aware of before the Commission started its work. In its conclusions the Sami Rights Commission has continuously emphasized heterogeneity, fluidity, multiplicity of traditions and histories. In these documents, Saminess of several different kinds, non-Saminess, as well as Kvæn,[11] Finnish, Swedish and Russian ancestry remains in ongoing articulation.

As importantly, for the occurring particular natural resource conflict, indigeneity is both present and absent in the new foundational narratives written by the Sami Rights Commission. Indigeneity is present as the foundational history of the region and, as follows, as the reason why the region must be decolonized, and both legally and historically rewritten. Indigeneity is also present as the foundation of indigenous rights to documents connecting the population of Finnmark to larger international communities rather than the non-Sami Norwegian population. However, in the overall conclusions and legal framework brought on by the process, indigeneity is made *absent*: the Sami Rights Commission took on a reconciliatory approach. As a result, all new legislation and all efforts to rewrite the legal nature of Finnmark apply to all citizens of the county, *regardless* of ethnic identity. Rights are, in other words, attributed according to long-term regional inhabitance rather than individual indigeneity. The same is true of the latest version of the Sami Rights Commission, the Coastal Fishing Committee (NOU 2008: 5). Indigeneity is embedded as the core of the document's foundational story. However, the recommendations of how to improve the rights situation for Sea Sami are, on principal, extended to all coastal inhabitants of Finnmark.

These documents exist as a backdrop; they are both absent and present in the process of protecting the indigenous fish. These two larger processes are, in other words relational, although the nature of indigeneity, regardless of its human or non-human nature, is played out in very different forms. To summarize, efforts to protect human indigeneity are built upon a foundation of *necessary messiness.*

11 Kvæn people are the people of Finnish ancestry that moved to the north of Norway before the end of the Second World War, and for whom Finnish language, ancestry and identity continues to be significant.

The same messy Saminess, however, became a threat to the protection of the wild salmon produced as a neo-liberal nature experiences-inducing commercial product.

In the Ministry of Environment's process, the DN was able to construct a parallel process, by insisting that salmon was different from white fish. This assertion enabled the institution to independently construct a new way of defining indigeneity, without referring to the other indigenous rights processes engaged in by other Norwegian ministries. The strategy, however, did demand continuous boundary work. The two fishing rights processes had to be deliberately kept apart because encounters would mean collisions (Law 2004 in Lavau 2008: 46).

Conclusions

In this chapter, governmental regulations is the topic, not in a discussion of what is included or excluded in the definitions of environmental crime, but in a discussion of what is included or excluded in the definitions of environmental *rights*. The bureaucratic events described here show two document trails where particular narratives of resources and rights holders were brought into being. In this document trail, each document was connected to others in complex assemblages passing information between institutions, confirming and co-producing one reality. In this process, definitions of ethnicity became progressively narrowed down in an increasingly excluding process. Numbers played a significant role in the narrative event unfolding. Numbers created the state of emergency and the need for action. Numbers played a significant role in pointing out the kinds of actions that should be taken. Numbers moreover served to depoliticize the chosen actions, by neutralizing and legitimizing choices made as the best for what was presented as the common good of mankind.

In this chapter I have provided a case study of how the human and the salmon indigenous were enacted, as in a state of ongoing ontic struggle. The messiness of the human indigenous was used as an argument to both pry the human indigenous apart from the salmon indigenous, and simultaneously to dissolve the human indigenous as a legal category. Interestingly, the documents I describe authorized the proposed separation of wild salmon and indigenous people with reference to the fact that the fish caught on the coast are indigenous mixed populations (St.prp nr 32, (2006–07)), adding to the messiness of Sea Sami indigenous practices. In the river, on the other hand, what can be rhetorically described as pure indigenous specimen are fished by the economically preferred human, the angling sportsman.

Comparing the performances of the human and non-human indigenous in the bureaucratic processes I refer to, it becomes apparent that while the non-human indigenous was taken for granted, defined according to genetic stock and place of origin, the human indigenous was contested. In Norwegian natural resource management, wild salmon and indigenous humans were co-constituted in unexpected ways. In the empirical case I have described, the indigeneity of salmon legitimizes the de-indigenization of people. According to the Directorate of Nature

Management (DN) the endangeredness of indigenous salmon produced indigenous human as a threat. A closer look at the DN documents, however, revealed that Sea Sami fishermen, the human indigenous, were considered as a different kind of threat than the threat it was described as, that is, a threat to the survival of the wild salmon as a species. In my opinion, sea Sami fishermen could as well be described as a threat to indigenous salmon as willed into being a neo-liberal actor.

Postscript

Natural resource management practices, such as those exemplified in this chapter, in their time caused the World Commission on Environment and Development (1987) to recommend a change in the then existing perspectives of the uses of local knowledge. Following the introduction of the new Nature Diversity Act in 2009, the Norwegian Ministry of Environment radically altered its approach to local knowledge. Paragraph 8 of this Act explicitly states that although scientific knowledge represents the foundation for nature management, local knowledge and specifically Sami knowledge must also be included. The Ministry and the Directorate of Nature Management have since then made significant changes to implement this Act. In the case of coastal salmon fishing in Finnmark, a new management regime has been suggested by the Ministry of Environment and the Directorate of Nature Management, together with the Sami Parliament. This new management regime is negotiated in a working group process where the above mentioned institutions were present together with representatives of fishermen's organizations, river owners' associations and the Finnmark Estate. The recognition of the existence of ontological politics, implicit in this initiative, offers hope of destabilizing existing bureaucratic nature practices, and of new opportunities, bringing other salmon-human relations into official vision.

References

Asdal, K. 2003. *Politikkens teknologier. Produksjon av regjerlig natur* [*Technologies of Politics. Production of Governable Nature*]. Dr. avhandling. Oslo.

Asdal, K. 2008. Enacting Things through Numbers: Taking Nature into Account/ing. *Geoforum*, 39(1), 123–32.

Barnett, H. 1999. The Land Ethic and Environmental Crime. *Criminal Justice Policy Review*, 10(2), 161–92.

Callon, M. 1986. Some Elements of Sociology of Translation: Domestication of the Scallops and the Fishermen of St. Brieuc Bay, in *Power, Action and Belief: A New Sociology of Knowledge?* (ed.) J. Law. London: Routledge, 196–223.

Cronon, W. 1992. A Place for Stories, in Nature, History, and Narrative, special issue of *The Journal of American History*, 78(4), 1347–76.

Eythorsson, E. 2008. *Sjøsamene og Kampen om Fjordressursene* [*Coastal Sami and the Battle over Fjord Resources*]. Kárásjohka: CálliidLágádus.

Goff, C. and Geis, G. (eds.) 1993. The Environment and Social Justice. Special issue of *The Journal of Human Justice*, 5, 1–128.

Halsey, M. 1997. The Wood for the Paper. Old-growth Forest, Hemp and Environmental Harm. *Australian and New Zealand Journal of Criminology*, 30(2), 121–48.

Halsey, M. 2004. Against Green Criminology. *British Journal of Criminology*, 44, 833–53.

Halsey, M. and White, R. 1998. Crime Philosophy and Environmental Harm. *Theoretical Criminology*, 2(3), 345–71.

Haraway, D. 1988. Situated Knowledges: The Science Question in Feminism and the Priviledge of Partial Perspective, in *Feminist Studies*, 13(3), 575–99.

Hinchliffe, S. 2008. Reconstituting Nature Conservation: Towards a Careful Political Ecology, in *Geoforum*, 39(1), 88–97.

Jacoby, K. 2001. *Crimes Against Nature: Squatters, Poachers, Thieves and the Hidden Nature of American Conservation.* Berkeley: University of California Press.

Kramvig, B. 2005. The Silent Language of Ethnicity, in *European Journal of Cultural Studies*, 8(1), 45–64.

Kohler, R.E. 2006. *All Creatures: Naturalist, Collectors and Biodiversity 1850–1950.* Princeton: University of Princeton Press.

Larson, B. 2005. The War of the Roses: Demilitarizing Invasion Biology, in *Frontiers in Ecology and Environment*, 3(9), 495–500.

Latour, B. 1985. Visualisation and Cognition: Drawing things Together, in *Culture Technique* [online]. Available at: http://citeseerx.ist.psu.edu/viewdoc/download?doi=10.1.1.115.5725&rep=rep1&type= pdf [accessed 15 June 2008].

Latour, B. 1988. Drawing Things Together, in A. Riles (2006). Documents: Artifacts of Modern Knowledge. Ann Arbor: University of Michigan Press.

Lavau, S. 2008. T*he Many Lives of Goulburn River. Sustainable Management as Ontological Work.* Ph.D. Thesis. University of Melbourne.

Law, J. and Mol, A. 2008. The Actor Enacted: Cumbrian Sheep in 2001, in *Material Agency: Towards a Non-anthropocentric Approach*, edited by Knapett and Malafouris. New York: Springer, 57–78.

Lien, M.E. 1988. *Fra Boknafesk til Pizza. Sosiokulturelle perspektiver på mat og endring av spisevaner i Båtsfjord, Finnmark* [*From Boknafesk to Pizza. Socio-cultural Perspectives on Food and Change in Eating Habits in Båtsfjord, Finnmark*]. Magistergradsoppgave. Sosialantropologisk institutt, Universitetet i Oslo.

Lien, M.E. 2007. Weeding Tasmanian Bush. Bio Migration and Landscape Imagery, in *Holding Worlds Together: Ethnographies of Knowing and Belonging*, edited by M. Lien and M. Melhuus. Oxford: Berghahn.

Lidskog, R. and Sundqvist, G. 2002. The Role of Science in Environmental Regimes, in *European Journal of International Relations*, 8(1), 77–101.

Low, N. and Gleeson, B. 1998. *Justice, Society and Nature: An exploration in Political Ecology*. London: Routledge.

Mol, A. 2002. *The Body Multiple, Ontology in Medical Practice*. Durham: Duke University Press.

NOU 1994: 21. *Bruk av land og vann i Finnmark i historisk perspektiv. Bakgrunnsmateriale for Samerettsutvalget* [*Use of land and water in Finnmark in historical perspective. Background material for the Sami Rights Commission*]. Samerettsutvalget.

NOU 1997: 4. *Naturgrunnlaget for samisk kultur* [*The natural resource base for Sami culture*]. Utredning fra et utvalg oppnevnt ved Kronprinsregentens resolusjon 10. oktober 1980.

NOU 1997: 5. *Urfolks landrettigheter på bakgrunn av folkeretten og utenlandsk rett, bakgrunnsmateriale for samerettsutvalget* [*Indigenous land rights on the basis of international law and foreign law, background material for the Sami Rights Commission*]. Samerettsutvalget.

NOU 1999: 9. *Til laks åt alle kan ingen gjere: Om årsaker til reduksjonen i den norske villaksbestanden og forslag til strategier og tiltak til å forbedre situasjonen* [*On the causes of the reduction in the Norwegian wild salmon stocks and the proposed strategies and measures to improve the situation*]. Utredning fra et utvalg oppnevnt ved kongelig resolusjon av 18. juli 1997.

NOU 2001: 34. *Samiske sedvaner og rettighetsoppfatninger. Bakgrunnsmateriale for Samerettsutvalget* [*Sami customs and rights perceptions. Background material for the Sami Rights Commission*]. Samerettsutvalget.

NOU 2005: 10. *Lov om forvaltning av viltlevende marine ressurser* [*Law for the management of wild living marine resources*]. Havressurslovutvalget.

NOU 2007: 13. *Den nye sameretten* [*The new Sami law*]. Utredning fra et utvalg oppnevnt ved kongelig resolusjon 1. juni 2001.

NOU 2008: 5. *Retten til fiske i havet utenfor Finnmark* [*The right to fishing in the sea alongside Finnmark*]. Kystfiskeutvalget.

Ot.prp. nr. 53, (2002–03). *Om lov om rettsforhold og forvaltning av grunn og naturressurser i Finnmark fylke* [*The Finnmark Act*].

Pedersen, S. 1988. Varangersamenes fiske i Tana for 300 år siden [*Varanger Sami fishing in Tana 300 years ago*], in *Varanger årbok*. Kirkenes: Sør-Varanger og Vadsø historielag.

Pedersen, S. 1994. Bruken av land og vann i Finnmark inntil første verdenskrig, i NOU 1994:21. *Bruken av land og vann i Finnmark i historisk perspektiv* [*The use of land and water in Finnmark in historical perspective*], 13–133.

Pedersen, S. 2001. Fra bruk av naturgodene etter samiske sedvaner til forbud mot jordsalg til ikke-norsktalende og Deanodat: Ei bygd innerst i Tanafjorden, in NOU 2001:34 *Samiske sedvaner og rettighetsoppfatninger. Bakgrunnsmateriale for Samerettsutvalget* [*Sami customs and beliefs. Background material for the Sami Rights Commission*], 289–418.

Pedersen, S. et al. 2010. *Sjølaksefiske i Finnmark i historisk perspektiv. Utredning til Finnmarkskommisjonen* [*Salmon fishing in Finnmark in historical perspective. Investigation for the Finnmark Commission*]. Kautokeino og Tana: Sámi Allaskuvla og *SEG*.

Riles, A. 2000. *The Network Inside Out.* Ann Arbour: University of Michigan Press.

Sankoff, P. and White, S. 2009. *Animal Law in Australasia: A New Dialogue.* Annandale: Federation Press.

Singleton, V. 2010. Good Farming: Control or Care? In Care in Practice: On Tinkering in Clinics, Homes and Farms, in *Care in Practice*, edited by A. Mol, I. Moser and J. Pols. Bielefeld: Transcript Press.

St.prp. no. 79 2001–02. *Om opprettelse av nasjonale laksevassdrag og laksefjorder* [*About the establishment of national salmon rivers and fjords*], fra Miljøverndepartementet and Innst.S. nr 134(2002–03), fra Energi- og miljøkomiteen på Stortinget.

St.prp. no. 32. 2006–07. *Om vern av villaks og ferdigstilling av nasjonale laksefjorder* [*About the protection of wild salmon and completion of national salmon fjords*]. Miljøverndepartementet.

Verran, H. 2010. Number as an Inventive Frontier in Knowing and Working Australia's Water Resources, in *Anthropological Theory*, 10(1–2), 171–8.

Walters, R. 2010. Toxic Atmospheres Air. *Critical Criminology*, 18, 307–23.

Ween, G. 2009. Blåfjella-Skjækerfjella. Om forvaltning og utøving av sted/natur [About the management and conduct of the location/nature]. *Norsk antropologisk tidsskrift*, 1(2), 95–108.

Ween, G.B. 2010. Book Essay: Indigenous Peoples, Self-determination, Knowledge and Identity, in *Forum for Development Studies*, edited by H. Minde et al., 37(2), 281–6.

White, R. 2003. Environmental Issues and the Criminological Imagination. *Theoretical Criminology*, 7, 483–506.

White, R. 2007. *Dealing with Environmental Harm: Green Criminology & Environmental Law Enforcement.* Briefing Paper no. 5. University of Tasmania: TILES.

Williams, C. 1996 (ed.). Environmental Victims: An Introduction, in *Social Justice*, 23(4), 1–6.

Index

Page numbers in *italics* refer to tables